The Social Construction of Emotions

The Social Construction of Emotions

Edited by

Rom Harré

Basil Blackwell

© Basil Blackwell Ltd 1986

First published 1986

Basil Blackwell Ltd
108 Cowley Road, Oxford OX4 1JF, UK

Basil Blackwell Inc.
432 Park Avenue South, Suite 1503,
New York, NY 10016, USA

British Library Cataloguing in Publication Data

The Social construction of emotions.
    1. Emotions   2. Interpersonal relations
    I. Harré, Rom
152.4   BF531
ISBN 0-631-15199-0

Library of Congress Cataloging in Publication Data

The Social construction of emotions.
  Includes index.
  1. Emotions — Social aspects.   2. Emotions — Cross cultural studies.   1. Harré, Rom.   [DNLM: 1. Emotions.
2. Social Environment. BF 531 S678]   86-8576
BF531.S63   1986   152.4   86-8576
ISBN 0-631-15199-0

Typeset by Joshua Associates Limited
Printed in Great Britain by T. J. Press Ltd, Padstow

Contents

Preface

In recent years the study of human psychology has been undergoing profound changes. As with most fields of human endeavour the efforts of many hardworking practitioners in human science has lagged somewhat behind the cutting edge of innovation, both in theory and method. Behind the more superficial changes to be seen in every branch of psychology there lies a deeper revolution – a decline in confidence in empiricism as the philosophical basis of good work. This deep-lying revolt appears in the rise of cognitive science, through which human action can be related to the reality of processes of thinking. It also appears in the shift towards research programmes which pay attention to the languages of mankind, their diversity, and the very distinctive practices within which they play a major role. This change of focus in research has been accompanied by a sudden realization that much of what passed for scientific psychology in the era of simplistic empiricism may be no more than a projection of local custom and practices, even local political philosophies.

The chapters in this book present a coherent approach to the problem of understanding and accounting for human emotions. They represent the work of a widening group of workers who have transformed their disenchantment with the sterile paradigm of psychology dominant in the recent past into a burst of creative work, both illustrating new methods of empirical research and contributing substantial results to the new corpus of knowledge. Sensitivity to language and awareness of human cultural diversity inform all of this work. We hope the book will help to promote many further studies in a field that is both intrinsically fascinating and of considerable practical human concern.

The plan for this work existed before its execution, so to speak. Some contributions could be taken straight from existing publications, while others were commissioned to complete a coherent whole. We are grateful

Preface

to the various editors and publishers listed in the acknowledgements for permission to make use of material that has already appeared elsewhere.

Rom Harré
Linacre College
Oxford

Acknowledgements

Chapter 2: 'Emotions and statements about them' by Errol Bedford is reprinted by courtesy of the editor, the Aristotelian Society, from *Proceedings of the Aristotelian Society*, LVII, 1956–7. Chapter 6: 'The acquisition of emotions during adulthood' by James R. Averill is reprinted from *Emotion in Adult Development* edited by C. Z. Malatesta and C. E. Izard. Copyright © 1984 Sage Publications, Inc. Reprinted by permission of Sage Publications, Inc. Chapter 7: 'Affect and social context: emotion definition as a social task' by J. Coulter is reprinted by kind permission of Macmillan, London and Rowman and Littlefield, Totowa, New Jersey from J. Coulter, *The Social Construction of Mind* (1979). Chapter 9: 'Envy' by J. Sabini and M. Silver is reprinted with permission from the *Journal of the Theory of Social Behaviour*. Chapter 12: 'Accidie and melancholy in a psychological context' by Rom Harré first appeared in *Personal Being* (Oxford: Basil Blackwell, 1983); 'Accidie and melancholy in a clinical context' by Robert Finlay-Jones is reprinted by kind permission of the *Australian and New Zealand Journal of Psychiatry*, 17, 149–52, 1983. Chapter 14: 'The domain of emotion words on Ifaluk' by Catherine Lutz is reprinted by kind permission of the American Anthropological Association from *American Ethnologist*, 9 (1), 1982. Chapter 15: 'A Japanese emotion: *amae*' by H. Morsbach and W. J. Tyler is reprinted by kind permission of John Wiley and Sons Ltd from Rom Harré, *Life Sentences* (Chichester: John Wiley, 1977).

PART I

Social Constructionism:
Theory and Method

1

An Outline of the
Social Constructionist Viewpoint

Rom Harré

The phenomenon of human emotion has begun to attract a great deal more attention from philosophers and psychologists in recent years. Past lack of interest can be explained in part by the predominance, since the seventeenth century, of a philosophical conception of emotions as simple, non-cognitive phenomena, among the bodily perturbations. Philosophers and psychologists of antiquity held more subtle views. For instance, Aristotle proposed a cognitive account of emotion in which factual beliefs and moral judgements have a central role in the causation and individuation of emotions. On Aristotle's account, while emotions give rise to affective impulses, they are generated by a state of mind, involving cognition-based construals and evaluations of some state of affairs in the world. 'Fear', said Aristotle (1941 edition), 'is a . . . mental picture of some painful or destructive evil in the future.'

Spinoza (1677) also held a loosely cognitive theory of emotion in which emotion feeling is 'accompanied by an idea of an external cause'. However, in general the emotions were conceived by philosophers as simple, involuntary and purely affective states. Though the emotions figured in theories which were regarded as of more central importance, for instance emotivist ethics and expressivist aesthetics, the emotions themselves were taken to be unproblematic, and not worthy of extensive study in their own right.

During the nineteenth century the emotions became a topic of interest for scientific study. This research, as represented by biological and phylogenetic theories, shared the prevailing philosophical conception of emotion as an essentially non-cognitive, involuntary phenomenon which, though capable of influencing intelligence, language and culture, was not itself essentially dependent upon these complex and historically conditioned factors. Darwin's (1872) theory of emotions as common to animals and man, based upon primitive states of physiological arousal involving innate instinctual drives such as self-preservation and pain-avoidance, and manifested in specific behavioural routines, was highly influential. A close relation between physiological responses and ethological displays had already been worked out in detail by Charles Bell (1826). Another version of the reductionist account can still occasionally be found. For instance, 'affective reactions to stimuli are often the first reactions of the organism and for lower organisms they are the dominant reactions, [hence] our evolutionary continuity with other species and the fundamental nature of affect' was penned only a year or two ago! (Zajonc, 1980) However, some contemporary theorists have begun to incorporate cognitive elements such as belief and judgement in their emotion theories (Leventhal, 1980). However, among academic psychologists (and some philosophers) these elements are still regarded as natural and as closely related to the basic drive and arousal factors which featured in the earlier theories. It is rather difficult to make sense of the idea of a natural belief, but its universalistic implications can at least be fairly well tested. However, the overwhelming evidence of cultural diversity and cognitive differentiation in the emotions of mankind has become so obvious that a new consensus is developing around the idea of social construction. This book is devoted to elaborating the theory and methodology of the new approach and to their illustration in a wide range of empirical studies.

There is another form of reductionism that is also noteworthy. Philosophers traditionally conceived of the 'higher' emotions as compounded out of basic or 'lower', and certainly simpler, emotions. These were thought to be prior to, and essential properties of, the more lately acquired higher emotions. Descartes (1952 edition), for example, claimed that 'pride' is a complex conjunct of 'gladness' and 'love' (or perhaps one should say that he claimed this about three seventeenth-century French emotions which roughly correspond to whatever we mean by the modern English words 'pride', 'gladness' and 'love'). Similarly, some more modern theorists have regarded the higher emotions as complex states involving lawlike combinations of those instinctual drives and physiological responses which were alleged to constitute the primary emotions. While 'fear' and 'anger' used to be common candidates for membership of this class, the number and type of emotions taken to be primary varies from one theorist to another. Izard (1977) postulates the existence of genetically determined behaviour patterns that represent 'several fundamental emotions'. Plutchik (1962) offers 'eight primary emotions', each of which is allegedly related to a basic adaptive pattern. Tomkins (1970) refers to nine primary emotions, each related to innately endowed patterns of neural firings. Recent work in the 'constructionist' style shows, however, that no simple, combinatory theory is empirically plausible. In the case of

emotions, the overlay of cultural and linguistic factors on biology is so
great that the physiological aspect of some emotional states has had to be
relegated to a secondary status, as one among the effects of the more basic
sociocultural phenomena (see chapter 6).

<h2 style="text-align:center">WHAT IS AN EMOTION?</h2>

Psychologists have always had to struggle against a persistent illusion that
in such studies as those of the emotions there is something *there*, the
emotion, of which the emotion word is a mere representation. This
ontological illusion, that there is an abstract and detachable 'it' upon which
research can be directed, probably lies behind the defectiveness of much
emotion research. In many cases the only 'it' is some physiological state
which is the basis of some felt perturbation. Swayed by the ontological
illusion, it is easy to slip into thinking that that state is the emotion. But in
the case of the emotions, what is there is the ordering, selecting and
interpreting work upon which our acts of management of fragments of life
depend. We can do only what our linguistic resources and repertoire of
social practices permit or enable us to do. There has been a tendency
among both philosophers and psychologists to abstract an entity – call it
'anger', 'love', 'grief' or 'anxiety' – and to try to study it. But what there is
are angry people, upsetting scenes, sentimental episodes, grieving families
and funerals, anxious parents pacing at midnight, and so on. There is a
concrete world of contexts and activities. We reify and abstract from that
concreteness at our peril.

With that caution in mind, we have to rethink the question, 'What is
anger?' or love, mawkish sentimentality, spleen and so on, to which the
research process must, among other questions, provide an answer, and
without a try at which it cannot start. Our answers are, as likely as not,
liable to reflect the *unexamined* commonsense assumptions of our local
culture. These assumptions can best be brought to light by a preliminary
study of how this or that culture or subculture uses that section of its
emotional vocabulary and other relevant linguistic resources, with which
we, from our more or less distant standpoint, can roughly pick out
episodes in their emotional lives. But it is not that these differences should
then be deleted to reveal what say anger really is. Anger can be only what
this or that folk use the word 'anger', or something roughly approximating
it in their culture, to pick out. We must be careful to suspend any
assumptions we may have about the viability of cross-cultural translations
of vocabularies and interpretations of practices, upon which any nativist
theory of universal emotions must depend, to wait upon proper and
careful empirical research. We illustrate this point extensively in Part III.
Instead of asking the question, 'What is anger?' we would do well to begin

by asking, 'How is the word "anger", and other expressions that cluster around it, actually used in this or that cultural milieu and type of episode?' The results may be startling. Unravelling the basis of usage will lead us deep into the heart of emotion theory, and bring to the subsequent empirical work, including the study of the physiology of the emotions, a sophistication it has sadly lacked.

The first step to a more sophisticated theory will be to show how, in research, priority must be given to obtaining a proper understanding of how various emotion vocabularies are used. Recent work (reported in Part II) has shown that the very idea of an emotion as a response suffered by a passive participant in some emotive event is itself part of the social strategies by which emotions and emotion declarations are used by people in certain interactions. This is not to deny that there are 'leakages' into consciousness from raised heartbeat, increased sweating, swollen tear ducts and so on. But these effects are incidental to what it is to be in this or that emotional state. It turns out that the dominant contribution to the way that aspect of our lives unfolds comes from the local social world, by way of its linguistic practices and the moral judgements in the course of which the emotional quality of encounters is defined.

Turning our attention away from the physiological states of individuals to the unfolding of social practices opens up the possibility that many emotions can exist only in the reciprocal exchanges of a social encounter.

Looking first at the uses of words not only sensitizes the investigator to his or her own ethnocentric presuppositions, but also allows for the possibility that other cultures may use closely related concepts in very different ways. There are cultures in which, though the term in question comes, so to say, under the same umbrella (that is, may be appropriate to apparently similar kinds of encounter), it is involved in the creation of different expectations and may incorporate rather different moral judgements. This feature is particularly prominent in the way words that roughly correspond to our word 'fear' are used in remote cultures (see Lutz, chapter 14 below).

But reliance on unexamined common sense can have another unfortunate effect on research methods which the linguistic turn can help to prevent. There has been a tendency to treat the study of a certain repertoire of rather simple emotions as paradigm cases, defining this part of the practice of psychology, in the way that Newton's *Opticks* was for so long a paradigm study for physics. Not surprisingly, given the conceptual naivety of much psychological research, these paradigmatic studies turn out to be concerned with those emotions which have an easily identified and readily measured physiological accompaniment. For example, one well known textbook mentions only depression, anxiety, lust and anger. Lust and depression are not emotions. Depression is a mood and lust a bodily agitation. Concupiscence might have been the emotion, but only lust is considered. 'Anxiety' may sometimes be used to refer to an emotion, but it is a generic term with a wide and vaguely bounded sense. We are left only with anger. There are about four hundred words for emotion in English, and there are many words in other languages that seem to pick out something like emotions for which there are no English equivalents. The standard fare is thin gruel. In this work we will be dealing in detail with about a dozen emotions only. But our aim is exemplification, not salience to life's little problems or completeness in the scientific sense. *Much* remains to be done, and what we offer here is a lead and an example.

With chapter 9 we begin a preliminary study of the 'green' emotions – envy, jealousy, spleen, spite and the like – through an investigation built around some of the uses of the word 'envy'. In the other chapters in part II as in chapter 9, the way words are used is intimately bound up with the situations, social contexts and moral imperatives of the display, feeling and interpretation of emotions. In part III we turn to variation on two dimensions: history within our own culture, and the exotic and remote cultures whose 'emotion' systems have recently begun to be untangled. These examples are meant not only to hammer home the point about cultural diversity, but also to illustrate the essential developments in methodology that will be highlighted in the rest of the chapters of this part.

What does the analysis of the differential uses of a vocabulary show? It makes abundantly clear that the study of emotions like envy (and jealousy) will require careful attention to the details of local systems of rights and obligations, of criteria of value and so on. In short, these emotions cannot seriously be studied without attention to the local moral order. That moral order is essential to the existence of just those concepts in the cognitive repertoire of the community.

The point can be illustrated in some recent work of Nadja Reissland. She found that the mothers of small children were unable to say whether quarrelling children were envious or jealous of one another. At first she thought this showed that the concepts were not clearly distinguished in the linguistic community of the mothers. She devised a test to see. The mothers were asked to imagine three characters N, M and O. N and M are seated at an outdoor cafe, very jolly together, sipping an aperitif. O sees them from across the street. In the first scenario, M is married to N, while in the second M is married to O. Unhesitatingly, the group thought that O would be envious of N in the first case, but jealous in the second. Here is a very simple example of the role of a moral order in the differential use of a pair of emotion words. What is at issue in differentiating the emotions are the rights, duties and obligations of married people, *in that culture.* How do we explain the mothers' original difficulty? They had no idea what moral order obtained with regard to matters in dispute among their children, the communal toys of a university developmental psychology department.

There are many other language games in which the words 'envy', 'envious','jealous' and so on play a part. For example, 'envious' can be used to express congratulations and avow a wish, as in 'I am envious of your trip to Athens.' Then there is the dog-in-the-manger use of 'jealous': 'Guard this jealously'; that is, 'Don't let anyone else get at it.' This is close to the pathological sense of jealousy that we ascribe to a woman who makes a scene if her husband 'so much as looks at another woman' (and of course vice versa).

Anger, like envy and jealousy, is a generic emotion – or perhaps it would be best to say a cluster of emotions – with diverging species in a number of distinctive language games. Here are brief sketches of three.

First, there is the case where somebody's actions are interpreted as gross violations of the injured party's moral status (for instance, an affront to dignity). Depending on the level of moral transgression, the emotion can range from annoyance to righteous indignation. In its pathological forms, this genus of emotion includes the taking of umbrage and being 'in a huff'.

Then there is the more complex case of 'nourishing' anger (see chapter 8). In this language game the anger 'felt' by the apparently injured party (A) is the (almost) exclusive basis for A's interpretation of the actions of B as transgressions against A's rights, dignity or the like. If A feels annoyed, then this is the best ground for holding that B's actions must have been offensive. Furthermore, if B tries to escape from the 'no win' situation by denying an intention to offend, then A has further cause for complaint and ground for indignation. B's defence implies that B (offensively) believes that A is the kind of person who would impose unjust interpretations on B's actions or facial expressions, just to nourish his or her anger.

Finally, there is a relatively new 'anger' language game that is played in T-groups and Rogerian therapy sessions. 'Let's let all that *anger* out!' This kind of talk suggests that there is a buried affective state, a kind of emotional boil, that can be lanced and the poison removed. But even a brief encounter with 'encounter' groups shows that there is almost certainly no such thing as 'buried anger'. The anger displayed by the members seems to be created by the therapy session itself. So the use of the word 'anger' in this and related language games bears only a weak family resemblance to its use in the more traditional cases cited above.

These language games involve a whole lexicon or cluster of related verbal expressions such as 'fed up with', 'mad at', 'furious with', together with an elaborate repertoire of para-linguistic displays built up as a culturally distinctive refinement and extension of the *native* possibilities of ethological display. For example, in one feminist T-group the members are reported to display their 'anger' by pounding the floor.

The extent to which local moral orders are involved in human emotions suggests that there might be considerable cultural variety in the emotion

repertoires of different peoples and epochs. In part III we offer a wide
range of illustrations in support of this hypothesis.

CONDITIONS OF WORD USE AS A THEORY OF THE EMOTIONS

Summarizing much recent work (see also Leventhal, 1980), we can set up
a three-component theory of the conditions for the use of emotion words.

1   Many emotion words are called for only if there is some bodily
agitation. These words cannot be names for the agitation, since it has been
clearly demonstrated that qualitatively one and the same agitation can be
involved in many different emotions. The advent of the James–Lange
theory could perhaps be explained as the result of concentrating on this
component alone.

Many emotions are manifested in typical behaviour displays. Such
displays are strongly influenced by cultural conventions. However, it
would be a mistake to include them among the conditions for the use of
emotion words. They are together with the utterance of emotion words,
among the very forms of expressive display, and as such must share the
deep grammar of emotion words themselves.

2   All emotions are intentional – that is, they are 'about' something, in a
very general sense. We are afraid of . . ., mad at . . ., jealous of . . ., chagrined
because . . ., sad about . . ., grieved for . . ., proud of . . . and so on. In some
cases some cognitive work has to be done to seek out the cause of a bodily
perturbation. This is particularly true of those emotions that involve the
flooding of the system with adrenalin. It would, however, be a mistake to
see the work of Schachter (1971) concerning this matter as a proof of a
cognitive theory of the emotions. His work on the role of presumed causes
in the identification of emotions is really a special case of the general
logical point that emotion words (states) are intentional. Some belief in the
existence of a suitable intentional object is a necessary condition for their
correct use. Sometimes the identification of the intentional object of an
emotion state does involve cognitive 'work', but not always.

3   Finally, the involvement of the local moral order, both in the
differentiation of emotions and in the situationally relative pre- and
proscription of emotions, indicates that there is a third set of conditions
for the use of emotion words – namely, local systems of rights, obligations,
duties and conventions of evaluation.

Must all three conditions be met for the use of all emotion words? There
are many cases where all three seem to be involved. For instance, 'anger'
seems to be correctly used in some central cases only when there is a

distinctive felt bodily agitation, when there is some action by another at which we can be angry, and when that action is able to be construed as a transgression. The qualification 'able to be construed' inserted into the third clause is needed to widen the theory to include the common phenomenon of 'nourishing' anger, described in more detail above. But there are also some emotion words whose conditions of use seem to collapse to just the moral criterion. Linda Wood has shown that there is no specific feeling, nor is it likely that there is a specific cortical state, associated with the emotion of loneliness (see chapter 10). Nor is there any standard behavioural display of loneliness. Wood found that those who complained of feeling lonely said in effect that they were more isolated than people of their sort (for instance, grandmothers) ought to be. Actual isolation, measured in terms of human encounters per day, was not so important in complaints of loneliness; the local moral order is the dominant factor here.

Pride is another puzzling emotion, at least if one tries to understand it within the old paradigm. There does not seem to be a distinctive bodily feeling. Instead, the somatic component seems to be derived from culturally idiosyncratic displays of this emotion. There is certainly an intentional object of one's pride, and only on condition that one has been worthy of 'victory' is it right to display a proper pride. Overstepping that mark can lead to accusations of hubris or vainglory. But we do say that someone is puffed up or swollen with pride, too. These metaphors may perhaps be traced to an element of the ridiculous in an exaggerated or excessive display. The matter deserves more research. The same could be said for 'hope', which also benefits from a cluster of characteristic metaphors, such as 'surging', 'springing' and the like. There are yet other non-standard cases. Chagrin is the sort of feeling we get when we have publicly set ourselves to achieve something and then have been forced to admit that we cannot carry it through. There has been a 'dent to our pride'. Is there a special bodily sensation? I doubt it, despite the usual practice of speaking of chagrin as a feeling. There is often something 'hang-dog' about someone who makes a public ass of himself. But many other postures could be adopted, partly depending on the extent to which one has 'laid it on the line' in undertaking a given task in the first place. The more over-confident the attempt, the more humiliating the failure. A modest demeanour is a good preparation for winning or losing in our culture.

I have been trying to build up a case, not only in support of a more complex psychological theory of the emotions than the intellectually anorexic accounts offered by recent academic psychology, but also in support of the claim that two social matters impinge heavily on the personal experience of emotion. These are the local language and the local moral order. The philosophical analysis of the emotion concepts carried by local vocabularies is supposed to reveal the deep grammatical rules by which we can express the conventions for their use. If this is to serve as a basis for a reformed and enlarged psychology, it seems to open up the possibility that there are culturally diverse emotion systems and repertoires. Historians and anthropologists have established conclusively that there are historically and culturally diverse emotion vocabularies. I claim that it follows that there are culturally diverse emotions.

THE CULTURAL RELATIVITY OF EMOTIONS

There are several modes of cultural variation among emotion systems. I briefly summarize here the conclusions of the empirical work reported in part III.

1   First, there is the inversion of a standard of valuation. In one of the ways we use 'fear' it is used to express an emotion proper to a context of threat or danger, when the intentional object of the fear is generally unambiguous. Fear belongs in a cluster of concepts along with 'bravery' and 'cowardice', which refer to typical culturally relative moral qualities. It may seem hardly worth remarking that in our culture the former is highly approved and the latter condemned. But as Catherine Lutz has shown (chapter 14), among the Ifaluk the word *metagu* is used in contexts that share some features with those in which we use terms from the 'fear' vocabulary, in particular the presence, real or imagined, of a threatening or dangerous object. But in other ways the concept of *metagu* is very different from 'fear'. Among the Ifaluk, those who are submissive and passive in *metagu* – provoking situations are commended, while those who display an aggressive stance are condemned. The moral qualities with which the concepts are associated are such that it would surely be a gross mistranslation to treat *metagu* as equivalent to 'fear'.

2   Second, there is the encouragement by one culture of what is suppressed by another. The Japanese are said to value and to encourage a peculiar form of 'sweet dependence'. This agreeable emotional state is almost a reversion to the infantile in its intensity, and may even be pursued by 'playing baby'. For most Europeans, indulgences of that variety are left behind in infancy, suppressed by both peers and adults. The Japanese encourage and amplify this phenomenon to create and sustain an emotion, *amae*, quite distinct from anything to be found in the adult repertoire of Western cultures. John McDoe (personal communication) has suggested that something like *amae* may be on the rise in the West with the recent emphasis on 'mothering wives'. Perhaps the 'tired businessman' who allows himself to be petted and cosseted at home is experiencing something like Japanese *amae*.

3   A strong form exists in one culture of that which is weak in another. Most of us feel uncomfortable when we see someone, even a stranger, behaving foolishly, rudely or otherwise badly. Spaniards feel this emotion especially acutely, so acutely that it is treated as a distinct emotion, *verguenza ajena* (perhaps: 'alien' or 'alienating shame'). Television programmes showing someone behaving badly can be almost unbearable to a Spaniard, owing to the force of *verguenza ajena*. There is a well-known Iberian cultural complex into which this seems to fit, namely, the cluster of customs and concepts built around the notion of *dignidad* (see chapter 11).

4   There may also be historical changes in the emotional repertoire of a continuous national culture. In the psychological literature of the Middle Ages and early Renaissance, long discussions of the emotion 'accidie' are particularly prominent. The history of accidie (Latin *acedia*) is closely bound up with changing conceptions of religious duty. The emotion is first reported under the nickname, 'the noonday demon', by Evragius, in Alexandrian times. Hermits who found it difficult to keep up their devotions through boredom were victims of it. But the boredom was not touched with guilt or shame. Rather, it was qualified by despair and sadness, the gloom that comes over one who has lost the warmth of God's regard. *Acedia* was associated with *tristicia*. Accidie disappears from the explicit repertoire of English emotions with the rise of Protestantism, and its disappearance seems to be accompanied by a more explicit relation between dereliction of duty in general and the twin emotions guilt and shame. The cure of accidie involves more than the mere resumption of the abandoned task: it must be taken up again joyfully.

5   My final category of culturally distinctive psychological phenomena are those I think should be called 'quasi-emotions'. These are felt states of being that are closely related to the physical conditions of life. The misery one feels when coming down with flu, and struggling home through a cold rainy night, is a particularly disagreeable quasi-emotion. But to turn to the bright side, there are the more agreeable winter feelings. Take the case of 'cosiness'. We say we feel cosy, that a particular sort of occasion or physical environment is cosy, and so on. I call 'cosiness' a quasi-emotion also partly because of its double meaning as a feeling and as a description of place. (The word may come from the Gaelic *cosh*, a small hole into which one might crawl and so be snug.) The interest of this quasi-emotion is heightened by the fact that, in some other European languages, words for similar but not identical states of being exist. There seems to be a marked absence of such terminology from Mediterranean languages though this is arguable. The Dutch word *gezellig* refers to a state experienced in somewhat similar circumstances to those in which we would use the word 'cosy'. However, my Dutch informants assure me that

one could not be *gezellig* alone. (The Dutch word derives from the word
for friend.) Thus the Dutch word picks out a quasi-emotion somewhere
between the English 'cosy' and German *gemutlich*. The latter, I believe, is
confined to companionable occasions. The Finns have the word *kodikas*
from the word *koti*, meaning home. (I am particularly indebted to
L. Helkana for explaining *kodikas* to me.) While the word can be applied
to rooms, ambiences – even people – it lacks the duality of cosy and
gezellig, since it does not appear able to be used to refer to anything like a
feeling, either collective or individual.

These kinds of cases could be multiplied a hundred-fold. There can be
little doubt that, even if there are some universal emotions, the bulk of
mankind live within systems of thought and feeling that bear little but
superficial resemblances to one another.

METHODOLOGY AND THE FRAMING OF RESEARCH PROGRAMMES

Enough of a sketch of the chapters to come has been given, I hope, to point
to some aspects of methodological enrichment necessary to study
scientifically what we can now see as the domain of the emotions. The first
enrichment involves the priority that must be given to linguistic studies.
What are the emotion vocabularies, and under what conditions are they
used? We have seen enough already to realize that the asking of these
questions forces both cognitive and moral features of the language games
of emotional display and ascription into the forefront of research interest.
   Once one begins to study the emotions in this way, another important
matter emerges. Emotions are strategic. They play roles in forms of action.
And actions occur in situations. So the investigation of an emotion must be
widened to include the social contexts in which their display and even their
being felt (for those cultures that recognize emotional feelings) is proper.
Thus the study of rules must be undertaken. Averill, in chapter 6, sets out
in some detail the kinds of rules the understanding of which is an essential
part of the research into emotions. But situations and contexts are not
bland backgrounds against which actors can do what they may. They are
distinguished from culture to culture by the kinds of dramas that may
unfold. As Sarbin shows in chapter 5, there are plots and in the telling of
emotions there are narratives which realize these plots. In chapter 14
Catherine Lutz gives us a subtle analysis of the emotion vocabulary of a
remote culture. In getting to know the semantic system within which
something like an emotion vocabulary works, she called for a native
assessment of meanings. In those accounts narratives were prominent. It is
easy to see, even in the summaries of that chapter, the kinds of plots and
situations in which this or that emotion cluster has a proper place.

Emotions do not just happen. They are part of the unfolding of quite standard dramatic scenarios.

In sum, our four or five worked examples illustrate a methodology which is based upon the elucidation of five basic features of the emotions:

1   the repertoire of language games available in a culture;
2   the moral order within which the moral appraisals which control both the meaning and the occasioned use of emotional terminologies are themselves meaningful;
3   the social function (acts) which particular emotion displays and emotion talk perform in the dramaturgically shaped episodes of this or that culture;
4   the narrative forms that the unfolding of the situations revealed in 1, 2 and 3 above realize;
5   the systems of rules by which these complicated forms of social action within which the emotional qualifications of actions and actors are maintained, changed, critically accounted and taught.

When, and only when, *all this hard work has been done*, we are likely to engage profitably in the tracking of the physiological details of the various bodily perturbations that severally accompany the activities which the bringing out of the above five features enables us to understand. The extent to which perturbations are important and how they are managed varies along dimensions that only the above methodology can reveal. For some cultures emotions are seen as 'located' in social relations; in others as residing in individual bodily reactions. In some cultures what is of little importance for us is 'hypercognized', to use Heelas's useful term, and what is central to us may be hypocognized, rendered of little account. And these complementary processes may be part of the social activity by which the emotions of a form of life are managed.

REFERENCES

Aristotle (1941)   'Rhetoric, *The Basic Works of Aristotle*, ed. R. McKean. New York: Random House.
Bell, Sir Charles (1826)   *Essays on the Anatomy of Expression in Painting*. London: Longman.
Darwin, C. (1872)   *Expression of the Emotions in Man and Animals*. London: John Murray.
Descartes, R. (1952)   The passions of the soul. *Descartes' Philosophical Writings*, trans. N. Kemp Smith. London: Macmillan.
Izard, C. (1977) *Human Emotions*, New York: Plenum Press.
Leventhal,   H. (1980)   'Towards a comprehensive theory of emotion'. *Advances in Experimental Social Psychology*, **13**, 139–207.

Plutchik, R. (1962)   *The Emotions: Facts, Theories and New Models*. New York: Random House.

Schachter, S. (1971)   *Emotion, Obesity and Crime*. New York: Academic Press.

Spinoza, B. (1677)   *The Ethics*. The Hague.

Tomkins, S. (1970)   Affect as the primary motivational system. *Feelings and Emotions: the Loyola Symposium*, ed. M. B. Arnold. New York: Academic Press.

Zajonc, R. (1980)   Feeling and thinking. *American Psychologist*, February.

2

Emotions and Statements about Them

Errol Bedford

I

The concept of emotion gives rise to a number of philosophical problems. The most important of these, I think, concern the function of statements about emotions and the criteria for their validity. A solution to these problems is offered by what I shall call the traditional theory of the emotions, and I should like to begin by discussing some aspects of this. According to this view[1] an emotion is a feeling, or at least an experience of a special type which involves a feeling. Logically, this amounts to regarding emotion words as the names of feelings. It is assumed that to each word there corresponds a qualitatively distinct experience which may, although it need not, find 'expression' in outward behaviour. If it does, this behaviour entitles us to infer the existence of the inner feeling, and therefore to assert, with some degree of probability, statements of the form 'He is angry.' Looked at in this way, emotions naturally come to be thought of as inner forces that move us, in combination with, or in opposition to other forces, to act as we do. Briefly, anger is a specific feeling which leads the angry man to show the signs of anger (e.g., striking someone) unless he is willing to, and able to, suppress them. It follows, I take it, that to explain behaviour by saying that a man acted as he did because he was angry is to give a causal explanation, although, admittedly, a causal explanation of a special sort.

This is the accepted view of the older psychological textbooks. Stout distinguishes, indeed, between 'emotional dispositions' (e.g., liking and disliking, hate and love) and 'emotions', but he affirms that the emotion itself in which an emotional disposition is actualized is 'always an actual state of consciousness' that, besides sensations and conative tendencies, 'also involves specific kinds of feeling which cannot be explained away as resultants or complications of more simple elements' (Stout, 1938, pp. 371, 375). Even James thinks that an emotion is a feeling, although he identifies the feeling with somatic sensations. In the famous passage in his *Principles of Psychology* he tells us that his theory is 'that the bodily changes follow directly the perception of the exciting fact, and that our feeling of the same changes as they occur IS the emotion' (James, 1890, II, p. 449).[2]

I am going to argue that this involves a fundamental mistake: the logical mistake of treating emotion words as names, which leads in turn to a misconception of their function. There might, all the same, be more to be said for this view if it were less inadequate at the psychological level, if it did not presuppose a richness and clarity in the 'inner life' of feeling that it does not possess. What evidence is there for the existence of a multitude of feelings corresponding to the extensive and subtle linguistic differentiation of our vocabulary for discussing emotions? This assumption gains no support from experience. Indignation and annoyance are two different emotions; but, to judge from my own case, the feelings that accompany indignation appear to differ little, if at all, from those that accompany annoyance. I certainly find no feeling, or class of feelings, that marks off indignation from annoyance, and enables me to distinguish them from one another. The distinction is of a different *sort* from this. (Perhaps I do not remember very clearly – but then is not this part of the difficulty, that the words 'indignation' and 'annoyance' do *not* call up recollections of two distinct feelings?) I might add that at the present time this is psychological orthodoxy. The author of the chapter on 'Feeling and Emotion' in a standard textbook (Boring, Langfeld, and Weld, 1948) remarks that 'there is little evidence that a peculiar, unique type of consciousness accompanies and identifies the different emotions' (p. 100).

In any case, does the truth of such a statement as 'He is afraid' logically require the existence of a specific feeling? I imagine that it would nowadays be generally conceded that emotion words are commonly used without any implication that the person they refer to is having a particular experience at any given time. But it may be said, granting this, that such expressions as 'is afraid', 'is angry', nevertheless gain their whole meaning from an indirect reference that they make to experiences, and can only be defined in terms of feelings. A man can feel angry as well as be angry; the expression 'is angry' may not name an experience, but 'feels angry' surely does, and all that can be meant by saying that someone is angry is that he is liable to, and sometimes does, feel angry, without first understanding what it is to be angry. I do not think, however, that this argument can prove what it sets out to prove, i.e., that anger necessarily involves a specific feeling. In the first place, 'feels angry' is often able to serve instead of 'is angry'. We can say, 'I felt angry about it for days afterwards.' A more important point is that one cannot understand what it is to feel angry without first understanding what it is to be angry. If we can assume the meaning of 'is angry', or teach it (ostensively or by a descriptive account), we can go on to explain 'feels angry' by saying that it is to feel as people often feel who are angry.

But how could we explain the expression 'feels angry' without pre-supposing that the person we are explaining it to understands 'is angry'? The only possible method open to us would seem to be this: to make him angry, e.g., by insulting him, and then to say to him, 'Well, feeling angry is feeling as you feel now.' The difficulty is that, if the view I am criticizing is correct, we cannot ensure in this way that we have taught him the meaning of the expression. We have to be certain that he has experienced a specific feeling. Yet it is logically possible that the insult (or other stimulus, and it is a crucial point that there is no *specific* stimulus) has failed in its object – it may have produced no feeling, or the wrong feeling, or so confused a mixture of feelings that he cannot discriminate the essential from the inessential. (The matter is, if anything, even more difficult from his point of view.) We cannot exclude this by arguing 'He is angry, therefore he feels angry', for how are we to know that he is angry? *Ex hypothesi* his behaviour is no proof of this. And having as yet no guarantee that he has grasped what the question means, we obviously cannot ask him whether he feels angry. Nor can we discover that he has understood the meaning of the expression by observing that he uses it in the same way as we do, for, *ex hypothesi* again, this will not prove that he means that same by it. The conclusion to be drawn, if I am right, is that being angry is logically prior to feeling angry, and therefore that being angry does not entail feeling angry, and, *a fortiori*, does not entail having any other feeling.

Now it may seem that this does not accord with the confidence we have in our beliefs about our own and other people's emotions, respectively. But is this really so? We do not first ascertain that a man feels angry, and then conclude that he is angry. On the contrary, we realize that he is angry, and assume (perhaps wrongly) that he feels angry. Behavioural evidence for a statement about emotions is evidence in its own right, so to speak, and not because it entitles us to infer to private experiences. For if we have good grounds for the assertion that a person is jealous, we do not withdraw this assertion on learning that he does not feel jealous, although we may accept this as true. It is, after all, notorious that we can be mistaken about our own emotions, and that in this matter a man is not the final court of appeal in his own case; those who are jealous are often the last, instead of the first, to recognize that they are. This is scarcely consistent with the view that the criterion for identifying an emotion is the recognition of the special qualities of an experience; it is intelligible if the criteria are different from, and more complex than, this. I am going to discuss these criteria shortly. For the moment, I only want to suggest that the traditional answer to the question, 'How do we identify our own emotions?' namely, 'By introspection', cannot be correct. It seems to me that there is every reason to believe that we learn about our own emotions essentially in the same way as other people learn about them. Admittedly, it is sometimes the case that we know our own emotions better than anyone else does, but there is no need to explain this as being due to the introspection of feelings. One reason for this is that it is hardly possible for a man to be completely ignorant, as others may be, of the context of his own behaviour. Again, thoughts may cross his mind that he does not make public. But the fact that he prefers to keep them to himself is incidental; and if they were known they would only be corroborative evidence, not indispensable evidence of a radically different sort from that which is available to other people. It is only in some respects, then, that each of us is in a better position to understand himself than anyone else is. Against this must be set the possibility of self-deception and a reluctance to admit that we are, for instance, vain or envious.

I must now meet what is, I think, the most dubious objection that is likely to be made to this – the alleged impossibility of distinguishing, from an external observer's point of view, between real anger, say, and the pretence of it. It is sometimes claimed that, although someone might behave as if he were angry, and give every appearance that he would persist in this behaviour, there would still be a sense in which he might be shamming. What then is the difference between being angry and merely pretending to be? It may be held that it can only lie in the fact that the man who is pretending is not in the appropriate state of inner feeling. Now this objection plainly rests on the attempt to assimilate being angry to other cases of 'being so-and-so' in which the only decisive evidence for whether someone is pretending or not is what he feels. One line of reply to it, therefore, would be to deny that there are any such cases. But it is doubtful whether this could be sustained. Pain is a specific sensation (or class of similar sensations), and it seems clear that being in pain does entail having that sensation, since 'I am in pain but I don't feel anything' is self-contradictory. If so, it is possible for someone consistently to pretend to be in pain, and yet to be deceiving us. We might, of course, be unwilling to believe anyone who, after showing all the signs of pain, confessed that he felt no pain; but the point is that, *if* what he says is true, it entails the falsity of 'He was in pain.' Can we say that being angry is similar to being in pain in this respect?

Let us contrast the case of a man who is angry with another, behaving in a similar way, who is only pretending to be. Now it may well be true that the former feels angry, whereas the latter does not, but in any case it is not this that constitutes the difference between the fact that the one is angry and the fact that the other is only pretending to be. The objection rests on a misconception of what pretence is. There is necessarily involved in pretence, or shamming, the notion of a limit which must not be over-stepped; pretence is always insulated, as it were, from reality. Admittedly, this limit may be vague, but it must exist. It is a not unimportant point that it is usually *obvious* when someone is pretending. If a man who is behaving as if he were angry goes so far as to smash the furniture or commit an assault, he has passed the limit; he is not *pretending*, and it is useless for him to protest afterwards that he did not feel angry. Far from his statement being *proof* that he was not angry, it would be discounted even if it were accepted as true. 'He was angry, but he did not feel angry' is not self-contradictory, although it is no doubt normally false. If in a particular case it is difficult – as it may be – to settle the question, 'Pretended or real?' that can only be because the relevant public evidence is inadequate to settle it. What we want is more evidence of the same kind, not a special piece of evidence of a different kind. Our difficulty in resolving the question, 'Is he really in pain?', on the other hand, arises from the fact that the only decisive evidence is evidence that he alone is in a position to give. (I think that even in the case of pretending to be in pain there is a limit, only it is exceptional in depending on a subjective condition. It is decisively passed if a person truly says 'I feel pain.' There may, of course, be inductive evidence for accepting or rejecting his statement.)

This is confirmed by the difference between the two questions, 'Do I really feel pain?' and 'Do I really feel angry?' Since there is little room for doubt about the answer, the former is not a query that anyone is very likely to put to himself; it may even be said that it is a meaningless question. But I am inclined to think that it could be asked as a classificatory question, as roughly equivalent to 'Is this pain or rather discomfort?' It is to be answered, if at all, by comparing the present feeling with other feelings definitely counted as pains, and considering whether it is sufficiently similar to be classed with them. One cannot resolve it by answering the question, 'Am I really in pain?' since the answer to that question must depend on the answer given to the first. By contrast, 'Do I really feel angry?' is one of a class of similar questions that are common in everyday life. This question does not concern the comparison of feelings; in answering it one is trying to decide whether one is angry or not, and the answer 'Yes' can be mistaken in a way that a similar answer to the question 'Do I really feel pain?' cannot be.

II

Having, I hope, cleared the ground a little by putting some preliminary arguments against the traditional theory, I now want to consider whether an adequate alternative to it is provided by a dispositional theory of emotions, and to discuss the criteria for the use of emotion words. Can the concept of an emotion be fully elucidated without using non-behavioural, indeed non-psychological, concepts? I will try to justify the negative answer that I think should be given to this question.

To begin with, statements about emotions cannot be said to describe behaviour; they interpret it.[3] The situation seems to be that emotional behaviour, so to speak, is far from being homogeneous. The behavioural evidence for 'He was angry' varies with the person and the occasion; in different cases it is not the same, and possibly it may not even be partially the same. Conversely, the same, or similar, behaviour can be differently, yet correctly, interpreted in different circumstances, for example as anger, indignation, annoyance, exasperation, or resentment. Accordingly, categorical descriptive statements, e.g., (1) 'He raised his voice and began to thump the table', and hypothetical descriptive statements, e.g. (2) 'If I had gone on teasing him he would have thrown something at me', are evidence for such statements as (3) 'He was very angry', but they are not part of what these statements mean. Clearly, on hearing (3), it would be proper to ask for details, and such details could be given in (1) and (2). (1) and (2) would therefore give additional information to that already given in (3). To put the matter another way, (1), (2) and (3) are independent of one another in respect of truth and falsity. (1) may be true when (3) is false (a man can thump the table and raise his voice – to emphasize a point – without being angry), and (3) may be true although (1) is false (for not all angry men thump tables). The same holds of the relationships of (2) and (3). The truth of (2) is perfectly compatible with joining in the fun; anger, on the other hand, is consistent with not being prepared to throw things. I think that this would still hold if other statements were substituted for (1) and (2). It does not seem to be possible, therefore, to analyse (3) into a set, however complex, of categorical and hypothetical statements that describe individual behaviour. (3) does not sum up, but goes beyond, the behavioural evidence for it, and it would always be logically possible to accept the evidence and deny the conclusion. Although when we say (3) we are in a sense talking about the behaviour on which its truth rests, anger is not merely a disposition, and cannot be reduced to a pattern of behaviour, actual or potential.[4] All that can be said about the logical relationships between (3) and such statements as (1) and (2) is that it is a necessary, but not a sufficient, condition for the truth of (3) that some statements such as (1) and (2) should be true, without it being possible to specify which.

This last assertion may be challenged in at least two ways. It might be said, first, that the phrase 'necessary, but not a sufficient, condition' ought to be changed to 'neither a necessary nor a sufficient condition'. But since the only ground on which this could be maintained appears to be the traditional view, I shall not discuss it any further. I will only add that I do not believe that we either do, or should, take any notice of anyone's protestations that, for instance, he loves his wife, if his conduct offers no evidence whatever that he does. At the other extreme, those who want to be thoroughly behaviouristic about emotions will argue that the phrase 'necessary but not sufficient' should be amended to 'both necessary and sufficient'.

What I am suggesting is that people who share the same information and the same expectations about another person's behaviour may possibly place different emotional interpretations on that behaviour, if their knowledge is confined to descriptive statements about it. It may be urged that this difference of opinion can be eliminated as further evidence of the same type comes to light, and that it can only be eliminated in this way. The assumption underlying this – that the criteria for assertions about emotions are purely behavioural – is not, however, borne out by an examination of the way in which we actually use emotion words. These words, when used without qualification, carry implications not merely about behaviour, but also about its social context.

Consider the distinction between two emotions that have a close similarity, shame and embarrassment. The behaviour of an embarrassed man is often not noticeably different from that of one who is ashamed; but there is an important difference between the respective situations they are in. In a newspaper article last year (1966), Mr Peter Davies, the publisher, was said to be 'to his mild embarrassment' the original of Peter Pan. The embarrassment is understandable, and the epithet appropriate, whether its application is correct or not. Yet we can say at once that, if the writer of the article had alleged that Mr Davies was 'to his shame' the original of Peter Pan, this would have been incorrect; it is scarcely conceivable that it could be true. The reason for this is obvious, and it is logical, not psychological, since it has nothing to do with Mr Davies's behaviour, still less with his feelings. It is simply that the fact that Barrie modelled Peter Pan on him is not his *fault* – it was not due to an act of his, and there is nothing reprehensible about it anyway. In general, it is true to say of someone 'He is ashamed of so-and-so' only if what is referred to is something that he can be criticized for (the criticism is commonly, though not perhaps necessarily, moral). It is, in other words, a necessary condition for the truth of the statement that he should be at fault. The word 'embarrassed' is not connected in the same way with blame and responsibility; the claim that it makes is the vaguer and weaker one that the situation is awkward or inconvenient or something of that kind. 'He was embarrassed' may impute a fault to someone else, but not to the person of whom it is said. (I do not mean that we may not also impute a fault to someone of whom we say this. Sometimes one puts oneself into an embarrassing situation, sometimes one finds oneself in it. I mean that we do not impute it *in* saying 'He was embarrassed' in the way we do if we say 'He was ashamed.')

It may be pointed out that we can, after all, be ashamed of the faults of others. But I do not believe that this is true unless we accept the fault as our own; when, for instance, our children, or even our friends, commit antisocial acts in houses that we introduce them to. It is most unusual to be ashamed of the deeds of total strangers, although it is possible provided that responsibility is accepted through identification with the stranger in virtue of a common characteristic – 'I was ashamed to see an Englishman lying dead drunk on the pavement.' A Frenchman would be unlikely to say this, although rising to a still higher level of generality he might change 'Englishman' to 'European'. (It is beside the point that such acceptance of responsibility may be irrational.)

The connection between shame and responsibility is not, of course, ignored in the traditional theory of emotions. It appears as the doctrine that every emotion must have an appropriate object; that it is impossible (psychologically) to experience the feeling specific to shame unless you recognize that you are open to criticism. But there are no limits to what men may feel; we can only set limits to what they can say. This is merely the misrepresentation of a logical point as a piece of implausible *a priori* psychology.

The point of the example is to show that, although knowledge of facts that is quite independent of knowledge of behaviour cannot by itself establish a given interpretation of that behaviour, it can be sufficient definitely to exclude it. I suggest, then, that it is possible to rebut the contention that, e.g., A is jealous of B's relationship with C by showing that the claim that such an assertion makes about the situation which A is in, viz., that he is in a certain marital, professional or other relationship (depending on the context) with B, is not satisfied. Certainly, the contention that A is jealous is as a rule rebutted by evidence about his behaviour which is inconsistent with its truth. The reason why the claim that A is in a certain relationship with B is usually unquestioned is that it is very rarely false; the assertion that A is jealous is not usually made unless it is already known that the claim is satisfied, although it is frequently made on inadequate behavioural evidence. In general, then, this criterion is relevant to the *assertion* of statements, rather than the justification or rebuttal of statements that have *already* been asserted – it leads us to pick one word rather than another. For example, the decision whether to say that the driver of a car which has broken down for lack of water is indignant, or merely annoyed or angry, depends on whether the radiator is empty through (let us say) the carelessness of a garage mechanic who undertook to fill it for him, or through his own carelessness ('annoyed with myself' but not 'indignant with myself'). Indignation, but not annoyance, seems to imply unfairness, particularly unfair accusation, or breach of an agreement. Thus, if the garage mechanic is later taxed with his carelessness, it could not be said that he was indignant, unless he was in a position to reply 'But you said you would do it yourself, sir' or something similar.

Statements about emotions may also involve another, and somewhat different, type of commitment, which has an even closer bearing on the elucidation of their function. It can be illustrated in the contrast between hope and expectation, and I think this throws some light on the question why one is, and the other is not, usually counted as an emotion. The most apparent difference between them is that hoping for and expecting an event express different degrees of confidence that the event will happen. To expect something is to believe that it is more likely than not to happen. In the case of hope it is only necessary that it should not be an impossibility. This is, however, not the only, nor the most crucial, difference. Phrases which express a low degree of confidence, e.g., 'I think it may . . .,' 'Perhaps it will . . .', cannot be substituted without loss for 'I hope that. . . .' The expression 'I hope that . . .' implies, in addition to a very vague estimate of probability, an *assessment* of whatever is referred to in the clause that follows. I think it is clear that one cannot hope for something, although one can expect something, without judging it favourably in some respect, or from some point of view. Compare (1) 'I don't favour a higher purchase tax but I expect it will be raised' with (2) 'I don't favour a higher purchase tax, but I hope it will be raised.' (1) creates no surprise; (2) demands further explanation. Does he think it bad for the country, but profitable to him personally because he has a large stock of goods on which he has already paid tax? Does he regard it as unsound fiscal policy in general, but advisable temporarily in an inflationary economy? Failing an answer to questions such as these, (2) is surely a puzzling remark, and (3) 'I don't favour a higher purchase tax in any respect, but I hope it will be raised' seems to me to be self-contradictory. (Since – to mention one reason – one can only favour events under human control, and hope is not restricted in this way, 'I favour . . .', does not precisely represent the implication of 'I hope that . . .', but it will do for the purpose of the present example. I need hardly say that it is not my intention to give an exhaustive – or, indeed, a more than roughly accurate – account of the particular concepts that I use as examples).

It is a psychological truism that men do not, with some exceptions, hope that their opponents will win; it is a truth of logic that they cannot hope that their opponents will win without approving of this in *some* respect. Thus, 'I hope that . . .' is commonly used to declare, or to commit oneself to, an allegiance, and although disagreement *about* hopes is disagreement about the interpretation of facts, disagreement *in* hopes is not – it is one of the forms that disagreement about value may take (e.g., 'I hope the Socialists will get in.' 'Well, I don't. I think it would be a disaster for the country.') This is a further reason why it would be absurd to say that questions of the form 'Do I feel regret for . . .?' 'Do I really hope that . . .?' could be settled by introspection. 'Do I really hope that the Tories will get in?' is plainly a question a wavering Tory supporter might put to himself. This may amount to asking himself whether, granted that he thinks a Tory government better than a Labour one, he is concerned enough about the election result, or whether he is not too indifferent to say, if he is honest, that he *hopes* for a Tory victory. If so, he will answer it not by searching his feelings, for they have nothing to do with the matter, but by reflecting, for example, that when the party's policy was attacked he did not bother to defend it, or by remembering that after all he has agreed to do some canvassing. But it is just as likely, if not more likely, that the answer to the question will be a *decision* about his allegiance, reached by reconsidering the merits of the two parties. (Contrast 'Do I really feel pain?' discussed above.)

To generalize from this example, emotion words form part of the vocabulary of appraisal and criticism, and a number of them belong to the more specific language of moral criticism. Normally, the verbs in their first-person use imply the speaker's assessment of something, and in their third-person use they carry an implication about an assessment by the person they refer to.[5] It is perhaps worth mentioning that there are certain cases in which a third-person statement gives the speaker's verdict on that person; a factor which certainly complicates discussions of character. Such terms as 'vain', 'envious', and 'resentful' are terms of censure.[6] There is an overlap between the lists of emotions, and the lists of virtues and vices that are given by philosophers. The overlap is not complete; some virtues (e.g., veracity) are not connected with emotions, and some emotions (e.g., regret) cannot be treated as elements of character and are not merits or defects.

So far I have discussed the conditions which appear to govern the truth and falsity of statements about emotions. While emotion concepts do not form an altogether homogeneous group, I believe that this is correct as a broad outline. But there is one respect in which it needs to be supplemented. This concerns the sense in which emotions (as opposed to statements about emotions) can be justified or unjustified, reasonable or unreasonable. It is fairly obvious, to begin with, that the behavioural criteria for the use of emotion words are not connected with the application of these predicates. The way in which a man behaves will determine whether he is or is not angry. But *if* he is angry, the behavioural evidence for this is not in itself relevant to the question whether his anger is justified or unjustified. On the other hand, if the claim that an emotion word makes about a situation is not satisfied, this is often indicated by saying that the emotion is unjustified or unreasonable. The attribution of the emotion, that is to say, is not withdrawn, but qualified.

An example will make this clearer. Suppose that B does something that is to A's advantage, although A thinks that it is to his disadvantage (e.g., B, a solicitor administering A's affairs, sells some shares that A believes [wrongly] will appreciate in value). Now it would be misleading to say simply, except to a fully informed audience, 'A resents what B did' – this surely carries the incorrect implication that B has injured A. To guard against this it is necessary to add 'but his resentment is quite unjustified', or some equivalent expression. A's belief that B has done something that affects him adversely is, however, a necessary condition if the word 'resentment' is to be used at all. The distinction between what the situation is and what it is believed to be is normally unimportant, and for this reason emotion words make an objective claim unless special precautions are taken to exclude or cancel it (e.g., 'He was afraid but no one else was' [there was no real danger]; 'Your surprise is quite unjustified' [the event was only to be expected]).

But this is not the whole story, and the question whether an emotion is justified or not does not always turn on an issue of fact. There is a second group of emotions (not, I think, necessarily exclusive of the first) in respect of which the qualifications 'unjustified', 'unreasonable' refer to a different implication, and have quite a different force. Contempt, disgust and pride are typical of this group. If I were to say that a music critic's contempt for Bartók was unjustified, I should not be asserting a fact; I should be challenging his assessment of Bartók. It is impossible to give any simple paraphrase of this remark, but it could be taken, in part, as more or less equivalent to saying that Bartók is a better composer than the critic allows. While the critic's assessment of Bartók determines, among other considerations, whether I shall assert or deny that he is contemptuous of Bartók, it does not determine whether I shall say that his contempt is justified or not; *that* depends on my opinion about his assessment.

How far can these distinctions be accounted for by theories in which emotion concepts are treated as psychological concepts? I am inclined to think that if an emotion were a feeling no sense could be made of them at all. It may be said that an emotion is unjustified when a feeling is inappropriate or unfitting to a situation. But I find this unintelligible. Feelings do not have a character that makes this relationship possible. In any case, the interpretation suggested is not what is meant by saying that, e.g., a critic's contempt is unjustified. In general, I do not think it can be maintained that logical predicates apply either to feelings or to sensations. What reasons could be given for or against a feeling, or for or against its 'inappropriateness' to a situation.? If someone were to say 'I felt a pang this afternoon', it would be meaningless to ask whether it was a reasonable or unreasonable pang. The matter is different if he says 'pang of regret', but the phrase 'of regret' does not *name* the feeling, as I have already argued, and the pang of regret is justified, if it is, not as a feeling, but because his regret is justified. Nor do these predicates apply to bodily sensations, such as feeling giddy or having a pain in one's leg. This, I think, explains the fact that, while we often say 'You ought (or ought not) to be (or feel) ashamed (etc.)', we cannot say this of feelings,[7] a point that has created difficulties for moral philosophers who adhere to the traditional theory about emotions. Sir David Ross, for instance, recognizes that 'ought' does not apply to feelings, and he assumes that from this it follows that it has no application to emotions, except in an 'improper use'. According to him, 'we cannot seriously say', e.g., 'You ought to feel ashamed' (Ross, 1939, pp. 45, 55). He is therefore constrained to interpret this remark as meaning that a certain feeling is 'right or fitting' in the circumstances, which, as I shall argue shortly, misconstrues its point. If, however, we do not presuppose that the primary function of 'I feel ashamed' is to report a feeling, there is no objection to allowing – what is surely the case – that 'You ought to feel ashamed' employs 'ought' in a perfectly 'proper' sense, indeed in the same sense as in 'You ought to apologize.'

A dispositional theory of emotions may be thought to be on stronger ground, since it can be argued that behaviour may be unreasonable or unjustified. To use a previous example again, to say that someone has an unjustified contempt for Bartók is to say, I take it, on this view, that certain categorical and hypothetical statements are true of him, and that these statements describe behaviour that is unjustified. In other words, the assertion that contempt for Bartók is unjustified means that a certain pattern of preferential behaviour is unjustified. But what is this pattern of behaviour? Presumably it will consist in doing (or being prepared to do) things of this sort: switching off when Bartók's music is announced on the Third Programme, wasting free tickets for a concert of his music, never buying records of Bartók, going for a walk when a neighbour plays his music on the violin, and so on; in short, choosing against this composer whenever a choice presents itself. Now let us suppose that contempt for Bartók is unjustified, as it undoubtedly is. Even so, this behaviour may be perfectly reasonable or justified, and therefore cannot constitute an unjustified contempt for Bartók. It is open to a different interpretation: that the person who behaves in this way is simply uninterested in this composer's music, or in modern music generally. Consistently to choose against something is not necessarily to condemn it, or to be contemptuous of it, because this choice is susceptible of rational explanation in other ways.

III

I must now amplify what I have said in passing about the functions performed by statements that refer to emotions. It is generally assumed that these functions are to report feelings, or to report, predict or explain behaviour. Now although some statements containing emotion words are used in these ways, and particularly as explanations, the force of the qualifications 'unjustified' and 'unreasonable' in itself suggests that this is much less common than might be thought, and my contention is that it would be a mistake to imagine that the primary function of these statements is to communicate psychological facts. Their principal functions are judicial, not informative, and when they are informative, it is often not merely psychological information that they give. Consider the following remarks, as they might be used in suitable contexts in everyday life:

1   'They are very jealous of one another'
2   'I envy Schnabel's technique'
3   'I feel ashamed about it now'
4   'I never feel the slightest pang of regret for what I did'
5   'I am quite disgusted with the literary men' (Keats)
6   'Well, I hope you are ashamed of yourself'
7   'His pride in the Company's record is unjustified'
8   'He is very disappointed in you'

I think these are all typical examples, and they have been chosen at random, except that I have taken care to ensure that in each case it is clear that the operative word is the emotion word; i.e., I have avoided such instances as 'He is very disappointed by your failure to get there in time.' Of these examples, the first is different from the rest, its point, I assume, being to inform the hearer that a certain relationship exists between the persons referred to, e.g., in a suitable context, that they are rivals in their profession. The other remarks have what I have termed, for want of a better word, a judicial function. (2) praises Schnabel; it resembles, say, 'Schnabel has a brilliant technique', although it is more tentative and personal, and implies more than this – it would only be said by another pianist. (3) is an admission of responsibility, or perhaps a plea in mitigation, and (4) is the justification of a choice. (5) and (6) imply highly unfavourable assessments. In (5) Keats condemns literary men, and he goes on (letter of 8 October 1817) to give part of his reasons for feeling disgusted by telling an anecdote about Leigh Hunt. The force of (6) seems to lie in its mixture of blame with imputation of responsibility – there are two general lines of reply to it, either (a) 'No, I think I was quite right' or (b) 'No, it wasn't my fault.' (7) is either a way of saying that the person referred to is taking more credit than he deserves, or of saying that the Company's record is not as good as he believes. The normal conversational point of (8), I think, would be to convey blame.

In general, then, the affinities of (1)–(8) are not with descriptive statements about what people feel and do, but with a different type of statement altogether. (4), for instance, is very close to 'My choice was quite correct (sound, justified)' and (8) to 'You have not done as well as he expected.' These are not put forward as exact paraphrases; I only wish to suggest that they do not miss the point in the way that any psychological interpretation does. We do not counter such statements as (1)–(8) if we disagree by challenging an alleged fact. If this is accepted, it can be consistent with a psychological analysis of emotion concepts only if either (a) a naturalistic theory of value is presupposed, or (b) these usages are treated as non-literal.

(a)   It may be said that a judgement of value is a report or expression of an individual's feelings, and that it would not be surprising, therefore, if emotion words (reporting or expressing feelings) had a function somewhat similar to that of value words. I can only make one or two remarks about this here. Earlier I discussed a moral emotion, shame, and tried to show that the concept of shame is logically dependent on the moral notion of wrong action. I believe, then, that there are specifically moral emotions in this sense only: that the use of some emotion words ('remorse', 'shame', etc.) presupposes moral concepts. There are not specifically moral (or for that matter, aesthetic) experiences, and consequently no judgement of value can be a report, or an expression, of an experience. In the case of example (3), no statement that merely reported a feeling could be equivalent to it, since such a statement would not be an admission of responsibility. To accept responsibility for a past action (in the ordinary sense in which it is the opposite of taking credit for something), one has to admit that one did the action and to concede that it was wrong. But there is no experience which, taken in itself, is inconsistent with refusing to admit the one or concede the other. Even if there were a specific experience which always accompanied the admission of responsibility, this would be something logically accidental.

(b)   It could be argued that, although such words as 'regret' and 'pride' name emotions in their primary sense, they are used in a different sense in the examples. This will not doubt be turned by some into the objection that a consideration of such usages can throw no light on the nature of the emotions. What does this amount to? There exist uses of emotion words that are unquestionably figurative or metaphorical, e.g., 'angry masses of cloud', 'the raging waves of the sea foaming out their own shame'. Statements (1)–(8) are precisely the literal uses that would be contrasted with these, and no one is likely to maintain, therefore, that they are figurative in the strict sense. It may more plausibly be argued that they are extended or derivative senses of emotion words. But what, then, are the senses from which they are extended or derived? No use of, e.g., 'envy', 'ashamed', or 'pang of regret' appears to exist which is more basic, primary, or literal than that of the examples. There is perhaps a temptation to suppose, because we associate emotion with violent feelings and behaviour, that the word 'disgusted' is somehow being used more literally when it is used by or of a man who is actually feeling nausea than it is by Keats in the sentence I have quoted. But all that this proves, it seems to me, is that the experiences of those who are disgusted are different on different occasions. No doubt, to be disgusted with the literary men is not the same as being disgusted with the state of the kitchen sink – the one criticism is moral, and the other is not – but there is a very close and intelligible connection between them which should not be obscured by treating one sense as more primary than the other.

IV

What kind of an explanation of behaviour are we giving when we account for it in terms of emotions? I should like, in conclusion, to sketch the general lines on which I think this question ought to be answered. As this is no more than a corollary of the preceding discussion, I can put it very briefly. The traditional theory gives the answer that emotion words explain behaviour by specifying its cause, i.e., a certain feeling or inner experience. But surely, when we ask what caused someone to do something, we usually neither expect nor receive an answer in terms of feelings. The answer takes the form of a reference to some external circumstance, if that is relevant, or to some thought, memory, obeservation, etc., that accounts for the action. If we refer to feelings at all, this appears to be a type of explanation that we fall back on as a last resort, because it is unilluminating and only one step removed from saying that the action is unaccountable. What seems to me to be wrong, then, on this score, with the traditional view is that it does not do justice to the explanatory power of emotion words. For the fact is that to know the feeling that may have preceded an action is not to understand it, or to understand it only very imperfectly. One can remember an action that one did many years ago, an action that one no longer understands, and the question 'Why did I do it?' can remain in the face of the clearest recollection of what it felt like to do it. If emotion words merely named some inner experience that preceded or accompanied behaviour, to explain behaviour by using them would not give the insight that it does.

A quite different answer to this question is proposed by Professor Ryle (1949) in *The Concept of Mind*. Referring to what he calls 'inclinations' or 'motives', Professor Ryle writes, 'The imputation of a motive for a particular action is not a causal inference to an unwitnessed event but the subsumption of an episode proposition under a law-like proposition' (p. 90). Again, 'To explain an action as done from a certain motive is not to correlate it with an occult cause, but to subsume it under a propensity or behavior-trend' (p. 110). And as I understand him, explanation in terms of mood-words is of a generally similar character. Mood and motive explanations, despite their differences, have this in common, that they are explanations by reference to types of disposition (p. 97). Now, although I have been simply following Professor Ryle in what he here denies, I find the positive side of this less adequate. It does not seem to me that emotion words explain merely in the relatively superficial way that dispositional words explain, if 'the glass broke because it was brittle' is to be taken as a model, however rough, of this kind of explanation. To refer to a man's laziness or fondness for gardening is to account for what he does on a particular occasion by removing the need for a *special* explanation of it; by showing that his conduct is not in any way surprising or unusual, but part of the regular pattern of things that he does or is likely to do. To assimilate emotion words closely to dispositional words is to give an incomplete account of their explanatory function; they explain behaviour more fully than could be done by saying, in effect, that it was only to be expected. ('To say that he did something from that motive is to say that this action, done in its particular circumstances, was just the sort of thing that that was an inclination to do. It is to say "he *would* do that" ': (Ryle, 1949, pp. 92–3)).

I would suggest that emotion words go beyond this sort of explanation in two ways. First, they set the action to be explained, not merely in the context of the rest of an individual's behaviour, but in a social context. 'He was rude to you because he was jealous' resembles 'I helped him because he was a friend' in accounting for his behaviour by the reference it makes to his relationship with other people. Second, emotion words explain by giving one sort of reason for an action, i.e., by giving a justification, or partial justification, for it. 'He refused an interview because of his contempt for journalists' explains the refusal by connecting it with an assessment made by the person whose behaviour is referred to. In this respect it has some analogy with, for instance, 'He reads Gibbon because he thinks highly of his style.' Emotion concepts, I have argued, are not purely psychological: they presuppose concepts of social relationships and institutions, and concepts belonging to systems of judgement, moral, aesthetic and legal. In using emotion words we are able, therefore, to relate behaviour to the complex background in which it is enacted, and so to make human actions intelligible.

NOTES

1   The details vary. For example, it is very commonly held that every emotion must have an object, and therefore that it is an experience involving a 'cognitive' element, not a pure state of feeling. 'We must hold,' writes McTaggart, 'that the cogitation of that to which the emotion is directed, and the emotion towards it, are the same mental state, which has both the quality of being a cogitation of it, and the quality of being an emotion directed towards it' ((1921 and 1927), II, 146). (I think it is important to ask what 'directed towards' could mean here.) Russell claims that emotions also involve bodily movements. In *The Analysis of Mind* (1921) he says that 'an emotion – rage, for example – (is) a certain kind of process ... The ingredients of an emotion are only sensations and images and bodily movements succeeding each other according to a certain pattern' (p. 284). To discuss the details of these theories would complicate, without

affecting, my argument, which is meant to show that an emotion is not any sort of experience or process.

2 James prints the passage in italics.

3 This is not to say that we do not also use the word 'description' in such a way that (3) (immediately below) might form part of a description of some incident. When I say that (3) does not describe, I am making what could be looked on as a technical distinction between description and interpretation, which is meant to indicate a difference of order between (3) and (1) or (2). Higher-order statements explain and interpret what lower-order statements describe.

4 Let me give an analogy. 'Jones is responsible for this muddle' is a statement about the behaviour its truth is dependent on, although it is not shorthand for a set of statements describing that behaviour.

5 But the words 'right', 'unreasonable', etc., when used to qualify third-person statements, sometimes serve as endorsements of, or refusals to endorse, this assessment on the speaker's part. I discuss this point below.

6 A point noted in respect of envy by Aristotle in *Nichomachian Ethics*, 1107*a*.

7 In the same, i.e., moral, sense. A doctor might maintain that his patient ought not to feel any pain when the physical condition is not as a rule painful, or when he has given a dose of morphine that would alleviate the pain of most patients. 'Ought not to' here means (roughly) 'would not normally'. He might equally be prepared to give a reason why a patient feels giddy, i.e., a causal explanation. This is not a reason *for* feeling giddy, which is an impossibility.

REFERENCES

Boring, G., Langfield, H., and Weld, T. S. (1948) *Foundations of Psychology.* New York: John Wiley.

James, William (1890) *The Principles of Psychology*. New York: Henry Holt.

McTaggart, M. E. (1921/1927) *The Nature of Existence*, vol. II. Cambridge: Cambridge University Press.

Ross, David (1939) *Foundations of Ethics.* London: Clarendon Press.

Russell, B. (1921) *The Analysis of Mind.* London: Allen and Unwin.

Ryle, G. (1949) *The Concept of Mind.* London: Hutchinson.

Stout, G. F. (1938) *A Manual of Psychology*, 5th edn. London: University Tutorial Press.

3

The Thesis of Constructionism

Claire Armon-Jones

In the last ten years a new set of emotion theories has emerged. These theories (as represented for example in philosophy by Coulter, 1979; in social theory by Sabini and Silva, 1982; in psychology by Averill, 1980; and in anthropology by Lutz, 1982) retain the standard use of 'emotion' as a term to cover phenomena such as fear, anger, sorrow, joy, compassion, grief, remorse, envy, jealousy, guilt, pity, gratitude and other affective states. However, they are united by the principle that emotions are 'socioculturally constituted'. The principle of the 'sociocultural constitution of emotion' is one aspect of a general theory concerning the sociocultural constitution of individual experience, a theory which originated in the critical positivist tradition of post-enlightenment social philosophy. Mead regarded individual experience and behaviour as not prior to, but constituted by, the social group of which the individual is part: 'the behaviour of an individual can be understood only in terms of the behaviour of the whole social group of which he is a member, since his individual acts are involved in larger, social acts which go beyond himself and which implicate the other members of that group' (Mead, 1934).

Mead's theory was influential in promoting studies of the interdependence between social frameworks and the shaping of individual behaviour and experience. Similarly, Montesquieu's (1750) analysis of the sociological basis of political constitutions and civil law provided an inspiration for cross-cultural studies of the relation between individual experience and the religious beliefs, norms, political and social ideologies of particular cultural systems.

One outcome of these analyses is a model of general experience as constituted by what it is conceptualized as, and of conceptualizations as essentially deriving from the language, beliefs and social rules – the 'world view' – of the agent's cultural community. It is this model which provides the background to the constructionists' principle of emotion as 'socio-culturally constituted'. The arguments which claim to justify this background model require more clarification than I will be able to provide in this outline. However some crucial aspects of what the constructionist means by 'socioculturally constituted emotions' can be outlined as follows:

1   According to constructionism, emotions are characterized by attitudes such as beliefs, judgements and desires, the contents of which are not natural, but are determined by the systems of cultural belief, value and moral value of particular communities: 'the capacity to experience either shame or guilt . . . involves cultural knowledge and reasoning conventions' (Coulter, 1979). '. . . our capacity to experience certain emotions is contingent upon our learning to interpret and appraise matters in terms of norms, standards, principles and ends . . . judged desirable . . . or appropriate' (Pritchard, 1976).

2   Constructionists defend the view that emotion attitudes are culturally determined by the claim that the attitudes involved in emotions are learnt as part of the agent's introduction to the beliefs, values, norms and expectations of his/her culture. The acquisition of culturally appropriate emotion attitudes requires that emotions should be understood as elicited as a result of the agent's having acquired a culturally appropriate construal of the situation in which the situation is presented, and understood in terms of those values, etc., of his/her community: 'types of situation are paradigmatically linked to the emotions they afford by convention. The link is neither deterministic nor biological but sociocultural' (Coulter, 1979).

3   Thus far constructionism differs from naturalism in regarding emotions not as natural responses elicited by natural features which a situation may possess, but as socioculturally determined patterns of experience and expression which are acquired, and subsequently feature in, specifically social situations. However, constructionism adds to the claims above the following 'prescriptive' thesis: 'emotions are a soially prescribed set of responses to be followed by a person in a given situation. The response is a function of shared expectations regarding appropriate behaviour' (Averill, 1980). According to constructionism, there is a prescriptive implication embedded in the cultural situations in which emotions feature in that an emotion is not merely warranted by the situation as culturally construed but is deemed by members of a community to be a response which ought to feature in that situation because its presence would demonstrate the agent's commitment to the cultural values exemplified in that situation. This prescriptive relation between the emotion and the values it reflects is alleged by constructionists to have a crucial role in contributing to the acquisition of culturally appropriate emotions and to the subsequent regulation of the agent's responses to emotion-warranting situations.

4   The rationale for (3), according to constructionism, is that emotions are constituted in order to serve sociocultural functions: 'the meaning of an emotion – its functional significance is to be found primarily within the sociocultural system' (Averill, 1980). Emotions are regarded by constructionists as functional in that the possession of culturally appropriate emotions serves to restrain undesirable attitudes and behaviour, and to sustain and endorse cultural values: 'emotions are statements about, and motivations for the enactment of cultural values' (Lutz, 1982). This functional account of emotion again differs from naturalism in that it requires that emotions are related in some way to agent responsibility. For example, according to constructionism, once emotion attitudes are acquired then agents can be held responsible for the adoption and expression of such attitudes in the contexts for which they are prescribed. Thus, unlike the alleged 'natural, passive state', the adopted emotion is able to demonstratively reinforce the social value which commands the response and the agent's commitment to the value.

THE IMPLICATIONS OF CONSTRUCTIONISM

Constructionist theories of emotion, are I think, important and worth examining not only because they go beyond traditional theories of emotion as natural phenomena but because they have radical implications for both philosophical and practical ethics.

What implications does constructionism have for philosophical ethics? The ethical theories of, for example Kant (1949) and the Emotivists (e.g., Stevenson, 1937) are opposed in their views of the relation between emotions and moral discourse. According to Kant, moral discourse should be expressive of objectivity and consistency in rational judgement concerning moral matters. The emotions, being capricious and unevenly distributed natural dispositions, should not be motivations for, or involved in, such judgements. According to Emotivism, moral discourse is essentially functional, its function being to express the emotions of the speaker and incite emotions in others. Kant's theory is compatible with the view that moral training can educate and exert a controlling influence on natural emotional dispositions. However, both theories regard emotions as phenomena which are ontologically prior to moral judgement and action. Whereas for Kant emotions, as natural dispositions, should be ignored in moral judgement, for the Emotivists these natural dispositions are necessary conditions of moral judgement. Also, it was certain assumptions concerning the nature of emotion, which prompted the criticisms of Emotivism. According to Urmson (1963), Emotivism is false because emotions are not within our power to choose or reject and therefore could not be objects of moral incitement or influence.

However, constructionism disputes not only the grounds for this criticism but also the theories it addresses. According to constructionism, moral sentiments such as 'guilt' and 'pity' are not ontologically prior to moral judgement because a grasp of certain moral rules is a precondition of the capacity to feel the moral sentiments. Thus far, constructionism reverses the Emotivists' account in regarding such sentiments not as causal conditions, but as dependent upon the prior understanding of moral rules and discourse. In particular, according to constructionism, it is because the moral sentiments involve moral attitudes such as the evaluation of an act as morally wrong that, *contra* Urmson, such sentiments can involve agent responsibility and be subjected to rational appraisal and criticism. Moreover, as Williams (1972) suggests, in criticism of Kant's ethical theory, moral worth and emotion are not separable, since emotion has a crucial role in conveying the sincerity of moral worth. Here constructionism develops this role of emotion by explaining it as a social function of emotion, and the constitution of the 'moral sentiments' as part of moral training.

What implications would constructionism have for practical ethics? If, as the constructionist claims, emotions are functionally constituted for the maintenance of particular value systems, then a moral issue arises in that such organizations of human experience not only are socially based, but also can be evaluated as desirable and just. For example, during the early stages of the First World War recruitment of British soldiers was increased by propaganda aimed at the creation of an attitude which would enhance the motivation of young men to fight. The attitude in question, 'courageous patriotism', qualifies as an emotion because it was clearly something felt, i.e., 'the fervour, shining eyes and heart swelling with pride', etc. Moreover, the emotion itself was not clearly separable from its intended purpose, in that to feel 'courageous patriotism' was at that time, by social definition, to wish to be in the battlefields saving one's country and to believe that in performing such actions one's integrity as a citizen and as a man was preserved. Hence it was from such specific ends that the emotion derived its particular quality and content. The ethical issue which would arise here is whether it is morally acceptable to create an emotion which obscures the realities of war, diverts the person from other desires (e.g., immediate self-preservation) and responsibilities (e.g., family) and suppresses other emotions (e.g., compassion for the construed opposition).

THE ASSUMPTIONS OF CONSTRUCTIONISM

My aim in this chapter is to examine certain aspects of constructionism chosen with respect to both their foundational role in constructionist theory and their amenability to philosophical analysis. Given the varieties of emotions and of emotion theories, I will not be able to test the arguments proposed for every emotion, nor will I consider all the philosophical issues which constructionism might inspire. Descriptive work has been done by theorists, including those mentioned here, on the question of how emotions are socioculturally constituted. However, little philosophical attention has been paid to the question of how it is possible that emotions could be socioculturally constituted. So we need to specify the theory of mind that is presupposed in the constructionist account, and to consider various versions of constructionism.

First, constructionism would appear to require a theory of mind in which emotions, as instances of psychological states, are defined as cognition-based. On the constructionist account culturally appropriate emotion attitudes are acquired by reference to those contexts for which the emotion is deemed to be desirable. This implies that, once the emotion has been acquired, then the agent's further ability to respond appropriately will depend crucially upon his/her ability to appraise a situation as warranting the emotion. The view that emotions depend upon appraisals is compatible with those contemporary philosophical theories which characterize emotions as cognitive in virtue of their dependence upon judgement and belief.

Second, and following from this, constructionism also appears to require a theory of mind in which emotions can be defined as in some sense world-dependent. The constructionist's account of emotions as responses appropriate to cultural contexts implies some kind of link between the emotion and external states of affairs. Post-Wittgensteinian philosophers have argued that psychological states such as emotion could not be identified via introspection alone because inner states lack the requisite identifying features. Emotions, they argue, are identified in part by behaviour, and in part by those external situations to which the emotion is directed. Constructionism is, it seems, committed to some version of this philosophical thesis in that, if it were possible to identify emotions via introspection alone, then the notion of 'appropriate context' would be redundant and could not have the explanatory role which the constructionist ascribes to it.

However, constructionism contains assumptions which go beyond the philosophical positions stated above. The philosophical theses make the minimal and general claim that emotions are world-dependent in so far as they are individuated by reference to behaviour and to appropriate object or situation types. But this thesis as it stands is still compatible with the naturalist views which constructionism disputes, since it is consistent with the claim that the external referents of emotions have a natural and universal status and give rise to responses constituted by natural beliefs and desires, etc. Constructionism maintains that emotions are constituted by non-natural attitudes, these being acquired in, and explicable by reference to, specifically sociocultural contexts.

This last claim requires that emotions are constituted by attitudes which are in principle learnable, and that such attitudes and their external referents are either irreducibly or significantly sociocultural in nature. The constructionist theses also require that emotions can be understood as prescribable for a social system, and that the sociocultural determination of emotion is revealed not only in semantics via its influence on our understanding of emotion terms but also in phenomenology via its penetration to the quality of emotion experience itself. So, while constructionism requires the minimal philosophical thesis above, in order to oppose the naturalist view constructionism also requires a validation of these further assumptions.

Third, constructionism opposes the traditional view expressed in philosphy in psychology that emotions are non-purposive forces which serve to disrupt rationality. Descartes and Darwin did allow that emotions are purposive in so far as they assist the survival of the individual. However, constructionism goes beyond this individualistic teleology in regarding the function of the emotions as essentially sociocultural and as serving individuals only as members of their community. This sociofunctional account of emotion exposes constructionism to the objection that it is not clear what kind of social function could be ascribed to phenomena such as ill-founded and negative emotions. Consequently, constructionism also needs to provide a plausible explanation of the way in which, and the extent to which, emotions can be understood as having a sociofunctional role.

CONSTRUCTIONISM VERSUS NATURALISM

The points made so far raise the question of how radical an alternative to the naturalist view of emotions constructionism intends to be. Here I will briefly outline two possible versions of constructionism which take the form of a strong and a weaker thesis. I will suggest that the weaker thesis is more plausible and is also sufficient to dispute some of the important premises of naturalism.

The strong thesis can be defined as one which claims that for any emotion, including the primary emotions, that emotion is an irreducibly sociocultural product. From this it would follow that no emotion can be a natural state, and therefore that the complex or sophisticated emotions cannot be regarded as cultural modifications of natural states. On this view the term 'emotion' derives from, and is central to, the sociocultural domain. The similarities between natural responses and 'emotions' are incidental. So to predicate the term 'emotion' of natural responses is to extend the term beyond its scope of legitimate application. This radical view gains support from two equally radical philosophical theses. First, the similarity between human and non-human behaviour cannot be used as evidence for the claim that emotions are natural states because emotions involve cognitions such as belief and judgement which cannot legitimately be ascribed to members of non-human species. Second, agents cannot be said to feel an emotion (E) unless they have a grasp of the concept E and can apply this concept to their own experience on appropriate occasions.

The weaker thesis can be defined as one which concedes to the naturalist the existence of a limited range of natural emotion responses. This view is implied by Averill, who states that 'the view that there is an invariant core to emotional behaviour which remains untouched by socio-cultural influences is essentially a reification of emotion in to a biological given' (1980). Averill's reference to emotions as 'untouched by socio-cultural influences' appears to allow for the possibility of emotion responses as featuring prior to, and extra to, sociocultural influences.

One advantage of the weaker thesis is that, in conceding the existence of natural emotions, it escapes some of the difficulties of the strong view. For example, on the strong view it remains unexplained why, if emotions such as 'fear' are never natural responses, the humans who undergo these emotions exhibit much the same types of behaviour as some non-human species. Here it seems implausible to argue that responses which produce the same, or similar, effects are nevertheless entirely different. Also, given that it is such effects which provide evidence for the ascription of beliefs and judgements, etc., then it is not clear why these inferences from behaviour to mental state should be confined to humans. If such cognitive features can be ascribed to non-human species, then they need not serve as evidence for the non-naturalness of human emotions. In particular, the fact that we often regard non-verbal behaviour as sufficient for the ascription of emotions such as 'fear' to other persons suggests that mastery by them of the concept 'fear' is not a necessary condition of their experiencing this emotion. These points support our intuition that some objects or situations are natural referents of emotions such as 'fear' in virtue of their possessing features relevant to extra-social needs such as survival. For instance, no cultural significance need be attached by persons to a charging bull in order for it to be construed by them as dangerous and as warranting fear.

The strong view, in denying the existence of any natural emotions, is committed to refuting the points above and is in this respect problematic. However, the weaker version raises the question of exactly what is being asserted. Is it that some emotions, such as non-primary emotion types, are entirely socioculturally constituted? Or is it that all emotion types are socioculturally constituted to some extent? The first option is vulnerable to the naturalist objection that, for any emotion type, we can provide an instance of that type which is not specifically sociocultural – for example, instances of 'compassion' as generated by natural, empathic distress at the suffering of another being. So the second option seems preferable. It enables the constructionist to demonstrate the extent to which both primary and non-primary emotion types are socioculturally constituted, a position which is compatible with there being instances of both types in which they are natural respnses to natural situations.

For the constructionist who adopts this version of the weaker thesis, the interest lies, I think, in the question of how much significance can be attached to the natural emotions relative to the socioculturally constituted emotions. For example, proponents of naturalism endorse the view that emotions, primitive and socialized, share the same biological bases and, where applicable, the same natural cognitions. Sociocultural variables, in so far as they feature in naturalist theory, have a peripheral influence, e.g., in reducing the intensity of the natural response and in determining the manner in which it is outwardly displayed. A proponent of this approach is Ekman (1980), who introduces the term 'display rule' to explain the cultural prohibition and control of natural emotion states. For example, he claims that the exhibition of 'grief' at funerals in certain societies is a natural response constrained by norms which permit its expression only if the griever is close to the deceased.

The crucial point here is that the naturalist's predication of the term 'emotion' to both primitive and socialized emotions is justified by the view that both phenomena are sufficiently similar to fall under the same term. The weaker constructionist's objection to this account would be that, in so far as emotions involve specifically sociocultural attitudes, feature in specifically sociocultural contexts and bear a prescriptive, functional relation to such contexts, the naturalist cannot extrapolate his account of natural emotions in order to explain them. Furthermore, the naturalist's account is of limited scope since the salient aspects of an agent's emotional responses form part of a mental life, the interests, goals and general attitudes of which largely reflect the agent's membership of his/her cultural community. So the issue presented by the weaker constructionist is perhaps a more subtle one, inviting us to consider whether our application of the term 'emotion' both to natural and cultural instances of a response leads us to ignore their discontinuities.

The sense in which emotions can be understood as constituted by specifically sociocultural attitudes, and the prescriptive relation which emotions bear to sociocultural beliefs and values, is an issue which I have examined elsewhere (Armon-Jones, 1985). In this chapter I will describe some contemporary philosophical critiques of traditional theories of emotion, focusing in particular upon those features of the contemporary views which are compatible with, and might therefore provide a framework for, constructionism. I will suggest that the contemporary philosphical characterization of emotions as cognition-based and as involving attitudinal components should be understood as providing a basis for the constructionist principle of emotions as socioculturally acquired responses. I will also, having examined some theories of the role of sensation, and the subjective element in 'emotion feeling', suggest that emotion feeling can be analysed as essentially constituted by the relevant attitudinal components. This claim is relevant to constructionism since, if sociocultural factors can determine emotion attitudes, then such factors should also be understood as determining emotion feeling via their determination of the attitudes by which emotion feeling is constituted.

THE REFUTATION OF THE TRADITIONAL THEORIES OF EMOTION

Philosophers traditionally defined the emotions as 'passions'. Passions were regarded as involuntary, non-cognitive phenomena which, like sensation and perception, are incorrigibly known simple impressions named by simple concepts: '[the passions] are received into the soul in exactly the same fashion as the objects of the exterior senses' (Descartes, 1952); '. . . a passion is an original existent' (Hume, 1978); '. . . [they] are so interior to our soul that it is impossible that they should be felt without their being in reality just as they are felt' (Descartes, 1952).

The traditional view is, first, subject to Wittgenstein's general critique of introspectionist semantics. According to this view, the inner feelings of both passions and sensations are contingently related to, and hence logically independent of, their expressions in verbal and physical behaviour. This view, Wittgenstein points out, renders the inner feelings themselves radically private. Against this, he argues that the inner feelings are not radically private but accessible since the terms via which we describe them depend upon objective criteria for their meaning and justification, and hence form a part of a shared public language: 'an "inner process" stands in need of outward criteria' (Wittgenstein, 1980).

Second, Wittgenstein points out that emotions and sensations are fundamentally dissimilar in that emotions, unlike sensations, are characteristically about an external object or situation, a reference which is apparent in the inclusion of a grammatical object in emotion sentences; for example, M is 'annoyed with x/afraid of x/grateful to x/angry that x', x being some situation, person, action or attribute in the world which provides the extension of the emotion. Thus far, the general characterization of emotions as involving 'a reference to something beyond the person himself or beyond his present state' (Pitcher, 1965) already moves away from the traditional view of the passions as inner processes, logically distinct from the external world.

The analysis of the meaning of emotion terms also suggests that there are logical restrictions upon the type of object to which an emotion can refer. 'Envy' and 'jealousy', for example, do not, within their grammatical rules, permit me to feel 'envious' or 'jealous' of myself, because these emotions share the feature that they are conceptually related to objects, the range of which excludes the subject of the emotion. By contrast, the subject can be included among the objects of emotions such as 'pride' and 'shame'. While M can also be proud or 'ashamed' of someone else, there must be some relation of responsibility or personal relevance here in order for M's emotion to qualify as 'pride' or 'shame'. For example, M's feeling 'proud' of his son's achievements requires that M regards himself as in some way responsible for, and able to take credit for, the events in his son's life. Similarly, although an agent can ascribe to himself the term 'annoyed' or 'angry', he cannot ascribe to himself the term 'indignant' if the act of negligence which gives rise to his feelings is his own fault: only if the act of negligence is the fault of someone else could he describe himself as 'indignant'. So there are generally restrictions upon the sort of object to which an emotion type can be directed (see Bedford, chapter 2 above).

THE COGNITIVE ASPECT OF EMOTIONS

The examples considered so far enable us to illustrate the contemporary philosophical view (e.g., Kenny, 1963; Lyons, 1980; Gordon, 1969) that emotions are dependent upon cognitions. In order to be 'envious' I must believe that the object of my 'envy', e.g., an attribute, belongs to another, and I must also believe that it is an attribute which I do not possess. Similarly, my being 'guilty' or 'ashamed' about an action requires that I believe that I am responsible for the action. However, while beliefs may be essential to the generation of emotions, they are not sufficient to constitute particular emotions because different emotions can be generated by the same belief. For example, the 'belief that x is dangerous' could provoke 'fear' in M and 'excitement' in S. The crucial differentiating factors are commonly the evaluative and appetitive attitudes which are also involved; for example, the difference between the two emotions above may be explained by the fact that S's 'excitement' about x is warranted by his desire to live dangerously, whereas M's 'fear' about the same x is warranted by his evaluation of x as menacing or threatening to him and his desire to avoid x.

Similarly, my feeling 'envious' requires that I hold the beliefs stated above in conjunction with other attitudes to which 'envy' is conceptually related, such as 'my evaluating the attribute as good' and 'my desiring the attribute for myself'. It is not a necessary condition of my being envious that I regard the attribute as desirable in all respects, only that, despite other opinions I may have about the attribute, I regard it as desirable in some respect. For example, while I may regard M's ruthlessness as undesirable in so far as it causes him to be selfish and inconsiderate towards others, I may also regard M's ruthlessness as desirable in so far as it gives him determination and assists his career. It would be correct to say that if I decide that, all things considered, M's ruthlessness is undesirable then I cannot be, or continue to be, envious. But I am not impelled to resolve my appraisals of the attribute in this way, in particular because they focus on different aspects and consequences of the attribute and are not therefore self-contradictory.

Exactly how the various attitudinal components which individuate the particular emotions are interrelated is a question debated by philosophical theorists of emotion. However, as a general theory the attitudinal acount disputes the traditional theories of emotion in the following respects. As opposed to traditional views, the beliefs, evaluations and appetitive attitudes involved in an emotion are cognitive in that they depend upon the agent's knowledge and his capacity to judge and compare. Also, if emotions are constituted by particular conjunctions of attitudes, then they are not, as the traditional views claim, simple but complex phenomena; i.e., M can explain his 'anger' avowal by stating the object of his 'anger', say, S's action; his belief, say, that the action was directed towards himself; his evaluation, say, of the action as an insult; and his desires, say, to seek revenge on S.

EMOTIONS AND INTENSIONAL OBJECTS

The attitudinal account also imposes restrictions upon the status of the object to which an emotion can be directed. If M's 'anger' is 'about x', then x is the extension of M's emotion. However, given that it is M's attitudes towards x which generate his emotion, then x, in its role of explaining M's emotion, has to be characterized intensionally. This distinction can be elucidated by using Aristotle's account of 'anger' (in his *Rhetoric*) as 'a desire for what appears to be a revenge for what appears to be an insult'.

Let us suppose that the referent of M's 'anger' in Aristotle's example is A's doing x: 'letting his tongue protrude from his mouth'. Here it is not x as extensionally characterized, but x as construed as, or believed by the agent to be, 'an insult' which is conceptually related to 'anger' and which explains his 'anger' as warranted by the action. Similarly, as we saw in the case of 'envy', the descriptions applicable to x such as 'ruthless' are not interchangeable *salva veritate* in their role of explaining M's 'envy', because it is the attribute only as construed in terms of its advantages (promoting A's career) which warrants M's 'envy'. So while it is towards an object x that the agent's emotion E is directed, and it is x which provides the extension of E, it is x under the agent's descriptions that explains x as an object of E in particular.

If an emotion depends upon the construal of an object under those intensional descriptions which warrant the emotion, then this provides considerable latitude, both in the range of token extensional objects to which a particular emotion can be directed and in the range of third-person evaluations concerning the warrantedness of the emotion. For example, token objects of M's 'depression' can run the gamut from 'the weather' to 'work' to 'personal relationships'. These objects have few extensional properties in common; however, they warrant M's 'depression' in so far as they share the intensional feature of 'looking bleak to M', etc. *A fortiori*, the third-person evaluation of an agent's emotion as warranted depends not only upon judgements concerning the extension of the object (e.g., that there really is an x of which M is afraid) but also upon agreement over the agent's construal as being a plausible construal of the object (e.g., that x can be construed as menacing or dangerous).

THE RELATION BETWEEN CONSTRUCTIONISM AND CONTEMPORARY EMOTION THEORIES

What relevance do the accounts outlined above have for constructionism? The characterization of emotion as attitudinal and cognition-dependent is crucial to constructionism in the following respects. According to constructionism, a socioculturally constituted emotion is an acquired response. This requires that the elements constitutive of the emotion are ones which are capable of being acquired by the agent. Consequently, it is essential to constructionism that an account of emotion be given in which emotions are neither identifiable with, nor have the same ontological status as, phenomena such as sensation and perception. This is so because, although perceptual skills, for instance, can be acquired, we also have reason to believe that perception and sensation are not essentially skills acquired by training but are natural phenomena which exist prior to the acquisition of any sociocultural frame of reference within which we might want to explain them. Hence, if an emotion was, as Aquinas believed (in 'The emotions'), a matter of a perception followed by a sensation, then this would cast doubt on the possibility of the emotion's being a socioculturally acquired phenomenon.

However, the contemporary accounts of emotion are consistent with constructionism in that the attitudes regarded by contemporary theorists as constituting emotions share the feature that they can in principle be acquired by training. While we regard some attitudes as natural (e.g., the desire to eat; the evaluation of wild beasts as dangerous), we regard other attitudes as dependent upon training and the introduction to a social custom (e.g., the desire to be polite; the evaluation of a Matisse as delicate; the belief that theft is a crime). Thus far, the contemporary accounts of emotion appear to provide an apposite framework upon which constructionists might build their explanation of how the attitudes which constitute the various emotions are socioculturally constituted.

Furthermore, the explanation of emotions as involving reference to an object or situation type enables the constructionist to demonstrate the extent to which such situations reflect the beliefs, values and expectations of particular cultures and the way in which such situations are used as contexts for the acquisition of the culturally appropriate emotion attitudes. Also, the constructionist can explain the agent's subsequent construals of situations as warranting certain emotions in virtue of the construal's involving attitudes which reflect the beliefs and values of the agent's community.

Finally, the attitudinal account opposes the Cartesian and Kantian view of emotions as opposed to the faculty of reason. If emotions are cognition-based, then this allows that they can be subjected to rational persuasion and criticism. For example, agents can be reasoned out of their 'anger' just because the emotion is based on attitudes which can themselves be critically appraised in respect of whether they form an accurate or reasonable construal of the situation. If the agent misinterprets the situation as an insult, then we expect and consider him able to relinquish his 'anger'. This point is relevant to constructionism because it allows that emotions can be endorsed or condemned with respect to the social appropriateness of the attitudes by which the emotion is generated, and that agents can be held responsible for the possession or absence of those emotion attitudes which are socially required for a situation.

EMOTIONS, SENSATIONS AND QUALIA

The analysis given so far has characterized emotion in terms of the attitude complexes to which the various emotion types are conceptually related. According to some attitudinal theorists emotion feeling is not reducible to attitudes, in which case the analysis is, as it stands, incomplete in failing to incorporate emotion 'feeling' itself. This alleged incompleteness of a purely attitudinal account has led to various compromise views in which emotion 'feeling' is reintroduced by supplementing attitudinal components either with the notion of emotion qualia or with physiological features.

The motive for the introduction of emotion qualia is the belief that emotion feeling has a subjective element which is not reducible to the belief, desire and judgement components of the emotion. This subjective element is regarded as a phenomenally distinct feeling which, though evident in the experience of 'being moved' by an emotion, can only be 'vaguely approximated' via evocation and metaphor and so cannot be entirely captured via attitudinal analyses. For example, Arnold qualifies her cognitive account of emotion by adding to it an 'emotion quale [which] consists precisely in that unreasoning involuntary attraction or compulsion' (Arnold, 1960). Similarly, with reference to emotion conceptualizations, Leventhal maintains that 'the verbal, conceptual system ... is a way of representing and communication about feelings but not a representation of the feelings themselves' (Leventhal, 1980). The implication of these remarks is that there is a gap between emotion feelings themselves and the means by which they are conceptually represented.

The introduction of emotion qualia to the characterization of emotion poses a difficulty for constructionism in the following respects. The constructionist wants to argue that emotions are socioculturally constituted in that sociocultural factors determine not only emotion attitudes and their expression in language and behaviour, but also the experiential aspect of emotion via their determination of emotion feeling. The 'qualia' thesis outlined above requires that it is a necessary condition of a state's being a felt emotion that the attitudes involved are accompanied by an irreducible subjective feeling. The qualia thesis poses a difficulty for constructionism in virtue of its individualistic implications. It postulates a domain of individual emotion experience which is not reducible to emotion attitudes and expression and therefore can remain exempt from the sociocultural factors which are alleged by the constructionist to explain these latter components. Hence if the experiential aspect of emotion amounts to irreducible qualia, then this casts doubt on the possibility that emotion feeling could be socioculturally constituted.

The 'physiological' thesis (e.g. Perkins, 1966) poses a difficulty for constructionism in virtue of its naturalistic implications. Physiological factors such as chemically induced arousal and increased motor activity are biological events understood to be basic, natural and involuntary. Hence if these events are necessary components of a felt emotion, then this limits the scope of the constructionist's argument in that it reduces those components of the emotion which could be explained as socioculturally constituted. For instance, such physiological events could not be prescribed nor subjected to social endorsement and condemnation. The constructionist could argue here that, even if emotion feeling amounts to physiological events, this is not inconsistent with constructionism since it is the agent's attitudes, themselves socioculturally constituted, which cause the physiological events in question. Hence the 'physiological' thesis does not provide a strong opposition since it does not necessarily support naturalism. However this approach is unsatisfactory in so far as it requires constructionists to relinquish their view of emotion feeling as culturally constituted in favour of its being a natural response caused indirectly by cultural factors. While constructionists could take this approach, they do not need to do so since emotion feeling can, I believe, be adequately characterized without appealing to qualia or to physiological factors as necessary constituents of the total emotion event.

THE CONSTITUTION OF EMOTION FEELING BY ATTITUDES

Here I want to examine a distinction which Wittgenstein draws between emotion and sensation because it is relevant to the problem posed for constructionism by the qualia thesis. Despite contemporary philosophical agreement that psychological predicates require outward, critical justification, the qualia thesis above implies an adherence to the belief that criteria are expressive of an inner quale or irreducible raw feel not only in the case of sensation but also in the case or emotion. But this raises the question of what the 'feeling' term in an avowal such as 'I feel x' (where x stands for an emotion predicate) could refer to. The difficulty here is that, although the account above may apply to sensation, the notion of a residual qualia is not plausible in the case of emotion. Why not?

Wittgenstein, as already noted, argues that the terms for both emotion and sensation feelings are conceptually related to those verbal and physical expressions to which they give rise. However while in the case of sensation Wittgenstein does 'not deny the existence of the inner process' (*Philosophical Investigations*, 304), in the case of the emotion 'joy', for example, he states: 'and of course joy is not joyful behaviour nor yet a feeling around the corner of the mouth and eyes. "But joy surely designates an inward thing?" No. Joy designates nothing at all. Neither any inward nor any outward thing' (Wittgenstein, 1981, p. 487).

From Wittgenstein's remarks on the failure of emotions such as 'joy' to 'designate anything' can be derived the following claims. First, the remark above is not meant to imply that 'joy' lacks any kind of referent, but is, as Green (1979) suggests, meant to criticize theoretical reductions of emotion to either inner feeling or outer behaviour, and to emphasize that no single item of verbal or physical behaviour can provide sufficient conditions for the ascription of an emotion.

Second, I would suggest that the reason why Wittgenstein confines 'reference to an inner process' to sensation terms is that sensation terms do refer to inner qualia in virtue of the fact that such qualia are not embraced by, and remain ontologically distinct from, the expressions to which they give rise and to which they are conceptually related. For example, the raw feeling of a pain cannot be constituted by 'my clutching my leg, believing that I am in pain, and making verbal avowals' because pain can be felt independently of such attitudes and their behavioural expressions. Hence Wittgenstein's claim that sensation feels are conceptually related to outward criteria in the form of the appropriate verbal and behavioural expressions is a purely semantic claim concerning conditions of meaningfulness for sensation terms, not an ontological claim about the existence of sensation feelings. The point here is that sensation terms refer to 'inner processes' just because, though conceptually related to, they are nevertheless ontologically distinct from, the attitudes and behaviour to which they give rise. Thus far it is not to emotion feelings but to sensation feelings that Leventhal's distinction between representation and feeling really seems to apply.

However, with reference to the emotion 'joy', Wittgenstein remarks:

> the gasp of joy, laughter, jubilation, the thoughts of happiness – is not the experience of all this: joy? Do I know then that he is joyful because he tells me he feels his laughter, feels and hears his jubilation – or because he laughs and is jubilant? Do I say 'I am happy' because I feel all that? . . . the words 'I am happy' are a bit of the behaviour of joy. (Wittgenstein, 1980, p. 151)

Wittgenstein is, I think, making two points in this remark. The first point is that we do not recognize our 'joy' as a result of observing our thoughts and behaviour. I do not infer that I am joyful via induction from 'hearing my jubilation'. Rather, I simply think and behave in a joyful manner such that my recognition of my emotion, as expressed in the avowal 'I am happy', is part of the expression of the emotion. The second point which emerges from the above remark is that 'the gasp of joy, laughter, jubilation, the thoughts of happiness' amount to – are identifiable with – the 'experience of joy'. Hence, unlike the case of sensation, in which attitudes and behaviour refer to an inner quale of which such factors are ontologically independent, in the case of emotions these factors are ontologically constitutive of emotion feeling.

A complication arises here because although, when considering the constitution of emotion feeling, Wittgenstein refers to 'the thoughts of happiness', he nevertheless appears to focus on the expression of such thoughts in the form of outward verbal and physical behaviour. But 'feeling joyful' need not be overtly expressed. I can 'feel joyful' without allowing it to show in my verbal and physical behaviour. This is compatible with the possibility that, on occasions, 'feeling joyful' can be fully manifested in its outward expression, and also with the claim that such outward signs provide the criterial justification from which the term 'joy' derives its meaning. However, if 'feeling joyful' need not be made manifest, then Wittgenstein's reference to the constitution of emotion 'feeling' by 'expression' needs qualifying.

Here we can define 'expression' as criterial for 'feeling joyful' in so far as it manifests in verbal and physical behaviour those attitudes which are themselves constitutive of emotion feeling. First, this qualification remains compatible with the general point of Wittgenstein's remark that the 'feeling of joy' is not an inner quale. The avowal 'I am happy' is an expression of 'joy', one which does not however refer to an inner quale but is expressive of the 'thoughts of happiness'. Second, I would suggest that the 'thoughts' in question can be analysed as the agent's complex realizations of the attitudes to which 'joy' is conceptually related. Let us suppose that M is 'feeling joyful about' x – 'the news that his wife is not terminally ill after all'. Here M's dwelling on the occasion of his hearing the news, his visions of his wife returning home, his plans for their future, etc., can be defined as realizations of those attitudes towards x which constitute his 'feeling joyful', such as his belief that his wife is not terminally ill, his evaluation of the news is good, his strong desire for her to live and remain his companion, and so on.

The points made so far suggest that the feeling of 'joy' is not an ontologically distinct inner quale but is constituted by those thoughts which provide the particular content of the attitudes to which 'joy' is conceptually related; moreover, that the 'feeling' term does not in this case refer to an inner quale but to those attitudes which are constitutive of 'feeling joyful'. This account of 'joy feeling' as constituted by the relevant emotion attitudes can, I think, be generalized to other emotions, as I will try to show. First, we need to clarify the relation between emotion attitudes and their expression in verbal and physical behaviour.

This relation can be clarified by distinguishing between the overt expression and the covert entertaining of emotion attitudes. For example, in overtly expressing his 'anger', the angry person tends to convey his feelings towards the offender via spoken appraisals such as (P) 'wretched bastard . . . get out!' and he may also behave in a violent manner; whereas in covertly entertaining an emotion such attitudes and behaviour remain undisplayed. Here the antagonist's claim that linguistic and behavioural expression does not represent inner feeling is correct in so far as overt expression can be a refined version of the inner feeling. For example, my 'feeling angry' can, and often does, amount to more than 'my shaking my fist' and stating P. But it does not follow that what is actually omitted from overt emotion expression must be omitted because of its alleged irreducibility to the attitudes constitutive of 'feeling angry'. In particular, the covertly entertained emotion is a mode of experiencing the emotion which shares the same features as the overt expression to which it is conceptually related; for example, in feeling inwardly angry the agent responds to the occasion of his being wronged by experiencing angry thoughts such as P above. However, P shares the same descriptive features as the overt communication. Here P, whether conveyed or merely thought, represents the agent's attitudes to the offender, e.g., the judgement that S has wronged him and his desire to 'seek revenge'. While in the case of a covert entertaining of 'anger' we may also experience violent urges, the urge again has the same descriptive features as the overt act of violence in that the urge takes form not of a sensation but of a bodily rehearsal of the display of 'anger'.

However, the distinction between overt and covert emotion feeling is not sharp. The angry person may convey his attitudes but restrain his behaviour. Alternatively, he may prevent a full statement of his attitudes by letting his 'anger' be known in a stilted or ambiguous way, e.g., 'it is remarkable how mean some people can be isn't it S?' etc. The two modes of emotion expression differ in the following respects. An overt expression of emotion feeling is frequently a communicative act and hence leads to particular consequences. One effect of overt 'sadness' is consolation or commiseration from others. Also, in communicating an emotion we do, I think, commit ourselves to being a possessor of that emotion. By contrast, undisplayed feeling can remain ambiguous and hence is more amenable to self-deception. If M suppresses the outward signs of his 'sorrow' then it is easier for him to pretend, or to persuade himself, that he does not in fact 'feel sad'. Nevertheless, both modes can be equally constitutive of emotion feeling. Just as the consequences of overt emotion expression may enhance feeling (e.g., M's display of anger may instigate a fight which in turn intensifies his angry feelings), so covert emotion feeling can be as intense, if not more so, than the display. (For example, 'anger' can build up for being suppressed; similarly 'grief, sorrow and fear' can feed upon themselves unless conveyed and discussed.) But if to feel these emotions is either to express overtly or entertain inwardly the relevant attitudes, then how, it may be objected, can this account allow us to measure the intensity of emotion feeling? How can the possession of such attitudes provide an account of the agent's being moved by an emotion?

So here we want to ask: What has to be added to these emotions for them to qualify as emotions by which the agent is moved? In the case of 'regret', for example, I would suggest that the recollections and wishes of the agent must first be vivid, in that agents could not reasonably be said to feel intensely regretful about an event which they barely remember. Second, such attitudes must be serious, in that to feel intensely regretful requires more than a passing acknowledgement of something that the agent wishes had not happened. In particular, a usual feature of intense regret is that the emotion is at least tinged with sorrow about the event. Third, such attitudes must be consuming, since to be moved by 'regret' the agent's recollections and wishes must not only be occurrent, but must also greatly or totally preoccupy the agent's attention. Similarly, in order to feel intense 'fear' the agent must not merely surmise, but must have a firm conviction, that the object x of his 'fear' is dangerous; he must construe x not as faintly threatening, but as vividly menacing; his attention must be totally absorbed by x and he must also have a strong or urgent desire to avoid x.

Here it seems reasonable to suggest that the inner array of events described above constitutes a typical state of feeling 'regretful' or 'afraid' and hence explains sufficiently what it is to be moved by these emotions in a particular case. Consequently, in the case of 'regret', for example, a report such as 'I wish that x had not happened', although a refined expression of the agent's attitudes, is not an 'approximation of the subjective element' but is at most a summary of, and at least a selection from, these attitudes. Hence the antagonist's reference to 'vagueness' as a descriptive feature of the subjective element seems misdirected. If I can only vaguely describe my 'regret' or 'anger', whether mild or moving, then I cannot properly be said to feel these emotions. Hence if 'feeling' is not easily conveyable via language and behaviour, this is because it is barely a feeling, not because it is a 'bare feeling'.

THE ROLE OF BODILY FEELING

So far I have suggested that emotion feeling is constituted by the appropriate attidues, whether such attitudes are covert or overtly displayed. Against this account the antagonist might object that it fails to explain why we have the term 'feel' in our emotion repertoire. Perkins, a proponent of the compromise view, argues that one role of the term 'feel' in the case of emotion is to designate bodily feeling: 'bodily feeling is indispensable to . . . our practice of . . . conceiving emotions as felt' (Perkins, 1966). This view requires some consideration as an alternative to the attitudinal account of emotion feeling advanced so far.

Perkins wants to argue that an emotion is a double aspect phenomenon such that attitudinal and behavioural components can qualify as a 'felt emotion' only if they give rise to some kind of bodily sensation. Sensation is understood by Perkins as a non-specific aspect of the total emotional event and hence differs from the traditional James-Langian account of emotions as individuated by, and reducible to, specific or unique disjunctions of sensation. On Perkins's view it is a necessary condition of an event x's being a felt emotion that a non-specific bodily feeling (S) features in the total emotional event. Perkins, in using the necessary condition S, seeks to provide a criterion for placing psychological phenomena in the class of 'emotion'. So far the criterion remains uninformative about the nature of particular emotions. He can avoid this objection by maintaining that it is in the realm of sufficient conditions that the nature of particular emotions is revealed. Nevertheless, we have to consider particular emotions in order to establish whether the criterion works for emotion generally. While it would be wrong to claim that S never features in an emotional event, the claim that S is a necessary condition for an event's being a felt emotion, is, I think, dubious.

If S does feature in an emotional event, then this occurrence of S is surely related to the intensity of the emotion feeling. And 'being intensely felt' is not a defining feature of emotion feeling. Extreme 'anger' or 'sorrow' might, on occasions, be accompanied by S. But S is not necessarily present in less extreme versions of the same emotion types. I can for instance be 'mildly angry' or 'faintly melancholy' without the presence of S; whereas Perkins's argument commits him to the view that anything less than an extreme case cannot qualify as a felt emotion. The antagonist might argue here that extreme emotion occurrences do necessarily involve S; moreover, that such occurrences provide the paradigms upon which mild occurrences are conceptually dependent. But first, even if this claim were true, it would not establish that S is a necessary feature of any instance of a felt emotion. Second, it is not clear that S is a necessary feature even of extreme, or intensely felt, emotions. As already argued, the crucial measure of the intensity of, say, 'envy' is the extent to which the attitudes involved are vivid, serious and occupy the agent's attention. Whether or not I feel any twinges or palpitations, if my thoughts are totally consumed by a 'strong desire for an object which I do not possess and which belongs to another', then I can be said to feel 'extremely envious'. This point applies equally to the emotions 'sorrow' and 'anger' discussed above. 'Anger', for example, may give rise to S, but the criterion of its being intensely felt is the quality and force of the attitudes and behaviour it generates. Hence if S is neither essential to emotions as moderately felt nor essential to emotions as intensely felt, then it would seem that it is not an intrinsic defining feature but a contingent fact about emotions that they can give rise to S.

THE ROLE OF THE TERM 'FEEL'

While the arguments of the compromise view are problematic, the re-emphasis on 'feeling' in the explanation of emotion is, I think important in that it serves to remind us that emotions can be qualitative, experiential states. This aspect of emotions is not, as I will go on to argue, incompatible with constructionism. However, it does provide an explanation of the use of the term 'feel' in our emotion repertoire. Here it is useful to examine some actual contexts in which we would tend, or prefer to use the locution 'feel x'. I do not wish to imply that the following examples are exhaustive; however, they do illustrate some ways in which emotion 'feeling' terms can have legitimate applications without referring to emotion qualia or physiological changes.

We tend to use 'feel' for occurrent emotions, e.g., 'I feel afraid of x (now', and 'am/is' for standing emotions, e.g., 'M is (tends to be) afraid of loud noises'; 'I am still in love with J'. However, constructionism can trade on the fact that, in general, sentences such as 'I feel x' (where x is an emotion predicate) are synonymous with 'I am x' and therefore that the feeling term does not designate anything over and above those attitudes constitutive of 'being x'. For example, 'I am/feel afraid (now)' are intersubstitutable without loss or change of meaning.

Another use of 'feel' can be derived from the fact that in the case of emotions the expression of which has a performatory role (e.g., to praise, blame, criticize or congratulate), it is possible to isolate the phenomeno-logical aspect of the agent's emotion reaction from the performatory aspect of the emotion. By this I mean that agents reserve the locution 'feel' for reporting their introspective emotion experience, reports which are confined to 'how' the agent feels and do not include a reference to the agent's possible intention in expressing E. Let us suppose that person J was wronged or failed the expectations of person M in some way. The communicative intention of a statement made by M such as (P) 'I am angry with you/ashamed of you, J' is to criticize J. Here it is surely the case that the force of M's negative appraisal would not be successfully conveyed to S via a statement such as 'I feel angry/ashamed with you', in that there is no reason to suppose that J would regard himself as admonished by a mere introspective report of how M happens to feel. The point here is that the performatory use of statements such as P (e.g., as a criticism of J) is not effectively conveyed by the 'feel' locution. However in those contexts in which M's critical intention is absent or no longer necessary, then M may revert to the 'feel' locution in describing his 'anger' or 'shame'. If M is musing to himslf or a neutral party about the situation concerning J, he may describe himself as 'feeling' or as 'having felt angry/ashamed' because he is attending to the qualitative, experiential aspect of his emotion and not to its performatory aspect, being his criticism of J.

The above account also suggests another use of 'feel', which is to express uncertainty as to whether we ought to 'be in' a particular emotion state. For example, 'I am angry about it' implies more strongly than does 'I feel angry about it' that the emotion in question is justified and reasonable. In particular, the overlap between the use of the term 'feel' to refer both to sensation and to emotion suggests that agents can use the term 'feel' to interpret their emotion as, like sensation, not self-initiated. In the 'anger' example above the use of 'feel' may have an excusatory function in that the strategic redescription of 'being angry' as 'feeling angry' enables the agent to entertain this emotion without assuming the responsibility which would subject the emotion to moral censure or rational criticism. For example, in a sentence such as 'I just feel angry about it, although I know I shouldn't be' the use of 'feel' can be understood as mitigating the acknowledged irrationality of the 'anger' by excusing its presence as involuntary.

The points above would appear to remain compatible with construc-tionism in the following respects. While, as I suggested, the locution 'feel' may be reserved for describing the phenomenological aspect of an emotion, this aspect shares the same form as the covert emotion feeling which itself essentially consists not of irreducible qualia, nor of physiological changes, but of those attitudes which are constitutive of the emotion. In the example above, M's retrospective report of having 'felt angry' would consist of the same desires, beliefs and evaluations concerning J as the overt performance, the difference being only that M is not, or is no longer, actually conveying his critical judgement of J's behaviour. Similarly M's report that he 'feels ashamed about J's failure of his (M's) expectations' would consist of the same attitudes (i.e., the desire and the belief that J could have met M's expectations, and the evaluation of J as at fault for having failed to do so) which are conveyed as criticisms in the overt performance. In this case the identity between the phenomenological report and the overt performance obtains in that M's report of 'feeling angry/ashamed' shares the same attitudinal structure as M's 'being overtly angry/ashamed'.

I would also argue that, although the locution 'feel' may have a role in expressing only the experiential aspect of the emotion, this focus of attention is a contingent and context-dependent feature, not a logical feature of emotions, since the ability of agents to confine their attention to the phenomenological aspect of their emotion – to 'how E feels to me' – logically presupposes their having a conception of the situation as appropriate to E and, in cases where it applies, of the performatory use of E. Here the constructionist can assert that in these cases not only is M's 'feeling' report a result of his original critical appraisal of J, but this performatory role of the emotion depends crucially on social expectations concerning those situations which are deemed to warrant 'anger' or 'shame'.

So far I have suggested some ways in which emotion 'feeling' terms are used to convey the phenomenological, as distinct from the performatory, aspect of an emotion. But this is not to deny that agents feel something while conveying their critical evaluation. This point is important because it allows the constructionist to explain how emotions can be qualitative states while simultaneously fulfilling some cultural expectation. In particular, on this point constructionism has a certain strength in being able to unify various disparate philosophical emotion theories.

To illustrate this, consider Bedford's claim that emotions 'form part of the vocabulary of appraisal and criticism' (Bedford, 1967). This claim expresses Bedford's view that emotion sentences have a performatory role in that they can be used to praise or condemn agents for their behaviour. Sentences such as 'I am ashamed of you', he suggests, serve a 'judicial function' rather than reporting the feelings of the speaker. Unfortunately, Bedford makes two unwarranted assumptions here: that performatory functions such as these are primary, and, following from this, that emotion predicates need not be treated as denoting psychological states 'at all'.

Beford's denial that emotion terms primarily denote psychological states is extreme and provokes a dichotomy in philosophical emotion theories between the performatory aspect of emotions, i.e., the use of emotions to convey appraisals relating to some standard or value, and the phenomenological aspect of emotions, i.e., as denoted by emotion 'feeling' terms. Also any theory which denies emotion terms a central role in reporting our mental life is neither plausible nor appealing. My analysis of emotion 'feeling' in the previous section was intended to show, among other things, the way in which emotion feeling terms are about experiential states.

However, Bedford's unwarranted conclusions need not be fatal to his general argument concerning the performatory aspect of emotions. If his account of the performatory aspect of emotion could be made compatible with an account of emotions as experiential states, then this would make his arguments both more plausible and more interesting. And here constructionism does offer an account which unites these two aspects in that it can explain emotions as culturally constituted responses which are simultaneously experiential and performatory. For example, self-ascriptions such as 'I feel ashamed' frequently serve the function of expressing the agent's feelings; but this expressive function is surely not incompatible with the ascription's being a self-criticism and an acknowledgement of the agent's act as wrong by reference to some social standard of desirable behaviour. In particular, this compatibility enables the constructionist to assert that the 'feeling of shame' in the above case is socioculturally constituted just because the attitudes which constitute the 'feeling' are explainable as internalizations of the beliefs and values of the agent's cultural community.

RECAPITULATION

In this chapter I have suggested that contemporary philosophical theories of emotion are consistent with constructionism in that the characterization of emotions in attitudinal terms not only rejects the traditional view of the emotions as simple, non-cognitive phenomena, but also provides a basis from which emotions can in principle be explained as acquired responses which are determined by sociocultural prescription and training. I have further suggested that the phenomenological aspect of emotion which has been emphasized by the recent theoretical interest in emotion feeling does not present a difficulty for constructionism because, unlike the case of sensation, emotion feeling terms do not refer to irreducible emotion qualia or to sensations; rather, the ontology of emotion feeling should be analysed in terms of the emotion attitudes by which the emotion feeling is constituted. I explained this acount by distingiushing between the covert entertaining and the overt display of emotion attitudes, and by introducing the notions of 'vividness, seriousness and inclusivity' of emotion attitudes as sufficient conditions of an emotion's being 'felt'. The advantage of this account is that it allows the phenomenological aspect of emotions to be accommodated within the constructionist's framework of explanation. Having considered some uses of the locution 'feel' which are compatible with the 'attitudinal' theory of emotion, I concluded by suggesting some ways in which constructionism can offer an account of emotion which unifies their social, performatory aspect with their experiential aspect.

REFERENCES

Aquinas, Thomas   The emotions. *Summa Theologia*, vol. 19, trans. Eric D'Arcy. London: Blackfriars and Eyre and Spottiswoode.

Armon-Jones, C. (1985)   Towards a constructionist theory of the emotions. Unpublished B.Phil thesis, University of Oxford.

Arnold, M. (1960)   *Emotion and Personality*, New York: Columbia University Press.

Averill, J. (1980)   A constructivist view of emotion. In R. Plutchik and H. Kellerman (eds), *Emotion Theory Research and Experience*. New York: Academic Press.

Bedford, E. (1967)   Emotions, *Proceedings of the Aristotelian Society*, 57; also in K. Gustafson (ed.), *Essays in Philosophical Psychology*. London: Macmillan.

Cannon, W. (1927)   The James-Lange theory. *Australasian Journey of Philosophy*, 39.

Coulter, J. (1979)   *The Social Construction of Mind*. London: Macmillan.

Descartes, R. (1952)   The passions of the soul. *Descartes' Philosophical Writings*, trans. N. Kemp Smith. London: Macmillan.

Ekman, P. (1980)   Biological and cultural contributions to body and facial movement in the expression of emotions. In A. Rorty (ed.), *Explaining Emotions*. London: University of California Press.

Gordon, R. (1969)   Emotions and knowledge. *Journal of Philosophy*, 66.

—— (1974)   The aboutness of emotion. *American Philosophical Quarterly*, 11.

Green, O. (1979)   Wittgenstein and the possibility of a theory of emotion. *Metaphilosophy*, 10 (3 & 4).

Hume, D. (1978)   *A Treatise of Human Nature: Book II*, 2nd ed. Oxford: Oxford University Press.

James, W. (1884)   What is an emotion? *Mind*, 9.

Kant, I. (1949). *Critique of Practical Reason*, trans. L. Beck. Chicago: University of Chicago Press.

Kenny, A. (1963). *Action, Emotion and Will*. London: Routledge & Kegan Paul.

Leventhal, H. (1980)   Towards a comprehensive theory of the emotions. *Advances in Experimental Social Psychology*, 13.

Lutz, C. (1982)   Parental goals, ethnopsychology and the development of emotional meaning. *Ethos*.

Lyons, W. (1980)   *Emotion*. Cambridge: Cambridge University Press.

Mead, G. (1934) Mind. *Mind, Self and Society*. Chicago: University of Chicago Press.

Montesquieu, C. (1750)   *De l'Esprit des Lois*.

Perkins, M. (1966)   Emotion and feeling. *Philosophical Review*, 75.

Pitcher, G. (1965)   Emotion. *Mind*, 74.

Pritchard, M. (1976)   On taking emotions seriously. *Journal for the Theory of Social Behaviour*, 6(2).

Sabini, J., and Silva, M. (1982)   *Moralities of Everyday Life*. New York: Oxford University Press.

Stevenson, C. (1937)   The emotive meaning of ethical terms. *Mind*, 46.

Urmson, J. (1963)   *The Emotive Theory of Ethics*. London: Hutchinson.

Williams, B. (1972)   *Problems of the Self*. Cambridge: Cambridge University Press.

Wittgenstein, L. (1980)   *Remarks on the Philosophy of Psychology*, vol. 1, trans. G. E. M. Anscombe. Oxford: Basil Blackwell.

— (1981)   *Zettel*, 2nd edn, trans. G. E. M. Anscombe. Oxford: Basil Blackwell.

4

The Social Functions of Emotion

Claire Armon-Jones

According to constructionism, emotions have a sociofunctional role:

> The meaning of an emotion – its functional significance – is to be found primarily within the sociocultural system. (Averill, 1980)

In this chapter I want to examine the sense in which emotions can be regarded as having social functions. Emotions are explained by the constructionist as functional in that they are constituted and prescribed in such a way as to sustain and endorse cultural systems of belief and value. In particular, emotions are alleged to involve internalized social values so that the agent capable of feeling the appropriate emotion provides an autonomous and reliable adherent to the values marked by the emotion.

What kinds of social function could emotions have? Functions postulated by the constructionist are the regulation of socially undesirable behaviour and the promotion of attitudes which reflect and endorse the interrelated religious, political, moral, aesthetic and social practices of a society. Here the constructionist uses the alleged social functions of emotions as explanatory priinciples such that, for any emotion which bears a prescriptive relation to moral values, for example, the agent's possession or adoption of that emotion in a relevant moral context serves a social function in endorsing the moral values which are exemplified in that context. Hence emotions such as guilt, compassion, resentment and anger, in so far as they have a moral role, are said by constructionists to contribute to the preservation of the moral rules of a society.

What kinds of social function does the constructionist ascribe to emotions which do not have a characteristically moral role – emotions such as 'hatred, jealousy, and envy'? The constructionist claims that such emotions do serve social functions because they involve culturally appropriate attitudes and are attached to cultural contexts. For example, an agent's hatred or envy of x, where x embodies some cultural notion of undesirability, or desirability, is regarded as having a special role for a community in expressing the agent's possession of culturally appropriate antipathies, expectations and aspirations.

PROBLEMS OF THE FUNCTIONAL ACCOUNT

As a general explanation of emotion, the constructionist principle of emotions as functional is subject to the following criticisms. To explain emotions as functional is simply to impose a teleological account upon phenomena which need not admit of this type of explanation. It would for instance be wrong to argue that, if 'x is jealous of y', and if x's jealousy has the additional effect of 'making y feel wanted in x's eyes', therefore the function of 'jealousy' is to 'make people feel wanted'. This reasoning not only generalizes from the particular to the universal but also confuses something's being an incidental effect with its being the intention, and the reason for the emotion. Using the same objection, we might ask why it should follow from an emotion's being an 'enactment of social values' that the endorsement of such values should be the function of the emotion, as opposed to an incidental effect. This objection requires that, in order to preserve the plausiblity of the constructionist thesis, the idea that emotions have a social function needs clarifying and qualifying. Here I think, constructionism can appeal to general principles of functional explanation.

The principle of functional identity allows that, if x is a function of y, then it is not the case that x is necessarily a function of y, because y can be replaced by any item n which is capable of serving the same function. The point of this caveat is that it releases constructionism from various undesirable commitments. For example, the constructionist wants to argue that the function of certain emotions E is to sustain the moral rules P of a society. However, this account is compatible with E's being replaced, or augmented by, other items, e.g., 'stringent moral laws', 'the practice of gossip', etc., which serve the same function P as that of E. Hence the constructionist is not committed to the view that E is a necessary condition of the existence of P. Applying this point to the examples above, the constructionist can assert that the function of M's 'anger' in endorsing a right is compatible with this right's being also expressed by a law protecting certain rights and with M's appealing to such a law. Similarly, the function of 'guilt' in regulating an agent's behaviour is compatible with such behaviour being regulated instead, or also, by other external means such as punishment.

However, the constructionist can argue that, while the use of E in sustaining P is not necessary, neither is it arbitrary, since E has a special role in expressing the agent's commitment to a value, one which would not be achieved by his/her dispassionate appeal to the relevant laws. 'Anger' at someone who violates my rights, for example, can have a special role in conveying the sincerity of my moral opinions. It can also be regarded as having a special role in criticizing the offender and in provoking repentance. In its critical role the 'anger', as an emotional display, conveys to the offender with immediacy and force that his/her behaviour is worthy of condemnation. Also 'anger', in involving the desire to injure, or seek revenge, poses an active threat to the offender, one which he/she could avert by repenting, but which I regard myself as entitled to convey.

GUILT AND SOCIAL FUNCTION

Here we need to examine some examples of emotions which can have moral roles with respect to the alleged connection between those roles and the serving of some social function. The constructionist wants to argue that moral behaviour is required by particular societies because it reflects and endorses their system of moral values; that agents who lack the capacity to 'feel guilty' for example are not able, or are less able, to act in a morally desirable manner; therefore that 'guilt', in so far as it prohibits morally undesirable behaviour, is functional in respect of its fulfilling the social requirement above. This requirement is supported by the fact that the capacity of an agent to 'feel guilty' depends upon his/her having a conception of notions of 'wrong' and 'moral wrong'. However, it could be objected that, although the capacity to 'feel guilty' depends upon a grasp of notions of wrong, 'guilt' need not be regarded as a social requirement over and above the agent's possession of these notions, because 'guilt' arises inevitably from one's perception of one's act as wrong. Therefore morally desirable behaviour is an immediate consequence, not a social requirement, of this perception.

The difficulty with this objection is that agents can evaluate their acts as wrong without 'feeling bad', which suggests that the relation between 'believing that one has acted wrongly' and 'feeling guilty' is one of neither logical necessity nor natural inevitability. So the constructionist could assert here that, although agents may 'feel guilty' as a direct and unmediated result of their evaluation of their act as 'wrong', in some cases this ability depends upon the agent's having acquired an understanding of the relation between 'wrong' and 'feeling bad'. In defence of this point, it is reasonable to suppose that in some cases a parent would not wait for the child to 'feel guilty' before ascribing 'guilt'. Rather, 'guilt' would initially be prescribed for those contexts in which the child 'ought to feel bad', i.e., contexts in which the child has committed an act which is judged by the parent to be a transgression against particular norms. Hence sentences such as 'you ought to feel bad about hitting your sister' would establish for the child a specific connection between 'wrong behaviour', 'objects of value' and 'feeling bad' in that the categorical respect owing to the sister provides the explanation of why the hitting is wrong and of why the child ought to 'feel bad'.

The above account of the acquisition of the attitudes appropriate to 'guilt' is compatible with the child's subsequent ability to 'feel guilty' as a direct result of its evaluation of its acts as wrong. Also, while 'guilt' is not an intrinsically moral emotion, contexts such as the one above are moral contexts for which 'guilt' would be prescribed as the emotion appropriate to acts which are deemed to contravene particular moral values. In defence of the constructrionist's functional account, it can be argued that, not only does the prescription establish for the agent a connection between morally undesirable behaviour and 'feeling bad', but the attitude of 'feeling bad' which is prescribed with respect to x, 'the object of value', constitutes a negative response to x. A negative response is analysable as one which causes the agent to experience x as unpleasant and as something to be avoided. In this case it is most likely that the agent's 'feeling bad' about x would have a deterrent effect, and that his subsequent ability to 'feel bad' about similarly morally undesirable acts would at least con- tribute to dissuading him from indulging in such acts; whereas this deterrent effect would not necessarily follow from the agent's dispassion- ate assessment of x as wrong. So here the constructionist could argue that 'feeling bad' is a social requirement in that, unlike the dispassionate assess- ment, it serves the function of actively deterring the agent from behaviour regarded as morally undesirable by his/her community.

The constructionist could also argue that, even in cases where 'guilt' does arise inevitably from the agent's evaluation of his/her act as wrong, there are social functions which this emotion is required to serve which are not ful- filled by the occurrence as it stands. In particular, the degree or intensity of 'guilt' which members of a society require an agent to feel can be said to depend upon the grossness of his/her transgression. For example, while an agent may have 'occasional pangs of conscience' about the 'heroin pushing' which provides his/her income, we would nevertheless condemn this 'mild guilt' because it fails to express the agent's sincere appreciation of the mag- nitude of the crime. The constructionist could argue that in this case 'extreme guilt' would be prescribed with the aim of inducing in the agent a degree of remorse which, unlike the mild case, would serve to reflect those moral sensibilities which we require him/her to possess, and which may be sufficient to discourage him/her from the 'hideous practice'.

Similarly, while an agent's understanding of the principles of his religion may be sufficient for him to 'feel guilty' about performing those acts defined by his religion as gross sins, it is plausible to suppose that 'intense guilt or shame' is required by the purveyors of such religious principles in that it serves the function of inciting sincere condemnation of those 'temptations caused by weakness of the flesh and spirit' and of maintaining negative and prohibitive attitudes to such sins. Here the religious confessional can be understood not only as a vehicle for the ritual dissolution of 'guilt' via God's pardon, but also as a vehicle for the intensification of 'guilt' in that the context of the confessional and the dialogue between priest and subject provides the appropriate causal conditions for intensifying the subject's 'guilt'. For example, if the subject accepts the invitation to dwell on the sin, and where possible take others into account, then the sins in question would be elaborated in such a way as to magnify the subject's emotion. Here it seems that not only can these sentiments be explained in terms of the religious convictions which warrant them, but their peculiar intensity can be explained in terms of the function which it serves in realizing, corroborating and sustaining those religious convictions.

THE FUNCTIONAL ASPECT OF EMOTIONS

While emotions can be understood as having a special function in sustaining values, this still leaves the issue of the status of the emotion itself, in particular of whether constructionism requires that it is a necessary condition of the existence of the emotion that it serve the social function of sustaining a particular value. Here we need to distinguish between two possible interpretations of the constructionists' 'functional' thesis. On the first interpretation, the emotion can be defined as intrinsically functional in that it depends for its existence upon its serving a social function. On the second interpretation it is an aspect of the emotion that it serves a social function. The first interpretation would derive from a radical version of constructionism in that the notion of emotions as intrinsically sociofunctional appears to rule out the possibility of natural emotions which exist prior to their alleged adaptation to a social function, and of emotion instances which are based on evaluations which do not themselves reflect, or depend in particular on, cultural beliefs and values; whereas a weaker version of constructionism would advance the second interpretation of emotion as having a sociofunctional aspect. One advantage of the second interpretation is that the constructionist who adopts it can go on to show the way in which the sociofunctional aspect is a significant and predominant feature of some emotion without contravening arguments for the existence of pre- and extra-social emotional responses. Also, the second interpretation conforms better to further general features of functional explanation.

A functional description of an item is selective in that it can ignore aspects of the item which are not relevant to its function. Hence, just as the colour of a piston is not relevant to the description of its function in contributing to the movement of a car, so we are entitled to claim that the possibility that emotion instances can be natural responses, can involve sensations or produce undesirable effects, e.g., crimes of passion, is not relevant to the description of their function in contributing to the maintenance of sociocultural systems of belief and value. The constructionist can assert that an effect of M's 'compassion', such as that of prompting others to 'play on his charity and goodwill', is incidental to the functional role this emotion can have in making a moral statement which serves to endorse sociocultural values. Similarly, that there are instances of 'anger' in which it is excessive, or is directed upon asocial objects such as the weather, is compatible with, but incidental to, the functional role of 'anger' in vindicating certain cultural values.

FEAR AND SOCIAL FUNCTION

The account of emotions as having a sociofunctional aspect can be exemplified with reference to 'fear'. Since 'fear' is understood by the naturalist as the archetypal primary emotion, it would appear to be the most resistant to the constructionists' explanatory principles and so deserves particular consideration. As already implied, the weaker constructionist would concede to the naturalist the existence of primitive 'fear' responses based on natural apprehensions of situations as menacing or dangerous; he/she would also concede that, having acquired a normative frame of reference for their emotion, members of a community are nevertheless still able to respond with 'fear' towards objects which are naturally fear-inducing but are not necessarily included within that frame of reference. However, the weaker constructionists' interest would lie not in the ontology of the primary emotions, but in their adaptation to particular sociocultural contexts.

Naturalists tend to endorse the empirical theory that, in so far as 'fear' could be said to have a purpose, then this purpose is related to the primitive survival instinct of the organism and/or to the survival of the species of which it is a member. Assuming for the moment that 'fear' attitudes can acquire some kind of sociocultural content, the question arises of what kind of social function 'fear' might have which could explain the social need for a kind of 'fear' which goes beyond its alleged natural functions.

One feature of 'fear' which would support its having a sociofunctional aspect is that 'fear' can be said to have an instrumental role in regulating a variety of other attitudes. 'Fear' is related to 'jealousy' as 'fear of losing the valued object', to 'guilt' as 'fear of punishment', to 'shame' as 'fear of humiliation and loss of integrity', etc. It has been proposed by Lutz and Howell that 'fear' has a social function in the Chewong and Ifaluk societies in that 'fear' is prescribed for morally significant contexts and is for this reason instrumental in sustaining social values. Here I want first to describe some salient aspects of this empirical work and go on to consider some implications it might have for the philosophical justification of constructionism.

Presuming for the moment that 'fear' is a viable working translation of native idioms, we can say that in both the societies studied by these anthropologists 'fear' is explained and conveyed to the child in similar ways. In the Chewong case 'fear' is explained as the response appropriate to particular fables. Subsequent 'fear', responses are apparently 'encouraged and praised' (Howell, 1981). Similarly, in the Ifaluk case, from the age of one year the child, when in appropriate 'fear' contexts, is 'told that it is afraid' (Lutz, 1982a). Those who appear to lack 'fear' have their attention drawn either 'to a stranger or to Tarita – an impersonated ghost' in an attempt to elicit 'fear', and the child's failure to display 'fear' is 'mocked' (Lutz, 1982a). In the Chewong case, their fables present a range of appropriate 'fear' objects such as 'the Malay, Chewong sicknesses and forest tigers', these being objects from which members of the Chewong community are uniformly encouraged to 'flee without hesitation' (Howell, 1981). In the Ifaluk case appropriate 'fear' contexts take such forms as 'wandering away from the domestic area and visiting members of a higher rank without food'.

Of particular interest here is that in both societies the contexts deemed appropriate to 'fear' are intrinsically related to their respective moral systems. The moral rules of Chewong society involve 'sharing, reciprocity and respect for scarce resources'. Transgression of such rules results, according to Chewong belief, in the immediate return of those objects, such as the Malay, which are presented in the Chewong fables. The moral rules of Ifaluk society involve 'obedience within the system of ranking, non-aggression and "maluwelu" – tranquil co-operation (Lutz, 1981). Transgression of such rules, e.g., aggression against a peer, is understood to result in the immediate reappearance of those 'fear' objects, such as 'Tarita', that are peculiar to Ifaluk society.

The sense in which 'fear' can be regarded as serving a social function for these societies is derivable from its contribution to the efficacy of their respective moral systems. For example, the child's ability to respond appropriately appears to depend upon its mastery of the appropriate expressive repertoire. The behavioural repertoire requires actions such as 'fleeing, acting shyly, submissive behaviour and giving food', only some of which would be appropriate in Anglo Saxon contexts. The mental repertoire requires not only a conceptualization of appropriate contexts but also a cognizance of the moral consequences of failing to respond appropriately. In the Chewong case 'not fleeing' is essentially related to the violation of social rules in that it is alleged to lead to a confrontation with objects which are themselves symbolized both as fearful and as modes of punishment. In the Ifaluk case 'fear' and moral rules are also explicitly connected, in that the Ifaluk themselves define 'general misbehaviour' as 'caused by an inadequate grasp of "fear" ' and the emotion 'malewelu' as an ability to feel 'fear' for one's own potential wrongdoing. Hence it is because the Ifaluk regard 'fear' as 'the emotion considered most responsible for obedient and good behaviour' (Lutz, 1982b) that failure to display 'fear' in appropriate situations is condemned.

Here the constructionists' claim that prescription plays a fundamental role in the acquisiton of culturally appropriate emotions does seem to apply. The prescription of 'fear' can be located in the Ifaluk practice of 'mocking' the child's failure to display 'fear' in appropriate contexts, for example in the presence of high-ranking persons. Similarly, the prescription of 'fear' is evident in the Chewong practice of 'approving' and 'encouraging' appropriate displays of 'fear', for example towards the Malay. Such practices are prescriptive in virtue of their being forms of praise and condemnation which themselves embody the requirement that 'fear' 'ought to be present because it is deemed desirable for the contexts in question'. In particular, the prescriptive force of these practices is implied by the fact that, if 'fear' was merely to be expected in such contexts, then it would remain unclear why praise and condemnation should occur. However, it is just because the peer does not expect a 'fear' response in such contexts that the response is prescribed. These points exemplify the constructionists' 'functional' account in that 'fear' in these societies is conceptually related to acts of transgression and can for this reason be understood as an emotion which serves the regulative function of sustaining the moral rules of these societies; moreover, that this social function is made possible by the prescription of 'fear' in culturally appropriate contexts.

IMPLICATIONS FOR NATURALISM

At this point the naturalist may object that, although in these societies 'fear' is prescribed, such prescriptions merely reinforce a universal and natural disposition by rewarding its expression in particular situations. This objection is problematic. The prescription of 'fear' involves the explication of the emotion by reference to those symbolic items which are expressive of 'fear' in these societies and which reflect their respective interrelated systems of belief, value and moral value. Such items take forms such as 'the Malay, high-ranking persons, Tarita', actions such as 'giving food, acting shyly, fleeing' and attitudes such as 'if I am bold the Malay will attack me'; 'if I visit the elders without food then Tarita will appear'; etc. Consequently, in order for the child to be 'afraid' in those contexts for which 'fear' is deemed appropriate, it must understand the significance of, and adopt the behaviour and attitudes appropriate to, such contexts. The acquisition of these responses depends upon both the demonstration of 'fear' using 'fear displays' and an explication of the meaning of such displays. Hence the child learns the appropriate repertoire by imitating these displays, the mastery of which is facilitated by the displays' being ascribed a meaning which coheres with the child's general conceptual scheme. With reference to 'anger', Lutz states: 'children's observation of parents "song" [justified anger among the Ifaluk] in particular situations enables them to learn the difference between right and wrong' (Lutz, 1982a). Here the child's adoption of 'anger' rituals is given substance by explanations of why 'anger' is appropriate in a given situation, e.g., by the description of those cultural rules, the violation of which gives 'anger' its point in Ifaluk society.

In the case of 'fear', the naturalist account may be correct in so far as natural fear responses are utilized. The explication of appropriate 'fear' responses may consist in part of the linking by a peer of the child's natural 'fear' – say, 'of the dark' – with other specifically cultural contexts in which it ought to be afraid. In this case the natural response would provide a basis for the subsequent adaptation of the emotion to social values, rules and expectations. However, it appears to be the case that 'fear' is mainly explicated and prescribed in those specifically cultural contexts for which it is deemed by members of these societies to be desirable. Hence the naturalist claim that 'fear' is socialized by the utilization of natural expression becomes problematic. It assumes that 'fear' would find natural expression in those cultural contexts for which it is deemed to be desirable, but it is not clear that 'fear' could find natural expresion in many of the contexts for which it is required.

For example, contexts such as the Malay and Elders do not, prima facie, possess features which naturally warrant 'fear'. Such contexts can only warrant 'fear' once their significance has been explained, an explanation which involves the description of those cultural rules which, as in the case of 'anger', specify the reason for 'fear' in these societies. Hence, although the child may in some contexts express natural 'fear', and although such responses may be utilized, the child's capacity to express the response which is appropriate to, and serves a function for, its community presupposes that it has an understanding of the significance of these contexts in terms of their relation to the beliefs and values of its community. So it would seem that the naturalist, in relying on the presence of natural expression, is not able to offer an explanation of the presence of 'fear' in contexts for which it is not naturally warranted. Hence constructionism has an advantage over naturalism here in being able to explain this presence of the emotion in terms of social explication and prescription and without appealing to natural 'fear' occurrences.

From the points above emerges a further difficulty with the naturalist account which lies in the assumption that, in the case of socialized 'fear' in these societies, the only variables under consideration are factors such as the cultural constraints imposed on the intensity of feeling, the type of display and type of context in which the emotion features. The inner feeling of 'fear' remains qualitatively the same as the natural feeling involved in its prototype, the primary emotion. We may presume that to 'feel afraid' in these societies may involve to some extent, and on some occasions, natural beliefs, e.g., that x is menacing, and natural desires, e.g. to avoid x. However, earlier I suggested that emotion feeling is constituted by those attitudes appropriate to the emotion. If we apply this claim to the points above then it allows us to assert that 'fear feeling' would not remain unchanged but rather would be qualitatively different to the extent that the attitudes constitutive of the emotion feeling are specifically cultural.

For example, in order for the child to be appropriately 'afraid', it must have a grasp of the contexts, behaviour and attitudes which are expressive of the emotion as culturally specified. Hence, to be appropriately 'afraid' in these societies is to entertain, or to overtly express, specifically cultural attitudes such as 'the belief that not fleeing will bring sickness, the evaluation of an Elder as angry, the desire to give food and act in a shy manner'. Not only do these attitudes come to provide the appropriate expressions of 'fear' but, given that such attitudes are constitutive of emotion feeling, we are entitled to assert that the cultural determination of the attitudes expressive of 'fear' also determines the particular quality of the 'feeling of fear' in members of these societies. Here a difficulty arises for the naturalist in that, while actions such as 'fleeing' take the same form, whether naturally or culturally determined, they are not identical in respect of the attitudes which give rise to them. In the Chewong case 'fleeing from the Malay' is justified by their beliefs concerning the danger which this tribe poses – their mysterious capacity to bring not only physical sickness, but also spiritual sickness and ill-fortune on the Chewong community. These beliefs clearly cannot be generalized in order to explain either natural or cross-cultural ocurrences of the response. So here it would seem that members of these societies, in prescribing 'fear', are endorsing a response which, in so far as it is related to cultural beliefs, values and moral values, is distinct from, and not strictly derivable from, natural 'fear'. While this distinction is compatible with the existence of natural 'fear', it does call into question the naturalists' account of socialized 'fear' as explainable in terms of natural 'fear' in virtue of their sharing the same qualitative features and causal conditions.

My reason for choosing the anthropological studies discussed above is that in relatively simple societies we may expect the processes of socialization and the relation between emotions and cultural systems to be reasonably explicit and hence easier to analyse. The extent to which the constructionists' explanation of 'fear' in these societies can be generalized to explain the role of 'fear' in more complex societies is a large question to which I could not do justice here. However, I think the points made above exemplify the constructionist explanation of emotions as socioculturally constituted, and as constituted in order to serve particular sociocultural functions.

THE ISSUE OF THE INAPPROPRIATE EMOTIONS

So far I have discussed emotions which, in virtue of their regulative nature and their relation to moral values, can be analysed as having a sociofunctional role. A question which arises here is whether this role can be plausibly extended to other emotions. Emotions such as 'excessive guilt', 'ignoble envy' and 'vindictive hatred' would appear to pose a difficulty for constructionism because, being undesirable, they are not readily analysable as being prescribable for members of a community and as having a sociofunctional role. Against the naturalist we might also argue that the oddness of some of them has little obvious bearing on their putative naturalness, either. So the question here is whether appropriate emotions such as these can be accommodated within the constructionist principles of explanation.

What is an inappropriate emotion? An appropriate emotion is defined by De Sousa as one which is 'warranted by the evoking object or situation' (De Sousa, 1980). This can be clarified by defining an appropriate emotion as one which is warranted because it is generated by true beliefs and/or accurate evaluations concerning the 'evoking object'. On this definition an inappropriate emotion is one which is not warranted by the 'evoking object or situation' because it is generated by false beliefs and/or inaccurate evaluations. The weak constructionist would, I think, concede that some emotions are unwarranted in virtue of the factual falsity of the judgements which give rise to them. For example, agoraphobia – 'fear of open spaces' – is based on the apprehension of such situations as in some way menacing to the agent. In this case the emotion is unwarranted because, as a matter of fact, such situations are not in the normal course of things dangerous. Conversely, 'fear of fire' *is* warranted, in virtue of its being generated by the true belief that 'fire is dangerous'.

However, the constructionist would qualify the definition above in maintaining that, while the warrantedness of an emotion may be dependent on the *de facto* features of the situation, its warrantedness will be largely dependent upon the cultural appropriateness of the agent's construal of the situation, a qualification which, given the arguments so far, needs to be respected. For example, while 'fear' may be generated by factual beliefs, it can also be generated by cultural beliefs, e.g., that 'x is a

Malay person/communist and x is dangerous'. Hence the warrantedness of the latter emotions will depend crucially upon the society in which they occur. In some societies these cases of 'fear' would be unwarranted because they are generated by attitudes which are not appropriate in those societies. Similarly M's 'guilt',as generated by the belief that he ought not 'commit adultery, vote against democracy, leave his family', etc., would, in a society which imposed no value on such principles, be unwarranted because it is generated by beliefs which, though not definable as *de facto* false, are inappropriate in that society.

The definition above allows us to eliminate at least one type of emotion from the range of alleged counter-examples to constructionism. For example, deviant emotions such as the aggression of delinquents present us with a problem not of unwarranted emotions, but of a conflict between cultural and subcultural values in complex societies, and a contradiction between different levels of appraisal and criticism. Delinquent aggression is warranted relative to the delinquent subculture. Moreover, while the aggression is socially censured as undesirable, it is at another level fundamentally permitted by the fact that the conception of 'delinquency' – 'of what it is to be and behave as a delinquent' – is fostered and transmitted by the society as a whole. Examples of 'deviant' emotions such as the aggression above are not inconsistent with constructionism. Rather, they suggest that the criterion of warrantedness for emotions in complex societies is not restricted to one overarching value but is necessarily adjusted to accommodate apparent conflicts of value.

THE UNWARRANTED EMOTIONS

However, there are cases in which we would regard an agent's emotion as unwarranted. For example, an agent's 'feeling ashamed' would be unwarranted if it is based on his malfounded belief that he is blameworthy. It would also be unwarranted if the intensity of the emotion is disproportionate to the extent to which he is blameworthy. Given that such cases do occur, then, how might the constructionist explain them?

The constructionist's thesis that an agent's emotions are socioculturally constituted is, I think, consistent with the possibility that the way in which a situation is interpreted will reflect individual differences of character and motivation, etc. However, the constructionist would maintain that, while such factors may explain why the agent comes to misconstrue a situation, the misconstrual can nevertheless be explained in terms of the agent's general comprehension of the beliefs and values of his community; moreover, the constructionist would maintain that the reaction by members of a community to emotions which cannot be explained in these terms says something about the constraints which communities impose on the emotional life of their members and the use of emotions in conveying the agent's possession of the appropriate sensibilities.

Consider the following example. Let us suppose that M's 'feeling ashamed' is based on his false belief that, or his overestimate of the extent to which, 'he is blameworthy in respect of his having shown interest in the needs and development of his son in preference to those of his daughter'. One point which emerges from this example is that the attitudes involved are culturally based. The belief that sons and daughters should have equal parental consideration is relative to particular historical periods and cultures. In some cultures (e.g. India) preferential consideration of the son is justified by the view that the son, given his money-earning and manual labour potential, is more highly valued than the daughter. The cultural nature of the context enables the constructionist to argue that there are two different senses in which the agent's 'shame' can be understood as unwarranted, and which relate crucially to the culture in which the unwarranted emotion features.

In Western society there may be various reasons why M's 'shame' is unwarranted. It may be unwarranted because he didn't in fact show preference to his son, because he didn't show sufficient preference to warrant 'shame', or because his preference was an inevitable consequence of his son's being more available in body and/or spirit for the father's consideration. M's actual misconstrual of the situation may result from his particular neurotic worries conerning his abilities as a father. But, given that his 'feeling ashamed' is based on his belief that he has transgressed his responsibility as a father to give equal consideration to his children, then his 'shame' bears the appropriate prescriptive relation to that transgression as the emotion he ought to feel if he endorses the value of equal consideration. So the constructionist can argue that while, given the factors above, M's 'shame' about his preferential treatment would be unwarranted, if the emotion featured in contemporary Western society, then it would be unwarranted only in respect of the token situation which the agent misconstrues: it would not be unwarranted in respect of the attitudes which give rise to it because the attitudes, though misapplied in a particular case, are, relative to contemporary Western culture, attitudes of the right kind. And they are attitudes of the right kind because they reflect M's adherence to the moral principle that 'children should be given equal consideration'.

By contrast, if M's 'shame' about his preferential consideration occurred in the context of Indian society, then the emotion would be unwarranted not because M's actual belief that he has given preferential consideration to his son is false, but because in this culture sons are alleged to deserve preferential consideration, and therefore he has no reason to be 'ashamed of his preferential consideration'. In this case M's emotion would be unwarranted because it demonstrates a peculiar set of attitudes, ones which do not reflect the values of his community. So it is reasonable to assume that M's 'shame' resulting from his beliefs concerning his preferential consideration is a kind of unwarranted emotion that is not likely to occur in such a community; moreover, that if it did occur then it would be rationalized by members of that community in terms of M's exposure to alien cultural values, or mental instability. In the case of misconstruals based on culturally appropriate attitudes, members of a society regard the emotion as normally subject to rational criticism by reference to just those beliefs and values upon which the misconstrual is based. For example, members of our society who suffer neurotic or excessive 'guilt' are often able to recognize that their emotion is irrational, an awareness which implies that they have a conception of those normal contexts for which the emotion would be socially warranted; whereas rational criticism would not even begin for a member of our society who suffered 'guilt about the rain floods', since the attitudes in question would be taken as a sign of mental instability.

However, it is significant that we do regard a person's persistent inability to recognize that his/her emotion is excessive, even where the attitudes in question are fundamentally culturally appropriate, as also a sign of mental instability. At least, we tend to disount such cases by judging the agent to be not wholly responsible for them. Rorty's (1980) 'inertia theory' can be understood as providing an account of such cases which is compatible with constructionism. She discusses examples in which the unwarranted response can be traced back to a warranted childhood response which persists, given sufficient eliciting situations, although no longer desirable. Here we could perhaps use the 'inertia' principle to explain certain cases of unwarranted emotions as responses which result from the over-prescription of the emotion in earlier contexts. By this I mean that, in a case of 'neurotic guilt', for example, the child's indiscretions are unduly criticized so that the prescribed response proliferates and extends from minimal to clearly unwarranted contexts. However, although the 'inertia' theory applies well to the constructionist principles of explanation, it is important to stress here that generally, and in normal cases, the constructionist thesis is not intended to defend a determinist view of emotions as inflexible, enduring responses which are grounded in early socialization. For example, De Sousa's account of emotions as 'reapplied to situations that are relevantly similar to the paradigm scenario' (De Sousa, 1980) needs to embrace the possibility that an emotion is only applied when, and for as long as, it is appropriate. While there are some points of overlap between adult and childhood emotions, different attitudes are regarded as appropriate for different stages of maturation; for example, 'adolescent love' takes specific forms (fantasy, sexuality, intensity) which differ both from childhood 'affection' (play, possessiveness) and from mature adult 'love' (responsibility, commitment). The relationship between emotions and maturation I want to discuss in more detail later, having first considered some further cases of inappropriate emotions.

So far I have suggested that some kinds of inappropriate emotion can be analysed as involving two types of unwarrantedness, neither of which would appear to be inconsistent with the constructionist thesis. In the first case, while the agent's misconstrual of a token situation may involve a false belief, one perhaps motivated by the agent's particular character, the misconstrual can nevertheless be understood as involving attitudes of a socially appropriate kind. The second case in which an emotion involves culturally inappropriate attitudes can be explained by the constructionist as non-paradigmatic, and as liable to deprive the agent of his status as someone in possession of normal sensibilities. Here I would suggest that the role of emotions in conveying an agent's intellectual and affective commitment to certain social beliefs and values is substantiated by the fact that there appear to be various social constraints imposed on emotions. These constraints are evidenced by the fact that agents are regarded as in possession of the appropriate intellectual and moral sensibilities provided that their emotions are of the appropriate intensity for a given situation (e.g., neither affective indifference nor excess) and involve the kinds of attitudes which could be subjected to rational criticism by members of a community.

THE SINFUL EMOTIONS

Here it may be objected that, while the claims above may apply to emotions such as 'shame' and 'guilt', the constructionist cannot accommodate emotions such as 'hatred, envy and jealousy' within his/her principles of explanation because these emotions are by definition undesirable and would therefore never be regarded by members of a society as appropriate to a situation. If these emotions are undesirable, then they would not be prescribed for a situation and cannot be regarded as serving any socially expedient function. Given these difficulties, then, the naturalist account would appear to be more persuasive. In this account 'hatred', 'jealousy' and 'envy' would be explained as natural drives arising from the disposition of the organism to protect its interests. The naturalist explains the suppression of such drives in the case of humans as made possible by the development of reason and self-control. The continuing existence of these emotions and their occasional excessive appearances is explained in terms of the ongoing conflict between the emotions and the above constraining mechanisms.

However, while the naturalists' account of the origination of these emotions may be correct, it is not clear that their account of the subsequent nature of these emotions is plausible, at least as a general explanation. For example, it does not follow from an emotion's involving negative attitudes that it cannot be prescribed or have a functional role. 'Guilt' involves the negative attitude of 'feeling bad', but this does not prevent it from being legitimately prescribed as the emotion an agent ought to feel in a given situation. So the constructionist could reply here that, while emotions may involve negative attitudes, it is the desirability of emotion attitudes for particular contexts and particular communities which justifies the possibility of their being prescribable and their having a functional role. Here it may be objected that 'feeling bad' can qualify as socially desirable because it is a form of atonement; whereas 'envy, jealousy and hatred' involve 'mean attitudes' which can only be understood as potentially destructive of both the individual and his/her community. The difficulty with this objection is that it perhaps confuses absolute moral assessment with the *de facto* assessment of the role of these emotions for a community.

For example, it may be correct to say that these emotions are exceptionlessly to be condemned from the viewpoint of some absolute moral standard. However, this moral standard overlooks the point that in practice there are cases in which these emotions can be understood as motivated by, and related to, sociocultural factors, a connection which can also be understood as prescriptive and sociofunctional. There are cases in which 'hatred' can be identified as a response which is deemed by members of a society to be warranted for certain contexts. 'Hatred of the Jews' was regarded by members of Nazi society as warranted; 'hatred' is a warranted response to black persons among members of the white South African community, and 'hatred' is a warranted response to communists among members of the American community. These examples suggest at least that it is not the case that, for any occurrence of 'hatred', that occurrence is deemed to be unwarranted by members of a community. Here it may be objected that it does not follow from the emotion's being warranted in a community that the emotion bears a prescriptive relation to its various cultural contexts. For example, the naturalist might argue that these instances of 'hatred' are not regarded as desirable: rather, it happens that the beliefs and values of these communities are such that they loosen the agent's constraints on his/her natural drive. Hence the 'hatred' is not endorsed as such but merely tolerated. However, the naturalists' case here is weak.

For example, there is no reason to suppose that the contexts above are natural contexts of the emotion, or that the quality and intensity of the emotion is explainable in terms of 'optimum or permissible drive level'. Here there would, I think, be no contention about the constructionist explanation of these cases of 'hatred' as culturally determined in respect of the objects upon which they are directed and the quality and force of the

attitudes involved. However, the more interesting weakness of the naturalist's account can be derived from an examination of those beliefs and
values which provide the cultural conditions of the emotion's being
warranted. For example, while 'anti-Semitism' was based on the belief that
Jews are bad, this belief was itself crucially related to the value imposed by
Nazis upon the Aryan ideal. Here it can be argued that the 'hatred' in
question was not merely warranted but was regarded by members of the
Nazi community as a desirable response in its role of vindicating the
Aryan ideal and the agent's commitment to, and endorsement of, this
value. This role of 'hatred' is substantiated by the fact that agents were
condemned, and in some cases punished, for failing express strong
contempt of the Jews. These points suggest that the naturalist's account of
these emotions as natural responses which are warranted only in respect
of their being tolerated by members of certain communities would appear
to be false.

The points above also suggest that the claim that emotions such as
'hatred' cannot be sociofunctional is also false. The functional role of
'hatred' in these cases can be located not only in its special affective role of
vindicating the agent's commitment to those values which are alleged to
warrant the emotion, but also in its role of perpetuating attitudes which
themselves serve to justify the practices of the communities in question.
'Hatred' involves critical attitudes, such as the appraisal of the object as in
salient respects 'unpleasant' or 'bad', and appetitive attitudes, such as the
'desire to avert or harm the object'. Such critical attitudes, in so far as they
are used to dehumanize the object of the 'hatred', can be regarded as
sociofunctional in that dehumanization is necessary to the agent's justification of his otherwise immoral treatment of the object. Just as 'hatred of
black persons' can be understood as part of the dehumanization necessary
to the justification of the white person's power over, and treatment of,
them, so 'anti-Semitism', in its role of dehumanizing the opponent, can be
understood as crucially related to the Nazi justification of their mal-
practices.

To what extent could the constructionist thesis be applied to emotions
such as 'jealousy' and 'envy'? First, we want to ask, Is it always the case that
the occurrence of these emotions is condemned as undesirable? In
considering this question we have, I think, to distinguish between various
meanings and degrees of intensity which these emotions can possess.
According to Aristotle (in his *Rhetoric*), 'we envy those whose possession
of, or success in a thing is a reproach to us.' However, Neu (1980) suggests
that the definition offered by Aristotle concerns only one sense of 'envy',
which Neu defines as 'malicious envy'. This sense of 'envy', which inolves
the 'wish that M did not have what M does in fact have', Neu distinguishes
from 'admiring envy' as involving the 'wish that I had what M has'.

The point of this distinction is that we can derive from it the claim that only 'malicious envy' carries the sinful implication of excessive and untempered greed; whereas 'admiring envy', if we consider some actual contexts in which it might occur, is not an emotion which we would be entitled to regard as worthy of condemnation. Let us suppose that 'A envies M's skill at hunting deer'. First, it would be wrong to argue that this case is reducible to 'admiration' because A's 'envy' involves the wish that A had M's skill, whereas 'admiration' would not necessarily involve A's desiring the attribute for himself. Second, assuming that M's skill is one that is valued by the society of which M and A are members, then it seems implausible to suppose that A's wish to possess the same kind of skill as M would be regarded as an undesirable aspiration. The type/token distinction can be employed here in that A's 'envy' might be condemned if A wished to actually expropriate M's skill. However, what A wishes for is the same kind of skill, a wish which does not threaten M's token possession of the skill.

A similar kind of distinction can be made in the case of 'jealousy'. It can be argued that it is only unreasonable of excessive occurrences of 'jealousy' that tend to be condemned. Moderate 'jealousy' of items such as money, spouse and property is generally regarded as warranted, a point reflected in the Concise Oxford Dictionary's definition of 'jealousy' as meaning, in one of its senses, 'zealous or solicitous for the preservation or well-being of something possessed or esteemed'. In particular, there are cases where we would regard moderate 'jealousy' as desirable. We would regard an agent's being moderately jealous about the fact that his loved one is about to be stolen by someone else as desirable, in that his failure to be moderately jealous would be taken as a sign of insensitivity and uncaringness. Here it may be objected that what we expect the agent to feel in the above example is not 'jealousy' but 'affection' or whatever, and that if his response was 'jealousy' in particular then it would nevertheless be condemned. First, against this objection it can be argued that we would only condemn expressions of 'jealousy' which, as selfish or obsessive, go beyond their acceptable role as expressions of caring and prudence. Second, the objection is, I think, again motivated by a moral stance to the situation. While 'jealousy' might not exist in a morally ideal world, this has no bearing on the fact that 'jealousy' does exist in this world and that certain degrees of 'jealousy', depending upon the culture in which it features, are regarded as both warranted and desirable. For example, a degree of 'jealousy' which we might regard as selfish possessiveness would in Arabic society be regarded as the proper attitude of a husband to his wife, and might be a warranted emotion to the extent that her behaviour counts as provocative in that society.

So far I have suggested that there are cases in which an agent's 'envy' or 'jealousy' would not be worthy of condemnation. Also, the examples above suggest that certainly the kinds of things about which we can feel 'jealous' or 'envious' can be explained by reference to cultural values, these being factors which can also provide the conditions under which occurrences of these emotions would be regarded as warranted; for example, the Arab gentleman's 'jealousy' of his spouse is warranted in virtue of his being a member of a community in which his status affords him a right to feel 'jealous' of his spouse. All the same, it is not clear that these emotions can be identified as having an explicit prescriptive relation to the cultural contexts in which they feature. While, if M is 'envious' of N's 'ability to paint', we might prescribe that he ought not to be envious, this emotion would surely not be prescribed for such a context. Why not? This restriction is rather puzzling because, given that M's 'envy' is of the 'admiring' variety, then it would be incorrect to say that the emotion is not prescribed because it is condemnable. Also, we would regard M as 'entitled' to feel envious in this context.

A possible explanation for this restriction might be derived from a conception which we tacitly employ between two types of emotion. Emotions such as 'guilt', 'shame', 'pity' and 'compassion' can be defined as unqualified in the sense that there is in principle no degree, or manner, in which they can be felt which we regard as bad. In cases where these emotions ought to be present in a situation, there is often a requirement that they should be maximally felt. On the other hand, we have a qualified conception of 'jealousy' and 'envy' as emotions which can in principle be, or become, bad. For example (though Neu does not suggest this himself), we may surmise that the relation between admiring and malicious 'envy' arises from the possibility that the desire for x, if persistently frustrated, may turn to begrudging resentment of those who already possess x. Similarly, 'jealousy' can become obsessive and destructive by the standards of any culture. So perhaps we do not normally prescribe these emotions because they possess this potential negativity. 'Pride' is similar here in that, although we do prescribe the 'pride' appropriate to an agent's achievements and efforts, we also regard this emotion as capable of turning into the bad 'pride' of vanity and egocentricity.

I want here to make some tentative suggestions which might render the above points consistent with constructionism. While the emotions considered are not normally prescribed, this could be made consistent with constructionism if the attitudes they involve can be analysed as bearing a prescriptive relation to the contexts in which agents are entitled to feel them. Here I will confine my attention to 'envy'. (However, similar arguments could perhaps be made for 'jealousy' and 'pride'.) First, the constructionist can argue that there are certain conventional aspirations which are regarded by members of a community as good. For example character aspirations such as wanting to be a 'charitable, considerate, courageous person', and role aspirations such as wanting to become a 'deer hunter, academic, business entrepreneur, housewife', etc., are deemed to be good relative to those cultures in which these qualities and roles possess a value. Second, the constructionist can assert with plausibility that these kinds of aspirations are ones which agents are not merely expected to possess, but ought to possess, and can be condemned for failing to possess; for example, M's confession that he finds deer hunting distasteful or tedious would, in a community which invested this practice with great social, practical and spiritual significance, be regarded as blameworthy, if not peculiar. So there is a sense in which these aspirations at least bear a prescriptive relation to certain contexts as ones which agents ought to have.

The crucial point here is that an agent's aspirations and his 'envy' overlap in that they involve the same desires; for example, a necessary condition of M's 'envying' N's skill at piano playing and of M's aspiring to acquire that skill is that M desires to play the piano for himself. This allows the constructionist to assert that 'envy' is warranted for certain cultural contexts because the desires involved in 'envy' bear a prescriptive relation to certain values as the desires which an agent ought to possess; moreover, that 'envy', though not prescribed as such, does have a role in expressing those desires and aspirations which reflect the agent's commitment to certain cultural values. For example, the reason why M's 'envy' of N's skill at 'deer hunting' is not blameworthy is just because this emotion serves to express M's recognition and endorsement of the value of this skill.

Another feature of 'envy' which would support the constructionists' thesis is that 'envy', unlike 'admiration', can be regarded as a motivational emotion. For whereas my 'admiring' M's possession of x is compatible with my not wanting x for myself, my 'envying' M's possessing x entails my desiring x for myself, a desire which provides one of the necessary causal conditions for my attempting to acquire x for myself. Here the constructionist can argue that it is the motivational aspect of emotions such as 'envy' which explains their having a functional role for a community in that an agent who feels 'envious' of certain culturally valued attributes and abilities will, where possible, be motivated to acquire them for him/herself.

EXPLICATION, GENERATION AND ENDORSEMENT: THE 'AGE PARADIGM'

In the previous section I examined cases of emotions which we would not normally regard as desirable. I claimed that, despite the unwarrantedness or negative nature of such cases, there is an underlying sense in which they can be understood as endorsed by a community and as having a sociofunctional role in vindicating its beliefs and values. I want to conlcude this chapter by making some suggestions as to how these points might be applied to the relationship between emotions and sociocultural paradigms of age and maturation.

On the naturalist view, the child begins with a set of natural emotions such as 'distress' and 'fear' which reflect basic needs such as comfort and security. With the spontaneous development of intelligence and social sensibility, the child learns to exercise self-control over these natural states by refining their quality and degree of intensity, and by learning to discriminate those situations to which the refined version is appropriate. The child who performs in the symbolic domain of emotion display (e.g., peer group aggression; atoning remorse) is regarded as channelling the basic state into more socially expedient forms. It follows from this view that there is a range of emotions which are not deemed applicable to childhood because they presume the attainment of an adult level of intellectual maturity, self-control and social sensibility. This is reflected in the kinds of concept which we select in order to define childhood experience. The child is defined as 'kind' rather than 'compassionate'; as 'fretful' rather than 'vexed'; as 'sulky' rather than 'angry'; etc. This age-dependence also applies, Slote (1983) points out, to the virtues. 'Innocence' and 'prudence', for example, are virtuous only relative to stages of life such as childhood, adulthood and old age. The 'prudence' of a 'schoolboy who takes out an insurance policy . . . in order to protect the interests of his future wife . . . seems immediately inappropriate, even pathological'.

Slote correctly identifies the relative nature of the virtues but assumes that this can be explained by a natural connection between certain attitudes, such as prudence and particular stages of maturation. We make the same assumption in the case of emotion. Certain emotions we regard as specifically applicable to childhood in that only a being who naturally lacked intelletual maturity, self-control, etc., could feel them. While the child may not have acquired the intellectual or moral depth necessary for the capacity to feel 'higher emotions' such as 'grief', I would suggest that the age-relativity of emotion ascription can also be understood as significantly socially based. The suggestion here is that age-related emotion ascriptions reflect sociocultural beliefs and values concerning intellectual and moral development which themselves embody particular conceptions of ideal age-specific emotions. These paradigms can be understood as realized and perpetuated via a community's explications of the emotions, and of childhood emotions in particular. On this view the child's enactment of emotions such as 'fretful', 'sulky', 'spiteful', etc., is crucially linked to the maturation hierarchy from which such emotion terms derive their role and meaning.

For example, in Western culture emotions such as 'fretful, cross-patch, boistrous' tend to be associated with, among other things, lack of self-control. Often such emotions are conveyed to the child via a critical comparison of his/her behaviour with that of a reference model. Consider the following example (P): 'Don't be silly, M. You are always a cross-patch when it comes to going to bed. Look at your elder brother J: he doesn't make such a fuss.' First, there is an interesting parity between this admonition and the Ifaluk explication of 'fear', which is that in both cases a central feature of the explication is the repeated definition of the child as being the possessor of the emotion in question. Just as the Western child is reminded that it is 'always a cross-patch', so, as already noted, the Ifaluk child, when exposed to fear-inducing contexts, is 'told that it is afraid'. Second, P implies (a) that J's being older is a condition of his having the virtue of self-control, therefore that if the condition of 'being older' is not satisfied then necessarily 'not self-control'; (b) that the agent to whom the sentence P is addressed has the persistent characteristic of being a 'cross-patch' because he is not self-controlled. (a) and (b) imply that, while the negative and excessive condition of being a 'cross-patch' is criticized, it is also explicated as a response which is expected and appropriate, given the child's level of development, and can in this sense be understood as tacitly condoned. The child's understanding of the emotion as remiss is part of its understanding of the emotion as expected and fitting of itself.

These points afford an opportunity to consider some further examples of emotion paradigms. Paradigms vary in scope, and for this reason can be understood as nested within each other. The age paradigm is involved as an aspect of general social paradigms of belief and value. Beliefs concerning maturation and moral development are essentially linked to general theories of human nature. The age paradigm is also involved in, but wider in scope than, the gender paradigm. For example, theories of maturation are applied uniformly to both sexes; however, beliefs concerning the rate and style of maturation are subdivided in accordance with norms of masculinity and femininity. The gender paradigm operates in those cases where the emotion term which is selected to identify a child's behaviour, and the frequency with which it is used is determined by the gender of the child. If the child is female, then the ascriber will tend to identify and explicate the child's behaviour Q as, for example, 'shy/ afraid' rather than 'cowardly'; as 'difficult/selfish' rather than 'angry': as 'impetuous/wilful' rather than 'boisterous'. In particular, the selection of a gender-appropriate emotion is prior to its being approved or disapproved. While Q may be criticized in a particular context for either sex, if the child is female it will be not 'cowardly/boisterous', etc., but 'shy/impetuous', etc., that she is chastized for, or told 'not to be'. So again, the female child's understanding of her behaviour as remiss will be part of her understanding of it as expected of her given her age and sex. She learns simultaneously both 'that she is' and 'what it is to feel shy, difficult, wilful' via repeated identifications and descriptions of her behaviour in these terms.

The rationale for the gender paradigm derives from cultural beliefs and values concerning masculinity and femininity. The principle of femininity is conceptually related to, for example, 'moderation, demureness and self-effacement'. These notions help to explain the patterns of childhood emotion ascription outlined above in that they represent ideals of feminine adulthood around which the concepts predicated of the female child are specifically structured. For example, it is because concepts such as 'wilful and difficult' embody the negative appraisal that Q is unsuitably immoderate that it is appropriate to predicate these kinds of concepts rather than, say, 'angry' or 'boisterous' to that gender whose behaviour is ideally moderate. Negative concepts such as 'wilful' and 'selfish' are related to the ideal of moderation where, for example, the female child learns as part of the explication of these concepts that as she becomes older she will also acquire the self-control and moderation deserving of her sex. By contrast, the principle of masculinity is conceptually related to 'self-initiation, enterprise and strength'. Hence if the performer of Q is male, then ascriptions such as 'boisterous', etc., will be favoured since these concepts, being complementary to notions such as enterprise and strength, serve to vindicate the ideal of masculine adulthood. Again, negative appraisals (e.g., 'don't be so boisterous, you'll break something') involved in the explication of the emotion do not extinguish it, but rather serve as reminders that, with the advent of maturity, self-control will transform 'boisterousness' into enterprise, confidence and other conditions of masculine entitlement.

To return to the wider age paradigm, the points outlined above suggest that the child has articulated for it a world of emotion experience which is tightly structured around aspirations towards adulthood, aspirations which however demand a conception on the child's part of a disparity between what is expected and defining of itself and what is expected and defining of the mature models towards which it aspires. Hence, explications of childhood emotion experience disseminate sociocultural conceptions of 'what it is to be a child'. Such explications, in Western society at least, tend to present the child as lacking those virtues such as 'strength, control, depth, effectiveness' which when eventually acquired entitle it to the rewards of adulthood, such as 'autonomy, significance and choice'. What implications do these suggestions have for constructionism? One implication which the constructionist might take up is the possibility that the childhood emotions are to some extent generated and perpetuated by the maturation hierarchy with which a society normally operates and in which such emotions have a role and make sense. This in turn calls into question naturalist theories of the relationship between emotion and natural processes of maturation, since it raises the possibility that certain emotions are not natural products of immaturity but rather are socially generated states. In particular, a difficulty arises with the naturalist notion of basic emotion states which are eventually constrained via self-control. The naturalist presumption that self-control is linked to maturation perhaps overlooks the extent to which an emotion must be generated before it can be prohibited. Bu this I mean that there is a sense worth examining in which the absence of control which is conceptually related to, and which is alleged to explain, certain immature states is in fact granted and realized via its role in a society's system of beliefs, values and ideals concerning maturation.

SUMMARY AND CONCLUSION

In this chapter I have posed the philosophical question of how it is possible that emotions could be constituted in such a way as to have a sociofunctional role. Having clarified and qualified the functional account in such a way as to render it a plausible and workable feature of constructionism, I went on to examine it by reference to some actual cases. This also afforded an opportunity to exemplify the relationships postulated by constructionists between the functional role of emotions and notions such as 'acquisition, sociocultural constitution and prescription'. Finally, I considered cases of inappropriate emotions such as negative and unwarranted emotions and posed some arguments which enable the constructionist to accommodate such cases within their principles of explanation. In defence of the functional account, I suggested that the capacity which emotions have for demonstrating the integrity of an agent's attitude can be regarded as sociofunctional in so far as emotions have a special utility in endorsing the sociocultural values which such attitudes reflect. I also suggested that certain emotions involve attitudes the regulative/motivational nature of which can be explained by constructionism as serving specifically sociocultural functions, e.g., of prohibiting morally undesirable behaviour/ generating appropriate incentives and aspirations.

While I have, for brevity, been selective about the emotions I have chosen to discuss, the philosophical arguments advanced in this paper do, I believe, support some of the main aspects of constructionism. For example, the thesis of constructionism goes beyond the claim that an agent's emotions will tend to reflect the community of which he/she is a member in asserting that emotions bear an internal, prescriptive relation to social values. Traditionally, an agent's appreciation and endorsement of social values was understood as a role made possible by his/her possession of the appropriate rational faculties. However, the constructionist thesis can be taken as broadening the scope of the agent's ability to perform this role.

First, the constructionist's thesis explains why the capacity to endorse social values could be possessed by emotions in that their attitudinal constituents can, as the constructionist maintains, be understood as involving prescriptive notions, e.g., beliefs that x ought to be respected, praised, condemned, desired, defended, etc. In such cases agents automatically feel grateful, guilty, angry in response to their perceived obligation, transgression or mistreatment. In so far as such spontaneous responses to the warranting situation involve prescriptive notions, then this does, as the constructionist maintains, suggest that the relevant values, and their relation to the appropriate appetitive attitudes, have already been internalized by the agent.

Second, the constructionist's thesis explains why this role is possessed by emotions in particular. According to constructionism, an emotion embraces the corpus of an agent's attitudes and therefore provides an effective internalization of social values. This explanation is, I think, plausible in that an emotion, as constituted by a complex of appropriate attitudes, is an integrated response which could therefore be said to commit agents to particular values with greater success than could be achieved by the mere rational comprehension of such values. In addition to these features, emotions could also be said to have a unique use in conferring an affective meaning on abstract rules and principles which assists their being realized in common practice and experience. The sentiment via which a moral rule is conveyed has a crucial role not only in demonstrating the sincerity of the agent's moral judgement but also in demonstrating to others the significance and importance of the rule.

Finally, it turns out that even the weaker version of constructionism casts doubt on some of the important assumptions both of naturalism and of ethical theory. Both these theories explain emotions as phenomena the natural and universal status of which provides a basis for our understanding of social and moral behaviour. However, the arguments of this paper support the thesis that emotions, in their socialized form, and as they feature in a society, have a significantly non-natural content and function. While this is compatible with the existence of natural emotion states, it does call into question the naturalists' claim that emotions generally are essentially explainable in terms of the natural drives and apprehensions from which they are alleged to be derived. Rather, to the extent that emotions reflect and sustain the religious, moral and political beliefs, interests and values of a community, then, contra naturalism and emotivism, the analysis of these interrelated systems should be prior to our analysis of the emotions which feature in, and support, such systems.

In particular, the arguments posed here suggest that it is perhaps wrong to view the fine-grained distinctions within, and differences between, cultural emotion repertoires as involving emotion terms which merely label the same fundamental emotion experiences, since emotion terms are conceptually related to distinct complexes of attitudes which themselves indicate differences of emotion experience. To the extent that such attitudes are socioculturally determined, this introduces the possibility that there is a range of emotion experience which is not naturally pre-existent but which, like intellectual and practical experience, is made available to agents via their acquiaintance with cultural systems and the language, social rules and practices which such systems involve. This in turn raises an issue concerning the ethics of the sociocultural constitution of emotion. If emotions do have a significantly non-natural dependence upon sociocultural beliefs and values, then this introduces the possibility of providing a revisionary moral analysis of emotions, the results of which would enable us to select and subsequently prescribe emotions which can be justified as of most benefit to social relations and to the welfare of the individuals involved. It is the above implications of constructionism, both for the analysis of the possible scope of emotion experience and for ethics, which, I think, discloses constructionism not as a replacement of Hobbesian scepticism with social determinism, but as a positive and enlightening theory.

REFERENCES

Averill, J. (1980) A constructivist view of emotions. In R. Plutchik and H. Kellerman (eds), *Emotion Theory, Research and Experience.* New York: Academic Press.

De Sousa, R. (1980) The rationality of emotions. In A. Rorty (ed.), *Explaining Emotions.* London: University of California Press.

Howell, S. (1981) Rules not words. In P. Heelas and A. Locke (eds), *Indigenous Psychologies: The Anthropology of the Self.* London: Academic Press.

Lutz, C. (1981) Goals, events and understanding: Towards a formal model of Ifaluk emotion theory. Paper presented at the 80th Annual Meeting of the American Anthropological Association. Los Angeles, December 1981.

—— (1982a) Parental goals, ethnopsychology and the development of emotional meaning. *Ethos.*

—— (1982b) The domain of emotion words on Ifaluk. *American Ethnologist*, 9, 9 February.

Neu, J. (1980) Jealous thoughts. In A. Rorty (ed.), *Explaining Emotions.* London: University of California Press.

Rorty, A. (1980) Explaining emotions. In A. Rorty (ed.), *Explaining Emotions.* London: University of California Press.

Slote, M. (1983) *Goods and Virtues.* Oxford: Clarendon Press.

5

Emotion and Act: Roles and Rhetoric

Theodore R. Sarbin

RELOCATING THE FOCUS: FROM AUTOMATISM TO CONTEXTUALISM

According to Stephen Pepper (1942), contextualism is one of four 'adequate' world hypotheses or metaphysical perspectives that guide thought and action. For academic psychology, with hardly an exception, the prevailing world hypothesis has been mechanistic – the root metaphor is the transmittal of force. More recently, especially among social and humanistic psychologists, the contextualist perspective has been adopted. The root metaphor is the historical act in all its complexity. The implication of adopting the historical act as the root metaphor is not just methodological, for instance that one will employ multivariate analysis. Rather, the implication is more fundamental. Change and novelty will become basic categories. Further, the phenomena of interest will be intentional acts, acts designed to transform or transfigure the world; and the acts are performed by persons as agents, not as mechanical automata. Equally important is the implication that the historical act (an act with a past and concurrent history) is told as a story. That language is an important feature of historical act analysis is self-evident.

In the following discussion of an old problem, I have been guided by the root metaphor of the historical act. Unlike many theorists in the recent academic tradition, I do not treat 'emotion' as detachable from social contexts.

To provide a poetic image the better to contrast the contextual with the prevailing mechanistic perspective, I quote from W. B. Yeats:

Invited address, American Psychological Association, Division 24 (Theoretical and Philosophical Psychology), 25 August 1984, Toronto, Canada. An earlier version was delivered at a colloquium at the University of Nevada, Reno, 27 April 1984.

O Body swayed to music
O Brightening glance
How can we know the dancer
from the dance?

The word 'emotions' has drifted into opacity at the hands of physiologists, psychologists and phenomenologists. The imagery is diffuse, and not easily communicable. Etymologically, emotion denoted outward-directed movement, as in migrations. The meaning was transferred to movements within the body. For the past 300 years or more, observers have focused on such perceived or imagined internal movements. The metaphors to describe such happenings have been drawn from many sources, the intent being to give form to vague internal happenings. Depending upon choice of metaphysics, the internal happenings have been described in the language of mentalism or in the language of physiology.

It would not be off the mark to say that emotion is a metaphor, and that its employment in folk contexts or in scientific contexts follows from a metonymic transfer from 'anger' to 'emotion'. In English, 'anger' could have provided the metaphorical basis for emotion. The appearance of the word 'anger' antedated by several hundred years the use of 'emotion' as a psychological category.

Prevailing theories detach emotions from context. When a theorist writes of anger, grief, pity, etc., there is hidden in the text an unrecognized implication that the phenomena represented by the specific emotion term can be detached from the context of action. Thus, emotion is generally discussed in the abstract, not unlike vision or digestion. This detachability is traceable to several sources. One is the ontological status assigned to such detachable substantives as mind, soul and psyche. Another source is the long-forgotten reification of an old metaphor: *the body is a container.* Still another source is the reification of the extended metaphor that emotion is located in the bodily container. The latter reification has given rise to the myth of the vissicitudes of the contents of the container under metaphorically marked conditions such as heat and pressure (Lakoff and Kövecses, 1983). Freud's hydraulics model was a modest extension of the myth.

From our present perspective, it is clear that emotion was introduced into our technical language as a metaphor for the passions. Passions have a unique status. They are assigned to a class of occurrences that 'happen'. They are regarded as if the person who suffers the passion is a passive victim – somewhat like the victim of microbial invasion. If passions were, in fact, nothing but 'happenings', it would be appropriate to look for causes in the workings of the 'psychic' apparatus and/or the somatic machinery. The uncritical acceptance of the concept of passions and its implied mechanistic causality has frustrated attempts to connect 'emotions' with the language of everyday life as represented by dramatists, novelists and poets. To perceive human behaviour as helped or hindered by 'passions' is to reintroduce the notion that social actions are driven by vaguely defined internal movements. To restore transparency to the concept of emotion, the myth of the passions would have to be put aside (not a likely outcome, given its entrenched status in psychological theories). Instead of a bodily happening, causally related to antecedents such as the Devil, Flesh, neuroanatomical processes, etc., I propose that we examine specific instances of conduct from a contextual standpoint.

The interactional imagery that I connect with the term 'emotion' is similar to that employed by ordinary people when they tell stories about grief, love, anger, fear, jealousy, pride and so on. The imagery is that of a multi-personed scene in which actions of one participant serve as a centre for subsequent actions by self and other. The meaning of emotion as a feature of social action is not the same as the meaning of emotion distilled by the experimental psychologist, the physiologist or the phenomeno- logist. The centre of attention for these traditional students of emotion is not in social life or drama, but in happenings inside the individual. For these scientists, situations are regarded only as potential stimuli for encapsulated internal physiological or mental happenings.

We have inherited from our intellectual ancestors a simple classi- ficatory scheme which was invented to talk about and to study the human condition. Intellect, will and emotion have been handed down to us as givens. This trinity remains as one of the fundamental guiding postulates of psychology, even though it is constantly challenged. Although few psycho- logists would today subscribe to the outworn faculty psychology as such, many continue to talk and work as if the three-way split of the faculties had continuing validity.

Emotion is not an old word. For psychologists, it replaces 'the passions', those happenings that are regarded as not being under the agency of the actor. For many writers, the passions are somehow connected to our animal heritage. They occupy a special place in theoretical structures in that they displace reason, the preferred faculty – the faculty that character- izes the human soul in all its nobility. This valuation is reflected in textbooks of psychology. As an undergraduate, I was taught that emotion was nothing but disorganized response, i.e., that the presence of emotion interfered with the smooth functioning of reason and action.

One outcome of the opacity of the term 'emotion' is the failure to achieve a common definition. Some writers talk of 'having' an emotion, others of the 'experience' of emotion; some equate emotion with visceral activity, some with the perception of visceral activity; some use emotion and feelings as equivalents, others argue that feelings are constitutive of emotion; others treat emotions as patterned organismic responses. Some cite reflexes as prototypic of emotion. The term is even applied to stimuli; some stimuli are emotional or evocative of emotion. Some writers say that emotion is an attribution, others that it is equivalent to anxiety. Some focus on facial expression as the diacritica of emotion.

To illustrate the difficulties in finding a common set of features, I quote from Paul Ekman's introduction to a book that extensively reviews research on facial expression and emotion:

> The lack of a clear definition of emotion presents problems for investigators some of whom have simply sidestepped the problem of specifying why the behavior they studied may be presumed to have anything to do with emotion, and also for the editor of this volume. Our selection procedure was to take into account, with few exceptions, any article that the author *said* was about emotion and where the face was studied in relation to other phenomena. (Ekman, 1972, p. 11)

The time has come to recognize that side-stepping cannot alter the fact that 'emotion' has too many and diverse meanings to be useful as a pivotal concept in a scientific enterprise. Even if a case could be made for the theoretical utility of the threefold description of conduct – intellect, will and emotion – the case could not be made for the ecological validity of such a division. Faculty psychology, or its modern derivatives, has little to offer the contemporary scientist who begins from the premise that human beings are actors in continuous interaction with the world, that their actions are compounds of judgements, evaluations and performances, enacted in social and linguistic contexts. Such a premise does not disavow the observation that the actor is *embodied*; therefore the scientist must recognize and take into account the fact that the actor is the current end-product of biological evolution.

ASKING THE WRONG QUESTION: FALLACIES OF REIFICATION

It has happened before – a metaphor coined to give poetic description to some phenomenon becomes reified. Once the figure of speech is literalized, unsolvable problems emerge, problems of the kind we are currently experiencing with emotion. When a term loses its metaphorical moorings, i.e., becomes reified, inevitably scientists, philosophers and even ordinary people believe they are justified in asking the question, What is emotion? Popper has written that this is the discredited method of the scholastics, and answers to such questions can lead only to more and more abstract verbal statements. A recent exchange between Zajonc (1984) and Lazarus (1984) in the *American Psychologist* exemplifies this proposition. A careful reading of their arguments maked clear that each is offering an answer to the question, What is emotion?

Zajonc argues that emotions are immediately given events, untrammelled by reflection, cognition, judgement, etc. His thesis centres on biological structures and the activation of processes that some writers label affect, others passions and still others emotional responses. He presents a large array of empirical studies to support his claim that emotion requires no antecedent cognitive action. Although cognition is also a term with unstable referents, he cites studies that appear to support the hypothesis that affect and cognition are independent processes.

Zajonc holds that affective reactions show phylogenetic and ontogenetic primacy. He cites theories such as those of Izard, Tomkins and Darwin to the effect that 'affect systems' are activated in much the same fashion as reflexes. No mediation is required. He further cites studies that suggest that affect and cognition are served by different neuroanatomical systems. He cites work on taste aversions and tonal preferences to support his contention that the affect system is independent of the cognitive system. In an effort to identify the causes of affective reactions, he looks for the mechanisms that make it possible for forces (energies) to be transmitted from organ to organ. The underlying world view is that of mechanism, and the job for the scientist is to find the connections between the elements of the machine. My reading of the arguments leads me to suggest that Zajonc's answer to the question, What is emotion? is to locate it in a category that would also include knee-jerks, eye-blinks and the startle pattern.

Lazarus, on the other hand, is a proponent of the view that emotions are influenced by antecedent and concurrrent cognitive appraisals. He, too, is concerned with the question, What is emotion? His answer is conditioned by the definition that every affect must have some judgemental antecedent. He cites a large number of studies that make clear the interaction of cognition and emotion. Between the lines of his argument is the assumption that the emotional response includes affect. The behaviour of interest, the dependent variable, remains a set of responses, usually assessed by observation of facial or bodily reactions, physiological measures and sometimes intentional behaviour. It seems that both parties share in one assumption – namely, that 'emotional states' exist, and are manifested through bodily process, overt expression and subjective feeling.

Unlike Zajonc, Lazarus regards the emotional response as mediated. The quality of the response depends upon the prior cognitive appraisal of the situation. The focus of their difference, then, is whether affect is mediate or immediate. If immediate, then emotion is like a reflex; if mediate, emotion is more like a two-stage affair. Both theorists appear to reflect a belief that there exists a definable entity called emotion.

Instead of extending the futile controversy over answers to the question, 'What is emotion? It would be better to begin a study from specific observations. Given such-and-such circumstances, how does a person

perform? What does he/she do or say? What are the features of the
ecological setting that may be the instigators or maintainers of certain
concrete acts? Suppose we observe the conduct of Smith, who is the object
of Jones's insult. What does Smith do? If he has been acculturated to the
concept 'insult', and if he has acquired the experience to make a judgement
about the intentions of Jones, then he is confronted with the problem of
maintaining his self-respect. The interpretations of the actions of Jones as
'insult' is a challenge to Smith's identity. At the same time that Smith
acquired the concept of insult, he also learned that retaliation or punishment was an integral part of the concept, and the appropriate response
was the adoption of the anger role. He also acquired certain metaphors to
communicate to self or other the vague visceral and proprioceptive
stimulus events that occurred concommitantly with the involved role
performance, e.g., 'the body is a container' (Lakoff and Kövecses, 1983).
Another metaphor was 'the contents of the container respond to heat and
pressure.' With these beliefs (the metaphoric origins of which have long
been submerged), Smith could transfigure a complex plot or scenario, a
personal drama, to 'feelings of anger'. Through this transfiguration, Smith
could invoke the myth of the passions ('the feelings came over me') and
claim that the anger was a *happening* for which he was not the agent.
(Later, I will extend the discussion of plots.)

RHETORIC AND DRAMA: THE ANALYSIS OF EMOTIONAL ACTS

As I remarked in my introduction, contextualism, the alternate metaphysics to mechanism, is best expressed in the language of 'historical acts'.
An entailment of this language is that we examine the actions of persons as
agents, taking into account as much of the social and nonsocial context as
possible. To give form to a contextual analysis of human actions. I, along
with others, have adopted a set of metaphors that have their origins in the
humanities. Victor Turner, for example, saw complex human actions as
social drama. Goffman has explicated the dramaturgical theory of conduct. Of course, Shakespeare provided a great impetus to theories based
on the ontological statement that life is theatre.

   The use of metaphors drawn from the theatre is consistent with the
current 'refiguration' of social science (as Clifford Geertz describes it). No
longer relying exclusively on energy, spatial and mechanical metaphors,
we are adopting metaphors that have their homes in the humanities. Not
only the theatre, but literary texts, game-playing and the language of ritual
are being raided for metaphors the better to construct theories of conduct.
This refiguration of social thought provides the background for my
employing metaphors drawn from two related humanistic disciplines:
drama and rhetoric.

I mention the drama only briefly. At least since G. H. Mead expounded his theories about role-taking, the theatrical term 'role' has had a prominent – if not always congenial – place in theories of social behaviour. It requires no great effort for any of us to translate our confrontations with others as episodes in a social drama. Routine interactions do not qualify as drama. Only when an act has the potential for creating strain are we likely to interpret the performances of people as if they were actors creating or following a script.

I have turned also to rhetoric as a source of metaphors. Contemporary authorities have revived the classical evaluation of rhetoric as the disciplined use of oral and gestural behaviour for the purpose of convincing or persuading others of the propriety or appropriateness of the speaker's values and actions. Rhetorical acts are confrontations of active beings in problem-solving situations, which rhetoricians call exigencies, or urgencies. An acknowledged authority on rhetoric. C. C. Arnold, makes the point that such acts are not confrontations of 'impersonally symbolized concepts . . . and vaguely specifiable human beings' such as one might find in a literary text. Rather, 'confrontations of *persons* extort and define commitments.' In the confrontations of oral rhetoric, a person has no choice but to 'stand with' his symbolic acts. His personal presence (even if only by voice) is itself 'symbolic, rhetorical action'.

Human beings have invented a variety of adaptive actions to deal with epistemological crises, the exigencies and urgencies of everyday life. Of the four classes of adaptive actions – changing beliefs, attention deployment, tranquilizing and releasing manoeuvres and rhetorical acts – the last named is the most powerful class of actions directed towards maintaining or enhancing one's identity.

Rhetorical acts are the stuff of which social and personal dramas are made. Two forms of rhetorical acts may be identified: 'dramaturgic' and 'dramatistic'. I employ these labels to distinguish the authorship of the rhetorical actions. Both are employed for the purpose of influencing the participants in a social drama. In dramaturgical action the actor engages in the strategic behaviour of impression management through the use of symbolic mirrors, through the donning of masks and other pretences, through deception, and through withholding information (secrets) (Goffman, 1961; Scheibe, 1979). The actor creates such strategic interaction scripts, making them up as he or she interacts with other actors. The actor is author/playwright. The intention is to persuade relevant others of the validity of the actor's expressed or implied claims. Like professional actors and debaters, the actors in the social drama monitor their rhetorical communications and make changes in the script as necessary.

These dramaturgical actions are nowhere better illustrated than in *Hamlet*. Nearly all the characters in *Hamlet* engage in deception, disguise, feigning, plotting and other strategic devices to achieve their ends.

'Hamlet, the noble prince, adopts a role of inauthenticity to bring Denmark back into the orbit of honor held under his father. Claudius, the evil king, employs secret stratagems, spies and surveillance to keep his kingdom secure from Hamlet's revenge' (Lyman and Scott, 1975, p. 17).

Rhetorical actions of the second kind – dramatistic – are employed by the actors in a social drama in parallel with dramaturgical actions. Dramatistic actions have a different authorship from dramaturgical ploys. In the dramatistic ontology, *life is theatre*. In contrast to dramaturgical rhetoric, where the actor is also the playwright, in dramatistic scripts the identity of the playwright is not easily reconstructed. Dramatistic scripts are patterned after half-remembered folktales, fables, myths, legends and other stories. Not taught and learned in any systematic way, the plots of these stories are absorbed as part of one's enculturation. Like the performances of dramaturgical actors, the performances of dramatistic actors are organized into recognizable patterns or roles. The contents of dramatistic roles are the compounds of valuational judgements, intentions and actions that are sometimes identified as emotions or passions.

Averill (1979) has made a case for referring to such occasions as grief, jealousy, anger, joy, etc., as transitory social roles. The judgement, bodily processes and performances together comprise the 'emotion' or transitory social role. Averill's analysis needs to be extended. 'Transitory' carries the connotation of temporary, short-lived, etc. Some dramatistic roles, such as grief, while not permanent, may be enacted over months and even years. Further, many everyday roles may be transitory, without the involvement characteristic of dramatistic roles.

To make good use of Averill's heuristic, I need to clarify the concept of role. One usage is that of the part in a play, the theatrical role. Except as a transparent metaphor, the theatrical role is not germane to our problem.

A second usage is where an agent takes on another identity; for example, a spy, a dissembler, an imposter. A certain political figure is a crook and pretends to be an honest person. Tootsie is an unemployed actor who pretends to be an actress. This variety of role-taking is better described as dramaturgic, as strategic, and is not central to such conditions as grief, anger, hatred, exultation, etc.

A third usage of role is the one most often used by social psychologists and sociologists: the expected conduct of a person, given his/her status or position in the society. These social roles may be conceptualized on a gradient one end of which is ascription (age, sex, kinship, birthright, ethnicity) and the other end, achievement (occupational and recreational statuses).

The fourth kind of role, and the one most pertinent to my analysis, may be called dramatistic. Grief roles, jealousy roles, revenge roles and so on are qualitatively different from social roles that are tied to positions in the social structure. These dramatistic roles may be likened to general literary stereotypes, such as the traditional lover, the picaresque rogue or the fool. Hamlet portrays the dramatic avenger; Richard III sets out to prove himself the villain *par excellence*; Othello is the prototype for the dramatic role 'jealous husband'; Iago is the scheming manipulator, the stereotype of envy, rancour and hatred.

I borrow the literary stereotype from belletristic sources to serve as a model for dramatistic roles. Such stereotypes also exist in the story-telling of fables, fairy tales, morality plays, bedtime stories, movies, soap operas and so on. The stereotypes are part and parcel of the myths and folktales of a society.

The foregoing discussion of the role concept brings into sharper focus Averill's proposal that the complex conduct that is ordinarily subsumed under 'emotion' be perceived as social roles. Because social roles are tied to social structure, I propose that the conduct of interest is better instantiated as dramatistic role performances, the metaphorical origin of which is reflected in literary stereotypes. At this point, we can dispense with the notion of literary stereotypes. Its only purpose was to help establish the difference between social roles, the patterned actions that maintain a collectivity, and dramatistic roles, the patterned action that maintain or enhance the self or identity. Dramatistic roles, e.g., grief, anger and jealousy, are patterns of conduct in the same sense as greetings and farewells are patterns of conduct. The patterns that are intimately tied to values, to conditions that involve one's identity, are indentified by many writers as emotions or passions.

Needless to say, dramatistic roles are not played *in vacuo*. The role enactments are integral to social dramas. Anger roles, grief roles, jealousy roles and so on are enacted to further an actor's self-narrative; and self-narratives, like other stories, follow a plot.

PLOTS AND THE LOGIC OF DRAMATISTIC ROLES

Contrary to the traditional view that emotional acts are irrational, dramatistic roles follow a logic. It is the logic of the self-narrative that dictates the course of action of the participants in a social drama. The logic is the plot of a story. The central actors, individually and collectively, perform according to plot structures. The plots provide a basis for retrospectively criticizing emotional acts as appropriate or stupid, justifiable or unreasonable, foolish or wise. Without such plot structures against which to assess the dramatistic roles, critical reflection would be impossible.

A full account of a dramatistic role includes intentions for the future, i.e., intentions to act in the interest of gaining status and power, of achieving an acceptable identity, of avoiding degradation. In his book that explodes the myth of the passions, Robert Solomon says: 'we intend to revenge ourselves in anger, to redeem ourselves in shame, to restore our dignity in embarrassment, to help another person in pity . . .' (Solomon, 1976, p. 190).

De Souza (1980) has proposed a similar line of thought. He argues that a person's 'emotional repertoire' (dramatistic role repertoire) is learned in the context of 'paradigm scenarios'. These paradigm scenarios are, in a manner of speaking, prototypes of social dramas and they reveal plot structures, some of which are acquired early in life. De Souza proposes that 'a child's instinctive responses to certain stimuli become a part . . . of an emotion. In simple cases the instinctive [reflexive] response to certain stimuli (smiling, crying) becomes an *expression* of emotion (joy, sadness, rage) but it does so only in the context of the scenario' (p. 285). The implication of this proposal for my analysis is that dramatistic roles are learned; they are not instincts or reflexes. Such roles are learned in the same school and at the same time as the plot structures that comprise our humanity.

The plot structure is often reflected in the images and metaphors of cultural myths which give form to the logic. The logic of anger, for example, is reflected in its plot structure described by Solomon as 'Court-room or Olympian mythology; oneself as legislator and judge; the other as defendant. Oneself as the defender of values, the other as offender' (Solomon, 1976, p. 289). The logic of contempt is represented in its plot structure as 'The other as a vile creature (and oneself, by contrast, as pure and noble). Typical metaphors: the other as a snake, a reptile, an insect, a spider . . . as degenerate or depraved' (1976, p. 294).

When actors adopt the perspective that the dramatistic role enactments are the products of their own valuations and intensions, they can offer an account of their conduct through an examination of 'reasons'. The causality of internal and external forces becomes irrelevant. Instead of asking, 'What caused me to feel ashamed?' the actor asks, 'What were my *reasons* for being ashamed?' The scientific observer may be guided by the same perspective. Search strategies and search outcomes are different for those who ask, 'What *caused* the person to weep?' from those who ask, 'What were the reasons the *person* wept?'

The implications of adopting a perspective that calls for the scrutiny of reasons rather than causes are manifold. Explanations of dramatistic encounters would be couched in the vocabulary of intentions, values, beliefs and reciprocal acts. Such explanations would contribute to the identification of any human episode as an historical act, the meaning of which cannot be divorced from its context.

ROLES, EMOTIONS AND INTENDED ACTS

The thesis that dramatistic roles are intentional acts is a radical departure from modern-day faculty psychology. To reject such a thesis, critics point to two observations: the first has to do with self-reports that contain descriptive phrases such as 'being seized by an emotion', 'being overwhelmed', 'being caught in the grip of an emotion', and so on. The second observation has to do with self-perceived bodily changes. The emphasis on bodily reactions has been instrumental in deflecting interest from emotions as role encounters to emotions as happenings. The fact of bodily reactions is used to support the claim that emotions are universal biological phenomena, the animal inheritance of our evolutionary ancestors.

Self-perceived bodily changes must be accounted for in a theory that treats rhetorical actions as the product of valuation and intention. As a first step, I refer to a dimension of role enactment that has proven useful in other contexts. Dramatistic roles, like social roles, may be enacted with various degrees of organismic involvement. I have suggested a dimension identified by eight reference cases. At the low end is causal role enactment, where little or no involvement is noted – usually the ritual exchange of routine actions, such as between a cashier and a customer at a supermarket. Next in order is ritual acting, 'going through the motions'. A greater degree of involvement is noted in engrossed or heated stage acting. More organismic involvement is observed in classical hypnotic roletaking, where, e.g., the person is analgesic. Next on the dimension is histrionic neurosis (often called conversion hysteria). Ecstasy is a reference case for highly involved role enactment, as in religious excitement. The high end of the dimension is illustrated by the actions of persons who believe they are the objects of sorcery and witchcraft. The organismic outcomes are sometimes irreversible.

At the low end of the dimension, role and self are differentiated, few organic systems are called into play, and little effort is expended. At the high end, role and self are undifferentiated, the entire organism is involved in the action, and a great deal of effort is expended (Sarbin, 1954; Sarbin and Allen, 1968).

When an actor makes use of his rhetorical skills to persuade others of the legitimacy of his identity claims, he monitors the action so as to present just the right amount of involvement. In the same way that each culture develops rules regarding optimal interpersonal distance, rules are developed for degrees of involvement appropriate to particular scenes. That is, the rhetorical act is subject to modulation. When an actor enacts a *dramatistic* role – say, the anger role – the degree of involvement is high. To make his point, the actor performs with increased vigour. It is important for the actor to communicate forcefully that he is responding to insult or injustice. William James said he could not conceive of anger without the display of 'vigorous actions'. The enactment calls for large expenditures of effort. Parenthetically, one of the stable categories of classical rhetoric is 'emphasis' (implying more than is actually stated). To achieve emphasis, the actor increases the vigour of his verbal and non-verbal communications. Not only angry roles, but grief roles, jealousy roles and exultation roles can be cited as instances where rhetorical acts provide 'emphasis'.

At any time prior to the dramatistic action, the actor can reinterpret the context and abort the role. Once the actor initiates vigorous role enactment, somatic side-effects occur that are not amenable to explanation by citing reasons. Bodily perturbations, such as increased heart rate, palmar sweating, respiratory changes, flushing, laryngeal constriction, glandular secretions and other reflex actions, once begun, are not under voluntary control. To explain these events, it is appropriate to regard them as happenings, and to search for causes.

The return to a neutral organismic base-line after vigorous action takes time. The physiology of recovery continues even after the dramatic role enactment has been concluded or aborted. The bodily effects have a semi-autonomous after-life. Although somatic events are side-effects of organismic involvement, they are none the less strands in the total context of any particular role enactment.

If the actor (or the scientist) focuses on the bodily perturbations that accompany and follow the role enactment, he can elect to interpret such happenings as 'the emotion'. Such an attribution is appropriate only for the physiological side-effects of increased vigour, but such a conceptual limitation is ignored by users of the myth of the passions. The part is assimilated to the whole, the somatic side-effects become coterminous with the complex of social and epistemic events that comprise dramatistic roles.

The self-report of 'being in the grip of an emotion' and similar self-reports is an attribution made by the actor. Instead of monitoring the context, including his/her own valuations and intentions, the actor pays attention only to the organismic happenings. Under such conditions, the inference is credible that the actor's behaviour is constrained by uncontrollable (and mysterious) biological forces. Needless to say, the somatic perturbations, once begun, run their course because of physiological, not social, constraints. When the actor employs bodily reactions exclusively as cues for constructing inferences about the causes of his conduct, he/she maintains the myth of the passions. Most important, the actor can convincingly deny responsibility for choosing one rather than another role.

A traditional theorist might ask, How about *feelings*? Are feelings not independent of acts, whether dramatistic or dramaturgic? A critical reading of theories of emotion reveals that feelings are sometimes treated as a synonym for emotion, and sometimes as constitutive of emotions. When I ask my informants to describe their feelings in connection with a recent event, the answers are uninformative except in so far as the actor tells a story, a self-narrative. The story provides meaning to the metaphors carried by the actor, such as, 'it was great', 'it was indescribable', 'it was the high point of my career', 'I felt like I would burst with pride'. Interviews with athletic champions illustrate my point: at the end of a contest, reporters ask the winner, 'How does it feel to be the winner?' or '. . . to have broken the record?' or 'What were your feelings when you won the gold medal?' An analysis of the responses reveals that the respondents first typically see their task as forming an opinion about a poorly under-stood internal state of affairs; second, after uttering the opinion ('It's a wonderful feeling'), they move away from the task of trying to pin down a 'feeling' and instead tell stories about the rigours of training, the role of the coach, family support, uncertainty of outcome, the meaning of the contest, etc. It is not productive to posit feelings as a special kind of sensation.

I am not alone in abandoning the myth of the passions and moving towards a recognition of the emptiness of the proposition that 'emotions' are detachable phenomena. I have already alluded to the ground-breaking work of James Averill (1979). Sylvan Tomkins (1980), long an advocate of emotion as a biological given, has enlarged his theory to incorporate scripts, scenes and plots. Congenial with my contextualist orientation is his declaration: 'What is important from the point of view of script theory is that the effect of any set of scenes is *indeterminate* until the future happens and either further magnifies or attenuates experience. The second point is that the consequence of any experience is not singular but plural . . .' (Tomkins, 1975, p. 219).

Joseph de Rivera (1977, 1984) has proposed a structural theory of emotions. He emphasizes the necessity for qualitative analysis of people as agents. Although he has not abandoned 'emotion' as a fundamental category, his research is predicated on observing people in action *vis à vis* other actors and things. At another time, I hope to show how 'the experience of emotion', a central category in the structural theory, may be illuminated by the narrativist approach.

Dramatistic role enactments are intimately bound to values. There is a need for a thorough examination of how rules are formed that guide a person to adopt one rather than another value stance. Hochschild's recent book, *The Managed Heart* (1983), makes a solid beginning towards under-standing the 'feeling rules' that influence the choice of dramatistic roles when the actor's values are in conflict with job requirements. She studied the effects of the conflict between an employer's requirement that an employee smile and act warmly and pleasantly in contexts that are degrading and insulting. The dramatistic plot structure (insult–anger–retaliation) is overlaid with dramaturgic (strategic) portrayals. Actions of this kind may be seen as reflecting inauthenticity. It is important to learn about the short-term and long-range effects of such inauthentic action.

SUMMARY

To recapitulate, I have set down the claims that involved actions can be profitably studied as dramatistic roles. I have also contended that the adaptive actions of participants under identity strain are rhetorical acts, the purpose of which is to persuade relevant audiences (including imagined audiences) of the legitimacy of the actor's identity claims. I distinguished between two classes of rhetorical roles: dramaturgical, exemplified by strategies of impression management; and dramatistic, exemplified by the complex of judgements, intentions and acts that flow from cultural sources. Such roles are the central feature of any social or personal drama. Dramatistic actions have a logic derived from long-standing cultural imperatives, the logic being contained in narrative plots. Sources of plots are found in myths, legends, folktales, parables, proverbs, morality plays and, of course, religious narratives.

One implication of the foregoing discussion of the contextualist root metaphor is that historical events pose special problems to the scientist. Change and novelty stand in the way of determinate prediction; the unique quality of social or personal drama makes it difficult to apply universal dimensions. Because love, grief, jealousy, joy and anger (and actions denoted by at least 400 other terms) have been called 'emotions', numerous writers have attempted to sort them into categories based on a limited number of dimensions. The lack of agreement as to what is constitutive of emotions, and the arbitrary detaching of 'emotion' from the social context, makes it extremely difficult, if not impossible, to construct a general theory of emotion. One implication of this conclusion is that 'emotion' be dropped from the psychologists' lexicon.

Because 'emotion' is such an entrenched concept in our thoughtways, some readers may reject my proposals with the declaration that there must be some stable referent, some reality, some utility, for the term 'emotion'. I know of no better response than a quotation from the social philosopher, Alasdair McIntyre (1971). The implication for a general theory of emotion is clear and vibrant:

> There was once a man who aspired to be the author of the general theory of holes. When asked, 'what kind of holes – holes dug by children in the sand . . . holes dug by gardeners . . . tank traps, holes made by roadmakers?' he would reply indignantly that he wished for a general theory that would explain all of these. He rejected *ab initio* the . . . pathetically commonsense view that of the

digging of holes there are quite different kinds of explanations to be given; 'why, then', he would ask, 'do we have the concept of a hole . . .?' (McIntyre, 1971, p. 260)

REFERENCES

Arnold, C. C. (1980)   Oral rhetoric, rhetoric, and literature. In E. E. White (ed.), *Rhetoric in Transition*. University Park, Pa.: Penn State University Press.

Averill, J. (1979)   Anger. In H. E. Howe and R. A. Dienstbier (eds), *Nebraska Symposium on Motivation, 1978*. Lincoln: University of Nebraska Press.

de Rivera, J. (1977)   *A Structural Theory of Emotion*. New York: International Universitia Press.

— (ed.) (1984)   The analysis of emotional experience. *American Behavioral Scientist*, 27, 675–832.

De Souza, R. (1980)   The rationality of emotions. In A. O. Rorty, (ed.), *Explaining Emotions*. Berkeley: University of California Press.

Ekman, P., Friesen, W. V. and Ellsworth P. (1982)   *Emotion in the Human Face*. New York: Pergamon.

Geertz, C. (1980)   Blurred genres: the refiguration of social thought. *American Scholar*, 80, 165–79.

Goffman, E. (1961)   *The Presentation of Self in Everyday Life*. Garden City, NY: Doubleday.

Hochschild, A. R. (1983)   *The Managed Heart*. Berkeley: University of California Press.

Lakoff, G. and Kövecses, Z. (1983)   The cognitive model of anger inherent in American English. *Berkeley Cognitive Science Report* no. 10.

Lazarus, R. S. (1984)   On the primacy of cognition. *American Psychologist*, 39, 124–9.

Lyman, S. M. and Scott, M. B. (1975)   *The Drama of Social Reality*. New York: Oxford University Press.

McIntyre, A. (1971)   *Against the Self-images of the Age*. New York: Schocken Books.

Pepper, S. (1942)   *World Hypotheses*. Berkeley: University of California Press.

Sarbin, T. R., (1954)   Role theory. In G. Lindzey and E. Aronson (eds), *Handbook of Social Psychology*, vol. 1. Reading, Mass.: Addison Wesley.

— and Allen V. L., (1968)   Role theory. In G. Lindzey and E. Aronson (eds), *Handbook of Social Psychology*, Vol. 1. Reading, Mass.: Addison-Wesley.

Scheibe, K. E. (1979)   *Mirrors, Masks, Lies, and Secrets*. New York: Praeger Press.

Solomon, R. (1976)   *The Passions*. New York: Anchor Press/Doubleday.

Tomkins, S. (1980)   Script theory. In *Nebraska Symposium on Motivation, 1979*. Lincoln: University of Nebraska Press.

Turner, V. (1974)   *Dramas, Fields, and Metaphors*. Ithaca, NY: Cornell University Press.

Zajonc, R. B. (1984)   On the primacy of affect. *American Psychologist*, 39, 117–23.

6

The Acquisition of Emotions during Adulthood

James R. Averill

The problem of the role of emotions in adult development could encompass three different issues: (1) the influence of emotion – and stress in general – on aging and development; (2) the way age-related changes in physiological and psychological functioning influence emotional reactivity; and (3) the acquisition of new, or the relinquishment of old, emotional experiences during adulthood. There is a growing literature on the first two of these issues although few definitive statements can be made. The third issue, which is the topic of this chapter, has been relatively ignored.

Let me begin with a few illustrations of what I mean by the acquisition and relinquishment of emotions during childhood.

1   Amok is an aggressive frenzy observed in several South-east Asian societies. It involves indiscriminate killing while in a trance-like state until the person running amok is himself killed. In its 'classical' form, amok did not involve psychopathology (e.g., a schizophrenic breakdown or neurological disorder) but was a ritualized response to certain socially defined situations (e.g., involving a loss of honour – see Murphy, 1973, for a historical review of amok). Van Wulfften Palthe (1936) reports that occasional Europeans living in South-east Asia have run amok; however, he could cite no case of a South-east Asian running amok while living in a European country.

2   Lucas (1969) has described the experiences of six miners trapped by a cave-in. After three days, parched with thirst, they took the first tentative steps towards drinking their own urine. The initial attempts resulted in gagging and vomiting. A resocialization of the emotions had to

Thanks are due to Bram Fridhandler and Ervin Staub for helpful comments on an earlier draft of this manuscript.

occur. Lucas draws on the literature of religious conversions to explicate the underlying processes. Although a bit overdrawn, the comparison is enlightening. The men had to create and internalize a new set of social norms that made the drinking of urine not only intellectually permissible but emotionally acceptable. By the time they were rescued, the men were drinking urine, if not with gusto, at least without disgust.

3   A common theme in feminist writings is the transformation of more passive emotional experiences, such as depression and lethargy, into more active states. Anger especially is viewed as a 'tool for growth'. Glennon (1979) quotes the following account by an anonymous participant in an informal feminist workshop:

> One woman becomes angry and pounds the floor and then suddenly another hears her and recognizes it and then all the women are angry. From an inarticulate moaning and pounding comes an angry fury as they rise together chanting 'No! No! No!-No more shame.' (Glennon, 1979, p. 83)

4   The life of Mahatma Gandhi represents the epitome of courage. Yet, in his autobiography, Gandhi (1958) describes himself as a child in the following way:

> I was a coward. I used to be haunted by the fear of thieves, ghosts, and serpents. I did not dare to stir out of doors at night. Darkness was a terror to me. It was almost impossible for me to sleep in the dark. (quoted by Gergen, 1982, p. 150)

Numerous other examples of emotional change during adulthood could be offered from ethnographic sources, autobiographical accounts and clinical case histories. Such examples tend to be too complex and lacking in detail to be demonstrative of any particular theoretical position. Nevertheless, they illustrate the type of phenomena that must be explained.

In this chapter I will analyse adult emotional development from a social constructivist point of view. This is not the only, or even the most common, view of emotion. My purpose, however, is not to provide a full account of all aspects of emotional development; that would be far too ambitious a goal. I hope merely to highlight some of the problems related to the study of adult emotional development and to adumbrate a few notions – particularly with respect to the rules of emotion – in order to facilitate further enquiry.

THEORETICAL ORIENTATIONS

Before we can speak meaningfully of emotional development, whether in adults or in children, we must have some conception of what we mean by emotion and by development.

A social constructivist view of emotion

I will only sketch in barest outline what I mean by a social constructivist view of emotion, ignoring the qualifications and other accoutrements typical of scholarly expositions. For details, the reader is referred elsewhere (Averill, 1974, 1976, 1980a, 1980b, 1982).

In cognitive terms, emotions may be conceived of as belief systems or schemas that guide the appraisal of situations, the organization of responses and the self-monitoring (interpretation) of behaviour. When conceived of in this way, the question arises, What is the source of emotional schemas? The more traditional answer to this question is that emotional schemas became hardwired into the nervous system during the course of evolution – that they represent innate affect programmes (Izard, 1977; Tomkins, 1981). By contrast, a constructivist view assumes that emotional schemas are the internal representation of social norms or rules.[1]

In more behavioural terms, emotions may be defined as socially constituted syndromes. By a syndrome I mean a set of interrelated response elements (physiological changes, expressive reactions, instrumental rsponses, subjective experiences). Some of these component responses may be biologically based (e.g., certain expressive reactions). However, the way the components are organized into coherent syndromes is determined primarily by social and not biological evolution. Another way of stating this same idea is to say that emotions are transitory social roles – that is, institutionalized ways of interpreting and responding to particular classes of situations.

The social rules that help constitute emotional syndromes tend to be open-ended, allowing a great deal of improvization. Among other things, this means that emotional syndromes are polythetic. A polythetic syndrome is one in which no single component or subset of components is essential to the whole. The rules of anger, for example, can be instantiated in an indefinite variety of ways depending upon the individual and the circumstances. No single kind of response represents a necessary or sufficient condition for anger or for any other emotion. The importance of the polythetic nature of emotional syndromes for the issues of development will become apparent below.

Perspectives on development

Any theory of ontogenetic development presupposes a theory of phylogenetic development, and any theory of adult development presupposes a theory of childhood development.

Phylogenetic development. A social constructivist view of emotion does not envision a completely plastic organism, the proverbial blank slate on which experience can write unhindered. *Homo sapiens* is a biological species, and millions of years of hominid evolution make some patterns of response easy to acquire and others difficult or almost impossible. But this being granted, it must also be recognized that the biological constraints on human behaviour are rather loose. Behavioural systems that have survived the course of human evolution (e.g., systems related to attachment, aggression, reproduction, etc.) are loosely organized, genetically speaking, and can be transformed and combined in an almost indefinite variety of ways.

Indeterminacy of behaviour is itself a biological adaptation, perhaps the most important of our species. But indeterminacy cannot last. The world in which humans evolved was – and in many respects still is – a dangerous place. Protection is provided by the group with its customs and practices, which themselves have evolved (socially, not biologically) through a slow process of trial and error (Campbell, 1975; Harré, 1979). The young child must be capable of acquiring these practices rapidly, or the child – and the group – will not survive long.

It follows from the above considerations that humans are by nature rule-generating and rule-following animals. Language acquisition offers a particularly salient example of this characteristic. When learning a language a person does not simply acquire specific responses – phonemes, words and whatever. Rather, the person learns the rules that make possible the production of an indefinite variety of meaningful utterances. Language is, of course, a specialized form of behaviour; but the capacity for language did not evolve in isolation. The ability to generate and to follow rules underlies a wide range of human activity – including the emotions, as I will argue below.

One other feature of human evolution deserves brief mention – namely, neoteny. This refers to the retention in adulthood of traits that are characteristic of earlier (infantile, juvenile) stages of development. Neoteny, like the indeterminacy described above, is more pronounced in humans than in any other species (Gould, 1977; Montagu, 1981). Of particular relevance to our present concerns is the fact that humans retain into adulthood some of the openness and potential for change characteristic of childhood.

Infant and childhood development. In analogy with *phylogenesis*, which refers to the origins of characteristics during earlier stages of biological evolution, we may speak of *paedogenesis* when referring to the origins of behaviour during infancy and childhood.[2] Ample evidence attests to the fact that intense stimulation of severe deprivation during the first few years of life can have profound – albeit highly variable – effects on later emotionality. Indeed, because the young child does not have the cognitive or behavioural skills to cope effectively with potentially threatening events, even seemingly innocuous occurrences (from an adult point of view) may have a major developmental impact. But beyond these widely accepted facts there is little agreement about the precise role and relative importance of paedogenesis for adult emotional behaviour. Let us examine the issue a little more closely.

Recently a minor paradigm shift has occurred in the study of infant emotional development. The nature and significance of this shift are difficult to convey in a few words. It involves, on the one hand, a change in the conception of the infant from a reactive to an active organism, and, on the other hand, a change in the unit of analysis from the infant *per se* to the mother–infant dyad (Trevarthen, 1979). The latter aspect is the more important for our present concerns. Although the infant can be conceived of a quasi-intentional agent that controls the conditions of its own development, the extent of its control is necessarily limited. This is not simply due to the undeveloped state of its behavioural and cognitive capabilities. It is also due to the nature of the developmental task. The infant is entering a world in which the meaning of an act has already been established. Therefore, it is up to the mother (or other caretaker) to interpret and complete the actions initiated by the infant and to put those actions into a meaningful framework.

Kay (1982) likens the above process to an apprenticeship. An apprentice cobbler, for example, may stamp out the soles of shoes, but the overall plan for making a shoe is provided by the master. Likewise, the infant may engage in certain behaviours, but the overall plan of the interaction is provided by the caretaker. The analogy may be extended further. The master cobbler may be expert in making shoes, but the cobbler's trade is only one aspect of a larger system of clothing manufacture and design; and the latter is, in turn, only a part of a still larger sociocultural matrix. The master cobbler need not understand the larger social and economic forces that make his occupation meaningful in order to ply his trade. Similarly, the caretaker need not understand all the factors that enter into the socialization process in order to engage the infant in meaningful interaction.

At first, the metaphor of an apprenticeship might seem stretched when applied to infant emotional development. It is important to remember, however, that the infant is not simply a passive respondent to stimuli, whether internal or external; rather, the infant is an active participant in an ever-widening circle of relationships.

An informative illustration of emotional development – or apprenticeship – among older children has been provided by Bateson (1976). The focus of his analysis is the socialization for trance (an emotion-like experience) among the Balinese. Bateson begins by breaking the socialization process into components. These components, he emphasizes, do not exist in isolation but are always a part of an ongoing process. They are, in a sense, analogous to the segments of an earthworm. 'Segmentation is itself not a quantity; it is a component or premise of the morphology of the worm' (p. 52).

With this rather graphic, if somewhat opaque, reminder, Bateson goes on to analyse the way Balinese children acquire the ability for trance. One of the components of socialization involves the phenomenon of clonus (i.e., the recurrent series of patellar reflexes that occurs endogenously when the leg is held in certain positions). Such automatic reactions, when placed in an appropriate social context, are used to reinforce the more general belief among the Balinese that the body can act in a semi-autonomous or ego-alien fashion. Thus, although clonus is not a component of trance itself, it does enter into the socialization for trance. Other components of socialization include a wide variety of symbols, rituals and 'paradigm experiences' that help make the trance seem a natural and self-explanatory state. As Bateson observes, 'the business of explanation and the business of socialization [for trance] turn out to be the same' (pp. 62–3).

Bateson's analysis of the *components of socialization* needs to be supplemented by an analysis of the *socialization of components*. As explained earlier, emotional syndromes can be broken down into component responses (expressive reactions, physiological changes, instrumental acts, subjective experiences). These components may undergo socialization independent of one another. For example, a person may learn to respond or to make certain kinds of judgements in a non-emotional context, and only later incorporate these components into an emotional syndrome. In this respect, the development of emotion does not differ from the development of many other complex patterns of behaviour in which a great deal of transfer of training may be involved.

In some instances, of course, the socialization of a component may also be a component of socialization (in Bateson's sense). This occurs when a component response is so closely tied to a specific emotional syndrome that socialization of the part must necessarily involve some socialization of the whole. Perhaps the best example of such components are verbal responses. As children learn the proper use of such terms as 'anger', 'fear', 'love' and so on, they are also learning to make the discriminations, both with respect to situations and to their own behaviour, that those terms imply. Stated somewhat differently, the acquisition of emotional concepts requires knowledge of many of the same rules that help constitute emotional syndromes. I will have much more to say about these rules shortly.

Adult development. At one time, it was common to speak of primary versus secondary socialization. Primary socialization presumably occurs during childhood and is more encompassing and enduring than secondary socialization. The problem with this formulation is that it is too global. Before one can speak meaningfully of differences between primary and secondary socialization, the specific behaviours being socialized as well as the conditions under which socialization occurs must be stipulated. In this regard, the only behaviour that has received detailed attention is language.

There is evidence, both physiological and psychological (Lenneberg, 1967) to suggest that there are differences between children and adults in the readiness and ability to learn language. There is also reason to believe, however, that these differences have been exaggerated and that their theoretical significance has been overinterpreted (see, for example, Ervin-Tripp, 1978; Neufeld, 1979). Consider the following facts:

1 The course of development differs depending upon the aspect of language involved. Phonology (sounds and their structure) tends to be acquired relatively early (during the first five to eight years); most older children and adults, especially, find it difficult to acquire a second language free of accent. The acquisition of syntax (the way words are combined to form sentences) is a more extended process, continuing into adolescence and beyond. Finally, the development of semantics (the meaning of words and sentences) continues throughout life.

2 There are large individual differences in the ability to learn a second language. Some adults can acquire even the correct phonology of a new language with relative ease. Does this mean that first and second language learning involves similar processes for some individuals but different processes for others?

3 The conditions under which first and second language learning occurs are usually quite different. The child is immersed in a total environment, completely dependent on communication with adults. The most intensive instruction in a second language cannot match these conditions. Even living in another linguistic group is not comparable, for a person's first language allows a degree of independence in thought and action that is not possible for the child. To an unknown extent, some of the differences in first and second language learning may actually be due to situational factors such as these.

4 As a person grows older, numerous physiological and psychological changes occur that influence the ease with which many kinds of behaviour

are acquired. Some, at least, of the differences in first and second language learning may be a function of more general changes in problem-solving ability, changes that have little to do with the acquisition of language *per se*.[3]

The above observations could be made *mutatis mutandis* with respect to emotional development. On the basis of much sparser evidence than we have in the study of language, it is often assumed that childhood emotional development is very different from adult emotional development. For such an assertion to have much theoretical significance, we would first have to distinguish which aspect of emotion is under consideration. For example, facial expression may undergo a different course of development from the appraisal of emotional situations. We would also have to take into account individual and situational differences, as well as more general physiological and psychological changes that might influence problem-solving in general.

To summarize briefly, I do not deny the importance of either phylogenesis or paedogenesis for an understanding of adult emotional behaviour. I do, however, question the almost exclusive emphasis that has often been placed on these developmental stages. Emotional syndromes are not innate, nor are they predetermined by events occurring during childhood. Quite the contrary: The most reasonable assumption to make – on both biological and psychological grounds, as well as for the sake of parsimony – is that emotional development continues throughout the life span and that the underlying processes are basically similar (although not necessarily identical) in all age groups.

And what, precisely, is acquired during emotional development? As described earlier, emotional syndromes can be broken down into more elementary components (expressive reactions, physiological changes, etc.) Some of these are biologically based; others are acquired in much the same way as any skill (such as dancing or riding a bicycle) might be learned. From a social constructivist point of view, however, the most important feature of emotional development involves the acquisition of the social norms and rules that provide the component responses with their meaning and co-ordination.

RULES OF EMOTION

This brings us to the core of the present analysis, namely, the rules of emotion. No attempt will be made to enumerate specific rules for any given emotion (such as anger or fear). Rather, I will delimit broad classes of rules that apply to emotions in general. The rules of emotion can be distinguished both according to type and according to scope (i.e., the

Table 1 Cross-classification of the rules of emotion

Type of rule	Scope of rule			
	Appraisal	Behaviour	Prognosis	Attribution
Constitutive				
Regulative				
Heuristic				

aspect of emotion to which they are primarily applicable). In neither case are the distinctions absolute; psychological reality seldom fits comfortably into the neat pigeonholes that we devise for analytical purposes. With this caveat in mind, table 1 presents a cross-classification of the rules of emotion according to type and scope.

In order to illustrate the three types of rules – constitutive, regulative and heuristic – represented in table 1, let us begin with a non-emotional example. Consider a game, such as chess. Some rules (e.g., pertaining to the layout of the chessboard, the nature of the pieces and the moves that are permissible) help constitute a game as a game of chess (as opposed, say, to backgammon). If there were no king, if pawns could move backward, and if rooks could be checkmated, then the game would no longer be chess. (Although, in the case of children, one might say they were playing *at* chess.) Other rules are primarily regulative. For example, in a chess tournament, it might be stipulated that a certain number of moves be made within a given time limit. Regulative rules do not determine the kind of game that is being played, but they do influence the way the game is played. The third type of rule presented in table 1, heuristic rules, determine the strategy of play. It is not possible to specify exhaustively or succinctly the heuristic rules for a game like chess. Such rules are the stuff of books and magazine articles (e.g., instructing players how to recognize situations in which one move might be more appropriate than another). Good chess players can be distinguished from poor ones by their (often intuitive) grasp of the heuristic rules of the game.

Constitutive, regulative and heuristic rules also apply to the emotions. For example, a person cannot be proud of the stars. This is not because of some biological incapacity; rather, to be proud of something, the existence of which is not connected with the self even remotely or by association, violates one of the constitutive rules of this emotion. No matter how glowingly one feels on a starry night, the responses cannot count as pride. There are also rules that regulate how pride should be experienced and expressed. To violate a regulative rule does not invalidate the emotion as an instance of pride, but it may make the pride 'sinful'. The biblical story of Satan illustrates this point. But while pride may lead to great falls, it is also the necessary foundation for great accomplishments. The trick, if one wants to call it that, is to be proud without being boastful, arrogant, pompous or conceited; but also without donning a false mask of humility. There are heuristics for pride; and from every indication, they are as difficult to master as the heuristics for chess.[4]

I will have much more to say about constitutive, regulative and heuristic rules shortly. But first, let me explicate briefly the other set of distinctions depicted in table 1. Rules of emotion may be distinguished depending upon whether they pertain to the evaluation of emotional objects (rules of appraisal), the organization of responses (rules of behaviour), the time course and consequences of the emotion (rules of prognosis) and the connection between the instigation, the responses and one's self (rules of attribution). Elsewhere (Averill, 1982) I have illustrated these four classes of rules as they apply to anger. Here, I can only indicate their general nature.

Rules of appraisal pertain to the way a situation is perceived and evaluated. Each emotion is characterized by its own set of appraisals. The appraisals determine what is sometimes called the intentional object of the emotion. For many emotions, the intentional object consists of three aspects: the instigation, the target and the manifest aim or objective of the response. Thus, the object of anger is revenge for wrongdoing; the object of fear is escape from danger; the object of love is union with the loved one; and so forth. The intentional object, it must be emphasized, is part of an emotional syndrome, not a cause of any particular episode. It is a meaning imposed on events, for whatever reason.

Rules of behaviour refer to the way an emotion is organized and expressed. As far as overt behaviour is concerned, this class of rules is rather obvious. Perhaps the only thing that needs to be added is that 'behaviour' includes physiological responses and subjective experience. This is perhaps easiest to illustrate by example. During the Victorian period, it was expected of young ladies that they faint when confronted with certain situations – provided they could do so safely and with decorum. In other words, there were (implicit) rules for fainting, even though ths is presumably an involuntary, largely physiological, response.

Rules of prognosis concern the time course and progression of an emotional episode. Some emotions may last only a few moments (e.g., being startled), while others may last for months or even years and progress through various stages (e.g., grief). If the appropriate time course for an emotion is violated, then the authenticity of the emotion may be questioned or hidden motives sought. Rules of prognosis may sometimes even extend beyond the limits of a single emotional episode. Thus, a person who asks, 'Am I really in love?' may be wondering not so much about butterflies in the stomach as about the long-term commitments he or she is willing to make.

Rules of attribution pertain to the way an emotion is explained or legitimized. These rules tie together the appraised object, the behaviour and the prognosis into a meaningful whole, and relate the entirety to the self. Stated somewhat differently, it is not sufficient to appraise a situation in a certain way or to make relevant responses; the entire syndrome must be interpreted and given meaning. When a response is interpreted as emotional, it cannot be judged by the same rules that govern rational, deliberate behaviour. But although emotions may be 'blind' (i.e., they do not follow standard rules of logic), they do have a logic of their own. (It is always possible to ask of an emotional response, 'Is it reasonable?') Also, a person cannot be held fully responsible for emotional responses because emotions are supposedly beyond personal control. We are 'gripped', 'seized' and 'torn' by emotion. Colloquialisms such as these do not describe intrinsic features of emotional responses. Rather, they are rule-governed interpretations of behaviour, reflections of our naive and implicit theories of emotion.

Referring back to table 1, 12 cells are created by crossing the threefold distinction among constitutive, regulative and heuristic rules with the fourfold distinction among rules of appraisal, behaviour, prognosis and attribution. Space does not allow a discussion of each of these cells. The reader will have to 'fill in the blanks', so to speak. One proviso should be mentioned, however. Depending upon the emotion, some of the cells in the table may be empty. For example, while rules of prognosis are prominent in emotions such as grief, they are much less important for emotions such as joy; similarly, some emotions (e.g., envy) are more subject to regulation than others; some require greater use of heuristics (e.g., love); and so forth.

Now let us explore some of the implications of the various kinds of rules represented in table 1 for an understanding of adult emotional development. Much adult emotional development involves the acquisition and refinement of heuristic rules. That is, the person learns to make finer distinctions when appraising situations; responses become more skilled; expectancies are more realistic and clearly established; and attributions to the self and others become more sophisticated. In short, the person becomes more adept emotionally without necessarily adding new emotions to his or her repertoire.

In spite of their importance, relatively little research has been devoted to a systematic analysis of emotional heuristics. Perhaps the most notable exception to this generalization is work done by cognitive-behavioural therapists on 'skills training' (e.g., Goldfried, 1980; Meichenbaum, 1977). As the name implies, skills training refers to the development of appropriate strategies for appraising situations and responding effectively.

The relative neglect of emotional heuristics stands in sharp contrast to the study of cognitive heuristics (e.g., by theorists interested in artificial intelligence). The reasons for this differential interest deserve brief comment. It is relatively easy to program a computer for the constitutive rules of a game (chess, say). Regulative rules can also be added if they are of any interest. The main problem in artificial intelligence is to program the computer to actually play the game in a manner that would compete with, or simulate the moves of, an accomplished human player. For this, the heuristic rules must be specified.

There have been few attempts to simulate human emotions (see Colby, 1981), and that is perhaps one reason why little attention has been devoted to an analysis of emotional heuristics. There is a second and more important reason, however. In comparison with heuristic rules, the constitutive and regulative rules of a game like chess are of relatively little psychological interest. In the case of emotions, the situation is quite different. Here, the 'rules of the game' (constitutive and regulative) are of primary interest. Until they are better understood, research on heuristic rules cannot proceed in a very systematic fashion.

Recently, a considerable amount of attention has been devoted to the rules that help regulate emotions and especially to the regulative rules of behaviour. (For example, the display rules for facial expressions discussed by Ekman and Friesen, 1975, fall in this category.) *Less attention has been devoted to the regulative rules of appraisal, prognosis and attribution; and still less to constitutive rules of all kinds.* In fact, not all theorists would even agree that 'authentic' emotions are constituted (and not simply regulated) by rules. Yet from a developmental point of view, constitutive rules are of prime importance, for only their acquisition makes possible truly new and different kinds of emotional experiences.

Emotional development – whether in childhood or adulthood – involves the internalization of the appropriate rules of emotion. When such internalization is inadequate or incomplete, characteristic disabilities may ensue. In the case of constitutive rules, inadequate socialization results in emotional syndromes that might best be described as *neurotic*. That is, the individual responds in a manner so unusual or bizarre that one does not know quite how to classify it. Examples would be the person who becomes 'fearful' of harmless objects (thus violating a constitutive rule of appraisal); whose 'love' is manifested in sadistic cruelty (violating a constitutive rule of behaviour); whose 'grief' is over in a day or prolonged for many years (violating a constitutive rule of prognosis); or whose 'anger' is the product of paranoid delusions (violating a constitutive rule of attribution).

The person who cannot conform to regulative rules may be considered *delinquent* rather than neurotic. An example would be the members of street gangs described by Toch (1969). These men often displayed anger that was well constituted (according to general cultural prescriptions) but inappropriately expressed. Lest there be misunderstanding, 'delinquent' does not necessarily refer actions that break the law. Rules of etiquette, civility and good taste are also regulative. Thus, persons who weep too copiously, who become envious at the well-deserved success of a friend, who remain angry too long, or who respond with too much cunning and forethought are all emotionally delinquent in the sense that I am using the term.

Finally, the person who has failed to acquire an adequate set of heuristic rules is neither neurotic nor delinquent in the senses described above, but simply *inept*. Illustrations of this state of affairs have been given in the preceding discussion.

Rather than further discussing the rules of emotion in the abstract, it might be more fruitful at this point to examine how a social constructivist approach can help clarify some perennial issues related to emotional development. Although these issues are multifaceted, in one way or another each involves a failure to take into account the rules of emotion and especially the distinction between constitutive and regulative rules.

FOUR VARIATIONS ON A COMMON THEME

A common theme in psychological theory involves the notion that some core aspect of emotion exists (e.g., some pattern of neurological activity, or a peculiar feeling), and that this core aspect remains invariant through time despite many variations in eliciting conditions and transformations in modes of expression. The four variations on this theme that I will consider are the following: (1) the identity of childhood and adult emotions; (2) the significance of events in childhood for adult emotional experience; (3) civilizing the emotions; and (4) getting in touch with one's own true feelings.

The identity of childhood and adult emotions

To what extent are adult emotional experiences similar to those of young children? For example, is the anger of an adult primarily an extension and elaboration of the anger of a child, or is the adult emotion fundamentally different? Most contemporary theories of emotion assume an essential continuity between the emotional life of children and adults. By contrast, a social constructivist view assumes that emotional syndromes can be acquired at any age; and that even when there is continuity (as between the anger of the child and that of the adult), the transformation may be so great that one can speak of the 'same' emotion in only a limited sense.

The problem of identity through time has always been puzzling. The Greeks posed the problem in an allegory about the ship of Theseus. This ship had its boards replaced gradually, one at a time, until not a single plank of the original ship remained. Was the ship still the same ship of Theseus? This is not an especially problematic case. But consider the following extension of the story. Suppose that, as each board was removed, it was carefully saved. After all the planks had been replaced, a new ship was constructed from the original boards. Are there now two ships of Theseus? If there were a dispute about the ships, which one has claim to being the 'real' ship of Theseus – that which showed the greatest continuity in time (with gradual replacement of planks), or that closest to the original in material content (being rebuilt from the original planks)? It is easy to imagine even further variations on this story. Suppose that, as the old planks were removed, they were destroyed so that a second ship like the original one could not be rebuilt from them. But also suppose that as the planks were being replaced, the ship was also being redesigned – its hull enlarged, the interior quarters rearranged, an extra deck added, and so forth. Eventually, the ship not only has completely new parts, but also a new configuration. Is it still the same ship of Theseus? And if not, at what point did the original ship cease to be and a new ship come into being?

Emotional development presents a puzzle not unlike the ship of Theseus. If we compare anger in the adult with the temper tantrum of an infant, there seems to be little in common. Yet, there is continuity, and it is not possible to say at any given point in time that now the infantile emotion has ended and the adult emotion has come into being. Because of this, we are tempted to conclude that there must be something, like a thread through time that lends unity to the entire sequence. What might that something be? The 'true' or 'authentic' emotion, perhaps?

According to our earlier definition of emotions as socially constituted syndromes of which no particular component is essential to the whole, there is no need to postulate an emotional *Ding an Sich* that somehow remains invariant through time. One can reasonably admit that an emotional syndrome (anger, say) is the 'same' in adulthood and childhood and yet deny that the adult and childhood emotions share any important features in common. Moreover, as any 'new' emotion must necessarily develop out of elements already present, there is a sense in which it is impossible to acquire as an adult an emotion that is completely different from anything that preceded it. But this says more about the way we use such concepts as 'new', 'different' and 'same' than it does about any invariance in underlying states.

The significance of events in childhood for adult emotional experiences

Earlier, I introduced the term *paedogenesis* to refer to the origins of behaviour in childhood. With respect to emotional behaviour, paedogenesis has been elevated almost to the level of dogma. That is, nearly all discussions of emotional development start – and stop – with childhood. To focus on emotional development in adulthood is rare. There is a sense, of course, in which all adult behaviour has its roots in childhood experiences. The child is the father of the man. But discussions of emotional development often go beyond this truism and imply that adult emotions, if not innate, are constituted during infancy and early childhood. Psychoanalytic theory, for example, assumes that adult emotional reactions are basically determined by events occurring within the first six years of life. Other theories may not be as explicit on this issue, but the tenor of analysis is generally similar.

Without questioning the importance of paedogenesis as a general principle, one can well ask why such theoretical emphasis has been placed on childhood experiences as determinants of adult emotions. The dogma – as opposed to the principle – of paedogenesis is based, in part, on the notion discussed above – namely, that adult emotions are only elaborate and transformed versions of their childhood counterparts. But it is also based on a particular view of causality.

Individuals have a bias towards seeking causes that resemble their effects in terms of salient features. Major effects should have major causes, and emotionally relevant effects should have emotionally relevant causes (Nisbett and Ross, 1980). To take a specific (but non-emotional) example, Taylor (1982) found that cancer victims often search their past for some significant event to which they can attribute their disease. It is difficult to accept the fact that a disease so serious as cancer can be the result of numerous small and – of themselves – innocuous insults to the body. Similarly, there is a tendency (not limited to laymen) to search for the causes of adult emotions – particularly if those emotions are unusual or dramatic – in specific and perhaps traumatic events that occurred during infancy or early childhood. The presumed events need not be actual, but may depend on the imaginings of the child; nevertheless, repressed or seemingly forgotten, they continue to exert their influence on adult behaviour.

From a social constructivist view, emotional development – whether in childhood or as an adult – typically follows a more subtle and non-specific course. Like the development of most other complex forms of behaviour, emotional development tends to be slow, piecemeal and cumulative; indeed, for the most part, emotional development is not even particularly emotional. Consider the case of anger. In the adult, anger is typically based on complex judgements regarding intentionality and justification (i.e., with respect to the behaviour of the instigator). The rules that guide such judgements are not peculiar to anger and they are not learned in all-or-none fashion as a consequence of some specific event. The same is true with respect to the expression of anger. The words spoken and responses made during anger are not necessarily different than the words and responses made in many other contexts. What makes them a manifestation of anger is the way they are organized and interpreted (experienced). In short, the development of anger – or of any other emotion – involves the acquisition of many components and the rules (of appraisal, behaviour, prognosis and attribution) that govern their organization and interpretation.

Civilizing the emotions

The sociologist Elias (1939/1978) has argued that much of the progress of Western civilization involved a taming of the affects. He cites many examples from medieval sources to illustrate attitudes and behaviours (e.g., regarding aggression, sexuality and alimentary functions) that today would be considered extremely crude and even inhuman. Elias also argued that children undergo similar progression, from the uninhibited expression of raw affect to the more refined and civilized emotional life of the adult.

Although most psychologists would probably agree that Elias has overstated his thesis, the view that socialization is primarily regulative is quite common. Consider the following observation by Tomkins (1979):

> Because the free expression of innate affect is extremely contagious, and because these are very high-powered phenomena, all societies, in varying degrees, exercise substantial control over the unfettered expression of affect, and particularly over the free expression of the cry of affect. (Tomkins, 1979, p. 208)

Consider again the distinction between constitutive and regulative rules. The view adumbrated by Elias, Tomkins and many others as well assumes that the rules of emotion are almost exclusively regulative, at least as far as fundamental emotions are concerned. However, if we admit that some of the rules of emotion are also constitutive, then the role of society becomes constructive as well as regulative. (Needless to say, in this context I am not using 'constructive' in its evaluative sense.) Indeed, much of the data reported by Elias could just as well be interpreted in this way. For example, the ferocity and bloodthirstiness extolled by the medieval knight are just as much social constructions as are the more benign emotions advocated by the most dedicated pacifist of today.

At this point the question might be raised, if emotions are social constructions, why does every society exercise substantial control over their unfettered expression? The paradox implied by this question is more apparent than real. Many, if not most, social products are subject to regulation – weapons, drugs, automobiles, financial and professional institutions and so forth. Once a person starts, it becomes difficult to think of a social product or institutionalized form of behaviour that is *not* regulated in one fashion or another. The emotions are certainly no exception to this rule.

Getting in touch with one's true feelings

In popular psychology, we often read or hear about people who are 'out of touch' with their feelings. To remedy the situation, groups devoted to 'consciousness raising' abound. If people need to get in contact with their feelings, at some point they must have lost contact (or perhaps never have made contact to begin with). But at what point? When do people normally establish contact with their feelings? At six months of age? At ten years? Or is this a matter of adult emotional development? The question is certainly an odd one, but let us speculate nevertheless.

People often 'discover' that they have lost contact with their feelings as they move from one sociocultural context to another. The move may involve physical relocation (e.g., immigration); it may be economic (e.g., getting promoted or losing a job); or it may be ideological (e.g., a religious or political conversion). Consider also the situation of women as they move from the home into the workplace; of men as they assume greater domestic responsibilities; of teenagers moving from high school and a family environment to a large and diverse university; of a gang member placed in a correctional agency; of the housewife after the last child has left home; of a person who retires after 40 years on the job. All such transitions involve some emotional readjustment; sometimes they also require fundamental changes in values and beliefs. It is precisely when old values must be abandoned and new standards acquired that a person may face the need to get in contact with his or her 'true' feelings.

The process of getting in touch with one's feelings is perhaps best exemplified during a religious or political conversion. How does the convert know when he or she has 'arrived'? In part, by experiencing the emotions considered authentic by the new reference group. But there is a catch here. If the emotions are recognized as social constructions, they would lose some of their air of authenticity. Why should one emotion be considered more authentic than another if both are socially constituted? The way out of this dilemma is to postulate that the new emotions reflect one's true feelings. They were there all along but had been submerged, repressed or otherwise denied awareness.

Of course, most social transitions do not involve such fundamental changes in values and beliefs (constitutive rules) that radically different emotions are evoked. For the most part, customary emotions may be adapted to fit new circumstances (e.g., instead of becoming depressed, the person may now become angry; or where anger was before, benign indifference may now prevail). Still, the underlying principles are similar.

Getting in contact with one's feelings is not so much a process of discovery as it is an act of creation.

CONCLUDING OBSERVATIONS

The acquisition of new emotions during adulthood, and the relinquishment of previously established emotions, is commonplace. Yet, such phenomena have been the subject of relatively little systematic investigation. The reasons for this neglect are more conceptual than empirical. Most theories view emotions as biologically primitive (innate) responses, or at least as behaviours that become well established in early childhood. From these perspectives, adult development is largely an issue of regulation (e.g., the inhibition or release of previously established tendencies). A neglect of adult emotional development is also fostered by the fact that most changes in affect (beyond childhood) are slow and continuous. Few of us experience salutory leaps in our emotional lives. Even falling in love – perhaps the best example of the acquisition of a new emotion experienced by most adults – has ample precedent in earlier development stages. When continuity in development exists, the problem of identity becomes problematic, and debates about what is truly 'new' or 'different' may obfuscate rather than clarify underlying processes. To complicate matters even further, most emotional syndromes are quite complex. Some aspects (e.g., cognitive components) are more subject to change than are other aspects (e.g., certain expressive reactions). This makes it easy to defend almost any thesis with respect to continuity and change, depending on the aspect of emotion taken as fundamental.

The present chapter has focused on the cognitive aspects of emotions; or, more accurately, on the social norms and rules that, when internalized, help to form the cognitive schemas on which the experience and expression of emotion depend. Much has been left unsaid, or has been said only cursorily – for example, about the process of socialization itself, and about the biological *anlage* or systems of behaviour without which the social construction of emotion could not proceed. Other chapters in this volume will help to rectify these deficiencies. If I have been able to illustrate some of the conceptual problems involved in the analysis of adult emotional development, then the primary goals of this chapter have been realized. If, in addition, I have encouraged the reader to explore further the advantages (and limitations) of a social constructivist view of emotion, then my goals have been more than achieved.

NOTES

1 To a certain extent, the contrast I am drawing here between biologically and socially oriented theories is a matter of definition. What I am calling emotions, for example, Izard (1977) refers to as affective-cognitive structures. Izard limits the concept of emotion to a much narrower range of phenomena than do I: namely, to the innate neurochemical processes, expressive reactions, feelings and action tendencies associated with a few fundamental states. But lest the differences in orientation be dismissed as merely a matter of definition, two points should be noted. First, the way basic concepts are defined is of central importance to any scientific theory; it helps determine the kinds of phenomena that need to be explained, and hence the locus of research. Second, a social-constructivist view rejects the notion that there are a few fundamental emotions, however defined, that can be identified with innate biological processes.

2 The term 'paedogenesis' (from the Greek *paedo*, child and *genesis*, origin) was introduced in 1866 by the German embryologist, Karl von Baer, to designate the condition in which larval and even embryonic forms (e.g., of insect, newts, salamanders) attain reproductive capacity while the remainder of the body is still in an immature state (Montagu, 1981). The term is still sometimes used that way today. The meaning given to 'paedogenesis' in this chapter – the origin of adult behaviour in childhood experiences – is more in keeping with the original Greek roots.

3 In this discussion of the development of linguistic competencies, I am ignoring an important distinction, namely, between first versus second language learning on the one hand, and the acquisition of language during childhood on the other. Many children learn a second language at an early age; conversely, under conditions of extreme deprivation, it is conceivable that the acquisition of a first language might be delayed until adulthood. For our present purposes, however, consideration of this distinction is not critical.

4 As is usual when concepts derived from one domain are applied to another, the extension of the concept of rules to the domain of emotion is to a certain extent metaphorical. The metaphor is perhaps most limited in the case of heuristic rules. I may be able to simulate a skilled performance by specifying a set of heuristic rules, but this does not mean that a person is following those rules when responding. It is important to recognize the limitation of the rule metaphor, not only in the case of emotion but also as applied to language and other psychological phenomena (see Shotter, 1976, for a detailed critique). However, the issue is not whether emotions are governed by rules in *every* sense of the word; the issue is, rather, whether there are *any* senses in which it is profitable to apply the notion of rules to an analysis of emotional phenomena.

REFERENCES

Averill, J. R. (1974) An analysis of psychophysiological symbolism and its influence on theories of emotion. *Journal for the Theory of Social Behaviour*, 4, 147–90.

—— (1976) Emotion and anxiety: sociocultural, biological, and psychological determinants. In M. Zuckerman and C. D. Spielberger (eds), *Emotion and Anxiety: New Concepts, Methods, and Applications*. New York: John Wiley.

—— (1980a) A constructivist view of emotion. In R. Plutchik and H. Kellerman (eds), *Theories of Emotion*. New York: Academic Press.

—— (1980b) On the paucity of positive emotions. In K. R. Blankstein, R. Pliner and J. Polivy (eds), *Assessment and Modification of Emotional Behaviour*. New York: Plenum Press.

—— (1982) *Anger and Aggression: An Essay on Emotion*. New York: Springer-Verlag.

Bateson, G. (1976) Some components of socialization for trance. In T. Schwartz (ed.), *Socialization as Cultural Communication*. Berkeley: University of California Press.

Campbell, D. T. (1975) On the conflicts between biological and social evolution and between psychology and moral traditions. *American Psychologist*, 30, 1103–26.

Colby, K. M. (1981) Modelling a paranoid mind [article with open peer review]. *Behavioral and Brain Sciences*, 4, 515–60.

Ekman, P. and Friesen, W. V. (1975) *Unmasking the Face*. Englewood Cliffs, NJ: Prentice-Hall.

Elias, N. (1978) *The Civilizing Process: The Development of Manners* (E. Lephcott, Trans.). New York: Urizen Books (original work published 1939).

Ervin-Tripp, S. (1978) Is second language learning like the first? In E. M. Hatch (ed.), *Second Language Acquisition*. Rowley, MA: Newburg House.

Gandhi, M. (1958) *All Men are Brothers*. New York: Columbia University Press.

Gergen, K. J. (1982) *Toward Transformation in Social Knowledge*. New York: Springer-Verlag.

Glennon, L. M. (1979) *Women and Dualism*. New York: Longman.

Goldfried, M. R. (1980) Psychotherapy as coping skills training. In M. J. Mahoney (ed.), *Psychotherapy Process*. New York: Plenum Press.

Gould, S. J. (1977) *Ontogeny and Phylogeny*. Cambridge: Harvard University Press.

Izard, C. E. (1977) *Human Emotions*. New York: Plenum Press.

Kay, K. (1982) Organism, apprentice, and person. In E. Z. Tronick (ed.), *Social Interchange in Infancy: Affect, Cognition, and Communication*. Baltimore: University Park Press.

Lenneberg, E. H. (1967) *Biological Foundations of Langugae*. New York: John Wiley.

Lucas, R. A. (1969) *Men in Crisis: A Study of a Mine Disaster*. New York: Basic Books.

Meichenbaum, D. (1977) *Cognitive-behavior Modification: An Integrative Approach*. New York: Plenum Press.

Montagu, A. (1981) *Growing Young*. New York: McGraw-Hill.

Murphy, H. B. M. (1973) History and the evolution of syndromes: the striking case of Latah and Amok. *Psychopathology: Contributions from the Social, Behavioral, and Biological Sciences*. New York: John Wiley.

Neufeld, G. (1979) Towards a theory of language learning ability. *Language Learning*, 29, 227–41.

Nisbett, R. E. and Ross, L. (1980) *Human Inference: Strategies and Short-comings of Social Judgment.* Englewood Cliffs, NJ: Prentice-Hall.

Shotter, J. (1976) Acquired powers: the transformation of natural into personal powers. In R. Harré (ed.), *Personality.* Totowa, NJ: Rowman and Littlefield.

Taylor, S. E. (1982) Social cognition and health. *Personality and Social Psychology Bulletin*, 8, 549–62.

Toch, H. (1969) *Violent Men.* Chicago: Aldine.

Tomkins, S. S. (1979) Script theory: differential magnification of affects. In H. E. Howe and R. A. Dienstbier (eds), *Nebraska Symposium on Motivation 1978* (vol. 26). Lincoln: University of Nebraska Press.

—— (1981) The quest for primary motives: biography and autobiography of an idea. *Journal of Personality and Social Psychology*, 41, 306–29.

Trevarthen, C. (1979) Communication and cooperation in early infants: a description of primary intersubjectivity. In M. Bullows (ed.), *Before Speech: The Beginning of Interpersonal Communication.* Cambridge University Press.

Wulfften Palthe, P. M. van (1936) Psychiatry and neurology in the tropics. In C. D. deLanjen and A. Lichtenstein (eds), *A Critical Textbook of Tropical Medicine.* Amsterdam: G. Kolff.

PART II

Case Studies in Contemporary Emotions

7

Affect and Social Context: Emotion Definition as a Social Task

J. Coulter

Sociology has had little to say about the nature of 'affective' or emotional conduct, perhaps primarily because, following Max Weber's lead, it has generally been hived off theoretically from the bulk of 'rational' action in human affairs, downgraded to a sort of appendage to social relations and consigned to a permanently residual status. Mistakenly thought of as beyond the scope of social convention and constraint, affective states have been allowed to fall exclusively within the province of psychology. In its turn, psychology has generated a variety of ways of handling the phenomena of affect, but few of them have remained consistent with, or controlled by, the conceptual structure of emotion-concepts, and this has entailed a serious neglect of the sociocultural dimensions integral to the very constitution of the phenomena under study. It will be argued here that such dimensions are *primary* in the consideration of affective states and conduct. Affect and rationality are much more closely interrelated than has been noted in the behavioural sciences, and both are throughout subject to sociocultural and sociolinguistic analysis. Affective states have too frequently been identified with feeling-states, or with other 'contents of consciousness'; they have also been theoretically 'reduced' to biological impulses or other visceral, vasomotor and biochemical transformations, or to the perception of such changes on the part of the organism. In the ensuing discussion, these issues are taken up in order to show how the relationships that obtain between particular sorts of emotions and social contexts (prior to or concurrent with their display) are analysable. The socio-logic of affect and affective states is a hitherto underdeveloped area outside of philosophy, and so we must begin with the clues bequeathed to us by the philosophy of mind.

EMOTIONS AS INTERNAL EPISODES

In one form or another, the basic categories of emotion – e.g., anger, fear, grief, shame, happiness, gult, disgust, regret, envy, pride, wonder, remorse, sadness, jealousy, embarrassment – will admit of combination with the concept of feeling; thus, we get 'feels angry', 'feels grief-stricken','feels ashamed', 'feels proud' and so on. Since we can also combine the notion of 'feels' with a wide range of sensation-concepts, as in 'I feel tired', 'she feels toothache', 'he feels hungry', 'she felt thirsty', 'I feel pain', the stage is set for the misassimilation of emotions to sensations (i.e., in the formal mode, the treatment of the categories of affect as if they functioned identically in our talk to the categories of sensation). This has been a pervasive mistake in the history of philosophical and psychological reflection on the subject. Hume (1739), for instance, remarked: 'when I am angry, I am actually possessed with the passion, and in that emotion have no more reference to any other object, than when I am thirsty, or sick, or more than five feet high.'

Clearly, this misses the point that we cannot even begin to *identify* the emotion we are dealing with unless we take into account how a person is appraising an object or situation. Although on some occasions it makes sense for us to say of someone that he knows his own emotion better than anyone else, we should not be able to sustain this as an invariant principle in our practical, judgemental affairs with other people; the reason why we may on some occasion reckon that a person knows his own emotion(s) better than we do is not because he has private access to internal feeling-states that define for him what his emotion is, but because, as Bedford has remarked in chapter 2 above, 'it is hardly possible for a man to be completely ignorant, as others may be, of the context of his own behaviour'. This does not mean that a person is to be thought of as analysing his own conduct and then *concluding* that he feels angry, jealous, etc., although this can happen when, e.g., someone is debating about whether or not he really feels jealous of another person. Rather, it is to be understood in terms of his routinely knowing (while others may not) some circumstances entitling him to be angry, jealous, sad or any of the affective states. If someone informs us that he *feels* angry, this may be treated as corroborative rather than indispensable testimony, but *the warranted ascription of anger does not depend necessarily upon a corresponding avowal, nor upon the presence of a particular feeling-state accompanying the anger displayed.* Wittgenstein (1967) observed that emotions are not genuinely localizable in the ways in which sensations can be, although the expression-behaviour of emotions (such as a tightening of the face, a rapid pulse, etc.) implies some characteristic sensations. 'But these sensations are not the emotions' (p. 488). He goes on to note that he would 'almost like to say: One no more feels sorrow in one's body than one feels seeing in one's eyes'. It is a further variant of the fallacious doctrine of perceptual introspectionism, which leads us to think that emotions are internal events. Various sensations may be bound up with syndromes of, e.g., fear, anxiety, grief and so on, but they cannot be thought of as *constituting* these emotions.

Melden has articulated the basic issue succinctly:

> When we ask ourselves whether someone is angry, our question is not whether such and such events are transpiring in the hidden chamber of his mind; nor do we, when we feel angry, turn our attention inward from the things that provoke us, the persons with whom we are angry, and the circumstances in which we show, display and vent our anger. (Melden, 1969, p. 206)

Because people can sometimes feign or suppress their felt anger and other affective states, it is a short step to the argument that there is a 'something' absent in the case of the pretence and present in the case of the stoically undisplayed anger, where the natural candidate for this 'something' is a sensation or feeling-state. However, if we treat self-reports like 'I feel angry' as circumstantially justified or unjustified *expressions of* anger, instead of as descriptions of internal events or states, then the 'something' that may be present or absent is nothing hidden in the chamber of the mind or body, but is some justifying or entitling (set of) circumstance(s). A sensation or feeling-state could arise and be avowed intelligibly in ways that are unoccasioned by the social and historical circumstances of a meaningful environment, whereas, by contrast, the appropriate application of affect-concepts to describe someone's state *depends upon* specific arrays of meaningful circumstances. What distinguishes grief from remorse and disappointment from shame is not a determinate inner feeling but responses, actions, appraisals and situations in the social world. It is not just that we cannot locate any neatly discriminable feeling-states uniformly correlated with (let alone constitutive of) the variety of emotions which leads us to propose that emotions and sensations are different sorts of phenomena; rather, it is that emotions cannot be hived off completely from the 'weave of life';

> 'Grief' describes a pattern which recurs, with different variations, in the weave of our life. If a man's bodily expressions of sorrow and of joy alternated, say with the ticking of a clock, here we should not have the characteristic formation of the pattern of sorrow or of the pattern of joy.
> 'For a second he felt violent pain.' – Why does it sound queer to say: 'For a second he felt deep grief'? Only because it so seldom happens? (Wittgenstein, 1968, p. 174)

Not only do emotions characteristically have meaningful objects or situations as their occasions, but such objects or situations *make emotions intelligibly present.* This is not a psychological point, but a logical one. It is not that it is impossible to experience some feeling previously associated with being ashamed in the absence of the recognition that one is open to criticism of some kind; the only argument being made here is that the *rational* avowal or ascription of shame is conceptually tied to the recognition on the part of the person of some responsibility for the object or situation of the shame, and a susceptibility to personal criticism for it. In Bedford's terms, changing the example,

> the decision whether to say that the driver of a car which has broken down for lack of water is indignant, or merely annoyed or angry, depends on whether the radiator is empty through (let us say) the carelessness of a garage mechanic who undertook to fill it for him, or through his own carelessness ('annoyed with myself' but not 'indignant with myself'). (chapter 2 above)

If the driver were to state that he was *jealous* of the situation, or *elated* by it, we should not understand his claim, even if he went on to say that this was how he actually felt. We simply do not know our emotional state or the emotional state of another by accepting the recognition of a sensation to stand for the emotional state. A man is not the final court of appeal in his own case; Bedford reminds us that 'those who are jealous are often the last, instead of the first, to recognize that they are'. And any such ratified recognition will hinge upon the appraisal of the specific meaningful circumstances operative in the particular case. Any affect-avowals made outside of the situated bounds of circumstantial justification or entitlement can lead to derogatory inferences as to the avowing agent's psychological condition; indeed, various self-imputed mental disorders rest upon the agent's recognition of a mismatch between his rational judgement of a situation's affect-affording features and his actual disposition to avow a specific emotion (for example, 'I know there's no reason to be afraid of television sets; but I just can't help myself . . .'). More commonly, however, ascriptions of affective disorders are undertaken by third parties (or in the third person), because it is usually found that irrational affective states are occasioned by a delusional version of the world taken to be true. *If* any television set had the property of radiating harmful energies, or of receiving one's thoughts and broadcasting them to the rest of the audience, we too might feel afraid of the object.

An emotion, unlike a sensation, may be described as reasonable or unreasonable, appropriate or inappropriate. A sensation, unlike an emotion, may be *had* as well as felt. We may, however, say something like: 'I had a pang of regret this afternoon' (where we cannot say that we had an anger or an envy), and this appears to be both a case in which we say 'have' an emotion and also one in which the phrase 'of regret' describes the sensation of the 'pang'. However, while it would make no sense to ask a man who reported having had a 'pang' whether it was really reasonable or justified, it does make sense to ask a man who reported having had a 'pang of regret' whether or not it was reasonable or justified. And this shows us that a wholly different language-game is being played with the word 'pang' in the two cases; 'the pang of regret is justified, if it is, not as a feeling but because his regret is justified'. Moreover, notice that we can intelligibly suggest to people that they abandon certain emotions on rational grounds, that we can argue them out of their anger, shame, embarrassment, disappointment, fear, etc., in ways that are not open to us in the case of sensations. In this sense,

> our capacity to experience certain emotions is contingent upon learning to make certain kinds of appraisals and evaluations. And learning how to make these appraisals and evaluations involves more than simply learning to identify some items of observation, whether 'private' or 'public'. That is, it is not like learning to identify headaches, toothaches, tables, or even moving trains. Rather, it is learning to interpret and appraise matters in terms of norms, standards, principles, and ends or goals judged desirable or undesirable, appropriate or inappropriate, reasonable or unreasonable, and so on. (Pritchard, 1976, p. 219)

(It might be remarked here that we probably do not learn to 'identify' headaches and toothaches as private phenomena, either; the argument has already been presented earlier.) Standards of judgement enter into the picture in the case of emotions; to feel some emotion is to feel in some way *about* someone or something, as Pritchard notes. And it is not to feel a certain way about anything physiological, unless one is, e.g., distressed or worried or panic-stricken about a physiological matter. The James–Lange theory of the emotions, according to which an emotion is a feeling of some visceral, vasomotor or other kind of internal, physical event(s), entirely confuses this point. While it is undoubtedly true that biochemical and physiological transformations of various kinds occur during or after various emotions are felt, this fact can only be established experimentally, and that presupposes an *independent* set of criteria for identifying the emotions in question; thus, emotions are not *identical* to feelings of any such kind. It is nonsensical to say that an angry person is angered *by* any bodily factors, except in special circumstances where these form the object or focus of his appraisal and attention. It looks as though there might be an exception to the claim that emotions are not identical to sensations of physical changes in the case of disgust. Here, one might think of the case in which a person is disgusted with the scene left by a murderer, where he experiences genuine nausea. But note that nausea is *not* identical to disgust, and the disgust which is felt in the given case is justified not by the nausea but by the immorality and inhumanity of the act whose results are witnessed. One may be disgusted with the corruption of a politician, but no nausea need be present as a warrant for the avowal of the emotion.

Schachter and Singer (1962) conducted a series of experiments that tended to show how mere physiological arousal is insufficient to induce a subject to report that he is experiencing a specific emotion, even though the arousal was almost identical to that present in certain sorts of emotional states. The experimenters injected epinephrine into volunteer subjects, a substance known to produce physical transformations similar to those found in persons undergoing various emotional reactions or in various emotional states. Some were told of the nature of the physiological reaction they would have, while others were told that there would be no experienced reaction whatsoever. Each subject was placed in a room with an actor who pretended to be either angry or euphoric. Those subjects who had been correctly informed about the reaction they would have to the injection did not become either angry or euphoric, whereas those who were told that they would not have a reaction tended to take on the apparent emotion of the actor. Those who did not know the physical basis for their feeling-state sought some way of accounting for it, and their taking on the apparent emotion of the actor in the room with them seems to have been a function of their appraisal of their sensation *in the light of* the available social information. Similar phenomena are discussed in some of Becker's (1967) work on drug use. The development of severe anxiety in cases where a novice has taken LSD-25 had usually been attributed to the pharmacological action of the drug itself. Becker, however, noted that, since such apparent drug-induced anxiety states or anxiety-psychoses were generally restricted to neophyte-users, some other explanation might be sought. He proposes that, when a drug user finds his subjective state altered in such a way as to fit his preconceptions of insanity or 'loss of mind', such an account of the experience may occasion panic. Even long-term users may experiment with a higher dosage than usual and experience effects unlike any previously known. Unless there are others present to counteract the 'loss-of-mind' interpretation of the experience, e.g., by redefining it as desirable rather than frightening, then panic may occur on the part of the user. Becker notes that those accompanying a drug-user while he is under its effects typically speak reassuringly about the drug's effects, instruct the user (if he is new to the drug) in how to compensate for perceptual distortion, and generally normalize the situation. 'Experienced users prevent the episode from having lasting effects and reassure the novice that whatever he feels will come to a timely and harmless end.' He concludes:

> the most likely interpretation we can make of the drug-induced psychoses reported is that they are either severe anxiety reactions to an event

interpreted and experienced as insanity, or failures by the user to correct, in carrying out some ordinary action, for the perceptual distortions caused by the drug. If the interpretation is correct, then untoward mental effects produced by drugs depend in some part on their physiological action, but to a much larger degree find their origin in the definitions and conceptions the user applies to that action. (Becker 1967)

The unavailability of anxiety-neutralizing definitions of the drug-using is claimed here to be decisive in the case of putatively drug-induced anxiety and panic.

Emotions, then, are not mere eruptions independent of appraisals and judgements, beliefs and conceptualizations. They are not to be identified with sensations or with physiological changes *per se*. They are generally amenable to reasoned dissuasion and inculcation. Moreover, emotions such as fear or jealousy may be cited as motives that commensensically explain actions. Mischel has pointed out that to say that jealousy was a man's motive for some particular action 'is not to say anything about the physiological arousal that energized his behavior, nor is it to say that he was in an emotional state . . . and we often use 'fear', 'jealousy', and so on, not to explain actions, but to signify emotional states that explain *a failure to act appropriately. . . .*' (Mischel, 1969, p. 263).

To say, for instance, that a man acted out of resentment is to relate his currently problematic conduct to the way in which he has appraised the situation in relation to prior social experiences; it is to assert of him that he knows or believes that someone or some institution or group has done something that has affected him adversely and that his present behaviour is informed by that knowledge or belief. Conversely, one could use the category to account for the absence of some otherwise conventionally required conduct on the part of a person. It is most routinely the case that emotion-concepts function in accounts that explain action that is in some way considered untoward or problematic within a situation, or that explain the absence of some otherwise obligatory or preferred course of action. Where actions are not 'noteworthy' *in situ*, by virtue of their situatedly clear motivational status, the categories of affect are rarely invoked in regard to conduct. Indeed, as Parsons (1951) long ago indicated, there are entire classes of actions which are undertaken according to the convention of preferred affective-neutrality.

Nothing in this account of emotions argues against the claim that we can *experience* emotions. However, it is clear that, as Kenny (1963, p. 62) remarks, 'only beings who are capable of manifesting a particular emotion are capable of experiencing it'. For example, emotions which can only be manifested by the use of language (e.g. remorse for a crime committed long ago, a longing for the arrival of a friend from a distant place, etc.) can be experienced only by language-users. As Melden observes,

No matter how much a dog may cringe with its tail between its legs when caught in the act of dragging its bone across the family's prize oriental rug, it does not feel guilt or shame. And no matter how endearingly it then proceeds to lick the hands of its master, it is not feeling remorse or asking to be forgiven for a shameful performance. (Melden, 1969, p. 206)

Whatever it is that the dog feels (fear? affection?), the ascription of categories such as guilt, shame or remorse apply only by analogical extension; warranted ascriptions of such categories properly depend upon the recognition by the offender of some standards of conduct, some rules applicable to him in the situation, and the understanding that violations are not merely unpleasant if uncovered, but wrong. It becomes clear that the capacity to experience genuinely either shame or guilt or remorse hinges upon a mastery of a natural language involving cultural knowledge and reasoning conventions.

Because of the connections between emotion-ascriptions and ascriptions of recognitions and appraisals of various kinds, such ascriptions are mundanely analysable for what they presuppose on the part of the ascriber. Were I to ascribe jealousy to you on the basis of your annoyance about your wife's having gone to lunch with another man, I should be betraying something about my *own* assessment of the emotional possiblities inherent in the situation, as well as making a claim about yours. The common retort of, 'What is there to be jealous (afraid, ashamed, embarrassed, etc.) about?' marks the disjunction that can arise when the ascription is being disavowed by reference to a discrepant analysis of the situation in question. However, there are (logical) limits to the possibilities of disjunctive emotion-affording appraisals. Without common ground, we could not teach emotion-concepts or recognize and avow emotions in intelligible ways. Types of situation are paradigmatically linked to the emotions they afford *by convention.* The link is neither deterministic nor biological, but sociocultural. It is, in a broad sense, moral; a person may be found morally deficient not to be, e.g., upset by the death of his father, moved by an act of extreme courage, angry at a miscarriage of justice – given, that is, that he concurs in the relevant description of the situation. Indeed, we may appeal to the conventional emotion-affording properties of a situation as grounds for claiming of someone that he is *hiding* his emotion, *concealing* his true feelings, in cases where his behaviour does not (appear to) express the appropriate emotion in the situation. moreover, since various forms of conduct may be characteristic *both* of an emotional state and of a reaction to a sensation or physiological process (e.g. crying), we require knowledge of the circumstances in order to disambiguate the behaviour on many occasions. If a person cries we can only know whether this is emotional behaviour or pain-behaviour if we know whether the circumstances occasioning the behaviour is emotion-affording or pain-causing. In some instances where a person has displayed what for a clinician is 'inappropriate affect', it has been found that the person has been reacting to an undetected source of acute physical discomfort which he has been unwilling to disclose. In other instances, children have been known to masquerade their emotional responses by claiming some slight physical injury or discomfort as the grounds for their crying, moodiness or irritability. Successful concealment of the circumstances informing behaviour can thus incur observers' errors in ascribing either emotion or physical sensation to an individual.

The psychologistic model of the emotions as internal episodes, then, fails to do justice to the constitutive connections between emotion-avowals and -ascriptions, and conduct, context, appraisal, belief and social convention. This model can never illuminate, only distort, our appreciation of the variegated ways in which emotions figure in the 'weave of our lives'.

SOCIAL ORGANIZATION OF EMOTIONAL DISPLAYS AND THEIR TREATMENT

In what follows, I shall sketch out, in a preliminary way, some suggestions for investigating the social structures of emotional displays and their treatment in various sorts of social interactions. An extract of data will be presented and discussed in terms of the analytical distinctions and issues raised above. Because there are no leads in the research literature on the study of actual emotional displays in natural settings, I am following a time-worn tradition of focusing upon an intuitively deviant case in order to illuminate conventional reasoning more sharply. The data are taken from an actual occasion in which two mental health social workers, a prospective mental patient already known to all present as psychiatrically diagnosed to be a hebephrenic schizophrenic, and her mother are speaking together. The diagnostic category of hebephrenic schizophrenia has no set extensional domain but broadly signifies a state of alternating emotional behaviour, in the absence of clear object or cause, on the part of the patient.

Data extract

MW01 = First mental health social worker
MW02 = Second mental health social worker
MPP = Mother of prospective patient

1   MW01   What d'ya want to tell me today? You were telling me a bit about yourself last time Sheila; tell me some more about yourself.

2	Sheila (prospective patient)	(laughs)
3	MPP	Go on then! (pause 2.0 secs) What's funny?
4	Sheila	(begins crying and looking imploringly at assembled company)
5	MPP	Don't. (1.5 secs) Shut up! What's there to be unhappy about?
6	MW02	Perhaps she's feeling ill.
7	MPP	Nah . . . she often cries . . . just like that when there's no reason to
8	Sheila	(begins to laugh, then breaks into sobbing)
9	MW01	Why are you crying, Sheila? Don't ya feel well today?
10	Sheila	(sobs even louder) (duration of 5 secs)
11	MW02	Tell us what's troubling you.
12	Sheila	(begins to laugh loudly and looks delighted)
13	MW02	Are ya laughing at me?
14	Sheila	No.
15	MW01	Are ya laughing at me? (Sheila begins laughing louder) What is it? (Sheila laughs more) Ya keep laughing at us what is it?
16	Sheila	Dunno
17	MW01	Ya do . . . don't wanna say, though, do you.
18	Sheila	No.
19	MW02	Why not?
20	MPP	Why not? (1.5 secs) Minute ago you were crying.
21	MW01	Is it those awful voices again?
22	Sheila	Mmmm.
23	MW01	What are they saying now?
24	Sheila	(still laughing) They co;:hm ta tanta::hlize me (breaks into sobs)
25	MW01	What do they say that's upsetting ya now?
26	Sheila	They scream at me . . . sometimes they tease me. (laughs)

Sheila's alternating elation and distress is not observably synchronized with any interactional events, and poses a problem for the assembled participants in locating the possible object or objects for these fluctuating emotional displays. Ordinarily, the location of an object that makes an emotional display intelligible does not necessarily cast light on the cause of the display – I can be elated *at* being complimented but *because* I am drunk, or angry *at* little things *because* I am suffering from dyspepsia, where to know its object is not thereby to understand its cause. Where the object of the display cannot be determined at all, or when determined is found to be irrational, issues of causality *do* become specifiable (albeit in defeasible ways). Thus, locating Sheila's auditory hallucination as the object of her emotional displays enables co-participants to find her apparently objectless and bizarre alternations of affect to be intelligible, and serves to specify the cause of her affective state in her mental disorder. Similarly, if co-participants had remained unable to locate the object of Sheila's emotional displays, then again her longer-term, over-arching condition of mental disorder could appropriately have been invoked as their possible cause. (There is, however, an interesting argument that would postulate affective psychiatric disorders as *consisting in* such bizarre affective alternations, rather than as the *cause* of them.)

Notice that the first reaction to Sheila's display of elation consists in an enquiry about it. Her mother, in utterance 3, asks her what is funny, searching for an object for the display. In doing so, she is presupposing that nothing in the interaction so far entitles or justifies the display. In turn 4, Sheila begins crying and looking imploringly at the co-participants. Again, her mother expresses her puzzlement by asking what there is 'to be unhappy about'. Her mother is clearly orienting to Sheila's behaviour as emotional and raising questions directed to locating the object or objects of the behaviour so constituted. However, in utterance 6, the second mental health social worker orients to Sheila's behaviour in terms of her possible *physical* condition, thereby constituting it as ambiguous between emotion and sensation-reaction. No observable circumstances have yet been determined which could enable co-participants to settle upon a consensual orientation to her behaviour: it could be *either* a display of emotions, or pain-behaviour interspersed with laughter. In utterance 7, Sheila's mother says that the present display (sobbing, looking unhappy) can be assimilated to prior cases in which there has been 'no reason' to behave in this way. If accepted by co-participants, this would provide for construing Sheila's conduct as *emotion-like* behaviour. After the ensuing bout of sobbing, however, the first mental health worker, in utterance 9, reverts to the physiological possibility by asking the girl whether she feels well, a locution signalling a primarily physical concern. After more sobbing, the second mental health worker asks the girl, in utterance 11, for what is troubling her. Formally ambiguous with respect to physical or life-circumstantial matters, the notion of 'troubling' her reopens an orientation to Sheila's conduct as potentially emotional in nature. The subsequent laughter on her part, and the cessation of distress-behaviour, reorients everyone present to a search for an object rather than a cause.

The alternating displays occasion alternating sorts of search-procedures on the part of co-participants; where the conduct is construed (albeit tentatively) as emotional, objects are sought; where it is constituted (again tentatively) as a sensation-reaction, causes (of a physiological sort) are presupposed in the questioning. The opacity of the possible object or objects of the behaviour construed as emotional provides for the persistence of the ambiguity it seems to have; where no object can be located in the meaningful environment for a display of this kind, the conventional options for conceptualizing the display appear to include construing it as something *other than* emotional.

In utterance 15, the first mental health worker responds to Sheila's sustained and heightened laughter by pressing hard for an explanation of its object. The laughter is being taken not as a reaction to anything physiological (such as a tickling or other animating sensation of that sort) but now as firmly affective behaviour. When Sheila says in utterance 16 that she does not know what she is laughing at, this is flatly contradicted by the mental health worker in utterance 17, and the contradiction is resolved by adding a reason for her denying knowledge of the object of her laughter, a reason that takes the form of an ascription of intentional concealment on her part. Sheila acknowledges that the ascription is warranted by agreeing in utterance 18 that she does not want to disclose the object of her laughter. (Note that one can often *agree* by saying 'No' – the token is not self-evidently negating.) Eventually, it is proposed by the same mental health worker that 'those awful voices' form the object of the emotional displays. Once concurred in as the object, it is revealed that changes in what the voices say occasion changes in Sheila's overt conduct. Now a synchrony has been located, as the object of the displays is rendered transparent.

Ordinarily, emotion like displays may be related synchronously to features of an ongoing meaningful environment or, where nothing therein observably entitles or justifies the display, to features of the agent's undisclosed thoughts or, further, to something physical, which thereby transforms the perception of the behaviour and constitutes it as non-emotional. The sort of search procedures that are initiated by someone's betraying the marks of some emotion in situations devoid of conventionally entitling objects will depend upon the analysis of the probability that the conduct is occasioned by (1) undisclosed objects or (2) physical stimuli. Since to suggest that someone is not disclosing something may be dispreferred in most ordinary situations, one would expect that the first search-preference would construe the conduct as occasioned by some physical stimuli wherever such a possibility would make sense. This would, as noted, logically entail the temporary abandonment of seeing the conduct *as* emotional. Having located an object for conduct constituted as emotional, questions about causation can be raised. In some instances, as in the above, the *kind* of object located *can* be informative as to the causation of the emotional display. (Note that 'causation' is here being construed singularly and locally; no causal propositions about affect can take the form of law-like statements of necessary and sufficient antecedent conditions for the display of a type of emotion. It has already been argued here that emotions may be rational or irrational, appropriate or inappropriate, justified or unjustified, in their contexts, and hence are normatively explicable rather than mechanically predictable phenomena.)

No matter how distant in time from the ongoing interaction is the object of an emotional display, it is rendered relevantly present in virtue of the device of postulating the operation of the memory and current reflection. For specific displays, some object is *requiredly* available and knowledge of it is ascribable to agents of the displays. Laughter is such a display. Where laughter is not seeable as physically occasioned, the agent is conventionally accountable for its object. Claimed ignorance of the object of laughter is unacceptable as an account, and may be warrantably disbelieved unless the agent makes out that his laughter consisted of imitation of others or that it was undertaken as a pretence of some kind. The latter two possibilities are contextually investigable, and may be employed as derogatory accounts for laughter where the known-in-common situation is consensually devoid of laugh-entitling features. In such ways, laughter may be construed in a setting as *devoid of genuine emotion.* Where it is treated as the expression of genuine emotion, then its object must either be contextually presupposed or tacitly available, or construed as available in the undisclosed but potentially disclosable thoughts of the person doing the laughing.

People normally have to deal with more complex emotions than fear, elation and other forms of affect which do not require any linguistic capacity on the part of those who manifest them: human emotions include a large range whose objects are 'abstract'. Characteristically, even those emotions warrantably ascribable to non-linguistic creatures are tied, in their human displays, to conceptually constituted abstract phenomena, although of course humans can *re*act with fear or elation directly in a way that is unmediated by linguistic constitution. Those emotions constituted by the orientation of the person to a *conception* of an event or situation can be transformed by alterations in the conception of that event or situation. Thus, Henslin has illustrated some of the ways in which the emotion of guilt, constituted by four different orientations to the suicide of a relative or close friend, can be 'neutralized' by adopting changed conceptalizations of the suicided person, the nature of the suicide itself, and/ or the factors thought to 'explain' the suicide (Henslin, 1970, p. 200). Henslin's is one of the only genuinely sociological approaches to the study of affect and its transformation available in the human sciences, and is itself admittedly a first approximation.

One word of caution should be noted here. It should not be thought that, because specific emotions can be transformed or eliminated by reconceptualizations of their objects (events, situations, etc.), there are no normative constraints oriented to by members in such transformations. We may say of someone who does not seem to recognize situatedly relevant normative constraints on his reconceptualization that he is 'not facing facts', or that he is 'making excuses'. Various sorts of situations have features socially pre-designated as fearful, hateful, provocative, frightening and the like, and once any given situation has been oriented to socially as belonging to a class of such situations, the possibility is open for a member's *re*conceptualization of it to be judged in some way untoward. Moreover, the categorization of a member as 'stoic' or 'hard-headed' in the face of some situation which conventionally entitles or justifies some specific emotion may be withdrawn if it is found that the member has not construed the situation along the convention-relevant dimension. Ascribed deviations from expressions of normatively required emotions are typically implicative for the ascription of personality; often more so than conformities.

There is a high degree of commonsense predictability involved in gauging the emotional responses or reactions to various classes of utterances and actions in everyday life. So much so, in fact, that we routinely ascribe the apparent affective consequences of an action to the actor as a part of his action itself, as when we say, e.g., 'he alarmed her', 'he frightened them', 'she angered him'. Such act-consequence elisions were even referred to as a class of actions *per se* by Austin in his category of 'perlocutionary acts' (1973, pp. 101–31).

REFERENCES

Austin, J. L. (1973) *How to Do Things with Words*, ed. J. O. Urmson. Oxford: Oxford University Press.

Becker, Howard (1967) History, culture and subjective experience: an exploration of the social basis of drug-induced experiences. *Journal of Health and Social Behaviour*, 8.

Henslin, James M. (1970) Guilt and guilt neutralization: response and adjustment to suicide. In Jack D. Douglas (ed.), *Deviance and Respectability: the Social Construction of Moral Meanings*. New York: Basic Books.

Hume, David (1739) *Treatise of Human Nature*, ed. L. A. Selby-Bigge. Oxford: Clarendon Press, 1888, Book II, Pt iii, Section 3; cited in Melden (1969).

Kenny, Anthony (1963) *Action, Emotion and Will*. London: Routledge & Kegan Paul.

Melden, Abraham I. (1969) The conceptual dimensions of emotions. In Theodore Mischel (ed.), *Human Action: Conceptual and Empirical Issues*. New York: Academic Press.

Mischel, Theodore (1969) 'Epilogue', in T. Mischel (ed.), *Human Action. Conceptual and Empirical Issues*. New York: Academic Press.

Parsons, Talcott (1951) *The Social System*. Glencoe, Ill.: Free Press.

Pritchard, Michael S. (1976) 'On Taking Emotions Seriously', *Journal for the Theory of Social Behavior*, 6.

Schachter, Stanley and Singer, J. (1962) Cognitive, social and physiological determinants of emotional state. *Psychological Review*, 69.

Wittgenstein, Ludwig (1967) *Zettel*, ed. G. E. M. Anscombe and G. H. von Wright, trans. G. E. M. Anscombe. Oxford: Basil Blackwell.
—— (1968) *Philosophical Investigations*, trans. G. E. M. Anscombe. Oxford: Basil Blackwell.

8

Anger and Similar Delusions

C. Terry Warner

Introduction

We are in the midst of a reassessment, in several disciplines, of long-standing assumptions about emotion. The most vigorous new work seems to be concentrating not so much on the cognitive aspect of many emotions, which is well enough recognized by now, but on the active, purposive and indeed strategic aspects; this work regards emotions as conduct – as manoeuvres or 'moves' in largely institutionalized social interactions involving clusters of people at once. Thus patterns of emotion, like rhetorical phenomena, are culturally indigenous. Their use is governed by expectations implicit in the moral order of the society and period in which they are to be found, expectations that pertain to such matters as rights, status and appropriateness. Among a given people, particular kinds of emotion arise, flourish and then pass into extinction, and at every stage are subject to diffusion, export and adaptation (see Harré, 1983; Sabini and Silver, 1982; Tavris, 1982).

Emotion and belief

In spite of increasing evidence for this 'social constructionist' view of emotion, its truth is far from obvious. On the contrary, in having an emotion – when, for example, we are ashamed, fearful, depressed, jealous, proud or head over heels in love – what we think is going on with us is a far

An earlier version of this paper was presented to the Utah Academy of Arts and Sciences, May 1984. Arthur King, Dennis Packard, Merlin Myers, Bernard Harrison, Eddy Zemach and Rom Harré have made suggestions that I have made use of, not necessarily as they might have wished. The influence of Harré in the final draft, and of King, are generally too pervasive to document specifically.

cry from anything that can be called conduct. We regard our emotion as a condition provoked or aroused in us – 'You are making me angry' – or as a condition that has befallen us – 'I think it's her son's rebelliousness that's saddened her so profoundly.' The cases that interest me most are the kind exemplified by anger, for in being angry a person is making a judgement that the object of her anger (whatever or whomever it is she is angry with), and not she herself, is responsible for her anger. So if it is true that in being angry she is engaging in a form of conduct in and by which she maintains that she is not doing so at all, but is passive, angry people are systematically in error in their beliefs about how things are with them.

I am interested not solely in anger, but in all emotions that have this property: when we are experiencing the emotion, we are certain we are being caused to have it. For convenience I shall simply treat one of these emotions, *anger*, as exemplary. It should not be difficult for the reader to generalize my conclusions to other emotions possessing the required property, such as contempt, (psychological) irritation, hate, embarrassment, dread, jealousy, self-pity, boredom and many, but not all, instances of what we call indignation, anxiety, guilt and indifference.

Now on the social constructionist view, systematically pursued or maintained conduct, including emotions, are embedded in complex social practices involving other people, whose responses are both anticipated and utilized. For this reason, the judgements in which particular avowals or expressions of emotion consist cannot be merely mistaken. In so far as the social practices that embed them are concerned, they are manoeuvres, stratagems, etc. The angry person's misunderstanding of herself is something she systematically sustains in a kind of morbid co-operation with others. It is not enough to say she is deceived: she is self-deceived; and, generally speaking, the others abet her self-deception.

How to account for the self-deception of angry people and people experiencing relevantly similar emotions is the problem of this chapter. It is a problem worthy of attention because the standard kind of account makes reference to psychical acts or processes of which the person is not aware – acts or processes that Freud called unconscious. On this view, the stratagems or manoeuvres in which self-deceiving conduct consists operate on a level or in a stratum unavailable to introspection: 'the unconscious'. There are two general difficulties with the notion of the unconscious. As is well known, it is internally inconsistent; I will talk about this difficulty in due course. But more to the point of this chapter, as an explanation of social behaviour, the unconscious is radically individualistic rather than social. (In Freud, the mentation that makes the expression of emotion an instance of conduct rather than a mechanical response is wholly internal; and the fact that this mentation is socially influenced does not make it less so.) Indeed, the inconsistency of the concept of the unconscious can be traced precisely to the individualism of it (though showing why this is so lies beyond this chapter). The problem before us, then, is to account for the sort of self-deception in which anger and similar emotions consist without reference to internal, unconscious processes, but instead by reference to the corporate social episodes of which such emotions are a part.

To develop an account of this sort, I shall

1 explore the self-deception that accompanies anger and similar emotions;
2 examine their 'strategic' aspects, by which they co-ordinate themselves with the strategies of others in patterned social episodes; and
3 explain how the agents engaged in these emotions deceive themselves as to the character of what they are doing, and construct this explanation without reference to unconscious stratagems or process.

My position will be that we deceive ourselves by adopting a self-deceiving rhetoric of moral conscientiousness and excuse – the rhetoric includes our avowals of emotion – and, by this means, presenting ourselves as morally justified. Such self-presentation is contrary to what a straightforward outsider can plainly observe of what we are doing. We make ourselves out to be acting conscientiously, whereas others can tell that, rather than acting conscientiously, we are merely making ourselves out to be doing so, which is a dissembling rather than a conscientious thing to do.

Before undertaking the three tasks I have outlined, it will be useful if I speak a bit more precisely about the theses I will defend.

To say that anger possesses the property I mentioned above – that the angry person believes she is being caused to be angry – is to say that she believes herself to be responding to a threat provided wholly independently of her will. It is this threat that she thinks is causing her to be angry. She believes herself a victim: whatever she is doing is undertaken only in her own defence. From an observer's point of view, we will want to grant that she may be wrong in this proto-theory of the genesis of her anger (though this is something *she* cannot concede without thereby ceasing to be angry). One way to capture this more tentative view is to say the anger is *defensive*; we would mean by this that the agent believes it to be an effect of an independent provocation, and we would take no position on whether her belief is true.

The received doctrine that we are not responsible for being angry actually consists of two erroneous doctrines, very closely related to each other. One of these doctrines amounts to a semi-sympathetic interpretation of the agent's view of her own anger. This interpretation allows that the agent may be mistaken in her judgement that she is caused to be angry by circumstances beyond her control. Yet it assumes that the judgement is

sincere and that she is responding straightforwardly to these circumstances as she (perhaps erroneously) sees them. This might be called *the
doctrine of sincerity or straightforwardness*. The second doctrine follows
from the first: though the angry judgement may be mistaken about *how* it
is being caused, it is not also mistaken about *whether* it is caused, and this
on account of its sincerity. At the very least, it is caused by the belief the
angry person has (sincerely held, if false) about how it is being caused, or
by the psychological state of having this belief, or by the onset of this belief.
This doctrine, which is also a sympathetic interpretation of the sincerity
doctrine, I shall call *the causal view of anger.*

Before sketching out my line of attack against these two doctrines, I
want to indicate briefly the dependency of the causal view of anger upon a
hard-edged distinction between judgement and feeling, or cognition and
affect. (The untenability of this distinction in this context will become a
point of issue later on.) This distinction is the means by which the causal
view grants the corrigibility of the angry individual's view of her anger
without altogether abandoning the idea that anger is caused. The self-
explanatory character of anger is assigned to a judgement-component of
the emotion – it is this judgement that is corrigible – which is accordingly
separated from a feeling-component.

That this is necessary for the causal view is made clear by considering
how the causalist would respond to the following objection: 'Suppose that
A, to this point angry at B, were to abandon her belief that B had done
what (up to now) she had supposed has been angering her. If this
happened, her anger would cease. This argues against the causal view and
for the *identity* of anger and the judgement it involves. In a clear case of
causality, if a person at first believed that a safety razor caused the cut on
her arm, and then changed her mind when she discovered fresh blood on
the shower door, the cut would not disappear. But when there is this sort
of change of mind about the cause of one's anger, the anger ceases. How
then can anger be contingent upon anything external, as the angry person
believes it is?' To this objection the advocate of the causal view would have
to respond as follows. The fact that A's anger ceases if her judgement
changes can be accounted for causally. The kind of causality her anger
imputes is not a direct causality. Her judgement against B respecting
whatever he is doing to anger her is separate from, and prior to, her angry
feelings, and it is this judgement, not B's act itself, that directly causes the
feeling. The production of the feeling is, as they say, cognitively mediated.
In the event that the judgement is correct, the object might be said by some
to be the cause A believes it is, by way of her perception, and otherwise
not; or the psychological state of making the judgement might be said to be
the cause, or the onset, of this state. In summary, the causal view of anger
must account for the corrigibility of anger, and the way it can do this
without abandoning the causality doctrine is by separating judgement

from feeling and regarding the judgement, but not the feeling, as corrigible. A might say, 'I was hurt. If you had said what I thought you said, you would have been responsible for what I've gone through. I can see now that it was all a tragic misunderstanding on my part.'

This response to the objection leaves intact the core conviction of the angry individual, namely, that she is not responsible for her anger. That is why I said the causal view is semi-sympathetic to that conviction. We can now isolate precisely the irreducible core that the causal view must maintain: the angry individual is not responsible for her angry *feelings*. She might under certain circumstances admit some responsibility for her judgement, e.g., 'I'm sorry; I should have listened to you more carefully.' But in no case will she admit responsibility for the feelings, since in her mind they are not the sort of thing that she *could* be responsible for. Respecting her feelings, she believes herself a pure patient. And in this belief she is not alone; the idea that we are not responsible for our defensive feelings is an almost unassailed dogma of our culture.

Two interlocking theses

A major difficulty with the causal view is that, as an interpretation of anger's defensiveness, it is incompatible with an interpretation of that defensiveness implicit in common usage. In other words, there are socially observable properties of angry conduct in the absence of which we would never ascribe anger, yet which are inexplicable if the causal view were true, and anger were straightforwardly defensive. The interpretation that alone can explain these properties, rival the causal view, is that anger is *resistant* or, in other words, motivated by ulterior considerations respecting others rather than straightforwardly caused. On this interpretation, the angry person's view that her anger is an effect of causes is not sincere; it is a *self-deception*. The straightforwardness doctrine is false. I will show how, in anger, we systematically distort both our understanding of the anger itself and what it is 'about'. The emotions of which anger is representative are so common in almost everyone's life that, because of them, most of us most of the time systematically misunderstand both ourselves and others.

This *thesis of self-deception* implies that the angry individual is not simply wrong about what, beyond her control, is responsible for her anger, but about whether *anything* beyond her control is responsible for it. This means that the causal view also is false. My denial of the causal view is an affirmation of the agent's responsibility for her anger; I'll call it *the thesis of agency*. This agency thesis does not, so far as I can see, reciprocally entail the thesis of self-deception. As the argument of this chapter is for the resistance, i.e. the self-deception, of anger, which is the stronger of the two theses, the argument will if successful hit both of my targets, and otherwise will hit neither.

What is at stake in trying to establish the self-deception thesis, and by means of this the responsibility thesis, is the interpretation of anger's defensiveness. In showing that the defensiveness consists in resistance, which is a public and social act rather than a private one, I shall keep a constant eye upon the self-deception literature. For it will turn out that the essentially social acount I give of the self-deceptiveness of anger will constitute a full-blown account of self-deception that at once accommodates all the observable aspects of self-deceived conduct and is free of the well-known conceptual debilities that have afflicted previous theories.

THE CAUSAL VIEW OF ANGER

Accusation and victimhood

There are two mutually entailing aspects of anger's defensiveness. The first is its accusatory quality. To an angry individual her anger seems to be the effect, in her, of someone else's conduct. 'I resent her for saying I'm not qualified for the job.' 'Of course I'm bitter. He up and dies without leaving me enough to pay the mortgage.' In her view, another person(s) is maliciously (or inconsiderately) and unfairly transgressing her rights or abusing her interest or violating her dignity, and the result is her self-protective, accusing emotion. She sees this other person as dealing unfairly (a question of rights) with her to her disadvantage (a question of interests), and therefore as morally responsible for the emotion.

Suppose that one individual heretofore angry at another were suddenly to concede that the other is not responsible for her anger. This concession would constitute a giving up of that anger. Were we not prepared to respond to the concession in this manner, we would be using the term 'anger' in an uncommon sense.[1] For example, imagine that we realize we have profoundly misunderstood the intentions of someone we have been angry with – someone, for instance, who has failed to keep an appointment after we have gone to great inconvenience to meet him. As we wait, increasingly upset, we re-examine our relationship to him. It begins to bother us, perhaps as it never has before, that so much in the past can be seen, on reflection, to manifest his disrespect for us, our time and our feelings. It bothers us also that we have been so naive as to overlook this repeated thoughtlessness. We are confident that he could have come on time had he wanted to enough, had it been among his priorities, had he not been selfish or insensitive. Then we receive a report that he has been in an accident. Suddenly what was mounting anger ends, and in its place we feel chagrin for having transgressed against a friend by unjustifiably bringing a charge against him in our hearts, which is to say, by unjustifiably becoming angry at him. We are chagrined because the unjustifiability of the angry charge renders it, in our own eyes, a transgression. Coupled with the chagrin is a sense of relief that we refrained from acting overtly on the anger while it lasted. Though anger has given way to chagrin and relief, it is still as true as it was a few moments before that we have been inconvenienced. The only thing that has changed is our belief, essential to the anger while it lasted, that the other party has transgressed against us and is therefore responsible for what we have been suffering.[2]

Indissociably connected with this accusing quality is a sense in the angry person of being passive, victimized and helpless. She feels she is a pure patient in the face of forces she cannot control. In the angry person's mind the accused can control some of these, if he but will; and that is precisely why she feels his victim. She does not believe merely that she is acting under duress or coercion. She believes she is not acting at all, but is passive. She not only bears no responsibility for her anger; she could bear none, however emotionally strong, resilient or self-controlled she might be. It is the very nature of this kind of emotion, as she understands it while having it, that she could not be responsible for it. At the same time, she does not necessarily think the other is the sole cause of her anger. She can freely admit that her own temperament and her history with him are factors that render her vulnerable to him. But she does believe his conduct to be an intrusion into prevailing and otherwise tranquil conditions, and therefore can be blamed for her agitation. The key here is that, as far as she is concerned, the causes and conditions she would identify for her anger are beyond her present control.

The accusation in an angry attitude is directed towards something beyond the attitude itself, whereas the sense of victimhood correlative to that accusation is self-conscious. In anger there is always a sense of being a victim with respect to rights or interests that are felt to be violated; in some cases this takes the form of self-pity. The accusation and the sense of being victimized are correlative because seeing another as provoking oneself is to feel provoked. Taken as a unit, this accusing/victimized attitude – this belief that the anger is a defence – is what we might call 'the angry view of anger'. The angry person incessantly puts forward an explanation of her anger by imputing responsibility for it elsewhere. She is essentially self-conscious, which is to say, self-regarding about whatever losses of rights, privileges or interests she feels she is suffering. She feels she is not the sort of person who deserves to be treated in this way.

Illustration of anger's self-conscious, self-explanatory character

Notice in the following banal episode, in which two people are angry at (with) each other, how this quality is progressively revealed as each party feels increasingly challenged about the legitimacy of his or her position.

Brent   It's ten minutes to eight, Alison, and . . .

Alison I know, don't tell me. I haven't even showered yet. Obviously this is one party *you* want to go to or you wouldn't care about being late.

Brent   Since we're seeing my friends, you're not going to hurry, is that it?

Alison Have I been standing around? After I got home from work I fed Sarah and got her ready for bed and you've only taken care of yourself.

Brent   If you really cared you could have been ready on time.

Alison Look, Mister, I've been working most of the day and then cleaned up the kitchen and got a babysitter just so we could go.

Brent   You think you're the only one who works around here. I come home early three days a week so you can take classes after you get off work, and I passed up a good promotion because you didn't want to live in Placerville, and all you can think of is how much you do and how little I do.

Alison You let me off duty for a few hours and you think you've made a big sacrifice. *You're* off duty just about all the time! What's the matter? Does it cut into your freedom when I get to go out for an hour?

Brent   So it's all my fault, is it? I'm always the one who causes our problems.

Alison Everything I said was true.

Brent   If you're convinced I'm so selfish, how can you stand me? Why don't you just leave?

Alison Here we go. The Great Victim rides again.

Brent   To hear you tell it, I'm always the one who's in the wrong.

Alison I never said that. Remember, you were the one who blamed me first.

Brent   I don't even feel like going to the party any more.

Alison I can't believe it. You need help. You're really sick.

Variant anger styles

A subcultural designation for the style of this exchange between Alison and Brent might be 'American assertive'. In other cultures, classes or subcultures, the style of offence-taking might well be different from theirs. In some such groups, for example, anger is typically even more volatile and sometimes, though not in all cases, less calculated and sinister and/or less durable (e.g., Tikopians, youthful Nuer males, Neapolitans). On the other end of a particular dimension, there are cultures, and classes within cultures, in which open altercation would be unthinkable or uncouth; in these, the accusation of another tends more pronouncedly to be a matter of making clear one's own victimized status. Some examples of this are ritualized clamour (Australian aborigines); accusing the object of one's anger of bewitching one (Tiv, Nyakyusa, Azande); histrionic suicide (Trobiander); and chilly silence (upper-class British). In some cultures the offender is treated with an intensified 'respectfulness' expressed by an increased formality of vocabulary and intonation (Korean). These matters are extensively treated in the literature of social and psychological anthropology.

What is common to these diverse cases is that the angry individual's offended status, and thereby his accusation, is unmistakably communicated by means of conventional and sometimes even ritual conduct that in its own way is just as defensive and, yes, self-assertive as the emotions of Brent and Alison during their falling-out.[3] To point out this commonality is to make no anthropological claim about the emotions characteristic of any peoples. Strictly speaking, it would be irrelevant to my thesis if it happened that some, many or even all known cultures lacked the defensive emotions I have defined. (Among the Nez Pece, multiple families lived in the same house for generations without trouble, and it is said that the Tasadays had in their language no word for anger or anything resembling it.) My interest is only in showing why any emotions possessing the accusing, self-victimizing properties I have specified cannot but be self-deceptions, whether and wherever these emotions happen to be manifest. In this paper I shall track the example of Brent and Alison through, with the proviso that a culturally different sort of accusing and self-victimizing emotion could have been chosen to illustrate my points.

The contrast of defensive emotions and other kinds

It is worth noting also that, although the expressions of anger between Alison and Brent are defensive, this is not true of everything we would be willing to call anger. It is possible, for example, that Jesus' castigation of the money-changers in the temple was not an accusation to the effect that those he drove before him were responsible for how he felt towards them. It is possible, in other words, that his attitude was more other-concerned, or perhaps even concerned for a principle, than self-concerned. It is possible, in other words, that it was more like love or integrity than hostility, even though appropriately called 'anger', or perhaps distinguished as 'righteous indignation'. I do not know whether this usage would be metaphorical or extended. One can chastise or reprimand – and be properly said to be angry – without feeling a victim.

These remarks suggest that to talk of accusing emotions like anger is to classify emotions in a manner different from their classification in the natural languages with which I am familiar. There may be emotions that impute causality but not malice or inconsiderateness to their objects, e.g., arousals such as instinctive fear of immediate physical threat. Such an arousal is not what I have been calling a defensive emotion. It seems certain also that some emotions impute no external causality at all, e.g. love, grief and joy. The lover who insists, 'I can't help loving you', or 'You made me love you' is an infrequent and, I think, marginal case. To love art, a child, one's companion of many years, gardening or silence, it is not necessary, definitely not usual, and perhaps even abnormal to insist by one's attitude that what one loves is making one love it. Defensive emotions, then, are but one kind of emotion, instances of which are distributed among the various groupings of emotions that we commonly make.

Inapplicability of the judgement/feeling distinction

The judgement/feeling dichotomy, required if the causal view is to account for the corrigibility of anger, breaks down when the attempt is made systematically to understand anger in terms of it. We have seen already that the judgement embedded in anger is not simply about the anger-object, but about the angry individual himself. What A is doing that is relevant to his being angry is seen by B not simply as conduct wholly external, but as conduct *just in so far as it affects him.* An unselfconscious judgement, or even an earnest assertion, *entirely* about another would be independent of anger and therefore would not be the sort of accusation that anger makes. The accusation that is anger, on the other hand, being explicitly or implicitly self-referential ('Alison, you are being unfair to me'), *cannot* be independent of the experience of anger. If the content of that judgement is that one is being psychologically or emotionally violated, it cannot be a sincerely made judgement without being also a feeling or experience of being violated (which the angry person takes himself to be). (This means that anger of the kind we are studying is not concerned wholly with another's deviation from a principle, but with violation of personal rights – of rights that constitute him the kind of person one is. The offence is experienced as a deep violation of what one is as a person.) Thus, what B thinks is his perception of A's offensive conduct can be *nothing other than* B's taking offence. There is no perception of offensiveness that is not also a taking of offence.

Someone might object that the perception and the feeling might be separate yet always concomitant. I consider this objection a concession that there are no good grounds, beyond a need to defend the causal view, for dividing anger into two components, a cognitive one and an affective one, judgement and feeling. These are abstractions drawn for some localized purpose from a total conduct in a total social situation engaging the organism totally, and in the present context are profoundly misleading.

So, agentively speaking, B's anger is not what the causal view of his anger implies it is, namely, a complex reaction consisting of several sequential moments, including an evaluative judgement and a subsequent affective arousal. It is not first a perception of offensiveness followed by a taking of offence. It is, instead, one thing, a totality, a being-offended-at-a-perceived-offence. Our taking-offence does not depend upon the other's offensiveness; it *is* (our perception of) his offensiveness. Our anger does not depend upon the other's malice (or callousness); it *is* (our perception of) his malice in so far as that malice has any power to anger us. Our anger-judgements concern both our adversaries and ourselves at once; it is not merely that we are blameless *because* they are blameworthy, but we are blameless *in* their blameworthiness. Our exoneration *is* their culpability. In anger, accusation equals self-justification.

In passing, we should note that from this point of view we can readily understand the perhaps infrequent but undeniable cases in which we perceive that another's angry act is maliciously intended towards us, and yet we are not reciprocally angry, but compassionate. A compassionate perception of malice is not a taking of offence, and *as perception* differs from one that is. Malice can be perceived; offensiveness against one's person cannot. This is because offensiveness is inextricably connected with the perceiver's sense of being violated in his personal rights, which sense involves a self-justifying appeal by the perceiver to a system of moral principles, principles with which he might or might not be concerned on this particular occasion. It is more accurate, therefore, to speak of taking offence than of being offended. At the same time, it is possible for one person, A, without taking personal offence, to perceive another, B, to be violating – i.e., offending against – the system of principles that constitutes him a person. For A to perceive this is for her not to see B offending or violating her personally, but instead undermining himself. One cannot be disenfranchised from the moral order by another, but only by oneself; hence, perceiving another in this way can be an accurate judgement, whereas taking offence cannot. Such cases tend to be ignored by people who hold the causal view of anger, and when they don't ignore them they tend in an *ad hoc* manner to adduce factors such as traits, dispositions and moods in order to account for them causally.

In a causal view, reciprocal anger is impossible

Unexamined, the causal view may seem to accord with our intuitions well enough, but in fact it has counterintuitive implications. In this section I shall give examples of such implications.

Angry people assume that the individual(s) they are angry at can be reciprocally angry at them. But in so far as they are angry, they do not and cannot really believe this. In his anger at A, B believes that A is to be blamed – is morally responsible for – his anger, and therefore that A could desist from her offensive attitude towards him if she wished. This makes that attitude different in kind from *his* anger, since he is certain that, given the provocation, he can't desist. If he were to suppose otherwise – if he were to concede that she is angry in the same sense in which he is angry– he would be conceding that she is exactly as free of responsibility for her anger as he believes he is for his, and therefore that she is not malicious and not morally responsible for his anger. This concession would constitute a giving up of his anger. In his anger he can't believe she is angry in the same sense in which he is angry.

Someone might say B could believe himself mistaken in his judgement against A: but though it is true that he might be mistaken, if he believed himself mistaken he would no longer be angry. He can allow that (he is mistaken and) she is really angry only if he is not angry. This is another of the counterintuitive implications. (An angry person might *say* that the individual at whom he is angry is reciprocally angry at him. 'Boy, is she ever angry at me!' But this does not mean that he believes she is angry in the same sense in which he is, i.e. justified in being angry. It means that she is accusing, not that she is legitimately self-protective.) It might also be objected that in being angry B can allow that A is angry *if* he is willing also to allow that she is mistaken in *her* judgement that *he* is maliciously feigning anger. But though he might well allow that she is mistaken, he would in doing so be conceding that she is not responsible for her anger, and this concession would be tantamount to his not being angry.

So under no circumstances can B or any other person consistently believe that two people can be angry with each other if he is one of these people: as far as he is concerned, the other person, the anger-object, can be angry only if he himself is not angry. And if he allows that she, the anger-object, *is* angry, he must believe her mistaken in her judgement about him and hence not be angry with her. Nor can anyone holding the causal view of anger consistently believe that any two people can be angry with each other unless he believes that each is mistaken about the other: if A is really angry then, if B is angry, A is mistaken about B, and the same is true of B.

It only compounds my case to realize that part of what B finds offensive may be his sense that A is capable of holding this very view about him: that he can't be angry because she is. Or, even further, that A may be holding that *he* has this view and is excusing himself by means of it, saying in his heart that *she* can't be angry because *he* is. There is no end to this kind of self-consciousness – or, I should say, this consciousness of 'what we must be doing together' – and no end to the even higher-level offendedness it can induce in the other.[4] The offensiveness of these anticipations of the other's metaperspective on the situation consists, I think, in a sense that it is a deep violation of one's own rights of autonomy and privacy. This goes some way towards explaining why in altercation with intimates we can feel outraged and indeed ravaged to the core of what we are.

Anger's resistance

The problems concerning the reciprocity of anger seem minor when compared with the inability of the causal view to account for the aspect of anger which I will call its *resistance*. Resistance is an accompaniment of being angry that cannot be reconciled with the causal interpretation of the angry person's defensiveness. It is a rival interpretation of that defensiveness. I want to mention three different, closely related, descriptions of the angry person's resistance. These will at first seem unrelated to the familiar, highly individualistic, notion of resistance. There *is* a relationship, however, and I will point it out in the next section.

First, if it were true, as the causal view maintains, that anger is a sincere and straightforward self-explanatory judgement (whether correct or mistaken) to the effect that it is a defence against threat, the behaviour of angry people would be strikingly different from what it is. A threatened person tries to flee from or to terminate the threat. But characteristically, an angry person does not behave in either of these ways. Instead he seems to cling to the threat, to make use of it, even to provoke it – sometimes, for example, by picking a fight out of the blue, by obsessively brooding over his wounded condition, by overstating his case in a manner that aggravates the other party, or by fueling up the quarrel if the other shows signs of letting it die. He may demand satisfaction but typically won't be satisfied. If the other leaves or even dies, he will, if he remains angry, tenaciously carry his grievance with him in his imagination.

A   I can't take this carping, snivelling attitude of yours any more.
B   Well then, leave. No one's forcing you to stay.
A   You think this marriage is holding you back in your career, don't you?
B   I never said that.
A   But you think it, don't you? Don't you?
B   Talking with you doesn't do any good. Let's just forget the whole thing, OK?
A   Oh, so you're not going to talk it out, huh? What's wrong. Afraid of the truth?

If A were merely defensive and not resistant (whether or not an external threat actually existed), she would not insist upon an interpretation of B's conduct that is unfavourable to her.

The behaviour of the angry person resists the demise of its provocation; it refuses to let its provocation die. In a non-psychoanalytic sense this can also be called its obsessiveness or compulsivity. Though from A's point of view she is merely defending herself against an external threat, whose victim she feels, from another perspective we can see that she is resistant to the loss of that threat, i.e. obsessive about keeping it alive.

B   Forget it, will you?
A   Why should I forget it?
B   Just get off my back.
A   How would you feel if I accused *you* of wrecking *my* career?

The causal view cannot tell us why A resists letting go of the threat she believes B presents. In other words, it cannot explain why what she calls a threat is, for her, an offence, a provocation. As we have seen, the threat itself, or even the perception of threat, whether accurate or not, does not explain this. This is because in the causal order the threat is unconnected with the system of rights to which she may or may not be making a self-justifying appeal at the moment. The offence, the provocation, as I have already pointed out, is an event in the moral order, not the causal one.

The second way to describe anger's resistance is as follows. The focus of debate between angry people, either spoken or silent, is almost always upon one issue: whose accusation is right? We might suppose that this issue could take one of two forms: (1) whether one or the other actually did, or meant to do, what one is accused of doing, and (2) whether one's doing it (or meaning to do it) was sufficient to anger one's accuser. But it cannot take the second form; from the angry person's point of view there can be no debate about the sufficiency of the provocation to provoke. Once it is seen as a provocation, the issue for him is settled.

> B   What I said was no cause to fly into a rage and attack me.
> A   I suppose you'd like it if I said that to you.

It is settled because, as we see here in the case of A, she actually has her angry feelings. If B is acting as she thinks he is, then in her mind there is no possibility that he is not causing her to feel offended – because she *is* offended, and *at* (*with*) *him*. The only question for debate is whether one or the other did what he or she is accused of doing, i.e., whether the accusing judgement is true or false.

But in spite of this fact, seldom is either of them willing seriously to consider the possibility of being mistaken in this judgement. Instead, this possibility is systematically resisted. If the causal view were sound, one would expect the protestations each makes of his or her own innocence to be considered by the other. Why not consider this possible way out of a miserable situation? The causal view provides no answer to this question. Indeed, except in infrequent cases, these protestations only infuriate the other more.

> A   Look, I haven't said a single thing that's unfair to you.
> B   Oh no, you're never in the wrong are you? You're even too good to live with.

This is but another version of anger's resistance to its own dissolution. On the causal view of anger, there is no accounting for this – no reason why the angry person would not be relieved to discover his anger-judgement mistaken.

Here is the third description of anger's resistance. We have seen that, so long as B is angry, he cannot understand A to be genuinely angry. Instead, he is sure that her accusations of him, and her protestations of doing her best to control herself in the face of his onslaught, are fraudulent. She cannot really have the anger-feelings she says she has. She is cynically using him; she is feigning. This assessment is in fact an aspect of his angry accusation of her. And for her part she senses this accusation, and in so far as she does she feels accused of feigning. Later we are going to see that, whether or not he is actually angry and accusing her in this manner – or indeed even knows of her existence – she feels accused simply in virtue of *her* anger. But she is in an unassailable position to know that she has her anger-feelings and is not merely pretending. Hence, since she knows her feelings are real, the charge that B makes against her – that she is not legitimately self-protective, that she is to some extent feigning – is preposterous. Yet she does not treat this charge as preposterous. She does not laugh at B's accusations or ignore them or even toss them off lightly, as one would the charges of a lunatic or a child. On the contrary, she is obsessive about the need to defend herself against them. She cannot let anything just drop, no matter how inaccurate or absurd. Indeed, it seems that the more outrageous his suggestions are concerning what she is trying to do to him, the more outraged she feels. She will say: 'I can't let him get away with that' or 'He's attacking my integrity', when what he's saying ought not to matter if it really were preposterous. She might say: 'But others might believe him', but she could just as well carry on like this if they were alone together on an island. The persistence of anger in the face of the perceived preposterousness of anger's provocation is a matter so curious that contemplation of it ought to throw almost all previous theorizing about defensive/resistant emotions into confusion. It is the aspect of anger that is least compatible with the individualistically oriented causal view.

THE AGENTIVE VIEW OF ANGER

We have seen that the viewpoint from which the resistance of anger can be recognized and its self-deceptive character entertained – I call it the agentive view – is one that rejects the idea that the angry person is sincere in her defensiveness. It is a viewpoint from which the agent is seen to be 'up to' something else entirely – something that the agent herself is unable to discover. Agentively speaking, anger is self-deception. It should be clear that I do not mean by this that defensive emotions might be instrumentalities by which people deceive themselves, as when one cannot think clearly because of being 'too emotional', e.g. infatuated or upset. I mean that these emotions might themselves be self-deceptions.

Before setting forth the agentive view, I want briefly to indicate, as promised, the relationship between the description of the angry person's resistance I have already given and the standard, individualistic, essentially clinical account of resistance. This clinical account is fraught with conceptual problems so great that it has created widespread scepticism in the past about the very notions of resistance and self-deception. Showing that the agentive view is free of these problems is a crucial part of my argument.

By the standard account, the causal view of anger fails not because it makes a causal judgement concerning its own genesis (which, as we shall see, is the agentive explanation of its failure), but because the causal judgement it makes is false. This account leads straight to the position that the resistant emotion-judgements we are talking about are unconsciously motivated. To see this, observe what happens when we try, as the standard account does, to give a causal alternative to the angry person's self-explanation in order to account for resistance. Since the threat the angry person perceives won't explain her nurturing response to it, there must be some other motivating belief that will explain it. What is this belief? It must be (1) a belief (or at least a suspicion) that the facts are not as favourable to her as she insists, and (2) a belief she is not sensible of having – a hidden agenda underlying her conduct, if you will. Such a belief she must be holding in a special cognitive status or on a special cognitive level to which he has no acknowledgeable access. It is commonplace now to characterize this state of affairs by saying she is motivated unconsciously. Thus we see how a search for a causal explanation of the angry person's resistance inevitably leads to the postulation of unconscious processes.

To add to this appearance of unconscious motivation, the angry individual resists too forcibly any suggestion that her case may not be airtight or that she seems to be contributing to her misery herself. When she manifests such resistance, it appears to observers that somebody has gotten uncomfortably close to the truth – that her preoccupation with the threat she says she is under is really her effort to ascribe responsibility elsewhere for what she is doing,a responsibility she unconsciously knows or suspects is hers. For if she did not in some peculiar manner or on some 'level' know or suspect it, we want to ask, why would she ever resist a probe that got too near?

Not merely anger, but self-deception in general, is standardly conceived to be unconsciously motivated. This unconsciously motivated or 'dynamic' self-deception is a problematic conception. According to this conception, an individual brings it about that she actively disbelieves something that she otherwise knows (believes, suspects) is true. A condition for her bringing this about is that she knows (believes, suspects) it to be true. Without this knowledge she would have no occasion for deceiving herself. (Presumably her motivation is the painful or embarrassing nature of the truth she thus knows.) So she must believe in one sense what she makes herself disbelieve in another. It was to avoid this obvious contradiction that Freud devised, and a long line of successors endorsed, the notion of unconscious processes: it is consciously that the self-deceiver comes to disbelieve what she believes unconsciously. But this move creates as many conceptual problems as it is designed to avoid, problems that render it completely unacceptable.

The treatment these problems require is too extensive to undertake here. But we can indicate here that one of the troubles with the notion of the unconscious is that it separates the resistant emotion from its motivation. Given the separation, the resistant individual must be thought to be reflecting, in an inner, and insulated, dialogue, upon what she is doing, and in addition to be denying or belying it by her responsibility-evading anger. Her self-conscious judgement that she is being victimized is preceded by and is in response to another, unconscious, self-conscious judgement she is anxious to belie. So it is the doctrine of the separation of resistance and its motivation that lies at the heart of the 'monodramatic' character of the causal view of anger.

This separation of the resistant act from its motivation, though apparently an epitome of commonsense, is simply unsupportable where anger is concerned. For it is but an alternate means of making the distinction, mentioned earlier, between judgement and arousal. Earlier we considered this distinction in regard to the accusatory aspect of anger, and saw that we have reason not to think of that aspect as affect-independent. Now, when the issue is resistance, we are considering the distinction in regard to a supposed self-reflective assessment, and will shortly see that here too we have reason to think this assessment an affect-independent judgement.

Here then is the challenge: to account for resistance without recourse to unconscious processes – without recourse, that is to say, to a motivation for resistance that is separate from the resistance. Whatever it is that the angry individual resists, it must be found in her accessible (conscious) experience of the social world she finds herself in. (No trait, pattern or disposition explanation will do when the task is to explain motivated resistance.)

This sort of motivation for resistance is already implicit in the agentive view of anger. Agentively, an angry attitude is an act, embedded in a social pattern of interactions, that takes itself not to be the act that it is; what the angrily resistant person takes herself to be is straightforward, which is to say, one who is *not* resistantly taking herself to be straightforward, for that is a resistant and unstraightforward thing to do. Fundamentally, it is her act of self-misconstruing that she is misconstruing. It is not something independent of that act that she is misconstruing; it is not something that could possibly be an object of reflection. Whatever self-monitoring might be going on is a systematic misconstrual of the self-monitoring that is going on. There is no room, therefore, for a self-reflective act of judgement to intervene between what she is doing and her act of belying what she is doing. Instead, what she resists admission of, by what she is doing, is precisely the same act as her resistance. Here, in the agentive view, is the suggestion of a motivation for getting or staying angry – a motivation for self-deception – that is not separate from the act of self-deception itself. In other words, it is a motivation that is not separate from the act that resists admitting this self-same motivation (which resistance takes the form of insisting that it is being provoked).

Search for a metaphor of defensive emotion as action

Before developing this account of self-deception, it will be helpful to have, for the cognitive aspect of anger, a metaphor that does a better job than *judgement* of capturing the self-consciousness or self-referentiality, as well as the purposiveness, of that emotion. One candidate is *self-assertion*. Because it is inextricable from the feelings of anger, what has been called the judgement-component might better be thought of as an act – an expression or avowal – that is *itself* resistant to admitting what it may apprehend, albeit self-deceivingly about itself. The resistance can be thought to consist in the contrariwise assertion made by the judgement: 'self-assertion' seems a fitting name for such an act.

We can go further. If anger is a kind of self-assertion, it is not necessarily a linguistic kind of assertion. It is more an assertiveness that may receive no verbal formulation at all, either spoken or silent. Much of the quarrel between Alison and Brent could have been, and no doubt was, carried on by means of offended looks, pouting or morbid feelings. I do not think it bizarre to say that the self-assertion – the avowal of self-justification – involved is the emotion itself and its behavioural expression. There is nothing about either cognition or conduct that coerces us into thinking that either judgements or assertions need be explicitly formulated. They need not have a particular 'logical form' in order to refer to or represent states of affairs. P. Saffra is said to have broken the hold upon Wittgenstein of the picture theory of propositional meaning by a contemptuous gesture of the hand familiar to Neapolitans; 'What is the logical form of that?' he asked (Malcolm, 1958, p. 69). We roll our eyes, purse our lips, fidget, wince, sigh, etc., and in so doing express our views – and other people get the message – even when there is no separate inner formulation of those views. The unarticulated informational content of such behaviour is what the current study of paralanguage in psychology is all about.

Yet, in spite of the advantages of self-assertion as a metaphor for the kind of thing anger is, someone might say: 'If anger is self-assertion, it must depend upon straightforward perceptions of the situation in which it is attempted, including an apprehension of itself. Even a self-assertion whose nature the asserter cannot appreciate while carrying it out (which is

the kind of self-assertion that anger would be) is a representation of itself.'
In answer to this objection, I can only say that the fact that the metaphor of
self-assertion doesn't forestall this 'representational' or 'reportorial'
interpretation is enough to send us looking for a better metaphor. What
might it be?

To answer this question, consider this. Anger seems less an attempt to
represent or even insist upon one's being a particular kind of person
coping with circumstances, and more an attempt (albeit an inherently
futile one) to *be* – to establish, make or constitute oneself – that way.
Anger seems a sort of *self-constitution.* It and the other defensive
emotions we are studying are, to use Sartre's phrase, 'magical transformations' of oneself and one's world.

But to this idea of self-constitution there are objections that must be
met. The most serious objection for my purposes is that if, *per impossibile*,
anger were conduct undertaken deliberately, it would be a cynical
misrepresentation, could not take itself seriously, and therefore could not
be anger. Further, when we act we may deliberate about doing so, may
forbear from doing so, etc.; but these things are not possible with anger.
Since for these reasons it appears that anger cannot be action, it must
instead be precisely what it takes itself to be, namely, not action at all, but
passion.

We must be cautious about objections like this, which during my earliest
thoughts about this subject would have seemed to me damning. For this is
an objection that arises *within* the causal view of anger. But outside of that
view, and within the agentive view, the story is otherwise. In anger, a
person perceives herself and her circumstance in a particular manner –
'under a certain description', as they say. This is not the accurate, agentive
description that is available to others. She has intentions and motives, to
be sure, but these pertain to the situation as she sees it. She might
deliberate, she might forbear, but only in respect of *her* understanding of
things. Hence she is not scheming about how she will assert or constitute
herself as angry, make herself justified, provoke others to provoke her or
otherwise misrepresent herself. She is instead concerned about how to
cope with provocation, whether to restrain herself, how much more she
can take, why she has to be the object of so much calumny, etc. It does not
follow from this that she is not doing what we can agentively perceive her
to be doing: it does not follow that *her* understanding is correct. Otherwise, she would understand perfectly what she was doing and her self-
deception would be impossible. (We must be careful to avoid
question-begging.) So her trying to cope with and defend herself in a
situation angrily perceived simply *is* doing what from a straightforward
observer's point of view (which is a point of view she cannot have) can be
seen as strategically and systematically making herself angry, victimized,
justified, etc. In the end, all we learn from the objection is what we already

know, that the agentive view of anger cannot be reconciled with the experience of anger. There is an interesting question that would take us in a different direction from the one I have chosen for this chapter. When operating within the causal view of anger, the issue before us was: Anger is a judgement that proffers an explanation of itself; can this explanation be true? Within the agentive view an analogous issue is: Anger is 'self-constituting'; it is an act that takes of itself as not responsible for itself. Can this self-constitution succeed? Can the angry individual ever coincide with what in her anger she takes herself to be? The answer, I believe, is that, the more she tries, the more incongruent with herself her self-image becomes. As long as human beings are angry, they are not, in spite of an existential cliché to the contrary, what they take themselves to be.

Assuming, then, that we have made legitimate our conception of anger as self-conscious action, we can say agentively that anger is defensive not in virtue of anything external, but in virtue of itself. The imputed anger-cause has powers to provoke anger if and only if it is perceived angrily. And now that we are able to say this much, we are in a position to formulate the fundamental question for this chapter. What does this defensiveness consist in? How does her imputation of causality to an object explain the angry person's obsessive resistance to the demise of her anger, or, in other words, her compulsivity in maintaining it?

DEFENSIVENESS, RESISTANCE AND OBSESSION

We seek reconciliation of anger's defensiveness with anger's resistance. To do so, we must account for the appearance the angry person gives of resisting admission of unconscious motives, but we must do this without countenancing the existence of such motives. To explain why such a person is resistant and nurtures rather than flees his provocation, it is insufficient to say that making himself a victim is simultaneously making another his victimizer. This answer fails to tell us why he would not simply let the anger die and thereby divest the anger-object of its angering power. It fails, in other words, to account for resistance.

There have been accounts that abandon the phenomenon of resistance; mine would be such an account if I were to stop at the insight that anger is an assertion of an emotional kind that asserts itself to be something that is, in fact, otherwise than what it is. On the strength of this insight, I could have said that the angry person deceives himself about what he is doing by doing it in the sense that he eclipses for himself the truth about his act (and the situation relative to his act) in performing that act. (See Solomon, 1973.) But in the absence of any other account of resistance, his only motivation for resisting would have to be the nature of what he deceived himself about, and of this (according to the view we are discussing) he has no inkling.

Another solution is only a little less unsatisfactory. It is this: Being angry means believing that one's provocation bears in upon one independently of one's own will or control. Given this perspective, 'letting one's anger die' can only mean relinquishing one's defensive feelings and intentions and thereby leaving oneself defenceless against the provocation, which in this perspective would retain its power to offend. As long as one's anger continues, one cannot see that abandonment would divest the anger-object of its angering power.

This answer tells why angry individuals would be unlikely simply to abandon their anger or let it die. But it does not tell us at all why they characteristically resists opportunities to let it die, e.g. when the object of their anger shows signs of withdrawing from the field of battle. We still need to know what there is about anger or its provocation that explains the phenomenon of resistance, and that does not, in explaining it, invoke unconscious processes.

We shall see that the answer is provided by the very property of anger that the causal view cannot account for. The threat A presents B cannot be preposterous in B's eyes; (I spoke earlier of another reason for his outrage, namely, that he feels violated in his person.) Angry at (with) him, A contends that he is maliciously or inconsiderately causing her anger and hence is not really angry at all, but feigning anger. But for his part, he knows directly that he *actually* has his anger-feelings and is therefore*not* merely pretending. So her anger at him, which he reads as an accusation that he is feigning, has got to be preposterous in his eyes.[5] Surprisingly, it will turn out that the very absurdity (in his eyes) of the charges against him is the property that makes these charges indispensable to his anger. Their absurdity is an aspect of his sense of outrage. It is this that simultaneously presents him with what he sees as an external provocation *and* justifies the position he is taking (i.e., convinces him that his anger is genuine). Nor, as we shall see, is it necessary or even relevant that A is levelling these charges: anger is a self-troubling activity in which one cannot fail to feel both assailed and justified by such preposterous charges, irrespective of what the anger-object is actually doing.

I take it that the strength of the argument I shall offer resides partly in its explicit Wittgensteinian recognition that anger is essentially avowal, which is to say a kind of conduct, rather than an inner experience of which angry expressions are some kind of report. To think it an experience, as B does, is to assess one's expressions on the basis of their accuracy, i.e. their truth: hence, in his own eyes, B has got to be right in the argument because he *really is* angry. But as Harré has pointed out repeatedly, the correct assessment of social acts is in terms not of truth but rather of sincerity. B is unjustified not because he is giving false reports of his inner state, a charge he knows to be preposterous, but because in the avowing conduct that is his anger (which includes his continuous monitoring of that conduct) he is insincere, dissembling.

In order to make my case, I shall offer a series of observations, each of which provides only an aspect of the total account of these matters. At the conclusion of this section it should be clear why I say that the very preposterousness of the charge, in B's eyes, is what makes it essential to his self-justification.

Anger's presupposition

Recall that B regards his anger-feeling not merely as not his responsibility, but rather as not the sort of thing which *could* be his responsibility. Given his view of it in having it, it is not the sort of thing he could produce in himself by taking thought, exerting his will, etc. Hence, in maintaining this view of his innocence and passivitiy in regard to his anger, he *presupposes* that he either (1) has the anger-feeling and is innocent and passive or (2) is not passive and does not have any anger-feeling at all, but is instead feigning his anger with an intent that can only be cynical and malicious. In other words, he presupposes that if he is not right about the cause of his anger-feeling – if he rather than A is responsible for it – then he hasn't got that feeling. But if he has got the feeling, then (in the absence of a mistake on his part, which, as we have seen, is a possibility he would in his anger reject) she is causing it. The agentive possibility, that he is responsible and yet has the feeling, is not a possibility as far as he is concerned, since the feeling is not, in his view, the sort of thing he could be responsible for.

A falsified world

Agentively speaking, both alternatives in the disjunction he presupposes (sincere or feigning) are false. Thus it is that anger brings into being not simply the interpretation of itself that it asserts to be the case, and that is false, but a complement of alternative interpretations of itself which are both false. It is this 'horizon' of possibilities taken together – it is the entire *outlook* in which the agent, B in this case, is either to be justified because innocent or condemned because malicious – that is the content of the angry person's self-deception. His self-deception is in this sense the falsification of the world, rather than simply the falsification of a situation within the world. That is, what is false is not just what he asserts about himself and his situation, but what he presupposes by that assertion.

Since as far as he can tell this outlook exhausts the possibilities, he cannot consider the agentive truth (which is that he is the author of his anger) without giving it a false interpretation. On his interpretation this truth can only mean that he is not really angry at all, but cynically pretending, whereas the agentive interpretation of this truth implies no such thing. His exhaustive horizon of false possibilities stands over against the truth about himself, which is not included in this horizon. The truth lies beyond the array of possibilities he can conceive. Correlative to this excluded truth about himself – B in this case – is the excluded truth about the anger-object, A, who for B must be either malicious or at least callous (if B is justified), or else caused to be angry by a malice of B's own (if B is not justified). In fact, A, the anger-object, is neither of these. The issue in B's mind is, Who is culpable here, A or I? Whereas the real issue is, Is the issue what B thinks it is? If he were not angry, would culpability be the issue? The answer is, No. That the issue in his mind is guilt and innocence is a function of his anger: a self-deception. The supposed cause for this effect does not exist apart from the effect itself. B will not be free from self-deception until this ceases to be the issue; until he is no longer angry; until he can perceive malice, if it is there, without perceiving offence.

Self-constitution as denial

Now the self-condemning alternative to his anger-judgement about himself and his anger-object is for B not merely an abstract or unsuspected possibility. That is, in constituting himself A's victim, he does not merely constitute a spectrum of alternative possible interpretations of his apparent anger, only one of which is his concern: on the contrary, constituting himself a victim is constituting himself as *not* being a victimizer. One cannot maintain mere innocence, mere justifiability, mere sincerity or, more obviously yet, mere freedom from responsibility. To undertake such self-assertion presumes that a question is being raised. A self-forgetful individual can be what he is, e.g., sincere or innocent, without regard to what he is not. But asserting or constituting oneself sincere or innocent by one's anger can only be in respect of some presumed (or presumed pending) charge. One can maintain one's innocence only by raising the issue of whether one is guilty (or acknowledging that issue if it has already been raised); one can maintain one's sincerity only by raising (or acknowledging) the issue of feigning; one's justification, the issue of culpability, etc. It is as if one assserted the favourable alternative by denying the unfavourable alternative – as if anger were a non-verbal way of saying, 'I am *not* the kind of person who could be morally responsible for this.'

The general point I am making is a central and poorly appreciated cornerstone of Sartre's conception of bad faith: self-constitution is actualizing one particular possibility over against others in a spectrum of possibilities all raised together by the act of self-constitution itself. The particular form of self-justification we call anger is a denial of being the sort of person who is insincere or malicious. Negation mediates the self-approval implicit in anger. One is not merely sincere, but sincere-as-opposed-to-feigning, etc. To be angry one must, in Sartre's words, become 'a Not upon the face of the earth'.

The indignation in anger

Let us move one step further. It might be thought that B's insistence upon his victimhood and his consequent innocence involves a denial of his culpability only in the sense of entailing it conceptually, so that all I've said could be true without B's actually being sensible of the condemnatory interpretation of his conduct that he denies. But in fact, this interpretation is one he feels the urgent need to deny, as if he were in the dock. The substance, as it were, of his accusations of A and his indignation in response to her accusations of him is his effort to exonerate himself in respect of whatever it is he is blaming her for, and this cannot but take the form of an active denial of his culpability in this very respect. A is defaulting on the psychological contract he and she have together, not he; she, and not he, is the agency behind his wounded responses and her purportedly wounded ones. So B raises *in his own mind* the troublesome possibility he denies in the very act of denying it. His maintenance of his innocence and her guilt is equally a denial of his own guilt and of her innocence. His is a *self-troubling* act. This point, crucial for establishing that what B is defensive about and resistant to admitting – what seems to motivate his over-elaborate protestations of innocence – is not pre-existent to or even independent of his denial of it, but an aspect of that denial.

So B is engaged in defending himself against the most intimidatingly personal kinds of charges completely apart from whether A, his anger-object, is actually levelling any of them against him, or even knows of his existence. In itself, anger is a kind of paranoia; just in virtue of being angry an indivudal conjures all the adversaries he must have in order, in his own eyes, to be angry justifiably, which is the only way one *can* be angry. His insecurity, then, his wrestling with self-doubt and guilt, his struggle to overcome a perpetual sense of unworthiness – all these are not less agitated, concerned or energetic than his anger itself, because they *are* his anger. The sense of being violated as a person, in regard to one's rights, is equally nurturing of the violation: a kind of self-induced social disequilibrium. A judgement always implicit in one's anger, and as central as any other, is 'I am not wrong about myself.' This judgement is implicit in such exclamations as 'Look, I mean what I say!' 'I'm not just kidding.' 'Why do you think I've been sobbing for the past week?' 'Don't think you're going to get away with this!'

It is in this way, then, that the agentive view accounts for his defensiveness. The angry person feels an urgency to defend himself against a possibility that (contrary to his belief) does not arise independently of his anger. There is a necessary connection between his denial of the possibility that he is a fraud and the urgency he feels to deny it. His self-deception does not consist in *directly* rendering the truth about his action inaccessible (by an internal act such as repression, for example), but in his creation of a possibility he feels a need to resist, which possibility, together with his asserted victimhood, excludes the truth.

Apart from this necessity, there are other reasons why B will tend to be defensive. For example, he will tend to construe any circumstantial evidence that is discrepant with his story as an attack upon his integrity. Obviously, if A is reciprocally angry at B, he will understand her anger – her self-defence against him – as an attempted condemnation of him; we have seen that this is because of the presupposition of his anger. But he will construe discrepant evidence in this way even if she *isn't* angry and therefore is not an accomplice to his anger. Since she *cannot* cause his anger-feelings in the way he supposes – they are constituted by him – she is necessarily innocent of his accusation against her. She is innocent not in virtue of anything she is or isn't doing, but in virtue of the nature of his anger itself. She is innocent in virtue of what *he* is doing. But this is an extraordinary sort of innocence he cannot possibly comprehend, precisely because he cannot (as long as he is angry) comprehend his anger as his activity. It is an innocence that consists in her being *neither guilty nor innocent* (in his sense of 'innocent'); that is, it consists in her being incapable of producing his anger because that anger is not the sort of thing external events can cause. But to him this extraordinary innocence – incapable of producing it in virtue of the kind of thing it is – can only be misunderstood by him as the more ordinary innocence – 'capable of producing it without actually having produced it'. Thus, any evidence that his accusation is not fully founded, any suggestion that A might be innocent in the first, extraordinary sense, will unavoidably be perceived by him to be evidence of his innocence in *his* sense – the ordinary sense – and *therefore* as an accusation of feigning, an attack upon his integrity, etc. All discrepancies or dissonance between his story and the circumstances threaten to condemn him, whether or not anyone means them to – and certainly whether or not they in fact do, for they do not!

We can learn something about the pressure to condemn himself that an angry person like Brent defends himself against by noting that sometimes, manoeuvring within the horizon of his self-deceived world, an individual will pre-empt this pressure by denouncing or even berating himself. We take Brent as our example because, as the preceding bits of dialogue show, he is the one most prone to self-flagellation.

B It's too painful to be dragged through all this again.
A Here we go again. You pick a fight and then accuse me of hurting your feelings.

> B   Look, I know you think you could have married a more successful person.
> A   If you start on a pity party again, I'm going to walk right out of here.
> B   I shouldn't have picked the fight. I don't know what's the matter with me.
> A   I can't stand you being such a wimp.
> B   When I get mad at you I guess it's because I think you can do everything and I can't do anything.
> A   I'm going to take my shower, Brent. . . .
> B   I wasn't really mad. I don't know why I do it. I guess I just resent not getting ahead in my job as fast as you are.

This self-deprecating 'turning-inward' of the anger has its own self-righteous satisfactions. When he needs to, Brent can say, 'At least I'm being honest with myself now.' If he makes the ploy that he rather than Alison is morally inferior, his excuse for his moral shortfall is just as effective as any superiority ploy might be.

The constant possibility of this self-humiliation tells us something about the indignation of someone like Brent when he is not condemning himself. He is, he believes, suffering at A's hands – yet in spite of this, as we just saw in the discussion of innocence, he feels a claim is being constantly made against him on her behalf. He feels what he construes to be a 'moral' summons or demand to recognize and acknowledge this claim. He is experiencing a pressure, counter to his claims on behalf of himself, to abandon those claims in the name of honesty. From his perspective, this would require him to make no consideration for himself in virtue of his suffering (which he is sure is real), but to give every consideration to A, whose conduct is wounding and angering him. It is no wonder that 'duty' for him is onerous. It calls upon him to relinquish his rights of protection and redress, to humiliate himself by conceding the claim presented on A's behalf that she is innocent. If made, this concession would be humiliating because, from his point of view, it would not be made in virtue of her conduct, i.e. because her present conduct entitles her to it (remember, he feels she is wounding him). It would have to be made *in spite of* her present conduct – in spite of the fact that she is wounding him. This means the concession would be made in virtue of something besides her conduct – for example, A's person, her rights or status, her inheritance, perhaps even her sovereignty, any of which implies his inferiority in regard to this something and his exclusion from full participation in the system of rights that constitutes him the person that he is. This pressure B feels to demean himself contributes both to what seems to him the irresistible provocation of these demands – 'How can I not be upset when she humiliates me like this?' – and to the justifiability of refusing these demands. 'They require too much. They are outrageous. Only a fool would grovel at her feet the way she wants me to.' (A similar story can of course be told of A's indignation.) Anger is indignant; it contains the seeds, at least, of paranoia, and also of self-hate. (This is true even, or perhaps especially, of those who angrily wield great power.) A possible next step for either party in *any* exchange of angry accusations is always something of this sort: 'Oh yes, I'm always the one who is in the wrong, aren't I? [quivering chin] I know I'm not the sort of person who's good enough for you. I just wish you wouldn't rub it in, that's all.'

The neutralization of all conceivable opposition

The absurdity of the felt attack brings us to the question, Why isn't the attack scoffed at or ignored? Why is self-condemnation the only perceived option? The answer is, it is the very preposterousness of the perceived claims against the angry individual that in his eyes establishes him as authentically angry, innocent of fraud and justified. He raises the self-condemning possibilities in a preposterous form, and it is this that creates his conviction that he is right. He is obsessed with the evidence against him because it *is* his justification, and yet contemptuous of it because it is absurd; it justifies him precisely *because* it is absurd. (I. A. Richards said, 'Contempt is a well-known defensive reaction.') The only conceivable opposition to the self-justifying claims the angry person makes is thus neutralized. We might say: the angry person nurtures this evidence against him by denying it, and precisely in order to be able to deny it. What other evidence could one cite for one's own sincerity and innocence than that the alternatives are preposterous? No other evidence could conceivably count. *We see that, without taking thought, even unconsciously, but because that is the only way he can see the situation*, the angry person indignantly considers the possibility of his fraudulence – he perceives it as a demand that he condemn and demean himself – and in the same stroke discredits it, because in view of his suffering it is preposterous.

On this account, no unconscious psychological process is involved in resistance. All the features of anger I have described are simply aspects of angry conduct responsive to others in a pattern of altercation expressed in a rhetoric of accusation and excuse. What is resisted is not a truth harboured in a consciously inaccessible psychical region, but the obverse of the act of resistance itself – a possibility raised only by denying it. We have not explained anger causally; instead, we have understood it as an act carried out as a component of an interactive pattern, anticipating and construing the responses of others.

SELF-DECEPTION

Bad faith

In my critique of the causal view of anger I said that characteristically a person who is angry concerns herself with whether the object of her anger actually did what he is being accused of. She is exercised to deny that she is mistaken about the accused. Yet her point of view allows that there is a possibility that she is mistaken, and that if she is there is no cause for anger. Why then is she resistant to the possibility of liquidating her anger by entertaining the possibility of a mistake? How does the agency view account for this?

The answer seems to be that, from the angry person's viewpoint, it is unlikely that any evidence against her position could suggest a *mere* mistakenness in judgement. If B had been trying to say something different from what A thought he was saying – something quite innocent – and if he had presented his case to her, she would have perceived his protestations as asking her to discredit her feelings and to denounce herself (unless of course she had abandoned her anger, or was in the very moment abandoning it). We have already seen why. What to us may look like an honest suggestion that she has judged mistakenly is to her the suggestion that she is the kind of person who would treat him perversely. I am not saying she cannot admit to being mistaken, but only that she will be giving up her anger if she does; hence, if she isn't giving up her anger we can understand why she isn't openly considering the possiblity of being mistaken, and (as is our common experience) pointing out her mistakes isn't likely to dissuade her.

> B   I didn't mean to attack you when I brought up the shower. I wanted to help. When I came home, I was feeling romantic and kindly towards you. That's the truth Alison.
> A   Oh, so I'm the one who picked the fight!
> B   (Controlled voice) No, I didn't mean that. I only meant that I wasn't trying to make you feel bad.
> A   So I made it up, huh? Why would I make up such a thing? Do you think I *wanted* to ruin the whole evening with another ugly fight?
> B   No. I'm trying to say that what you thought I said to upset you, I didn't really say, so there's no need for us to be angry with each other.
> A   That's it! Just gloss over it. You come home and start talking about how late I am, after I've done all the work, and I'm supposed to say, 'Oh thank you, my Lord, for pointing out my shortcomings to me.' You expect me to believe you? You think I'd be upset if you hadn't come home making insinuations?

There can be no admission of mere mistakenness unless the angry attitude and conduct have been or are being abandoned. It is precisely because our accusing emotions, such as contempt, hate, sadness, self-pity and embarrassment, as well as anger, *are* avowals and not merely inwardly held experiences reported by expressions of emotion that our beliefs do not determine our feelings. Cognitive therapy to the contrary, the beliefs ingredient in these emotions change only with, and not prior to, the relevant changes of emotion. (It might be possible to test this claim empirically.) Notice too that, however ill-founded or trivially motivated or irrational one's anger may seem to others – however, easy it may appear to correct it with a little information – it is in one's own view a response to an affront or a wrong. There is no anger the angry individual does not experience as a passion for justice.

There is an intuitive insight in Sartre's work on bad faith for which we can now provide a conceptual explanation. He said that bad faith is a determination in advance to be persuaded by inadequate evidence, to be unfulfilled by the evidence, to take as the normal ground for conviction a condition of being not quite convinced. In Sartre's work, there is no adequate accounting for this 'determination'. But the agency view provides an account. The existence of one's own anger-feeling (together with the logical obstacles to consider whether one might be mistaken) is enough in the angry person's mind to establish the culpability of the anger-object. *Post hoc ergo propter hoc.* What objective evidence there may be, one way or the other, is inaccessible as such. Given one's experience of a feeling that can only seem the effect of offensive conduct, it is all but inconceivable that one could be wrong.

B Ask Fred if I wasn't singing your praises when we were driving home.
A So what if you were? It was probably to make him jealous or to try to make up for the bad things you've said about me.

In a sense, the evidence against the anger-object is the anger itself. The angry individual is convinced *a priori* that the case against her *must* be deficient, and she contents herself with almost any supporting evidence, even though partial, inconclusive, speculative or even imagined, that is validated by that conviction.

The appearance of unconscious processes

In the study of self-deception, the trick is to take the phenomenon of resistance seriously without invoking unconscious processes. This I have done in respect of certain self-deceptive emotions. The account I have given of these emotions does not appeal to unconscious processes, yet it shows why such processes appear to be taking place. From a point of view that construes anger-feelings on a 'passive reception' model the resistance I have described – resistance to the demise of the provocation – cannot fail to be thought of as resistance to admitting an unconscious belief, motive or intention. What gives rise to this appearance of the effects of an unconscious belief is a genuine resistance, but it is not a resistance to admission of such motives. It is instead something in the angry person's interaction with the object of her anger that she resists, namely, a moral claim against her, the ludicrousness of which is the core of her self-justification. The accompanying appearance of an unconscious motive for resisting this claim is an artefact of her anger (and of the sympathy of observers); it is not an internally held truth that her act elipses. There is much indeed that the angry person does not know about herself or her situation, as we have seen, but this does not reside in an unconscious. It resides instead in an outlook publicly available to everyone besides her – an outlook that she does not and cannot enjoy because of being angry. Thus, the agentive view accounts for resistance – indeed, the sort of resistance whose motives cannot be acknowledged – without appealing to anything unconscious.

One way to state the problem with the classical conception of self-deception in this assumption, which as far as I know has not been called into question before, what the self-deceiver resists (e.g., the possibility of her own malice and fraudulence) is the very belief about which she deceives herself. On this assumption, the *only* mode of self-deception available is *concealment* from herself – e.g., relegation of a belief-content to a 'level' not available to consciousness. This is because the assumption entails that the belief about which she deceives herself is the same that she would openly believe were she not self-deceived. To suppose that beliefs are thus invariant through a range of psychological states, from straight-forward attitudes to self-deceptions, is to assume that self-deception is a matter of the *status*, such as a 'below-awareness' status, of a belief. On the agentive view, on the other hand, what she resists in her anger – the possibility of her own malice and fraudulence – is *not* what she is deceiving herself about. It is not what she would believe upon coming out of self-deception. It is an artefact of the anger itself, and it would not be a possibility – it would disappear – without the anger. Thus, what she denies in self-deception, like what she affirms, is not possible to deny (or affirm) apart from the self-deception. On the agentive view, her self-deception is not a matter of concealing a belief, but a matter, we might say, of believing perversely, and this in turn is a matter of participating insincerely in that 'form of life' in terms of which she learned to maintain herself as a person.

So now we know that self-deception must be possible because we know that anger is possible (and also the other defensive/resistant emotions). But we've always known that self-deception is possible; what we've needed to know is, *how* is it possible? And now we are faced with the same question about anger. It is true that the classical contradiction in self-deception theory is gone, but this minimal answer is not enough. We want to ask, If the agentive account is sound, why would one ever adopt the 'rhetoric' of anger and similar delusory emotions? We can't appeal to provocation to answer this question, since anger is the author of its own provocation. Why would self-justification be anger's desperate concern if the issue of whether one is justified in the anger does not exist without the anger? This is a question I treat in a separate paper (Warner, 1986).

NOTES

1   This is not the occasion to discuss the epistemological status of remarks such as these on the meaning of a word, but if it were, it would address the difficulties of discovering, in any other way than I discovered it, what we mean by 'anger'. And how did I discover it? I discovered (learned) it by becoming a representative member of a community that uses this word, helped by myriad responses to my attempts from other such representatives, until I became one of those in whose verbal conduct, the responses of others to me, and the written and recorded traces of these interactions, that meaning is now reposited. In other words, I became participant in those social forms that Wittgenstein called 'language games', which are institutions of conduct mediated by speech. I would also address the difficulties inherent in establishing 'empirically' how others in this community use the word 'anger' independently of how I use it, when in order to do so I must presume agreement about the meaning of many other closely related words, whose meaning for us would not remain unaltered if we discovered that 'anger' means something different from what we thought.

2   It is possible to regard angry people as others operating on one 'meta'-level or another, relative to those they are angry with. In the example, being justified in our treatment of another consists in our moral assessment of whether the other is justified in his response to us. Our response to him is mediated by our contemplation of his justification relative to the moral order that we have in common. Later, I shall return to these considerations.

3   Harré has pointed out to me that, in some cases, the conduct may be an 'amplification' of the offended status, as with the Australian aborigine and the Trobriander, and in other cases, such as the increasing deference of the Korean, a 'minimization' of it. I put these qualifications in scare quotes because they themselves are part of the anger. They are part of the self-justifying manoeuvre that is taking place. For example, the Korean's deference can be thought of as a move in a metagame, by which he can punish more effectively by displaying himself as morally superior to those at whom his anger is directed.

4   Harré pointed out to me the relevance of these considerations to the opportunities for and limits of reciprocity in angry interactions. For an account of these 'metagames', see R. D. Laing's Sartrian description of interactions as essentially political (Laing, 1972) and Harré (1979).

5   There are no doubt other reasons why his anger, with its implicit charges, is absurd. For example, as Harré has pointed out to me, it undercuts the conditions of personhood and respect of personhood on which the relationship is constituted, and also, obviously, the possibility of the altercation they are having with one another. But this sort of absurdity is not blatantly held before in B's attention, like the (perceived) accusation that he is merely feigning.

REFERENCES

Harré, Rom (1979)   *Social Being*. Oxford: Basil Blackwell.
—— (1983)   *Personal Being*. Oxford: Basil Blackwell.
Laing, R. D. (1972)   *Knots*. New York: Vintage Books.

Malcolm, Norman (1958) *Ludwig Wittgenstein, A Memoir*. London: Oxford University Press.

Sabini, J. and Silver, M. (1982) *Moralities of Everyday Life*. Oxford: Oxford University Press.

Solomon, R. C. (1973) Emotions and choice. *Review of Metaphysics*, 27 20–41.

Tavris, Carol (1982) *Anger: The Misunderstood Emotion*. New York: Simon and Schuster.

Warner, C. Terry (1986) Immorality and self-deception. In press.

9

Envy

J. Sabini and M. Silver

I am envy, begotten of a chimney-sweeper and an oyster-wife. I cannot read, and therefore wish all books were burned. I am lean with seeing others eat. ... But must thou sit and I stand? Come down, with a vengeance!

Christopher Marlowe, *The Tragical History of Doctor Faustus*

ENVY AND THE SEVEN DEADLY SINS

Traditionally, envy has an important place in the account of human misbehaviour. Cain slays Abel because Abel's sacrifice is more pleasing to the Lord. A Greek is cautioned to avoid the envy[1] of the gods as well as that of his fellows (see the Athenian justification for the institution of ostracism: Ranulf, 1974). St Thomas Aquinas excoriated envy as one of the seven deadly sins, which not only are evil in themselves but spawn other transgressions. Recently, Helmut Schoeck (1969), a sociologist, hypothesized that deep-seated envy and the fear of the envious are primary energizers of society's ills – both revolution and social stagnation. Heider (1958), in a less-sweeping analysis, proposed that envy is one of a group of negative affects caused by the positive state of another: a person is envious when he wants what someone else has just because that person has it. According to Heider, this feeling, in part, derives from an 'ought force' – people who are similar should have similar outcomes.

Although much has been written about the sources and deleterious effects of envy, to our knowledge no one save Heider has given sustained attention to a linguistic or phenomenological analysis of envy itself. This may be because we usually think of envy as a feeling, in the sense of an immediate unitary experience. Although questions are often asked about the causes of this experience, the experience itself is treated as a given, not susceptible to dissection. Yet 'envy' is often used in ways that do not manifestly involve experiences, i.e., to characterize an individual or supply a motive for action. We shall analyse the ways the concept of envy is used;[2] perhaps we shall then discover something about envy as an experience.

Depending on the context, 'envy' may refer to an emotion ('He was overcome by envy'), a reason for action ('He acted out of envy') or a characterization of an action as a transgression of a moral order, i.e., a sin. 'Sin' suggests that envy is part of a system of norms treated by a community as objective, i.e., having an existence independent of particular purposes at hand (see Berger and Luckmann, 1966, Schutz, 1973). This objective aspect of envy, open to commonsense discussion, clarification and debate, can be captured by the analysis of commonsense talk. We shall first examine envy as a sin and then turn to the subjective facets of the phenomenon – envy as a motive and as an emotion.

Envy is a curious sin. It is felt to be a nastier, more demeaning, less natural sin than the others. It is also puzzling – why people are envious is less obvious than why they are greedy or lustful. Merely look at 'envy's' entry in a dictionary of thoughts (Edwards, 1936): 'Every other sin hath some pleasure annexed to it, or will admit of some excuse, but envy wants both' – Burton. 'Other passions have objects to flatter them and which seem to content and satisfy them for a while, but envy can gain nothing but vexation' – Montaigne. As Rochefoucauld has pointed out, 'We are often vain of even the most criminal of our passions; but envy is so shameful a passion that we can never dare to acknowledge it.'

To articulate the odd qualities of envy, we need other sins to compare it with. The seven deadly sins provide us with a list of some of the more common, serious flaws in human nature – greed, sloth, wrath, lust, gluttony, pride and envy. Moreover as it is a traditional collection, and since envy is already a member, we can be sure that our frame of comparison is not solely determined by its convenience for our analysis.

What do the seven deadly sins have in common? Most generally, these words characterize a 'self' as demeaned, lowered or spoiled (see Goffman, 1971, for the notion of a spoiled identity). These sins typify a person as greedy, lustful, arrogant, lazy, etc.; yet the typification is not supported by other evidence about the self,[3] but by the particulars of the person's misbehaviour. This is also true of other sins: if we say that a person is a murderer, then the behaviour to which our charge points is killing.

However, the misbehaviours to which the seven deadly sins point have a distinctive feature. Consider the accusation that a person is greedy. The behaviour to which we point is that of acquiring goods. Killing another person is held to be wrong in itself in a way that acquiring a possession is not. Each of the seven deadly sins, apparently excepting envy, implicates behaviour that is not in itself evil. When I call someone greedy, I point to his acquisitiveness, but I do not call acquiring goods, in itself, evil. *Sloth* is a sin, but rest, a commandment. Although *lust* is considered evil, enthusiastic conjugal sex meets with clerical approval. Righteous indignation is a mark of virtue; *anger* is a sin. A priest denounces our *gluttony*, but may wish us a hearty appetite without being a hypocrite. *Arrogance* is evil, but self-assurance is said to be the seal of maturity. The six deadly sins other than envy *involve acts having goals which are not in themselves evil but which have been done inappropriately or to excess.* Moreover, not to pursue the very goals which are the ends of the proscribed sins is held to be pathological. Frigidity, anorexia and cowardice require explanation; sexuality, appetite, and self-assertion do not. It is easy to understand why these sins are, to quote Nietzsche, 'human, all too human'. To convince someone that we are incapable of lust or gluttony is to convince them that we are more or less than human. The deadly sins, then, point to charcateristic flaws of our common nature. Envy is out of place on this list, as it does not appear to point to a natural goal. This is the paradox of envy.

Envy as reason and cause

Envy is also advanced as an *explanation* of action (see Schoeck, 1969); yet if we consider the other sins, we shall see that they are rarely used with explanatory force. One way to explain an action is to point to its goal, but in most cases the other sin words are applied to behaviours where the goal is patent. To accuse an adulterer of lust does not report a goal for his acts, as if what he hoped to achieve by his adultery were mysterious.[4]

Perhaps sin words are used as causal explanations as opposed to explanations in terms of reasons and goals. In everyday talk we often give a causal account of an action when it appears to have no sensible goal (see Peters, 1958). (For present purposes we are bracketing the question of the ultimate compatibility of cause and reason explanations: see Melden, 1961; Alston, 1967.) A causal explanation of general paresis is sought precisely because shaking, stumbling, losing one's memory and dying are not the sorts of behaviour for which sensible goals can be found. Given that the goal of a sinner's misbehaviour is only too transparent, what aspect of it remains to be accounted for by a causal explanation? The only aspect of behaviour that sin words might explain is what caused a person's *transgression* in the pursuit of a normal goal. Although these sin words imply a lack of restraint, they do not, in themselves, supply its cause; at most they are stand-ins for a causal explanation. For instance, in Catholic theology original sin is held to be the real cause of the failure of restraint to which the sin of lust points. Similarly, a hypothalamic disorder is held by physiologists to be, in some cases, the cause of overeating – gluttony. Envy seems to have more explanatory force than the other sins; it appears to give a real causal account and not to be merely a stand-in for one. 'He overate out of gluttony' seems otiose; 'he maligned her out of envy' seems explanatory. We hold in abeyance how envy functions as an explanation. We shall be particularly interested in whether envy has more explanatory force than the other sins, and if so, in what way. But we first turn to envy as an emotion.

Envy as an emotion

Envy can be a feeling that possesses a person, takes hold of him, often to his dismay. Envious thoughts may come to us unbidden – even when we wish we could join in the celebration of a friend's success. Envy is often a conscious feeling, i.e., it is episodic, as in 'I had a pang of envy' or 'I felt envious for a moment.' Yet we must be careful when we speak of envy in this manner. Using a phrase like 'the experience of envy' may mislead us into assuming that answers have been given before we have explored which questions are to be raised. For instance, do we experience one mental content when we report an experience of envy, or is envy a way to characterize a class of contents? Are there particular experiences which in themselves constitute envy, or is it necessary that we have these experiences in a particular context? How does the presence or absence of the feeling of envy qualify our judgement of whether a person is envious? As is our wont, we shall explore these questions in regard to some of the other deadly sins, and then, having created a framework, we will turn to envy.

What might be passing through the mind of someone who is guilty of the sin of lust – fantasizing a sexual tryst, focusing on chest or crotch bulge, perhaps experiencing a genital tingle? But having these experiences is not equivalent to being guilty of lustful thoughts. We doubt that this description would currently be taken as evidence of lust, even by a conservative clergyman, if it were to refer to the thoughts of newlyweds on their wedding night. A Victorian, on the other hand, might hold that these thoughts would be lust if entertained by a woman, though not by a man. (St Paul might damn them both.) Lustful thoughts are not just thoughts with sexual content, but rather are thoughts of sex which are held by a particular community *to be inappropriate to their context.* Although the other sins can be shown to fit this mould, the sin of envy is again problematic. Although all thoughts about sex are not necessarily lustful, all lustful thoughts are about sex. What are envious thoughts about? Are they all inherently envious, or does context separate the sinful from the moral?

Often, people argue that they could not have acted out of envy, as they didn't feel envious. Is this a compelling argument with the other sins, or does it appear credible because of some odd quality of envy? Consider lust – suppose a friend says he was not guilty of lust, because he was not horny that day – he just happened to find himself in bed with a woman: does this modify our judgement of lust? No. If his partner were married and not to him, then our judgement of lust will depend upon our sexual ethic and not upon knowing his prior mental state. Is the prior experience sufficient, even though not necessary, to determine that someone has acted lustfully? No. There are many chaste horny people, either through extraordinary effort of will or, more typically, through lack of opportunity. Hence, pointing to a prior feeling can neither support nor defeat a charge of lustfulness.

Although a prior feeling is irrelevant to the moral characterization of an action, it may be a part of a causal explanation; for example, 'I woke up that morning and couldn't think of anything but sex. If I hadn't been so horny, I would not have accepted her invitation and ....' Here a heightened sensitivity is given as one part of a causal account of why something happened. So for the other sins, a prior mental experience does not enter into moral characterization of acts, although it may furnish evidence of an unusual sensitivity, which could enter into a causal acount. But envy, perhaps because it lacks an obvious goal, seems to require the *experience* of envy in a way greed or lust does not. If someone denies that he acted enviously because he did not feel envious, is he denying that a certain experience entered causally into his action?

Summary

We have thus far argued that the other deadly sins involve a person's transgressing in the pursuit of a typical human goal which is not, in itself, evil. We have also pointed out that sin terms rarely have explanatory value but are merely stand-ins for a causal account. We have touched on the relation between experience and behaviour for these sins. At first glance, envy does not fit the pattern of the other sins; we have pinpointed sources of this peculiarity. In the next section we hope to show how envy, like the other sins, may be analysed as a characterization of a person that is grounded in particulars of his behaviour and experience. In doing this we will see the manner in which envy does parallel the other sin terms, and we will attempt to show how the paradoxes of envy arise and how they may be resolved. Our approach will be to focus first on presentations of self in interactions affected by the issue of success. We will then see how the characterization 'envy' emerges from the problematics of such situations.

ENVY AND SELF-PRESENTATION

There are many ways to lose standing in 'the local scheme of social types' (Garfinkel, 1956) and wind up with a depreciated self. There are depreciations that we are fully responsible for and those that we merely fall into: crimes, faults, failures, gaffes and missteps. We may be depreciated through another person's malice: be falsely accused, snubbed, ridiculed, taunted or spat upon. Most curiously, a loss of esteem may just happen to us, not through our fault or another's spite, but merely because selves are linked in the social world. A person may be diminished inadvertently, as a by-product of someone else's success. It is often held that, if an individual feels diminished by another person's accomplishments, then it must be due to his own idiosyncratic sensitivities, perhaps a 'low self-esteem'.[5] But when particular cases of success and failure are considered, what others have or have not achieved is a background to our assessment. It is not only, as social comparison theory holds (Festinger, 1954), that a person evaluates his assessment of his own status by comparing his assessment with that of others, but also that his status, as evaluated by himself or others, is inherently comparative. Is there a question as to which of the two following events is a greater loss: being rejected for a position that all of one's friends have attained, or being rejected when they too have failed?

How can a person defend an eroding position? If this erosion is caused by something she has done or has been accused of doing, then she has many options for remedial action. She may deny the charge and even return one, calling her accusers malicious or rude. She can give a justification (showing how her apparently inappropriate behaviour was, in fact, appropriate) or an excuse; or she can accept the charge while pointing to mitigating circumstances. She can belittle the import of the charge by admitting that it describes her behaviour but also claim that, although it constitutes a major flaw in someone else, because of her particular position it is not a major flaw in her (e.g., an inability to add is a major failing in an accountant but a peccadillo in a poet). Barring all else, she might apologize, stating that her action was unfortunate. If these accounts are not tenable, then she could acknowledge that the act was typical of her behaviour in the past, but that she has reformed (Goffman, 1971). As a last resort, if she cannot lessen the loss of face, then she can at least avoid those who know of it.[6]

The remedial actions we have discussed can be used only when the individual and her audience are aware that there is something that must be answered for. This occurs when a moral charge has been made, or when the act is of the sort that typically calls for an explanation, apology or excuse. Consider, however, the predicament of someone indirectly demeaned by the accomplishment of another. The defence of her lowered status must be made in the absence of an accuser or an overt charge. She has done nothing; hence she has nothing to retract or justify. Nor can she point to the other person's deliberate harm-doing, for there hasn't been any.[7] The options open to her to prevent or minimize diminution of self are severely restricted and hedged with difficulty.

This situation can also be uncomfortable for the individual announcing his success and even for witnesses. Consider a social occasion in which a success demeaning one participant is announced. The person demeaned has a problem in preventing an erosion of his esteem. Yet he also, as a party to the interaction, is expected to participate unreservedly in the acclaim undermining his position. The person who has succeeded is also in a difficult spot. He understandably wants his success known. Moreover, if he does not announce his success during the encounter, he may insult those present, his reticence being taken as evidence that their approval is irrelevant to him. On the other hand, any excess or poor timing in his announcement may leave him open to the charge of being a braggart. If he attempts to underplay his accomplishment, he must do so skilfully. Otherwise, he will be guilty of false modesty, or, even worse, he may be seen as implying that his attainment is so easy the others should have achieved it also. Even a third party who cannot be demeaned by this particular success faces a problem: he must celebrate the success of one without tactlessly underscoring the lack of accomplishment of the other. Examining how a skilful third party can carry off this delicate manoeuvre will exhibit tactical possibilities without bringing up additional complexities of personal gain or loss.

How can he carry it off? He may take the fortunate person aside and congratulate her privately; he is then free to ignore or play down the matter in front of the person who might be hurt. If such an opportunity does not present itself, he must make his congratulations in the presence of the person whose position may be undermined; he will have to moderate his use of superlatives. Better yet, he might link the success to the other person's support, if this is at all plausible. He will also have to attend to the temporal limits of the celebration by changing the topic at the appropriate moment. He might, if he can find a suitable context, pick a topic that will allow for the failure to display his accomplishments.[8]

What if a person whose status is threatened were to use these strategies? It is doubtful we would call him tactful. Using such techniques for selfish rather than altruistic ends seems wrong, further demeaning their user. Yet it can be misleading to identify a characterization of an action with its presumptive motive. Judgement of an action, as we have found in our analysis of the deadly sins, depends more on the appropriateness of the action to its context than on the goal of the actor.

Suppose someone who is speaking has gone on too long. Changing the topic would be merely an appropriate response to a tedious monologue. Consider a braggart for whom you supply the missing modesty by taking him down a peg. If this were done with finesse, in an amusing manner at the right moment, your response would be an entertaining repartee, not a transgression. Everyday conversations involve a measure of self-presentation; they also involve changes of topic, turns at display, affirming team aspects of individual accomplishment, etc. If each of these parts is played without mishap, the propriety of the interactions is not called into question, even in the case where one or more of the participants could be seen as demeaned by the success of another. But what if one of them blows his lines, for example, changes the topic too quickly, or brings up his own success in a forced, clumsy manner? It is in this case that the question of ulterior motive arises – not because we had not realized that the parties in the interaction were displaying themselves or attempting to limit the display of others, but because, until this moment, these aims were part of the natural fabric of the conversation.

As Peters (1958) points out, in commonsense talk the question of motivation arises when a transgression of social norms is believed to have occurred. In such contexts, talking about motives, in part, supplies the goal that the person was pursuing when he transgressed. Of course, should they be pressed participants in almost any interaction could supply such goals for perfectly blameless behaviour (self-enhancement, for instance, is one common goal of ordinary conversation). However, supplying a motive in commonsense talk both points to a goal and characterizes its pursuit: saying that a person acts out of envy both describes the person's goal and has the force of characterizing that goal as inappropriately pursued. When someone inappropriately pursues a goal of self-protection, common sense is likely to use the epithet 'envy'.[9] This is especially true if he has done so by limiting the import of another's success or in some other way devaluing that person.

Let us closely consider this analysis of the commonsense use of 'envy'. It assumes the truism that people wish to have worthy selves. The transgressions, or sins, that occur in pursuit of this end are broadly of two sorts – those of pride and those of envy. The charge of pride (arrogance, boastfulness, being a braggart) arises when the transgression is in the service of self-enhancement; the charge of envy arises when the transgression is an attempt to prevent self-diminution. Since an attribution of envy presupposes that the actor's self has been diminished, or at least that he perceives this to be the case, to be seen as envious is doubly damaging. Not only has he committed a transgression, but he has tacitly acknowledged his lessened worth.

Not every situation of inappropriate *self*-protection is proper grounds for a charge of envy. A student who, after failing an exam, calls its fairness into question in a patently self-serving manner is a whiner and complainer, but not necessarily envious. However, if he remarked on the unfairness of the test only after being informed that acquaintances had gotten A's, his behaviour might warrant a charge of envy.

Only those situations in which the advantages, attainments, etc., of other people demean an individual provide a context for the charge of envy. 'We also envy those whose possession of or success in a thing is a reproach to us' (Aristotle, *Rhetoric*, book 2, chapter 10).[10] But for a person's behaviour to warrant this charge, it must not merely be an inappropriate response to being demeaned, it must be an attempt to protect against being lowered – or at least must be interpretable as an abortive or blocked attempt to do so. One might burst out weeping or commit suicide because of another's success. These actions, though inappropriate, need not be envious. They may be signs of a painful recognition of, or perhaps incorrect belief in, the diminution of one's status, rather than an attempt to cope with a diminution.

There is one other element in our analysis of envy: the method of self-protection is by undercutting the other person. If we redouble our own efforts because we are shamed by a rival's attainments, we are not envious. In fact, if our efforts are honourable, we are exemplifying the competitive spirit, indulging in virtuous emulation.[11] A coach, in the movies if not in life, may stimulate the waning spirit of his team by dwelling on how the other side's superior performance is making fools of them. Although being put down by the other side's performance is here a goad to competition, we wouldn't call this extra effort envious, even if it were to involve poking, gouging and other unfair play. The team might be guilty of poor sportsmanship, but in so far as they are attempting to prevent themselves from being demeaned *by trying to win the game*, they are not acting enviously.

We have thus far examined the question of when an action gives rise to a *charge* of envy. But when we call a person envious, we are typically not judging a single action, but a character, or self. The fact that envy refers to both actions and selves adds further complexity to our analysis. 'Envy', to borrow and extend the use of Ryle's phrase (1949), is a 'mongrel categorical' term, one that both characterizes a single act and makes a claim about the actor. Because of this duality, commonsense actors may introduce evidence to support or refute a charge of envy in a specific case by mentioning facts that are not about the action under discussion and might hence seem to be irrelevant. These facts are about the person's typical ways of perceiving and reacting to situations involving his esteem. An action by someone who often brags is more easily seen as envious than the same act by someone else known for modesty. An individual who is obviously sensitive to slights, snubs and other signs of lowered status will similarly be more liable to be seen as envious. An evidence of fragility in a person's feelings of self-worth may feed into the assessment of whether or not he is envious. The judgement that a person is envious is not reached simply by counting the number of times that he has committed envious actions. Judgements about selves are not collapsible in any simple way to judgements about actions.

Envy as sin, motive and emotion: a question of fit

We now return to the question raised earlier: whether envy fits into the pattern of the deadly sins. We noted that the other sins have goals which are not evil in themselves. Their pursuit is considered normal, natural, obvious, not requiring special explanation; it would be the failure to pursue these goals which would require a special explanation. What made these behaviours sinful was not their end but the inappropriate manner of their pursuit. The sin of envy, on the other hand, seemed less human, as it did not appear to involve a natural goal. We have attempted to demonstrate that there is a natural goal of envious behaviour and that, as with the other sins, it is its inappropriate pursuit which constitutes the sin. When we say that a person is envious, we are, in part, implying that a goal of her behaviour is to prevent herself from being demeaned. We have detailed a number of ways, both appropriate and inappropriate, that she may attempt to do this. When we say that a person, in pursuing this goal, is envious, we ground our statement by pointing to a particular class of inappropriate behaviours – behaviours that directly or indirectly attempt to belittle another person.

Our analysis has, in a sense, debunked the mystique of envy by removing its mysterious quality. We have argued that the goal of the envious person is no more perverse than that of the miser or lecher. But if his goal is so obvious and natural, why do thoughtful commonsense actors find envy so perverse?

Let us look again at our comparison of envy with the other deadly sins. Adultery is obviously a member of the class of sexual acts; whether it is evidence of lust depends only on our sexual ethic – our evaluation of its appropriateness. Inappropriately belittling someone, on the other hand, may be an aggressive act, an envious act, a thoughtless act or an arrogant act. It is only when we can connect someone's act of belittling to a goal of self-protection that we see it to be a token of envy. To be greedy, a person need attempt nothing more than to acquire a good; an envious individual is attempting to belittle another person in order to do something else, i.e., to protect his self-worth. Envy's perversity derives from the fact that demeaning somebody is an end – something that the envious individual is trying to bring about – but not the ultimate goal. What makes envy natural – self-protection – is not what betrays the act as envious – undercutting another person. What is immediately perceived is not the ultimate goal – self-restoration – about the indirect manner of achieving this goal – demeaning another person. The sexuality in a sin of lust is patent and unavoidable; *the self-protection in the sin of envy is obscured by envy's secondary but more overt end, the demeaning of another.*

ENVY AS AN EXPERIENCE

We have treated envy in the perspective of sin. This vantage makes salient the active, goal-pursuing nature of the phenomenon and slights its passive, afflicting, involuntary quality. Thus, it naturally places envy in the context of talk about motives, but obscures perhaps the most prominent aspect of envy, that it is an emotion that comes on a person, torments her and preoccupies her against her will. Although the perspective puts to one side what is most prominent to first reflection, it does so in order to fix on what is distinctive about envy.

Consider a relationship stricken by envy. A friend joyfully shares the news of her fine achievement. The less successful friend wishes to, wants to, intends to and indeed tries to create a sincere congratulation fitting with the excellence of her accomplishment and the warmth of their friendship. But he botches it. The congratulations come out forced, choked, diminished and cool. What is more *prominent*, compelling, about this unfortunate mishap is its unwilled, afflicting character: that it is an *emotion*. But what makes it *distinctively* envy is his failure to come forth with his friend's due. The failure takes on meaning as envy because it is what he would do if in this context he were trying to undercut her accomplishment, i.e., if he were moved by envy. The emotion takes its meaning from the motive. Reversing this perspective and treating the most prominent aspect of envy – that it can be an emotion – as if it were the key to understanding the *motive* envy (as has been done most recently in a rather extreme and diffuse form by Schoek, 1969, in his treatise on the effects of envy) obscures our understanding of envy by treating it as a mysterious homogeneous entity, an essence, whose contingent effects can be collected but whose nature remains untouched. Working on this assumption produces the paradox that each new fact can only increase envy's oddness; e.g., envy is: the sin against the brother (i.e., to those whom we owe the best, we do the worst – Aristotle, *Rhetoric*, book 2); a torment to the envious; more likely to be provoked by small than large differences in lot; etc. Until we use a conceptual analysis of envy, these facts perplex us rather than help us understand.

Starting from the view of envy as an emotion fixes us on envy's aspect as an experience – a content of consciousness – since this is such a prominent part of emotion. Yet, as shown in our previous analysis of the deadly sins, this approach is misleading. For example, when we say that a person is feeling lustful, we do not imply that lust is the content of his consciousness but, rather, that sex is. Sometimes recognition of a reduced position due to another person's accomplishment leads to thoughts that undermine the moral worth of that other person. One may merely notice the other person's unworthiness, or be obsessed by it. On occasion the actor may recognize that his criticism or feeling of outrage is inappropriate. He may realize that his criticism is ungrounded or overblown, that the other's moral failings are none of his business, that his concentration on these failings betrays an obsessive preoccupation. He may also recognize that it is his own diminution by the other's accomplishment that has occasioned such moral charges. If an actor comes to believe that he has reacted in such an inappropriate way as a defence of his reduced self, then he would be said to realize that he has experienced envy. The fact that he has characterized this reaction as envious does not mean that it ceases to occur. It may keep popping into his mind, along with an awareness of tight muscles and pounding heart, even though he realizes that the reaction is inappropriate. Such a recognition may lead to a further reduction in his self-esteem. This realization of the flimsiness of 'self' shown to him by his unwilled and uncalled-for defensive reaction is one of the torments of envy – knowing that he is envious. On the other hand, it is possible to feel demeaned by another person's accomplishments, also feel critical of him, and yet not believe that there is any connection between these two attitudes. Or it is possible to recognize the connection but not believe that the critical attitude is inappropriate; rather, it may be perceived as a justified response to his arrogant behaviour. In this case we might be right, but at another time, even though we did not believe that we were envious, someone else, if she could show that our feelings were overblown or overpersistent, would be warranted in asserting that we were possessed by envious thoughts. She might even convince us that we were envious.

We have argued that some form of criticism, undercutting or demeaning – either overt, implicit or experienced – is necessary for envy. Yet people sometimes firmly believe that someone is envious and may even offer evidence for their assertion, though they cannot point to any belittling. We would argue in such cases that some of the criteria for a person's being envious are manifestly fulfilled, for example, his being shown up by the other person's success. And this leads to the inference that the person is envious, i.e., that the other criteria are also fulfilled. The force of this inference, that the person is envious, is that the person would like to, or has some tendency to, begrudge or belittle the other person's success. If it could be shown that this was not the case, then the inference that the person was envious would be wrong.

As Kenny (1963) would point out, our position is somewhat overdrawn in that commonsense actors do accept 'partial cases' as instances of emotion, even though they deviate from the standard case of emotion. For instance, the paradigm case of fear involves an assessment of threat, a typical symptomology (shaking or trembling) and *qua motive* an attempt to avoid this threat. Yet we meaningfully talk of objectless fear. Consider the case of someone who cowers under a bed and says that he feels afraid. Even though he has not mentioned perceiving a threat, one would infer that he must have done. Yet what if he were to deny perceiving any threat? Must he be lying? To characterize this case *without being misleading*, one would have to call it fear and point out that it is an odd case of fear. In so far as one can grasp, talk about, this odd case, it is because of the features it shares with the standard one.

IMPLICATIONS FOR THE EMPIRICAL STUDY OF ENVY

We have treated envy as a word in a language, a concept people treat as objective. A virtue of this approach is that it restrains the tendency to view envy (or emotions and motives generally) as an entity causally and, hence, contingently related to its consequents: envious actions. Following the logic of this 'realist' view, we might assess the strength of an envy motive, perhaps by a TAT-based procedure, and then discover the relations between 'high envy' and such hypothesized consequents as belittling another. Yet if we did not discover such a relation, wouldn't we say that we were not, in fact, studying envy? Belittling another person is part of what we mean when we say that someone is envious. Treating this as an empirical discovery and not a conceptual clarification is misleading and leads to studies whose persuasiveness actually trades on our under-standing of the meaning of the terms we use – a practice all too common in 'empirical' social psychology (Peters, 1965). Our 'nominalist' approach does not preclude empirical investigations on 'the effects of envy', but it refocuses this research and is a necessary prolegomenon to it.

Instead of searching for the causes of envy, for instance, we might look at the way that selves are linked in our objective moral universe, how people commonly and idiosyncratically interpret or react to this linkage, and the moral failings attendant on these reactions. Envy as a feeling is subjective in that some people suffer greatly from it and others are not touched. As an example, Scheler, in 1910 (tr. 1961), pointed out that women were considered to be the envious sex. Imagine this were true. Instead of looking for the biological or biographical antecedents of women's susceptibility to this particular emotion, we would first look at the determinants of objective comparability in a particular social structure at a particular moment. At the turn of the century, given the restriction on women's entry into careers, politics, etc., the dimensions on which middle-class women, at least, were comparable with each other, e.g., attractive-ness, domestic ability, clothes or husband's earnings, were fewer and *more widely shared* than those in which middle-class men were comparable. This is not a fact about feminine personality *per se*, but about women's position in life. There are further questions to be asked about the idiosyncratic, personal reactions of individual women; understanding this social, structural aspect of comparability gives us a background against which to study its personal expression. Note that the focus of investigation has now shifted from the study of the determinants of envy to how individuals interpret and react to social comparability.

The lability of self-worth is common to depression as well as envy. There are many ways a person may react to a belief that his worth has been lowered. He can try harder, show how the other's accomplishments are really in a different area from his, show how selves are linked such that the other person's success enhances his own; or he may perceive a diminution and do nothing. In the empirical study of envy, we would look for the determinants of why an individual put down another as opposed to emulated the other, competed against the other, dwelt on his demeaning, did nothing and so forth. *The determinants of the selection of any of these responses are different from the determinants of why the person was sensitive to or imagined a particular self-diminution.* Of course, which response is made is related to opportunity as well as personality. We are not denying that some people are more prone to envy than others (Farber, 1961; Daniels, 1964). We believe that this is a most important issue and one we have not addressed. We have attempted to clear the ground for such an analysis.

NOTES

1   This is also sometimes translated as jealousy of the gods. Envy and jealousy have overlapping uses and also areas in which their meanings are clearly distinguishable. If my lover runs away with another man, I might be jealous of him, but not envious. I might be envious of him also if his *savoir faire* in seducing my lover highlights my lack of it (see Kingsley Davis, 1936, for a provocative analysis of jealousy; also Simmel, 1899/1955). One entry for 'jealousy' in the Random House *American College Dictionary* is 'envious resentment against the successful rival or the possessor of any coveted advantage'. Hence in talking about reactions to a success, envy and jealousy may be interchangeable.

2   Our theory treats a central, moral use of the term envy; the way 'envy' is used when a person complains that he is bothered by his own envy or that he has been maligned because of the envy of others. Another common use of 'envy' is as a compliment: 'That's wonderful, I envy you.' Here presumably the speaker is not confessing a delict but doing something else, i.e., saying that 'that' is so wonderful it is the sort of thing which could tempt a person into sin. Compare this with 'your kid is so cute I'm going to kidnap him' or 'that Cezanne is so marvellous I could just steal it'. As Heider suggests, these confessions as compliments are most likely to be used just where they don't literally apply (kidnappers are usually more disciplined).

3   'Self-worth' or 'self-esteem' would be more commonly used here. However, these phrases suggest subjective feeling rather than an objective social fact. In our usage, the self is an object that can be known by the actor and others and has value as determined by socially grounded standards of comparison (see Goffman, 1959; Blumer, 1964). We would reserve 'self-esteem' and 'self-worth' for the particular impression that an actor has of the value of his self. This impression may only loosely fit the facts of his accomplishments. A person may be in error about his own value.

4   In certain exceptional cases, sin terms can furnish a goal for action, and thus have explanatory force. For instance, we might explain that a prostitute's sin is

one of greed, rather than lust. The explanatory power of 'greed' in this example derives from its pointing to a deviation from the obvious goal of a sexual act.

5   We might even say that a person who feels demeaned by another's accomplishments is prone to envy. It is tempting to immediately treat the concept of envy in this connection. Yet to do so at this moment would confuse the issue. Only when the full complexity of this social situation is presented will we be able to elucidate the connection between the sort of depreciation and envy.

6   The extent of a person's objective loss is analytically distinct from the extent of his reaction to that objective loss; e.g., he may perceive that his social self is being lowered yet do nothing to prevent it. Perhaps status in the particular group doing the lowering is irrelevant to him; he isn't a member of the community. At the other extreme, the awareness of a minor loss may possess him, and he may find himself preoccupied with his lowered status.

7   There are other instances of this predicament in the social life; e.g., it underlies the stickiness of dealing with being ignored. The difference between being ignored and being snubbed hinges on the fact that the ignored cannot point to any special dereliction in the distribution of attention; being ignored is cumulative, not involving any overt violation of constitutive rules of social interaction. Hence, it is extremely difficult to deal with.

8   This strategy is delicate. You must choose a topic that will not in any way undercut the success of the person who is celebrating. Typically, the further this area of accomplishment is from the celebrant's, the better. In addition, you must be careful to pick an area of commensurate worth, or you will heighten the contrast and humiliate exactly the person you are trying to protect.

9   Sometimes even an expression of admiration may be seen as a sign of envy if it is stuttered, stammered, delayed or otherwise misplayed. In these cases we would say that the congratulations were insincere. Insincerity is a difficult concept. It is often taken to involve a mismatch between what a person says or does and what he 'really feels', i.e., a disconsonance between expression and internal state. Yet one can sincerely avow love while experiencing a gas pain. Can one sincerely congratulate another while *regretting* his success? This appears to be a difficult feat, but it is possible since it is what is meant by good sportsmanship. In fact, one can congratulate the winner of a race for his superb skill even while telling him you wished that the race had come out otherwise because you had bet on his opponent.

10 We have so far stressed that the linkage among the statuses of individuals is an *objective* phenomenon. Any social actor can understand that a person may be demeaned by certain successes of other poeple, or that someone may attempt to protect himself from being demeaned. This objective aspect of the phenomenon provides us with a necessary background for our understanding of personal differences in reactions to other people's attributes or accomplishments. Using this socially shared knowledge allows someone to recognize that another person is feeling intensely envious even if he himself has never experienced a pang of envy. Some people appear to be much more prone to feelings of envy than do others. It is likely that this is related to idiosyncrasies in the way an individual perceives himself; i.e., he is

susceptible to accomplishments of others that would not even be noticed, or would be considered irrelevant, by the rest of us.

11   Focusing on another's accomplishment and our lack is *likely* to lead to envy but need not. It might result in simple admiration, even though tinged by sadness or depression. Consider two examples both involving depression caused by another's success, but only one announcing envy. In a letter (*New York Review*, 1977), Edmund Wilson described how reading a draft of *The Great Gatsby* saddened him by showing how far he was from mastering a style shown in its polished form by Fitzgerald: 'I was re-reading *The Great Gatsby* last night, after I had been going through my page proofs, and thinking with depression how much better Scott Fitzgerald's prose and dramatic sense were than mine. If I'd only been able to give my book the vividness and excitement, and the technical accuracy, of his! Have you ever read Gatsby? I think it's one of the best novels that any American of any age has done.' Wilson admits depression, and even makes clear how it is Fitzgerald's particular accomplishment that perfectly brings out his own failings; yet he does not come across as envious. Why not? In this passage Wilson is clearly admiring Fitzgerald, there is no trace of backbiting, begrudging, demeaning. In contrast, let us consider a passage from a novel by John Powers (1975):

His family was extremely wealthy. He was good looking and smart, he was a great athlete and he could play seventeen different musical instruments, all at the same time. Worst of all, Earl Benninger had such a pleasant personality that it was impossible for anyone, including myself, to dislike him. Earl Benninger was a very depressing person to be around.

The narrator of this passage appeared to be envious, albeit in a minor key. The force of the passage is not that the protagonist was depressed, but that Earl was depressing; the narrator can be seen as demeaning Earl by making, or at least hinting at, a moral reproach. Since he said that Earl's behaviour is blameless, the reproach is inappropriate and, hence, evidence that he is envious.

REFERENCES

Alston, W. P. (1967)   Wants, actions and causal explanation. In H. N. Castaneda (ed.), *Intentionality, Minds and Perception*. Detroit: Wayne State University Press.

Berger, P. and Luckmann, T. (1966)   *The Social Construction of Reality*. New York: Doubleday.

Blumer, H. (1964)   *Symbolic Interactionism: Perspective and Method*. Englewood Cliffs, NJ: Prentice-Hall.

Daniels, M. (1964)   The dynamics of morbid envy. *Psychoanalytic Review*, 51(4), 45–57.

Davis, K. (1936)   Jealousy and sexual property. *Social Forces*, 14, 395–405.

Edwards, T. (ed.) (1936)   *The New Dictionary of Thoughts*. New York: Standard Book Co.

Farber, L. (1961)   The faces of envy. *Review of Existential Psychology and Psychiatry*, 6(2), 131–40.

Festinger, L. (1954)   A theory of social comparison processes. *Human Relations*, 7, 114–40.

Garfinkel, H. (1956)   Conditions of successful degradation ceremonies. *American Journal of Sociology*, 61.

Goffman, E. (1959)   *The Presentation of Self in Everyday Life*. New York: Doubleday–Anchor Books.

—— (1979)   *Stigma*. Harmondsworth: Penguin.

Heider, F. (1958)   *The Psychology of Interpersonal Relations*. New York: John Wiley.

Kenny, A. (1963)   *Action, Emotion and Will*. New York: Humanities Press.

Melden, A. I. (1961)   *Free Action*. London: Routledge & Kegan Paul.

Peters, R. S. (1958)   *The Concept of Motivation*. London: Routledge & Kegan Paul.

—— (1965)   Emotions, passivity and the place of Freud's theory in psychology. In B. Wolman and E. Wagel (eds,) *Scientific Psychology*. New York: Basic Books.

Powers, J. (1975)   *Do Black Patent Leather Shoes Reflect Up?* New York: Popular Library.

Ranulf, R. (1974)   *The Jealousy of the Gods and Criminal Law at Athens*. New York: Arno Press.

Ryle, G. (1949)   *The Concept of Mind*. London: Hutchinson.

Schoeck, H. (1969)   *Envy: A Theory of Social Behavior*. New York: Harcourt Brace and World.

Schutz, A. (1973)   *Collected Papers*, vols 1 and 2. The Hague: Martinus Nijhoff.

Simmel, G. (1899/1955)   *Conflict and the Web of Group Affiliations*. New York: Free Press.

10

Loneliness

Linda A. Wood

Loneliness is one of the most powerful human experiences, not only because it signals the absence of social connections, but also because the failure to experience loneliness appropriately calls into question one's very nature as a social being. Loneliness can thus be considered a fundamental or basic emotion. But it is rarely viewed in this way. In fact, loneliness is a most paradoxical experience for a number of reasons, not least of which is its problematic status as an emotion. My aim in this chapter is to argue for a social constructionist view of loneliness as a way of dealing with the paradox of loneliness, and to lay out the foundations for a social constructionist analysis. I begin with a brief discussion of some of the reasons for the problematic status of loneliness and some of the paradoxical aspects of the experience of loneliness. I then argue for the utility of a social constructionist perspective on loneliness and examine variations in that construction, particularly across the life-span, but with some attention to individual, gender and other differences. Finally, I discuss social constructions of loneliness as embedded in narratives, and conclude with some suggestions for research on loneliness. Many of the ideas discussed here were developed in the course of research projects I have conducted over the past several years, most notably one on loneliness among the rural elderly (Wood, 1981), but I will not be presenting empirical findings in any systematic fashion. For reasons of space, I shall also be unable to draw out the connections between loneliness and the considerable literature on related concepts such as attachment. Even so, my account of loneliness from a social construction perspective can be only illustrative, not exhaustive.

I wish to thank R. O. Kroger for his helpful comments and suggestions. I acknowledge gratefully the support of the Social Sciences and Humanities Research Council of Canada, the encouragement of the Gerontology Research Centre, University of Guelph, and the contributions of the participants in the rural elderly research project.

THE PARADOX OF LONELINESS

Is loneliness an emotion?

In the literature on emotion, loneliness is almost never mentioned; the major exception is the appearance of loneliness as one of many emotions that are presented in lists in certain types of research (e.g., Averill, 1975). But loneliness is never included by emotion theorists in lists of primary or basic emotions, regardless of how these are distinguished (e.g., by physiological componemts or ontogenetic primacy). One possible reason for this omission is that loneliness is not associated with any obvious physiological manifestations. Although there is no clear agreement on whether emotional experience requires any physiological involvement, either particular or general, most accounts of emotion give some attention to physiological factors as initiating, correlated or consequent factors. In the case of loneliness, however, there is very little discussion of physiological or biological components. Informants' descriptions of loneliness sometimes include what appear to be references to bodily involvement (e.g., tightness in the chest, emptiness in the stomach), but it is not at all clear whether they are describing bodily experiences, or using these expressions metaphorically.

But the lack of any plausible physiological components of loneliness does not account fully for its neglect in the emotion literature, because that literature mentions other emotions for which the physiological aspects are uncertain, for example, envy and jealousy. Perhaps the time-frame for loneliness is too long for it to be seen as an emotion in the traditional sense. Although participants in my research sometimes reported 'emotional experiences' which they described as loneliness, they used the term 'loneliness' more often to refer to cognitions or states of longer duration, such as attitudes, or life conditions (Wood, 1983). Discussions in the loneliness literature of loneliness as a 'feeling-state' recognize, albeit implicitly, the uncertainty of its status as an emotional experience. The issue of time-boundaries on the experience of loneliness has been unjustly neglected, although there is some attention in the attribution literature to variations in the time-course of loneliness and their relationship to inferences about causal stability and to motivational properties of loneliness (Peplau, Russell and Heim, 1979). However, there is no agreement on the precise time-boundaries of emotions.

Loneliness has recently come to be viewed as a social problem (Peplau et al., 1979). In this respect, it differs quite sharply even from other 'negative' emotions. For example, anger is not usually considered to be a social problem, although one among its presumed behavioural manifestations – aggression – is certainly seen this way. But this difference between loneliness and other emotions, while important, does not provide a logical reason for its neglect as an emotion.

In contrast to its infrequent appearance in the literature on emotion, loneliness is referred to implicitly or explicitly as an emotion or feeling in the literature on loneliness. I think that in part this reflects a basic assumption that loneliness *ought* to be an emotion, or that there *ought* to be an emotion like loneliness. In fact, one of the striking aspects of loneliness in contrast to other emotions is its overt moral aspect, although this is rarely discussed in any detail. Yet, the literature on loneliness is infused with moral or 'ought' elements. There is, for example, a moral position embedded in the most frequently used definition of loneliness, that is, as the experience of a discrepancy between existing, and expected or desired, social relationships (Wood, 1978). But this type of definition has not been sufficiently explored, nor have its moral implications been pursued. Some discussions do point out that our expectations and wishes are more than predictive: they are also normative (e.g., Peplau et al., 1979). But the 'ought' implied in such definitions of loneliness is abstract at best; it has not been applied to particular situations or relationships. There have been anecdotal and illustrative examples, as well as some sociological discussions, of expectations for certain relationships, for example, that one ought to have a girlfriend or boyfriend at a certain age, ought to have friends, and ought to maintain family relationships (Gordon, 1976). But there has been no systematic consideration of the relationships one is supposed to have, of the moral force of these expectations, and of their implications for one's worth as a person. Further, there are at least two aspects to the moral issues: with respect to relationships one is supposed to have, as noted above, and with respect to when one is expected to be lonely or is expected not to be lonely. Failure to meet these expectations is not simply surprising: it is seen as 'wrong'.

There has been some attention in the literature to the idea that 'admitting to loneliness' is equivalent to declaring that one is not a worthy person. As Gordon (1976) expressed it, 'To be lonely is to have failed' (p. 15). Gubrium's (1975) single elderly respondents rejected any judgement that they were lonely, not only because they did not believe themselves to be lonely, but also because they resented the negative connotations which they associated with such a judgement. A colleague to whom I mentioned this chapter said he was angry or insulted when people used to assume that he must be lonely because he was single. When I was introduced to a middle-aged man as an expert on loneliness, his first response was, 'Tell me how I can get to be lonely.' His query was ostensibly directed towards finding privacy and solitude, but its message in the context was, 'I'm not one of those.' It has become commonplace to note that, at least in some parts of North America, there is a sanction against acknowledging that one is spending Saturday night or a major holiday such as Christmas alone. This is demonstrated by the eagerness with which people account for such events: 'My essay is overdue'; 'I'll be leaving the next day to join my family.'

But if it is 'bad' to be lonely, it is also bad, perhaps even worse, not to be lonely when one is supposed to be. Many authors have observed that failure to display the appropriate emotion is negatively sanctioned. The important point here is that, even though an emotion is prescribed, this does not mean that it is condoned. That is, prescribed emotions can be negative and excessive (Armon-Jones, 1985; Wood, 1983). For the recently widowed, failure to admit to profound and debilitating loneliness calls into question one's adequacy as a spouse, one's devotion to the deceased. To be alone on Saturday night without an excuse, and not to be lonely, implies that there is something wrong, that the person does not form attachments, that people are not important. So loneliness may as well be admitted to oneself and to others. Larson, Csikszentmihalyi and Graef (1982) found that high school students reported only moderate feelings of loneliness when they were alone on weeknights, but intense feelings of loneliness when they were alone on Friday and Saturday nights. People in these situations face a difficult dilemma: They must choose between displaying loneliness, which is both required and negatively viewed, and avoiding a display of loneliness, in which case they are negatively evaluated for failure to display the appropriate emotion (Wood, 1983).

Writers who have pointed to the negative connotations of loneliness have suggested that these connotations in themselves constitute a problem, that they are 'wrong', harmful and can cause needless suffering. In identifying such moral aspects of loneliness, these authors are attempting to be helpful. But implicit in such discussions is the idea that loneliness should *not* be a moral issue. In attempting to deny the place of loneliness in the moral order, such analyses may effectively, if paradoxically, suggest that loneliness is morally 'neutral', and thus may contribute to a particular way of thinking and talking about loneliness that itself has moral implications.

Is loneliness social or nonsocial?

The central paradox of loneliness is that it is at one and the same time the most non-social and the most social of experiences. The essence of loneliness seems to involve private experiences – of separation, of a lack of sharing, of one's isolated individuality, of the *I* not the *we*. It thus may seem odd to consider it as a social phenomenon. And indeed, loneliness has been discussed for many years by clinical psychologists, but not by social psychologists until quite recently. However, loneliness must also be social, at least when it is defined in terms of discrepancies or problems in relationships. It is social because there must be some agreement, some shared understanding, of what might be possible in relationships in order to appreciate that something is missing.

But these sorts of definitions do not go to the heart of loneliness; they concern its sources rather than its essence; they are social only because loneliness is defined by the absence of the social. I want to argue that there is something very social about loneliness in its essence, in that loneliness involves failed intersubjectivity.[1] By intersubjectivity, I mean the mutual understanding that characterizes and derives from an interaction in which there is 'phenomenological awareness by social actors of the independent, subjective life-world of another' (Forgas, 1981, p. 15), an understanding which rests upon commonality of the taken-for-granted meanings. Intersubjectivity is a characteristic of a relationship, of mutual experience, rather than of individual experience. And the tacit understandings involve the world, not just individual characteristics. Further, partial intersubjectivity and the lack of intersubjectivity (although this is rarely total) are also characteristics of relationships. In themselves, they do not constitute loneliness; they may well entail a shared perception about the relationship. Even where they do not, loneliness is not inevitable. For example, one person may deny (as in some ethnomethodological studies) the partial intersubjectivity which does exist; this would be likely to evoke anger, or perhaps bewilderment, depending upon the relationship and the circumstances. Or one person may deny that there is a lack of intersubjectivity and thus may produce anxiety or even fear. Public acknowledgement of the lack of intersubjectivity, of the absence of communal meanings, may create confusion or embarrassment.

But loneliness does not involve the simple absence of intersubjectivity. Rather, loneliness, is the individual experience of *failed* intersubjectivity, the perception that the degree or type of intersubjectivity is not appropriate for a particular relationship, and, further, that this perception is not shared. Thus, although the essence of intersubjectivity is social, with respect to the locus of experience loneliness is non-social, is individual, because of the lack of shared understanding, because the experiencing individual is aware of not sharing the same taken-for-granted meanings.

The nature of the failures involved in different relationships will be different, because the relationships also involve different tacit understandings, in both breadth and type. Loneliness can be characteristic of an ongoing relationship, for example marriage, or can arise because a particular relationship no longer exists, for example after divorce or the death of a spouse. Or it may occur because there is insufficient total intersubjectivity in one's overall set of relationships, or where there is failure to have at least one relationship in which a person is sufficiently known.

The level at which or extent to which one wishes to know and be known will obviously vary by person as well as by relationship (Scheibe, 1979). A person may not wish to be totally known and knowing with one's spouse, for example; such total intersubjectivity can be experienced as boredom. And individuals may differ in their tolerance for the lack of intersubjectivity, which may be what we mean when we describe someone as a 'private' person. They may also differ in their tolerance for levels of failed intersubjectivity, for loneliness.

The expression 'failed intersubjectivity' is not usually used in connection with loneliness, but it does seem to capture the essence of loneliness and in some respects to go beyond the standard definitions. Compare, for example, the definition of loneliness as the experience of discrepancy. What does it mean, after all, to say that the quality or quantity of one's relationships is less than desired or expected? This is often brokwn down into various functions of relationships, such as mutual self-disclosure, emotional support and the like. But intersubjectivity cannot necessarily be broken down into these sorts of constituent elements. Rather, it may derive from some combination of such elements, or may even transcend them, so that actual levels, for example, of self-disclosure, or even the perceptions of such levels, may be largely irrelevant. And the taken-for-granted aspects of intersubjectivity concern many things other than the self.

The discrepancy definition is too broad in another sense: it encompasses too many failed expectations. Rook (1984) suggests that the discrepancy idea needs to be refined because dissatisfying interpersonal situations do not always evoke loneliness. She suggests, for example, that a marital relationship which does not meet expectations might result in resentment rather than loneliness. And one can imagine other circumstancs, for example, a disappointing sex life, which might provoke frustration rather than loneliness. What I am proposing here is that failure to meet expectations will be interpreted and experienced as loneliness only when it involves failed intersubjectivity. This view of loneliness captures what Rook refers to as 'a disturbing and persistent sense of separateness from others', which is, at least for some people, the 'core of loneliness' (Rook, 1984, p. 1391). It is not only that 'lonely' people think that others do not understand them; they also do not understand others: there is an absence of shared understandings. One of the respondents in my research with the rural elderly (Wood, 1981) reported that the loneliest time in her life was when she was forced by circumstances to have sustained interaction with a sister-in-law with whom she shared very few assumptions about the world on both an articulated and a taken-for-granted-level. This suggests one reason why it is so difficult for people to describe their experiences of loneliness. They cannot articulate failed intersubjectivity precisely because it encompasses the unarticulated, the taken-for-granted.

There is one final point. I have noted above that loneliness cannot be defined independently of social relations; that the nature of these relations is its essence, its content. In this sense, loneliness is different from other emotions, which may be dependent upon social relations in various ways, but for which social relations are not central. For example, anger may be directed towards others, and Sabini and Silver (1982) have argued that anger involves judgements that a transgression has occurred. But the transgressions need not involve the substance of a relationship (e.g., its intimacy, its 'strength'). For example, one could become angry at seeing someone usurping the subway seat of another person. Even jealousy seems to involve threats to the existence or maintenance of a relationship, rather than to its nature as such. And although people sometimes talk about loneliness in connection with 'non-social' events, such as failing an exam, it turns out that what is actually involved is the lack of opportunity to commiserate with another, to share the experience. Thus, loneliness is paradoxically more social than other 'emotions'.

What are some of the implications of this analysis of loneliness? To view loneliness as failed intersubjectivity is to provide a common core for understanding the seemingly disparate experiences of various groups. For example, rituals entail a great deal of intersubjectivity, and indeed, the provision of such shared experience is one of their important functions. Groups without rituals no longer have access to such intersubjective experiences, and may be considered 'susceptible' to loneliness. This might be a characteristic of some adolescent groups, who respond by constructing their own rituals (in which it is often difficult for outsiders,e.g. parents, to grasp the taken-for-granted meanings). Immigrants may find it difficult to sustain their rituals at times when this is most important, for example, when confronted with what can be an almost total lack of intersubjectivity. More generally, loneliness is likely to occur in relationships between members from groups who do not share many understandings, for example, from different cultures, and from different social classes. And the rhetoric of sexual equality may foster expectations about shared understandings that are rarely realized in male–female relationships, and that may thus entail greater loneliness than there would be if intersubjectivity goals were more modest. (See Garfinkel, 1967, for a discussion of all of the tacit understandings which are part of gender role enactment.) Long-term relationships, even of enmity (Harré, 1977), may be sustained in part because of the degree of intersubjectivity they entail. And the relative absence of loneliness in isolated groups (e.g., in some rural communities) may reflect the degree of shared understandings that have been built up rather than the number of interactions, as such, among members.

The idea of failed intersubjectivity may help us to understand 'appropriate' and inappropriate loneliness. For example, if a person says that she was lonely because she could not communicate intimately with total strangers, we would view this as inappropriate, as involving unreasonable expectations for shared understanding. Further, such a communication about loneliness would perpetuate failed intersubjectivity; whereas appropriate communications about loneliness (e.g., 'I cannot talk to my husband') could be seen as creating or at least involving intersubjectivity, for example, when shared with another married woman. (She would not have to ask what you meant, at least not in middle-class North American culture.) This view of loneliness is another way of integrating the concepts of existential and personal loneliness (see Wood, 1983), such that both involve the absence of the taken-for-granted, but with respect to different relationships, and with respect to what is possible versus what is actual. Finally, this notion allows us to consider the possibility of shared loneliness, within a dyad or larger group. For example, a couple whose child is about to leave for college may share the belief that their child is entering another world which is closed to them, in which the tacit understandings are different from those in their world.

Let me summarize the argument here. Loneliness is both individual and social. It is individual because it refers to the person as separated; it is social because what the person is separated from is other people. It is social because it concerns, indeed derives from our capacity for, intersubjectivity; it is individual because it involves experience which is not shared, the failure of intersubjectivity. In the next sections, I will propose that we can account for the apparent paradox or dualistic nature of loneliness by viewing loneliness as a social construction of failed intersubjectivity; that as a social construction, loneliness can be seen as a blending versus an opposition of the individual and the social. But we may note here that loneliness is basic because intersubjectivity is basic. As Schutz (1970) suggests, intersubjectivity is the essence of social life; without it, social action is impossible. Understanding of the other's life world is essential for a predictable and consensual social order. Intersubjectivity is also related to the basic paradoxes of existence: that persons can consider themselves, and be considered, both as subject and as object, and that the central life-span task involves a dialectical process of managing independence and togetherness.

THE CONSTRUCTIONIST APPROACH TO THE PARADOX OF LONELINESS

Historical perspectives

In the sociological literature, a distinction is drawn between social conditions and social definitions, and social problems are viewed as social constructions that may be generated even in the absence of any supporting conditions. Analyses of social problems as social movements (Blumer, 1971) and of the social career of social problems (Spector and Kitsuse,

1973) show how social actions and social constructions serve not only to identify, but also to create and to perpetuate, social problems. In a previous section I noted that loneliness is frequently viewed as a social problem in North America. It is therefore worthwhile to consider loneliness as a social construction. What might a social construction analysis of loneliness look like? In the first part of this section, I focus briefly on historical aspects of scientific and media constructions of loneliness as a general concept. I then consider social construction analyses of emotion and how these might be applied to loneliness. The following section addresses the constructions of everyday people and the specific variations which there are in constructions of loneliness. I recognize that there is clearly both an overlap and a reciprocal relationship between so-called researcher's constructions and everyday constructions; I separate them here solely for analytical purposes.

We might begin with the idea that social scientists have, in fact, constructed two problems: being lonely, and not being lonely. There are numerous articles which claim that being lonely is a widespread and serious condition. For example, in their preface to the NIHM monograph, *Preventing the Harmful Consequences of Severe and Persistent Loneliness*, Peplau and Goldston state that:

> Loneliness is a pervasive problem. It has been estimated that one American in four has experienced loneliness in the past few weeks; perhaps as many as 10 percent of the population suffer from severe and persistent loneliness.... The significance of these figures is highlighted by evidence linking loneliness to depression, suicide, delinquency, alcohol abuse and other mental health problems. (Peplau and Goldston, 1984, p. viii)

The condition of 'not being lonely' is less well formed as a problem, although I have tried to demonstrate above that such a construction is present implicitly if not explicitly in many accounts of loneliness. In any case, both of these constructions are tied to specific historical developments in North America. I will treat these very briefly, because I wish only to suggest why and how loneliness has come to be constructed as a problem.

It is commonplace to note that there are a number of social and demographic changes which have occurred in the twentieth century: family disintegration (as indicated, e.g., by rising divorce rates); increasing proportions of people living alone; geographic and social mobility; urbanization; population aging; the increasing role of television in daily life. Some of these changes are well documented; some have been overemphasized or greatly exaggerated. Nevertheless, such changes, in conjunction with values which are perceived to be dominant in North America, such as individualism and self-reliance (Weiss, 1984), are believed by many to be associated in some way with the current 'epidemic' of loneliness.

During this same period, there appears also to have been a systematic change in the way in which loneliness has been viewed, although this is not as yet well documented. I suggest, very roughly, the following sequence. Until at least the beginning of the century, the term 'loneliness' appears to refer most frequently to the physical absence of persons; it was used to describe both persons, as physically isolated, and places. In the 1930s and 1940s, loneliness was used to describe the pathological consequences of physical and social isolation for children (e.g., Zilboorg, 1938). In the 1940s to 1960s, loneliness was used to describe the distress of physical separation, first in adults, and later in children (Duvall, 1945; Bowlby, 1960). During the 1950s and 1960s loneliness was viewed as a psychiatric condition of social isolation (e.g., Fromm-Reichmann, 1959). In the 1960s, we see the beginning of attempts to distinguish loneliness from both physical and social isolation (e.g., Townsend, 1963). And by the 1970s, loneliness was treated as a feeling quite separate from isolation, although sometimes described as being weakly associated, for example, in studies in which lonely people report having less contact with others (see Perlman and Peplau, 1984).

There appear to be two trends in the changes in the use and meaning of loneliness. First, loneliness is seen less and less as an extreme condition (physical, social or psychological) and more as a normal experience. Second, the meaning of the term seems to shift from being alone as a physical state, to a feeling associated with being physically alone, to a feeling associated with being socially alone, to a feeling associated with social relationships in the abstract.[2]

The change in the use and meaning of loneliness has been accompanied by popular perceptions that loneliness has increased. There is no 'evidence' that loneliness as such has increased – surveys and epidemiological studies have begun only recently. But this development is in itself evidence that there has been an increase in attention to and concern about loneliness, and this increase can be documented systematically in both the popular media and the scientific literature, for example, by looking at the change in the number and frequency of articles on loneliness. The increase in these social constructions of loneliness is reciprocally related to an increasing awareness of and willingness to admit to loneliness by the general population. And both are tied to the increased 'psychologizing' of loneliness in North America. This trend is in turn related to perceptions of the social changes I have noted.

Specifically, then, we have two North American social constructions of loneliness. The construction of the problem of 'being lonely' is a reflection of concern about the suffering created by the breakdown of relationships, about the 'painful' personal experience of failed intersubjectivity which arises because of the social changes which have occurred. The concern is manifested in the development of therapies, treatment programmes, workshops and so on to reduce or prevent loneliness. At the same time, we have the construction of the problem of 'not being lonely'. This reflects concerns about the social changes themselves, about the social breakdown signalled by the failure of intersubjectivity. It functions to train people to be lonely, to keep them concerned about and tied into relationships when these appear to be falling apart. This construction is an antidote to the problems of untrammelled individualism and independence. It is reflected in the stereotyping of groups and of behaviour which might be seen as threatening to the preservation of traditional relationships, for example, in negative stereotypes about homosexuals.

There is very little reference in the loneliness literature to the construction of loneliness as a problem, even in discussions of 'the loneliness industry' (Weiss, 1984, p. 8), which includes the professional contributions of researchers. Rather, it is simply taken for granted that loneliness is a major problem which requires treatment. Similarly, there is little discussion of the social construction of 'not being lonely' as a problem, although Peplau and Goldston (1984) do suggest that it is 'probably undesirable that loneliness be eliminated entirely from the repertoire of common human experience' (p. viii). But I believe that this sort of analysis is necessary if we are to address adequately the potentials of human relationships and social life.

The analysis also suggests one reason why loneliness has been neglected in the literature on emotion: namely, that, unlike other emotions, loneliness is a recent construction; it does not have a long historical standing (see chapter 12 below). There are, however, good grounds for treating loneliness as an emotion, principally because it will allow us to address directly the moral aspects of loneliness. This requires a treatment of emotion in a moral context. Fortunately, such an approach is one of the thrusts of recent developments in social constructionism, which involves more than an analysis of scientists' constructions of social problems, but extends the analysis to everyday life, including 'internal' psychological experience, and to everyday activities of both researchers and 'ordinary' people (Gergen, 1985). The analyses of emotions as social constructions will also help us to understand 'how' loneliness can be an emotion, and to deal with the other paradoxes of loneliness I have described earlier.

Emotion and loneliness

In the social constructionist view, emotions are understood as 'socially determined patterns of ritual action' (Armon-Jones, 1985) or as 'socially constituted syndromes' (Averill, 1980). Emotions are normatively explicable, not mechanically predictable (Coulter, 1979). The question with which we are concerned is Wittgensteinian rather than ontological; that is, we should ask, 'Under what conditions do we use the term "emotion"?' not 'What is an emotion?' (Harré, 1984b; Sarbin, 1984). A number of social construction theories of emotion have been proposed (e.g. Armon-Jones, 1985; Averill, 1980; Coulter, 1979; Harré, 1984a; Sarbin, 1984). I shall consider here a blend of these accounts because they are similar in their implications for the analysis of loneliness.

Specifically, there are a number of elements that are or might be involved in the correct use of the emotion vocabulary: (1) physiological; (2) feeling/phenomenological; (3) display; (4) cognitive interpretation (including appraisal of the situation, labelling of the emotion, interpretation of the cause of the emotion, and interpretation of the emotion as passion *v.* action); (5) moral assessment. The constellation of elements required may vary somewhat for different emotions, but in general, only certain of these elements would seem to be necessary to speak of an emotion: namely, the interpretation of the emotion as passion, and the moral assessment (at least, in Western cultures – Harré, 1984b). The physiological element, in contrast, is not essential. This does not mean that physiological components are unimportant (see Sarbin, 1984). But it does mean that such components are essentially arbitrary; that one must merely select some physiological aspect or, in the case of loneliness, talk as if there were some such aspect. I suggested earlier that people were using physiological terms metaphorically when they talked about loneliness. Such talk serves to show – indeed, to constitute – the experience as intense. We might say that people reify these metaphors to warrant their interpretation of loneliness as a passion, in part, at least, because of its moral implications for the self.

Loneliness can be viewed as one of the emotions that require only the minimal elements, that is, the interpretation as passion, and the moral assessment. There is no need to belabour the point that on this view most of the paradoxes described earlier (e.g., the lack of any physiological involvement, the moral aspects) are unproblematic for considering loneliness as an emotion. That it has not been so considered in the emotion literature may reflect not that any particular element is missing, but that the total constellation of elements is both smaller and different from that involved in the traditional emotions. But the appreciation of loneliness as an emotion requires brief further consideration of both the moral element and the patterns of action involved.

First, if an emotion is explicitly a passion, it can be only implicitly moral, because it could be argued that morality does not enter into events and experiences over which we have no control, that is, over occurrences. But an analysis of talk about loneliness shows the equivocal relationship between action and occurrence. For example, Townsend (1963) found that, when asked in the presence of her daughters whether she ever got lonely, one elderly respondent said, 'Sometimes I do when they are all at work.' However, on a subsequent visit when she was alone, she told the interviewer that she was 'never lonely really, but I like my children to call' (p. 172). Townsend mentioned this incident to illustrate a methodological difficulty in the assessment of loneliness. But it also demonstrates several other points relevant to a constructionist analysis: (1) the older person thinks that old people are expected to be lonely; (2) the statement about loneliness has perloctionary aspects; that is, it affects the children's actions; (3) the statement functions as a self-fulfilling prophecy; for example, 'If I say I'm lonely, although I'm not, then I'll have visitors, and then I won't be lonely.' This example also elucidates another paradox of loneliness, namely that, although it is difficult to think of emotions as social problems, it is clear that some moral choices can constitute social problems. (See also de Rivera, 1984, on emotions as choices.)

Second, the interpretation of a set of responses as passion implies that cognition is relatively unimportant, aside from the label attached to the experience. Lazarus (1984) and some others would certainly dispute this. But I want to suggest that there is more to cognition than the label, or appraisal, or causal interpretation, that there is a 'content' to the experience of emotion, both behaviourally and cognitively. To paraphrase Armon-Jones (1985), to experience an emotion is to perform and practise the physical, verbal and *mental* actions criterial for and expressive of that emotion. In learning that we ought to experience a particular emotion, we also learn what to do and think. Emotion involves the internalization of social representations of broad scope, including a range of attitudes and desires. In the case of loneliness, the content consists mostly of mental actions, that is, attitudes about other persons, about relationships and so on (see Wood, 1983, for examples). This emphasis on content is tied to the importance of the moral character of loneliness and can be related to its several aspects. Whereas the label of loneliness is tied to the morality of loneliness itself, the content of loneliness concerns the oughts and shoulds of relationships. This relative emphasis on mental rather than behavioural content is perhaps yet another reason why loneliness has been neglected as an emotion.

The moral aspects of emotion are not to be underestimated. It is part of the constructionist position that 'emotions serve a social function in maintaining particular value systems' (Armon-Jones, 1985, p. 1). Tavris (1984), for example, has noted that anger has some constructive moral and social uses, and de Rivera (1984) has suggested that anger preserves values and closeness. As I have argued, loneliness also has a social function in particular sorts of societies, and may, like anger, serve to maintain or recapture closeness. Armon-Jones (1985) has suggested that emotions, as broad internalizations of social representations, have a special status within constructionism. I would like now to pursue briefly a line of reasoning that suggests that loneliness is an even more special case for constructionism.

I have argued that the basic paradox of loneliness is that it is simultaneously both social and non-social. On the one hand, it appears to represent a most individual, private, inner, psychological experience. But a consideration of loneliness as failed intersubjectivity, and the application of ideas about the social construction of emotion, suggest that loneliness is profoundly social – indeed, public and collective – in its identification, its contents and its expression. I think that the argument can be extended and the paradox 'resolved' by locating it in the larger dualities identified by Harré (1984a, 1984b) in his discussion of the social structure of emotion. I can here only sketch the resolution; it requires a much more detailed development than space permits.

Harré presents a structure that considers a dimension of display, with public and private poles, and a dimension of realization, with individual and collective poles. The structure thus defines four quadrants: the two with which we are concerned here are the public–collective (social) quadrant, and the individual–private (personal) quadrant. The social constructionist view is that what transpires individually and privately is appropriated from the public – collective realm. Harré suggests that emotions be considered as individually realized, but public–collectively or social defined. This is appropriate also for loneliness. What I want to propose is that intersubjectivity, or shared subjectivity be considered as *collectively* realized.[3] Loneliness as failed intersubjectivity then represents a movement along the realization or location dimension from collective to individual. It is in this sense, in its origins in and dialectical tensions with the social, that loneliness, of all the emotions, is most centrally located in the public space of social construction.

Variations on the constructionist theme

I have described the general way in which loneliness is socially constructed. But clearly, there will be variations in the constructions of different historical periods, different cultures and different groups. There will be variations with respect to the precise nature of the elements involved, that is, moral assessment, content, interpretations and so on. In this section I will consider how some of these critical elements might differ in the constructions for different groups. I will focus upon age differences, which have been largely ignored in social construction accounts (with the exception of Armon-Jones, 1985 and Averill, chapter 6 above) and in the general emotion literature; the attention that has been given to age has focused upon early development.

Constructions of loneliness for different age groups differ with respect to many of the elements that might be involved. First, the extent and intensity of physiological components will be likely to be seen as greater for younger than for older people because of expectations that ageing is associated with a flattening of affect. The moral assessments involved will also differ, with respect to the experience of loneliness itself, to the reporting of loneliness and to the kinds of relationships involved. Thus, increasing age will be seen as accompanied by greater loneliness. Loneliness will be seen as acceptable (perhaps even required in some instances) for old people, but not for very young people. Older people see 'complaints' of loneliness *as* complaints, as 'whining', whereas younger people see them as signs of social stigma (Gordon 1976). And the types and extent of relationship networks expected of older people will be diminished compared with those of younger people (because of loss of friends through death, decreasing mobility and so on for the aged).

The interpretation of the causes of loneliness is also likely to differ: for older people, it might be in terms of chronic conditions (e.g., poor health); for younger people, the cause may be seen as a matter of poor social skills. I note parenthetically that the current loneliness literature seems to focus both on deficits in social skills and on relatively young people. Most recently, discussions of loneliness have been extended to younger children (e.g., Asher, Hymel and Renshaw, 1984), who have been relatively ignored since the much earlier work on infants and children. The cognitive content of loneliness as described above will change with age; for example, an older person might be thinking, 'I miss my dead friend', whereas a young person will say to her/himself, 'I wish I had a date tonight.' The behavioural content will also change, principally in the direction of increasing passivity with age. That is, for younger people the social syndrome of loneliness will include active attempts to establish new relationships, whereas for the older person it may involve reminiscing about past relationships.

An examination of age differences in constructions of loneliness also illustrates some other important points about such constructions. First, we may object that some of the elements that I have described are simply stereotypes (although I would argue that these are involved in constructions of loneliness), or at least are highly 'subjective', and we may want to ask about the objective conditions or the reality on which such constructions are based. For example, we may want to ask about real physiological changes with age, changes in demography and so on. However, the physiological changes that accompany ageing are complex, and by no means well understood, and their implications for emotional experience may be contradictory (Schultz, 1982). It is the constructions of such changes which may be important for emotional experience, and, indeed, for further physiological changes. But ageing is itself a social construction (somewhat like gender – see Kessler and McKenna, 1978), which leads us to seek 'facts' about ageing, such as the increasing proportion of elderly, the increasing numbers of 'old' elderly and so on.

The way in which age has been constructed is associated with the identification several years ago of the elderly as the most lonely, or one of the most lonely, groups in society. Today, however, there appears to be a consensus that it is adolescents and young people who in fact are the most lonely (a reconstruction of the epidemiology of loneliness based on several large-scale surveys – see Perlman and Peplau, 1984). Practitioners and the media, however, sill frequently-identify the elderly as lonely. For example, a church deacon recently stated that 'The greatest enemy of the elderly is loneliness' ('Grandmother', 1985). Such statements point to the political aspects of the social constructions of loneliness among various groups. These constructions can shift the focus from problems of transport, economics, health care and housing to problems of social and family relations.

There is another important aspect to social constructions. The idea that loneliness was a serious problem for the elderly was in part based on the responses of older people to questions such as, 'What do you see as the most serious problem for the elderly?' When asked, however, if loneliness was a problem for them, many of them said, 'No, not for me personally.' This suggests that, in examining constructions of loneliness connected with different age groups, we need to consider not only how social scientists, and people in general, construct this experience, but how the different age groups construct their own experience; that is, we need to ask, whose constructions, about whom, are at issue.

Further differences in constructions of loneliness can be seen in a brief consideration of groups other than age groups. For example, discussions of sex differences in loneliness allude to some elements of a social constructionist perspective. Specifically, it has been found in several studies (see Perlman and Peplau, 1984) that women are more likely to report being lonely than are men. This finding is often interpreted as indicating that women may not necessarily be any lonelier than men; they may just be more willing to admit it. This may simply reflect differences in the moral assessments of loneliness, namely, that it is more acceptable for women to be lonely, because this is an emotion which is 'gentle', which is related to love rather than to anger. However, Armon-Jones's (1985) discussion of sex differences in emotion suggests that this analysis is incomplete. If women are assumed to be more concerned about and dependent upon relationships than are men, a syndrome is more likely to be constituted as loneliness by (and for) women than it is for men.[4]

There are clearly also differences to be expected in the constructions of loneliness for people of different marital status. For example, we would expect differences between married and single people in the interpretation of the cause of loneliness, and also in its content, both cognitively and behaviourally.

There are relatively few cross-cultural studies of loneliness, or of loneliness in other cultures. Most such studies have been conducted in European countries (e.g., Berg et al., 1981). One obvious possibility is simply that loneliness is less likely to be constituted as an emotion in some cultures and may not exist at all in societies in which there is no individual transformation of the social, if there are any such cultures (Harré, 1984). But even where it is so constituted, we might expect several differences compared with North American constructions. For example, with respect to the moral assessment of loneliness, Weiss (1984) suggests that Americans are 'more likely to see the lonely as inadequately self-reliant', whereas Western Europeans 'might see the lonely, not as weak, but as suspect, perhaps dangerous, because they are not members of communities' (pp. 7–8). And because concerns about relationships may differ cross-culturally, we might also expect differences in interpretations of the cause of loneliness, and in the attitudes and conditions that in part constitute loneliness.

Similar considerations might apply to constructions of social class differences in loneliness. Several studies (see Perlman and Peplau, 1984) have reported that loneliness is more prevalent among lower-income groups. This finding may reflect unexamined assumptions in North America about differences in moral worth by social class. It is interesting to note that one exception to this finding is Berg et al.'s (1981) study of Swedish elderly, although there are obviously several possible resons for the difference between this and the North American studies. And there are a number of studies that suggest that the marital relationship is viewed differently by middle-class compared with working-class women (e.g., Lopata, 1969), suggesting that several elements of loneliness constructions may also vary for the two groups.

Finally, if we adopt a social constructionist perspective, how would one consider individual differences in loneliness? One way would be to look at the person's construction of loneliness in the context of his or her relationships, occupation, life stage, cultural background and so on, and to compare it with others in similar situations.

We could obviously consider many other groups, and treat the constructions in more detail. But this would have limited utility. It would entail treating the elements separately, when we need to consider them together, in context, as suggested for individual differences. Further, it treats the groups as non-overlapping, whereas we would want to consider constructions for 'compound groups', for example, by examining cross-cultural differences in age constructions of loneliness, or constructions for widowed elderly. In the next section I sketch a contextualist approach to the problem of integrating the diverse elements of the constructions of loneliness relative to specific groups.

THE NARRATIVE IN THE CONSTRUCTION OF LONELINESS

Narrative, emotion and loneliness

> Only animals live entirely in the Here and Now. Only nature knows neither memory nor history. But man – let me offer you a definition – is the story-telling animal. Wherever he goes, he wants to leave behind not a chaotic wake, not an empty space, but the comforting marker-buoys and trail-signs of stories. He has to go on telling stories. He has to keep on making them up. As long as there's a story, it's all right. (Swift, 1983, p. 53)

One approach that can be taken within social constructionism is the study of narrative (Gergen, 1985; Sarbin, 1984). Social constructions of categories, of persons, of actions, are viewed within the context of emplotment, of a story, which is itself socially constructed. Narratives, or stories, are important to both scientists and laypersons because they structure and account for our experience. When confronted with an event for which a story is not readily available to us, we seek one out, either in the scientific literature or in the culture. If we do not find a satisfactory story, we seek to construct one, and we often form groups to help us do this, for example, parents of SIDS babies, widows, or 'loneliness' groups. From this perspective, 'social support' may gain its primary importance because it is a source of narrative, not just of information, money and the like. The narrative can serve to help us interpret our experience because it entails an integration of the multiple aspects of experience. The complexity of this integration, and its embeddedness in larger contexts, are two reasons why our social constructions can be so resistant to change, as Gergen (1985) has noted.

The importance of accounts is partially subsumed in the work of attribution theorists, except that in this tradition not all of the important elements are included, and those which are discussed tend to be treated in isolation. But a narrative must include more than causal explanations. It must also encompass the development and unfolding of the episode, the kinds of persons involved, their relationships to each other, the implications of the episode and of their actions for the value of their selves, and whether or not they are to be seen as agents or patients, as controllers of events or as sufferers of circumstances. The logic of action, and corresponding notions of blame and responsibility, are in the plot (Sarbin, 1984). But a story not only describes action, it also has implications for action; it says what to do about the problem it entails, For example, if stories of anger contain a link between anger and aggression, we are likely to choose aggression to deal with problems which we locate in anger stories. The story also prefigures subsequent episodes. For example, one of the implications of developmental and life-span stories is that people will grow out of the problem. Finally, like all social constructions, narratives do more than provide explanations, accounts of action and so on (Gergen, 1985); as I have illustrated, they also serve performative functions. They can themselves be seen as actions.

Sarbin (1984) has argued for a narrative approach to understanding emotion, and there are several reasons why this might be useful. In this approach, emotion is not just part of the story, it is the story. Harré (1984b) notes that there are some emotion terms, for example, *amaeru*, that cannot be translated into English, whose sense can only be conveyed by telling a number of anecdotes and giving literary examples (see part III below). Sarbin (1984) has found that, when asked to describe their 'feelings', informants first give an emotion word or metaphor, but invariably follow this with a story. So the necessity to translate foreign emotion terms by a narrative also applies to English terms, except that we happen to have a word for them, which might be seen as a kind of shorthand, or general classification label. Emotion stories are one category of a class of narratives in which the protagonist is viewed as a patient, as not being in control of at least some aspects of his or her experience. Other stories in this class might concern children, victims and the so-called mentally ill.

An advantage of the narrative approach for viewing emotion, and particularly loneliness, is that it can incorporate and integrate all of the elements that may be involved, including any physiological aspects, whether these are viewed metaphorically or not. The complexity of the social construction of loneliness can be captured within the narrative not only because the story can incorporate a label for the emotion, but also because it has content. The characteristics of the people, settings and events that form the narrative together become a loneliness story. There are different statuses and roles, life events and life histories associated with different ages, which also suggests that the loneliness of different ages may differ on many elements. In the next section, I suggest how these elements might be constituted into loneliness stories for different age groups. I note here, however, that one way of approaching the construction and deconstruction of narrative is to employ the ethogenic framework for the analysis of social episodes (Harré, 1974). This framework points to elements in the phenomenology of action generation (definition of the situation, persona, judge and rules) and to the sequence of actions, both overt and covert, through which a particular act or social outcome is achieved. The rules involved are both constitutive and regulative. Constitutive rules define the nature of the act (or label the emotion); regulative rules prescribe relevant actions (see chapter 6 above). And as noted earlier, both sets of rules have strong moral implications in the case of loneliness.

Loneliness stories

> I wouldn't be surprised if lonely people secretly yearn to be taken in for
> cross-examination from time to time to give them somebody to talk to about
> their lives. (Kundera, 1981, p. 163)

I have tried to show above why the narrative approach is useful for
understanding emotion, and thus for understanding loneliness. Stories
would seem to be a particularly good way of thinking about loneliness
because loneliness involves not having someone to whom to tell one's
story. It is a story within a story. But the story of loneliness may also be a
story of someone with no story (e.g., the schizophrenic or the amnesiac),
or of someone with the wrong story. And the story one is unable to tell may
as much be the 'little' episodes of everyday life as the story of one's divorce
or of other cataclysmic happenings.

I shall give here only two brief examples of loneliness stories, and then
try to show the various ways they might figure in the experience of
loneliness. The lonely adolescent story (the 'standard version') describes
the process of going through puberty, of attempting to establish one's
separate identity and independence from one's parents, and of forming
'romantic' relationships. The story is characterized by fluctuations in
display and behaviour (complaints of nothing to do, restlessness, moping,
frantic activity) and in interpretations of the cause of loneliness (my
friends are unreliable; I have poor social skills), and by clear and reiterated
interpretations of passion (I don't know what comes over me). Questions
about moral worth are prominent. Loneliness is experienced metaphorically as hunger.

The story of the lonely elderly widow is quite different. The level of
activity is generally depressed, the causal interpretation is clear and stable,
and there is a sense of being in a condition consequent to an occurrence,
rather than a sense of passion as such. Loneliness is experienced metaphorically as pain. The stories are not totally dissimilar: for example, they
may both be punctuated by episodes of crying and contain similar
cognitions such as 'I wish I had someone to talk to.' Both may be connected
in different ways with versions of 'self-pity'.

What are some of the implications of enacting such stories? Changes in
loneliness may occur because people change stories as they move through
different developmental phases. For example, the adolescent girl may give
up the lonely adolescent story as she matures, without immediately talking
on the 'lonely single' story. Or the young single man may give up the lonely
single story as he ages to the point of becoming a 'bachelor'. (This example
may have less relevance today; bachelorhood no longer seems to be
recognized as a distinct life-style, at least in North America.) In this way,

people might be seen to 'grow out of loneliness'. Loneliness may also wax and wane as people take on or give up other sorts of stories, as time passes or as circumstances change (for example, the lonely immigrant story). Perhaps the problem that some people have is that they cannot give up a particular story even when it is no longer appropriate. For example, in North American culture, complaints of the widowed or divorced can be seen as going on too long. In contrast, in Mediterranean and some other cultures, the widowhood story is or at least has been a life story. And the moral implications, the implications for self-worth, are different depending upon whether the story is seen as appropriate. This may even apply to 'chronic loneliness', or loneliness as a life story. This story will be viewed differently if it is embedded in another life story, for example, of physical handicap, than if there is no such other life story apparent.

Stories about loneliness for different ages groups direct us to the historical dimensions of narrative, because such stories involve cohort differences as well as age differences *per se*. For example, stories told about and enacted by older persons may reflect their formulation during a time when loneliness was used to describe a state of physical and historical isolation rather than a psychological condition. Historically, it is likely that loneliness stories as I have described them have appeared relatively recently, and have become entrenched as North American and Western European myths only in the last twenty or thirty years. Prior to the onset of Renaissance individualism, psychological identity appears to have been essentially group identity, such that the self did not exist outside of social definitions. It would not have been possible or necessary to imagine psychological separateness, and thus there could not have been loneliness of the kind we know today. Even in the early part of the twentieth century, discussions of psychological loneliness in both professional and popular literature are relatively infrequent, and seem to refer to a severe and entrenched sense of separation from others, for example, as embodied in 'schizophrenia'. Perhaps the essence of schizophrenia stories is that they present the most extreme loneliness narratives it is possible to imagine or create while retaining a human protagonist, because they involve the almost total failure of intersubjectivity. As I suggested earlier, what seems to have happened in the past fifty years or so is the transformation of loneliness stories from exotic, extreme tales such as those describing episodes in which people are extremely isolated physically (journeys to the Pole, solo transatlantic crossings and so on) or psychologically (as in schizophrenia), to 'ordinary' stories – stories of ordinary people in ordinary circumstances.

A large number of loneliness stories could be told, displaying great variation in their particular details. What might they share in common? Is there a universal loneliness narrative? At a less concrete level, loneliness stories might appear as stories of problems of attachment, of the maintenance of relationships, or of social integration. And one would expect that the different forms would appear more frequently and with greater elaboration in some cultures or groups than in others. At the most abstract level, however, all stories of loneliness will have as their central theme the failure of intersubjectivity.

CONCLUSIONS

There are a number of implications for future research on loneliness. First, we should direct our attention to social constructions of loneliness as embodied in ordinary language, particularly in narratives. Stories can be examined for the elements that I have identified above, including those that are intrinsic parts of emotion and those that are part of the context of emotion, and we can analyse how they are interrelated. We can seek to identify which elements are necessary and sufficient, and to uncover the 'feeling rules' (Hochschild, 1983) involved in emotion stories. One approach to this task would be to employ the ethogenic analysis of social episodes in conjunction with classical experimentation (Wood and Kroger, 1986). And we should carefully compare narratives across a variety of groups, for example, by looking at differences in stories told about and by women and men. We need also to examine more thoroughly the place of loneliness in the moral order, and the moral dimensions of various sorts of relationships. And should consider further the performative aspects of loneliness stories; that is, to look at what is achieved by different kinds of talk about loneliness, for example, in self-presentation or in giving advice.

Our understanding of loneliness would be enhanced by systematic, extensive historical and cross-cultural analyses of accounts of loneliness in serious and popular literature. And we should include the accounts of social scientists as these have appeared in theory, in research and in measurement.

In all of these projects, we should give careful attention to the language of loneliness. We should look at the etymology, and at historical and current usages of English terms other than loneliness, such as isolation, solitude, homesickness and self-pity. We should look more closely at languages other than English, for example German, in which there are both process and state terms for loneliness, namely, *Vereinsamen* ('to become lonely') and *Einsamkeit* (loneliness). And we could begin to compile the metaphors employed in loneliness discourse, particularly those that refer to physiological processes.

Perhaps most of all, we need to look directly at the idea of inter-subjectivity, to find out how people in everyday life understand this idea, how they describe it, what language they use in discussing it. Indeed, we should try to determine if they discuss it at all. Our efforts in this direction could proceed in the context of more general ideas about 'ways of knowing', such as Scheibe's (1979) work on sagacity and acumen. We need to know more about what is known. Work in ethnomethodology on what is taken for granted in everyday conversations may be helpful on this point. And we should consider intersubjectivity in different types of relationships and in different cultures.

None of this research should be carried out without a careful consideration of the implications, especially for participants, of bringing people to an awareness of their constructions, particularly of the 'passions' and of hitherto implicit understandings. Our constructions and research projects do not just have implications for action: they are actions (Gergen, 1985).

There is nothing in social constructionism that suggests that people do not suffer in very real, intense and profound ways, that they do not 'live' their constructions and stories of loneliness. But we must find new ways of addressing both loneliness and its broader implications. We can begin, as I have tried to do here, by re-examining our own constructions as social scientists and philosophers. We give a good deal of attention to negative emotions and to 'social problems'. We must also direct our energy to positive constructions, to the rewriting of loneliness stories, to the construction of stories in which there is the broadest possible shared understanding. Loneliness is not just part of everyday life: it is at the centre.

NOTES

1 J. Manusco (personal communication, 21 June 1985) has pointed out the relationship between this conceptualization of loneliness and Kelly's (1963) sociality corollary: 'To the extent that one person construes the construction processes of another, he may play a role in a social process involving the other person' (p. 95).
2 This analysis suggests that Harré's (1984b) 'quasi-emotions', which he describes as states of being closely related to physical conditions of life, can also be viewed as 'emotions-in-progress'. That is, a term begins as a description of external physical conditions, but is gradually appropriated to describe 'internal' psychological conditions, i.e., feelings and emotions.
3 I merely note here that this raises the possibility of a class of 'shared' emotions, which would be found in the social quadrant.
4 A simplified version of this point is Gordon's (1976) suggestion that loneliness does not mean the same thing to men and women.

REFERENCES

Armon-Jones, C. (1985) Prescription, explication and the social construction of emotion. *Journal for the Theory of Social Behaviour*, 15, 1–22.

Asher, S. R., Hymel, S. and Renshaw, P. D. (1984) Loneliness in children. *Child Development*, 55, 1456–64.

Averill, J. R. (1975) A semantic atlas of emotion concepts. *JSAS Catalogue of Selected Documents in Psychology*, 5, 330.

—— (1980) A constructivist view of emotion. In R. Plutchik and H. Kellerman (eds), *Emotions: Theory, Research and Experience*. Vol. 1: *Theories of Emotion* (pp. 395–39). New York: Academic Press.

Berg, S., Mellström, D., Persson, G. and Svanborg, A. (1981) Loneliness in the Swedish aged. *Journal of Gerontology*, 36, 342–9.

Blumer, H. (1971) Social problems as collective behaviour. *Social Problems*, 18, 298–306.

Bowlby, J. (1960) Separation anxiety. *International Journal of Psychoanalysis*, 61, 1–25.

Coulter, J. (1979) *The Social Construction of Mind*. New York: Macmillan.

de Rivera, J. (1984) The structure of emotional relationships. in P. Shaver (ed.), *Review of Personality and Social Psychology*. Vol. 5: *Emotions, Relationships and Health* (pp. 116–45). Beverly Hills, Cal.: Sage.

Duvall, E. M. (1945) Loneliness and the serviceman's wife. *Marriage and Family Living*, 1, 77–81.

Forgas, J. P. (1981) What is social about social cognition? In J. P. Forgas (ed.), *Social Cognition* (pp. 1–26). New York: Academic Press.

Fromm-Reichmann, F. (1959) Loneliness. *Psychiatry*, 22, 1–15.

Garfinkel, H. (1967) *Studies in Ethnomethodology*. Englewood Cliffs, NJ: Prentice-Hall.

Gergen, K. J. (1985) The social constructionist movement in modern psychology. *American Psychologist*, 40, 266–75.

Gordon, S. (1976) *Lonely in America*. New York: Simon & Schuster.

'Grandmother on way to priesthood' (1985) *Globe and Mail*, 18 May.

Gubrium, J. (1975) Being single in old age. *International Journal of Aging and Human Development*, 6, 29–41.

Harré, R. (1974) Blueprint for a new science. In N. Armistead (ed.), *Reconstructing social psychology* (pp. 240–59). Harmondsworth: Penguin.

—— (1977) Friendship as an accomplishment: an ethogenic approach to social relationships. In S. Duck (ed.), *Theory and Practice in Interpersonal Attraction* (pp. 339–54). New York: Academic Press.

—— (1984a) *Personal Being*. Cambridge, Mass.: Harvard University Press.

—— (1984b) *The Social Construction of Emotions*. Talk given at Oxford University, June 1984.

Hochschild, A. R. (1983) *The Managed Heart*. Berkeley: University of California Press.

Kelly, G. A. (1963) *The Psychology of Personal Constructs*. New York: W. W. Norton.

Kessler, S. J. and McKenna, W. (1978) *Gender: An Ethnomethodological Approach*. New York: John Wiley.

Kundera, M. (1981) *The Book of Laughter and Forgetting*. New York: Penguin.

Larson, R., Csikszentmihalyi, M. and Graef, R. (1982) Time alone in daily experience: loneliness or renewal? In L. A. Peplau and D. Perlman (eds),

Loneliness: A Sourcebook of Current Theory, Research and Therapy (pp. 40–53). New York: John Wiley.

Lazarus, R. S. (1984) On the primacy of cognition. *American Psychologist*, 39, 124–9.

Lopata, H. Z. (1969) Loneliness: forms and components. *Social Problems*, 17, 248–62.

Peplau, L. A. and Goldston, S. E. (1984) Preface. In L. A. Peplau and S. E. Goldston (eds), *Preventing the Harmful Consequences of Severe and Persistent Loneliness* (pp. vii–x). Washington, DC: US Government Printing Office.

—— Russell, D. and Heim, M. (1979) The experience of loneliness. In I. H. Frieze, D. Bar-Tal and J. S. Carroll (eds), *New Approaches to Social Problems* (pp. 53–78). San Francisco: Jossey-Bass.

Perlman, D. and Peplau, L. A. (1984) Loneliness research: a survey of empirical findings. In L. A. Peplau and S. E. Goldston (eds), *Preventing the Harmful Consequences of Severe and Persistent Loneliness* (pp. 13–46). Washington, DC: US Government Printing Office.

Rock, K. S. (1984) Promoting social bonding. *American Psychologist*, 39, 1389–1407.

Sabini, J. and Silver, M. (1982) *Moralities of Everyday Life*. Oxford: Oxford University Press.

Sarbin, T. R. (1984) *Emotion: A Contextualist View*. Invited address delivered at the meeting of the American Psychological Association, Toronto, Ontario, August 1984.

Scheibe, K. E. (1979) *Mirrors, Masks, Lies and Secrets*. New York: Praeger.

Schultz, R. (1982) Emotionality and aging. *Journal of Gerontology*, 37, 42–51.

Schutz, A. (1970) *On Phenomenology and Social Relations: Selected Writings*. Chicago: University of Chicago Press. Edited and with an introduction by H. R. Wagner.

Spector, M. and Kitsuse, J. I. (1973) Social problems: reformulation. *Social Problems*, 21, 145–59.

Swift, G. (1983) *Waterland*. London: Heinemann.

Tavris, C. (1984) On the wisdom of counting to ten: personal and social dangers of anger expression. In P. Shaver (ed.), *Review of Personality and Social Psychology*. Vol. 5: *Emotions, Relationships and Health*. Beverly Hills, Cal.: Sage.

Townsend, P. (1963) *The Family Life of Old People*. Harmondsworth: Penguin.

Weiss, R. S. (1984) Loneliness: what we know about it and what we might do about it. In L. A. Peplau and S. E. Goldston (eds), *Preventing the Harmful Consequences of Severe and Persistent Loneliness* (pp. 3–12). Washington, DC: US Government Printing Office.

Wood, L. A. (1978) Perspectives on loneliness. *Essence*, 2, 199–201.

—— (1981) *Loneliness and Life Satisfaction among the Rural Elderly*. Paper presented at the joint meeting of the Canadian Association on Gerontology and the Gerontological Society of America, Toronto, November 1981.

—— (1983) Loneliness and social identity. in T. R. Sarbin and K. E. Scheibe (eds), *Studies in Social Identity*. New York: Praeger.

—— and Kroger, R. O. (1986) Can we revive the classical experiment for social psychology? *Canadian Psychology*.

Zilboorg, G. (1938) Loneliness. *Atlantic Monthly*, 161, 45–54.

11

A Regional Variation: Emotions in Spain

Eduardo Crespo

WHAT ARE EMOTIONS?

In recent years we have seen a resurgence of interest in the study of emotions among psychologists. Investigations and publications on this theme have multiplied to provide us with a rich and interesting variety of empirical data. However, in reviewing current literature, the primary impression one receives is of confusion, as much on the plane of definitions as of explanations. Usually no definition is offered of what an emotion is; some authors consider it to be a self-evident concept that need not be defined. On the other hand, there is a considerable discrepancy between various investigators when they do set about giving a definition. There is no agreement on the type of process that is considered necessary and sufficient to denominate this or that emotion (physiological agitation, formal cognition, phenomenological experience, manifest conduct, social rules, etc.) in such a way that they can be considered to be emotions ('pride', for instance) and not something else.

These definitional problems are important and obstructive, when the concept of emotion is considered as a basis, a scientific concept, within a naturalistic and empirico-experimental framework.

Our position, however, is that the imprecision and ambiguity in respect of the significance and extension of the concept of emotion arises precisely because it is not a scientific concept in the naturalistic mode, but a concept in everyday use which takes its sense from the social theories which the subjects maintain in order to give sense to their existence, their own and others' actions, as well as their own identity. We propose to consider emotions and emotion concepts within the perspective of ordinary

The author wishes to acknowledge the help of Rom Harré in preparing this chapter and to thank him for translating it.

language. The aforesaid ambiguity and imprecision are not, then, scientific defects, but a data base on which to found an analysis of the different and changing explications of ordinary use. That which subjects understand by emotions will be a point of departure for a non-naturalistic social psychology, in which the emotions are considered as social constructions, labile and subject to negotiation – and not as facts of atemporal and transcultural significance. Our point of interest will not be physiological reactions and behaviours, that which is supposed to be the element upon which emotions, with their dynamics of social significance, are based, allowing one to entertain, for example, what Ortega y Gasset (1917) called the 'shot silk' emotions, tenderness and nostalgia, an inextricable mixture of pleasure and sadness. Only a social being is capable of maintaining these states of mind and of endowing them with meaning, despite their apparent contradiction and inexactness.

THE CONCEPT OF EMOTION

If we consider the concept of emotion as an element of any theory of human action, the first thing that manifests itself is the relative novelty of the term in languages like English and Spanish. In fact, it is a neologism, a term taken from French, which was not accepted into Spanish until quite recent times. The Academia de Lengua Espanola did not accept it, for example, until 1843, and even though it can be supposed to have had a use prior to its official acceptance, it is a term which certainly did not appear in the Spanish classics of the seventeenth century (Cervantes, Lope de Vega, Calderon, etc.). It appears in English for the first time, according to the Oxford English Dictionary, at the end of the sixteenth century, around the same time that the term gained general currency in France, as a derivative of *emouvoir*.

These etymological and historical data make clear that, for the development of a social psychology of the emotions, it is necessary to consult the historically changing character of social theories concerning the human person. If biological capacities for reaction and adaptation to the environment are, for all practical purposes, universal and transhistorical, the socially effective concept of human nature is historically changing and culturally differentiated. That which is manifest in us is not that which sustained affective actions and reactions in the past. We must assume that the effective concepts of human nature have changed (including the concept of the nature of those who form the community of scientists, which is based on a theoretical concept of common use).

It is curious, in such a case as this, how persistent are expressions which reflect an older mode of thought, such as the use of the expression, 'fear penetrates us'. This, as Ortega y Gasset points out in *El Hombre y la Gente*

(1957), reflects an old Indo-European conception, in accordance with which the emotions – like illnesses – are something exterior which invade us, which insinuate themselves inside us. How different is this hetero-centric idea of the emotions from our current homocentric and individual-istic conception, where the limits of the subject are thought to be coincident with the limits of his or her physical body. To speak of anger and pride, love and misery, envy and happiness in terms of passion, emotion or sentiment is not a question just of terminology, or style. It reflects conceptions and shadings which are not socially neutral, but which have implications for the system of attribution of responsibility, of excuses and obligations.

An interesting field of investigation would be the historical comparison of the explications of the 'life of affect', the terms in which it has been conceived, the subjects of different affective states, their moral character, etc. We can consider, as has been pointed out elsewhere (Harré, 1983), that there are emotions which have apparently disappeared but of which we have a well attested history. Such is the case with *acedia*, a term with an emotional referent which has disappeared from both English and Spanish, and which is maintained more or less as an archaism, but which is still significant in Italian and Portuguese (see chapter 13). The Spanish essayist Miguel de Unamuno (1916) wrote an interesting article on 'acedia', where he defined it as 'the insipid and sterile fruit of desire without hope' which leads on to the death of desire, to sadness and the peculiarly Spanish form of ennui, becoming *desanimado*. It is possible that the biological reactions of medieval monks affected by accidie were the same as those of our depressives; what is certain is that our evaluation and the consequences for us, as persons, predominantly socially defined, are clearly distinct, in that the social facts are different and are realized in distinctive social worlds.

EMOTIONS AND SENTIMENTS

Though the term 'emotion' is fully accepted in Spanish today and is in current use, its extension is slightly different from that which it has in English. 'Emotion' is a general concept which signifies 'an affective altera-tion which accompanies the experience of an incident', according to the Ma. Moliner dictionary, such as a state of expectation. The dictionary of the Real Academia defines it as, at bottom, an organic disturbance. In this sense its significance is the same as in English. The difference shows itself in that the concrete emotions (sorrow, happiness, sadness, guilt, envy, etc.) are treated in ordinary language as 'sentiments'. Though it would not be wrong to say 'an emotion of sadness' the usual characterization is as 'senti-ment of sadness, of guilt', etc. This detail might appear trivial and without major significance, but we belive that the characterization of the affective states in terms of emotions or sentiments implies a subtle difference in the way personal action is conceived.

The concept of emotion, we believe, brings with it a connotation of the transitory and the organic, that which is implied in considering the affective states as 'natural' processes, relatively independent of volition and, therefore, of morality, passive and, in a certain sense, independent of the permanent values which characterize a person. We have emotions, which come and go, as do our hunger and thirst, but *they are not our own*. They occur to us, and they are more or less agreeable and stimulating.

The concept of sentiment, however, has slightly different connotation. The affective states characterized as sentiments are considered to be processes more stable than emotions, more personal, less in a biological than in a moral sense. The sentiments are still not always controllable, but they are part of us. An expression in common use in Spanish is 'to have good or bad sentiments', which is a description of a wholly moral connotation, having no implications about the having of good or bad experiences or emotions.

As for the term 'passion', though it has ceased to be used in our societies, it was a central concept for the explanation of human action in other times (Vives, 1538). The passions were inclinations, desires and tendencies characteristic of a person, that were the object of considerable moralization and work. (Ascetic gravity, surely, is an example of emotional work.)

The distinction between emotion and sentiment (and in this case, passion) is not a clear and precise distinction, requiring the sort of conceptual treatment we give to empirico-experimental effects; it is an imprecise distinction because imprecision and ambiguity mark the distinctions of everyday usage. However, they point to the existence of two distinct systems of socio-moral implications. These implications constitute active elements of our collective life, such as elements of evaluation and sanction, of the generation of respect and responsibility.

However, it would be a mistake to consider these terminological systems to be static and universal. If the language we have been considering is an outstanding catalyst of social theories, we must not forget that these theories, however imprecise, ambiguous and contradictory, are, like society itself, in a state of conflict and permanent change. There exist diverse theories, confronting one another from time to time, because there exist diverse collective subjects. We should think of that upon which our distinction between emotions and sentiments is based as constituting an organizational element of two different ideologico-moralities of human existence: one, in terms of emotions, leads us to understand life as experience, more exactly as an aggregate of experiences. It is an individualist conception, conforming to that which we have to be when we are experiencing. In this, our responsibility consists, by definition in looking for the greatest number of experiences possible; our moral is 'maximize experiences – agreeable emotions'. The practice of psychotherapy serves, in a certain way, to sustain this vision. It treats bad emotions as independent of ourselves, so that good emotions can be externally imposed and substituted for them. The difference between those who experience good and bad emotions is a personal question (individual), a matter of habit and stimulation from the environment.

The other conception of human life, borne upon a description in terms of sentiments, supposes that life is to be considered more as a moral career than as an accumulation of experiences. The life of feeling does depend wholly on environmental situations and the events a person participates in, on the more or less habitual ways of conducting ourselves in them, without reference to moral character. The emotions, like the desires, in this case are properties imputable to the subject.

These different theories are active elements in the processes of social reproduction and change, in that they provide such powerful explanations of worth that they can be used as justifications and excuses in the daily maintenance of social order. The inevitable semantic ambiguity, which horrifies scientists, is properly the ground of negotiation of the meaning of action. A determinate vision of the world becomes dominant when the ambiguities are converted to the obvious, the 'natural' and the unambiguous by the members of some social group. In the terrain of the life of feeling we can find ourselves in a situation of negotiation and conflict for imposing a conception of an emotion: if the emotions are 'natural reactions', external to the 'quality' of the person who experiences them, reactions which 'naturally' demand their expression and consequential realization, the appropriate action becomes 'naturally' justified.

We can consider, then, that the concept of sentiment – in contrast to emotion – emphasizes the personal, understood in terms of affective participation in action. The substitution of a mode of thought/talk in terms of sentiments by a mode in terms of emotions supports a running together of the senses of agency and responsibility. Certain psychotherapeutic practices are contributing to this backwards step, mediated by the treatment of personal feelings as (emotional) reactions.

The concepts of emotion and sentiment can serve not only to characterize more or less transitory states of changing feelings, but also to characterize people as personalities. Our intuition suggests that the connotations of the term 'sentimental' are slightly different in Hispanic and Anglo-Saxon culture. While in the latter it is clearly a pejorative characterization, in Spanish it is ambiguous, admitting the possibility of a positive ascription. One of the most loved characters in the work of Valle-Inclan, el Marques de Bradomin, was described as 'faithful, catholic and "sentimental" '. This is a characterization which, in Castillian, could be called 'entrañable', a term whose rendering as the English 'affectionate' is not quite faithful to the sense in Spanish. 'Entrañable' refers to the 'innards' (viscera) and expresses with exactitude the affective reactions which are produced by certain topics, objects and situations charged with human significance. But 'entrañable' is evaluative, not a wholly descriptive term. It is used of a person who has left a trace of the quality of his feelings, of the goodness of his sentiments. It is a concept which suggests a form of being in which pragmatic values are not the only ones, though the values of that may not necessarily be the absolute highest.

THE SUBJECT OF EMOTIONS

Normally one supposes that it is an individual who is the subject of emotions, but this individual must be considered as a person, that is to say, as a subject whose identity is given by the social relationships which he or she maintains. In some cases, however, we must consider the existence of a collective subject of emotions; this would be the case for example in national pride and other collective *sentimientos*. The participation of an individual subject in such sentiments comes to be determined by the type of relationships he or she established.

More interesting, perhaps, are certain vicarious emotions, which are forced upon us directly by the rules for the maintenance of 'cara', face-saving rules in a determinate group. As a concrete example, consider the typically Spanish emotion, *verguenza ajena*. This is the change of feeling brought about in us in front of the incompetent or otherwise inadequate conduct of another person. The sentiment of shame, in this case, is completely outside the actions of the subject, who neither participates in the action nor is guilty of nor responsible for it. This brings home to us that the norms of self-presentation, the rituals of interaction, the rules for the maintenance of an impression – in short, the social order in its 'primary moment' – constitutes a property of the person who is thus automatically implicated in the regrets consequential on its breakdown. It is not necessary to have a direct relationship with the humiliated actor. It is enough simply to be a spectator of the action. But *verguenza ajena* is not only a surrogate sentiment, it is a terrible weapon to disqualify (devalue) an action and an actor. Those who make us feel *verguenza ajena* are considered to be ridiculous, and that, in a culture like the Spanish, is a terrible stigma.

On the other hand, to be the subject of emotions is not all there is to being human. Even if the physiological reactions can be considered universal, the emotions and sentiments are not: they are socially distributed. There is a primary distribution which corresponds exclusively to the conditions of life (Torregrosa, 1984). It appears logical to think that the enduring conditions of existence (poverty, unemployment, cultural isolation, racism, etc.) favour certain affective processes and make others impossible. This is an idea which has been developed for social psychiatry, and which academic social psychology, with its obsession for finding universal laws, has greatly neglected.

But there is a second social distribution of the emotions, a function not so much of the conditions of existence as of reference groups (though both things are intimately united). A clear case is the differentiation between the sexes. Men and women are considered socially to be subjects of distinct types of emotions. This distinction is deeply institutionalized, and appears as a datum of nature. Tenderness, for example, would not be a sentiment appropriate for men in our culture; by the same token, modesty would be basically feminine. These stereotypical ascriptions fulfil a series of functions, but, like so many social facts, they are the subject of continuous maintenance in daily life. The constant changes in the practices of ordinary discourse concerning these themes are of great interest. We must suppose that there is a battle for self-definition in emotional terms. An important aspect of the various feminist movements is that they are aimed precisely at this target.

The same point applies to expressive conduct as well. Weeping is a good example. Social tolerance of weeping ranges from an absolute repression, frequently connected with an image of feminity ('a man doesn't cry!'), to an obligation in the funerals of certain cultures (where the hierarchical position of the deceased is displayed in the hiring of professional mourners, 'wailers').

But not only is there a difference between men and women, there also exist emotions and sentiments proper to children, to the police, to soldiers and to priests. The case of children is especially interesting, for it appears that very early they acquire the habit of manifesting a double adult/infant code, handling interactional situations by means of shift from one code to the other. In the face of firm demands, or in support of exigent requirements, it is possible to observe a species of infantilization, activity controlled at base by behaviours and sentiments which adults consider to be proper to infancy, and with connotations of ingenuousness and irresponsibility. There are also capacities, when the situation requires them, of acting on the basis of adult schemas – in general, in a group of equals.

EMOTIONS AS SYNDROMES

From a psychosociological perspective, the significance of the emotions is given fundamentally by the structure of the semantic fields on to which they are 'inscribed'. It is impossible to understand each affective process (fear, happiness, sorrow, etc.) in isolation, in virtue of nothing but the ambient stimulus conditions which provoke them. Shame, for example, is a reaction appropriate to certain situations (of a threat of diminution of one's proper expressive worth, for example) in virtue of the existence of other socially acceptable *potential* reactions. This semantic network constitutes a social, not a personal, given. In the case of shame, to continue with this example, we consider that its significance is given by the relation it has with other affective processes, such as pride, humiliation and ridicule. The significance of ridicule, in the case of Spaniards, is culturally differentiated. It is our intuition that Spanish culture, in a general way, is more demanding in the conditions necessary to avoid ridicule (etymologically, not to give motives for laughter or mockery). Pride acquires its characteristic, in large part, as the right – a felt security – not to be a motive for ridicule or laughter. Other classical treatments (Balmes, 1845) indicate that pride should shun adulation, given that it is susceptible to depreciation. In reality the conjunction of sentiments pride–shame–ridiculousness–humiliation have reference to 'face work', the maintenance of a proper public presentation in some scenario. In the face of this conjunction of emotions and sentiments, 'publics' would exist as a world of private sentiments, still social, of guilt and remorse, which axis is not so much a public presentation as a system of interiorized values. This difference expresses clearly an ancient Spanish adage, which recurs in Lope de Vega and Cervantes, and which emphasizes that 'shame is more valued in the face than as a stain in the heart.' The face and the heart are the corporealizations of two different relational schemas, whose respective sanctions are shame and guilt.

The significance of a concrete emotion is given not only by its relation with other emotions but also by its relation to socially recognized structures of character. This is the case, for example, for fear and cowardice, for courage and valour. (In this sense English and Spanish cultures appear slightly different: in Castillian, courage (*coraje*) has a connotation of agressiveness, which it appears to lack in English.) Structures of emotions characterize structures of character and of personal identity. Fear, for example, admitted to be an uncontrollable reaction in the face of danger, real or imaginary, is ready to be converted into a mark of character, an element in a public identification, and subject to evaluation.

In summary, we consider that a psychosociology of the emotions should be able to distinguish the social theories which distinct groups maintain concerning the propriety and adequacy of their distinctive affective processes. From a psychosocial point of view, we are able to take account of the idea that emotions are socially distributed, and that in this distribution language plays a primordial role. This distribution is neither necessary nor static, but constitutes an element of changing social order and disorder. Following this, we are able to think of an historical development of the emotions, a development that need not necessarily be conceived as an ascent, but which can be regressive. We consider that an interesting line of investigation would be the study of how distinct social groups and persons in interaction negotiate from day to day the sense of their actions in emotion terms.

REFERENCES

Balmes, J. (1845) *El Criterio*. Buenos Aires: Espasa-Calpe (1939).

Harré, R. (1983) *Personal Being*. Oxford: Basil Blackwell.

Ortega y Gasset, J. (1917) Azorín: primores de lo vulgar. In *Obras Completas*, vol. 2. Madrid: Alianza Editorial.

—— (1957) *El Hombre y la Gente*. Madrid: Revista de Occidente.

Torregrosa, J. R. (1984) Emociones, sentimientos y estructura social. In J. R. Torregrosa and E. Crespo, *Estudios Básicos de Psicologia Social*. Barcelona: Hora.

Unamuno, M. (1916) De las trisezas españoles: la acedia. *Obras Completas*, vol. 3. Madrid: Editorial Escelicer (1968), p. 755.

Vives, J. L. (1538) *El Tratado del Alma*. In J. L. Vives, *Obras Completas*, Madrid: Aguilar.

PART III

The Diversity of Emotions

12

Emotion Talk across Times

Rom Harré and Robert Finlay-Jones

I

Accidie and Melancholy in the Psychological Context

Rom Harré

The analysis in chapter 1 of the conditions according to which emotion words and displays are used gave us bodily perturbation, belief as to intentional object, and moral qualities and imperatives as the 'components' of emotion. There are then four features that can vary: vocabularies and socially recognized displays; what are taken to be emotionally significant or salient bodily states; an ontology of relevant objects, people, states and happenings; and the local moral order. None of these could be expected to be historically constant. With the disappearance of *hauteur* goes a repertoire of stances and gestures and a vocabulary and grammar of disdainful expression. With the decline of naive superstitition goes a fear of graveyards. With the diminishment of the heroic goes the feeling of *hubris*. With the decay of a moral order, accidie was lost to view. In this part of the chapter we review the decline of the importance of this emotion and the loss of the word as a distinguishing tool, and suggest that there may be evidence to support the idea that accidie is with us once again, though lacking a supporting vocabulary. Melancholy too has faded from popular esteem, and the change in its importance may be related to the disappearance of accidie.

I am grateful to J. B. Bamborough, Principal of Linacre College for much help and guidance for the brief study of the history of the concept of melancholy.

ACCIDIE: AN EXTINCT EMOTION

Accidie is an emotional state; *negligentia, pigritia* and *otiositas* (negligence, laziness and idleness) were among its typical manifestations, while *taedium, desperatio* and *tristitia* were associated or consequential emotions. Medieval moral psychologists analysed accidie in detail, since for many not only was it the major spiritual failing to which those who should have been dutiful succumbed, but to feel it at all was sin. By the fifteenth century the popular conception of 'the sin of sloth' had ceased to be a state of mind and had shifted to manifest behaviour (or lack of it). 'Sloth' had taken on its modern connotation.

I offer accidie as an example of an obsolete emotion,since I think modern people do not associate any specific emotion with laziness or procrastination in the carrying out of tasks that duty demands. Rather, emotions cluster around occasions of reprimand, real or imagined, and urging. They can range from guilt to a kind of indignation, such as 'I was just about to do it, when you interfered!' However, there is reason to think that something like 'accidie' talk may be needed once again.

The basic idea of accidie was boredom, dejection or even disgust with fulfilling one's religious duty. It appears for the first time in the works of Evagrius (AD 346–9) as 'the noonday demon' which distracts a hermit from the duties of the ascetic life. From its earliest identification it had a double-sidedness: on the one hand, negligence (a behavioural matter); on the other, a kind of misery (a matter of feelings). By embedding the negligence in a moral order (one's duty to God), an emotion (*acedia*) was born, according to just the formula for linking feelings and behavioural manifestations with moral matters through a causal interpretation that we have used, in reverse, to analyse contemporary emotions. The range of feelings is quite wide, including sorrow, bitterness, misery and *taedium cordis*, weariness of heart.

The association of laziness with misery, out of which accidie was born, meant that a certain ambiguity affected the prescriptions for extirpating it. In so far as it involved a failure to carry on with a tiresome, uncomfortable or boring task, the cultivation of fortitude formed part of its remedy. But dutiful behaviour without joy (*gaudium*) was an inadequate response. *Acedia* was truly overcome only when delight in the exercise of one's proper activities returned.

A detailed history of the appearance, flourishing and disappearance of the emotional state of *acedia* can be found in Wenzel's excellent work, *The Sin of Sloth: Accedie in Medieval Thought and Literature* (Wenzel, 1960). Not only is there a shift from emotional state to typical behaviour as the referent of the term, but there is also a long, analytical struggle to relate *acedia* to *tristitia*. In catalogues of the sins and their progeny the relation undergoes several reworkings. In some, *acedia* is a species of *tristitia*. But in later works (e.g. Aquinas), *acedia* is the root of spiritual vice, and *tristitia* is experienced as among its typical manifestations. The essential issue is the dependence of the very existence of the emotional state on a moral order (duty to God fulfilled in spiritual exercises). Idleness and procrastination are still among our failings, but our emotions are differently engaged, defined against the background of a different moral order, roughly the ethics of a material production. (See for example the emotional state called 'Oblomovism', described by Goncharov and taken up by T. S. Eliot. I owe the comparison to a conversation with Don Campbell.)

MELANCHOLY: AN OBSOLETE MOOD

I think it would be correct to say that melancholy, which was of such interest to medieval moral psychology and which played such a large role in seventeenth-century personality and clinical psychology, is no longer within the reach of our current terms of talk. Though we understand what it is to be melancholy, we never confess to this feeling. Bored, depressed, nostalgic – yes. Melancholy – no (though White does include it in a *written* list of moods). A sane but gloomy person would be astounded if his medical adviser diagnosed his troubles as a case of clinical melancholy. Yet Marsilio Ficino made a career out of treating it, and Robert Burton wrote a very large and famous book anatomizing it. Melancholy is obsolete. Yet its role in medieval and Renaissance psychology was supreme. Some authorities hold that belief in the psychology of melancholy coloured and transformed the admissible forms of personality expression of an entire nation – the English.

'Melancholy' began its long history as the name of an illness, a bodily malfunction affecting the mind. Ficino's distinction of obnoxious melancholy (*atra bilis*) from congenial melancholy (*candida bilis*) retains the association with an illness brought about by a biochemical imbalance in the body (in those days expressed as an excess of black bile). According to Logan, in *The Voices of Melancholy* (1973), the concept of melancholy developed through the Middle Ages in two contexts: medical practice, in which the theory remained fairly stable, and moral psychology, where it was analysed among the passions. Klibansky et al., in *Saturn and Melancholy* (1964), emphasized the extent to which medieval characterology, based on the physiological theory of the four humours, was an echo and re-echo of certain texts, particularly that of Vindician. Excess of one humour caused illness which was cured by increasing its contrary. The seasons of the year and times of the day severally amplify the associated humour. Autumn and night were the times of melancholy. In the course of this period, 1100 to 1300, the melancholic and the three other 'complexions' shifted from the status of illnesses to that of temperaments, though without wholly losing their pathological connotations.

Hughes de Fouillori is extensively quoted by Klibansky et al. (1964). The text falls into two parts: a short summary of the physiology of black bile, and a detailed account of the associated emotions or passions in the context of moral theology. Thus, 'by black bile we may . . . mean grief, which we should feel for our evil actions. But we may also speak of a different sort of grief, when the spirit is tormented by the longing to be united with the Lord.' Later in the same passage the dual nature of the melancholic person is emphasized: 'Bowed by cares, sometimes wakefully directed to heavenly aims.' Popular psychology of the late Middle Ages, according to Klibansky et al., evidently elided and transcended both the medical pathological and the moral psychological theories to create a genuinely psychological treatment of temperament. Klibansky et al. quote mnemonic verses, which for the melancholic include:

> Invides et tristes, cupidus, dextraeque, tenacis,
> non expers fraudis, timidus, luteique, coloris.
> *Envious and sad, eager and skilful, tenacious,*
> *having no part in cheating, fearful and of a foul and*
> *   yellowish complexion.*

> Auctumnus, terra melancholia, senectus
> (frigida et sicca appetit et non petit rubea et clara).
> *Autumnal, earthy, melancholy, senile*
> *(cold and dry in his tastes, and he does not aim at being ruddy*
> *   [cheerful] and bright).*

By the late Middle Ages the complex of favourable and unfavourable features of the melancholic temperament were well established, and, as Klibansky points out, the unfavourable features were emphasized throughout popular and technical literature alike. They cite a marvellous description of the melancholy temperament from the Teuscher Kalendar (Augsburg, 1495), in which the melancholic is cold and dry like autumn, the earth and old age. He is timid, lazy, slow of movement, hostile, sad, forgetful, indolent, clumsy, has 'but rare and weak desires' 'owing to his sadness'. At the same time, it was widely held that only among men of this temperament could true genius be found. Later we have the entertaining spectacle of those who sought to be geniuses, cultivating the melancholy cast of mind, staring out from high towers on autumn nights. Women's melancholy seems to have had no such redeeming features.

By the sixteenth century melancholy had become the main focus of interest of psychology. I shall first summarize a good standard treatment (Bright, 1586) and then turn to one of the great psychological texts of all time, Burton's *Anatomy of Melancholy*.

Bright takes pains to distinguish true melancholy from 'that heavy hand of God upon the afflicted conscience, tormented with remorse of sin and feare of his judgement . . .' (p. iii verso). Melancholy has a physiological origin in 'an increase and excess of the melancholicke humour'. In a thoroughly modern manner, Bright identifies melancholy with a particular interpretation of a physiological state: 'when any conceit troubleth you that hath no sufficient ground of reason, but riseth only upon the frame of your brain . . . that is right melancholicke' (p. 133). The interpretation is typified by 'envious they are, because of their own false conceived want whereby their estate, seeming in their own false conceived fantasy much worse than it is . . . maketh them to desire what they see others to enjoy . . .' (p. 133).

Quite unlike modern depression, melancholy can sustain, indeed can even be the condition of, powerful intellectual endeavours: 'melancholie breedeth a jealousie of doubt in that they [the melancholic] take in deliberation, and causeth them to be more exact and curious in pondering the very moments of things – the vehemence of their affection, once raised . . . carrieth them . . . into the depths of what they take pleasure to intermeddle in' (p. 130). Melancholics are both 'diligent and painful, wary and circumspect' and 'doubtful and suspicious', the latter engendering the former.

With Burton, melancholy is neither an occasional disease nor a specific temperament, one among four. It is a complex affliction to which all are prone, consequential on the general conditions of human life. Burton's work, *The Anatomy of Melancholy*, has provoked two radically opposite judgements in modern authors. According to Klibansky et al., 'the assumption of the generality of melancholy and the uniqueness of each particular case' . . . 'is an entirely literary assumption . . .' (1964, p. 147). Bergen Evans, in *The Psychiatry of Robert Burton* (1946), interprets the general/particular distinction as a subtle and empirically well-grounded part of the empirical psychology of the conditions. Melancholy, says Burton, is a 'settled humour . . . *morbis, sonticus* or *chronicus*'. But the extent of the disorder and the problems of its treatment can only be grasped by a 'sheer, indefatigable listing of innumerable symptoms', (p. 47). Evans might surely be right.

In two respects Burton's treatment goes beyond that of Marsilio Ficino. It is a 'symbolizing disease', appearing in distinctive forms, but it is a condition in need of diagnosis, since 'the soul is carried hoodwinkt and the understanding captive'. However, 'there is in all melancholy *similitudo dissimilis*, like men's faces, a disagreeing likeness still' (pt. 1, s. 3, mem. 1, subs. 2). In essence, Burton's theory seems to be that there are 'quite natural inward causes' of unfounded 'fears and sorrows' which become the dangerous state of melancholy by virtue of wrong interpretations, as for example by being 'bewitched or forsaken of God' (pt. 1, s. 3, mem. 3). By showing 'to melancholy men ... the causes whence they [the symptoms] proceed', they can 'endure them with more patience' (pt. 1, s. 3, mem. 3), a remark reminiscent of the analysis by Schachter (1971) in *Emotion, Obesity and Crime.*

Secondly, Burton sees melancholy not as a temperament, among others, but as a condition arising out of quite normal physiological states, by some excess. Melancholy, 'in disposition ... goes and comes upon every small occasion of sorrow etc.' 'And from these melancholy dispositions no man living is free ...' (pt. 1, s. 1, mem. 1, subs. 4). Melancholy to Burton is 'a chronic or continuate disease, a settled humour ... not errant but fixed ... and as it were long increasing, so now being (pleasant or painful) given to an habit, it will hardly be removed' (pt. 1, s. 1, mem. 1, subs. 4).

Despite the enormous variety of ways in which dangerous degrees of melancholy are manifested, including unwillingness to speak for fear of uttering obscenities, urges to suicide, hyperchondria etc., 'suspicion and jealousy are general symptoms' (pt. 1, s. 3, mem. 1, subs. 2), leading to a particular kind of attentiveness to all around them, and to morbid fancies of persecution. And again, 'Inconstant are they in all their actions ... restless [yet] if once they be resolved, obstinate ...'. And again, 'what they desire they do most furiously seek ...'; 'prone to love', but 'love one dearly till they see another, and then dote on her'.

But why melancholy? As I understand it, it is the connection with the gloom and despondency that overcomes him or her whose abnormalities and inconstancies lead them into isolation and a kind of miserable idleness near to accidie.

The author of Aristotle's *Problems* (xxx, 1) quoted in Logan, *Voices of Melancholy* (1973) remarks, 'Those, however, in whom the black bile's excessive heat is relaxed towards a mean, are melancholy, but they are more rational and less eccentric and in many respects superior to others in culture or in the arts or in statesmanship.' The suggestion that either as temperament or as mood melancholy subserves and promotes intellectual activity is a common theme throughout its history. Burton is very largely concerned with the pathology of melancholy and the cure of its myriad manifestations. The dual nature of melancholy was an important part of seventeenth century psychology. As Babb (1951) puts it in *The Elizabethan Malady*, it was on the one hand 'a degrading mental abnormality associated with fear and sorrow', a malady sibling to our contemporary 'depression', and on the other 'a condition which endows one with intellectual acumen and profundity'. In the twin poems 'L'Allegro' and 'Il Penseroso', Milton displays both images. I offer these lines as an elegant summary of the psychology of melancholy. From 'L'Allegro' we have:

> Hence loathed Melancholy
> of *Cerberus* and blackest midnight born

> In Stygian caves forlorn
> 'Mongst horrid shapes, and shrieks, and sights unholy
> Find out some uncouth cell,
>   Where brooding darkness spreads his jealous wings,
>   And the night-Raven sings;
> There under Ebon shades, and low-brow'd Rocks,
>   As ragged as thy locks,
>   In dark *Cimmerian* desert ever dwell.

In these ingenious lines most of the pathology of melancholy is touched upon. In 'Il Penseroso' Milton gives exactly equal attention to 'constructive melancholy':

> But hail thou Godess, sage and holy,
> Hail divinest melancholy.
>
> Thee bright hair'd Vesta long of yore
> To solitary *Saturn* bore:
>
> Come pensive Nun, devout and pure,
> Sober, stedfast, and demure.

The cherub Contemplation and 'mute silence' are among the followers of Melancholy; the connection of melancholy with the scientific approach to nature dominates the last few lines:

> Find out the peaceful hermitage,
> The Hairy gown and Mossy Cell,
> Where I may sit and rightly spell,
> Of every Star that Heaven doth shew,
> And every Herb that sips the dew;
> Till old experience do attain
> To something like Prophetic strain.
> These pleasures *Melancholy* give,
> And I with thee will choose to live.

What does this story show? A theory being used to bring into order, and compose into a sort of unity, a variety of feelings, beliefs and environmental factors, engendering both a distinctive mood and a temperament (and personality) of which that mood is characteristic. The original physiological theory upon which the four-temperament analysis of human personality was based soon became enormously elaborated with astrological ideas. All of this vast apparatus of belief provided a powerful cognitive structure by which to organize one's experience. In the course of the long history of melancholy, the accounts of it take on a prescriptive force over and above their original role in the medical symptomology. By the time of Milton and Burton, melancholy is something one might aspire to and at the same time something of which one might desperately wish to be relieved.

II

Accidie and Melancholy in a Clinical Context

Robert Finlay-Jones

A CLINICAL AND DIAGNOSTIC PROBLEM

The subject of this part of the chapter is a state which has been referred to as 'disgust with life in general' (Altschule, 1965). It consists of a set of symptoms which has been periodically diagnosed (and, some would argue, mis-diagnosed) as a depressive syndrome for 25 centuries.

I first met this state when I asked a number of women living in an affluent area of London to complete the 30-item General Health Questionnaire, or GHQ, a screening instrument for detecting states of anxiety and depression (Goldberg, 1972). When they were interviewed subsequently using the Present State Examination (Wing et al. 1974), many of the women who had been detected as 'probable cases' by the GHQ were rejected by the diagnostic computer programs CATEGO and Index of Definition as being neither cases of anxiety nor cases of depression (Finlay-Jones and Murphy, 1979).

One response to such a finding is to ask whether these so-called 'false positives', who will be referred to here as 'undiagnosed subjects', differed from true cases in their symptoms, or from true normals in their social characteristics. They did, in both ways and from both groups. Compared with the normal women, the undiagnosed subjects were socially isolated and were either unemployed or had menial occupations. Secondly, they tended to answer the GHQ slightly differently to the true cases, although there was considerable overlap. Although they had lower scores overall than the true cases, there were nevertheless two questions which the undiagnosed subjects answered more often than the true cases. They answered positively to question 4, that is, 'I have not been managing to keep myself busy and occupied' and to question 30, that is 'I have found at times that I could not do anything because my nerves were too bad.' Note the emphasis on doing things. They were not able to keep busy; they could not do anything. They also complained of feeling anxious and depressed, but not as intensely or as frequently as the true cases did.

Robert Finlay-Jones, 'Accidie and Melancholy in a Clinical Context' is based on an address given in Sydney in December 1972 to mark the retirement of Professor L. G. Kiloh, School of Psychiatry, New South Wales.

So here was a group of women who complained of not being able to do anything, who were socially isolated and were either unemployed or did menial tasks, and who complained of depression and anxiety but who were not diagnosed as cases of depression or anxiety by more stringent criteria. What was the matter with them? Were they bored? Were they filled with the *taedium vitae*, the weariness which comes from leading a monotonous and lonely life? Were they lazy? Were they sinful? The answer to each of these questions would have been 'yes' at some time in the last two thousand years. Today they would probably be called mildly depressed. Their complaints of having difficulty in doing things might be explained away as a class-related style of expressing emotional distress. But at various points in the last two millenia it was regarded as important to diagnose them as suffering not from depression, but from a condition called *acedia*. The rest of this paper describes some aspects of *acedia*, how it was confused with depression, and why attempts were sporadically made to distinguish the two.

ACEDIA AND DEPRESSION IN THE HISTORY OF CLINICAL PSYCHOLOGY

We can begin to trace the history of this condition by recalling the temptations faced by the monastics of the early Christian church as they mediated in the desert outside the fourth century city of Cairo. John Cassian, writing in 415, listed them as the eight cardinal vices (Bloomfield, 1951/67). Seven of them are familiar to us: they are gluttony, lust, anger, avarice, vainglory, pride and depression (Latin: *tristitia*). The eighth, *acedia*, is not. What does the word mean? The Greek origin of the word means 'non-caring'. An alternative spelling in English is accidie. Cassian defined *acedia* as 'quod est taedium sive anxietas cordis'. This important phrase can be literally translated as 'that which is tedium, also known as "anxietas" of the heart'. Sir Aubrey Lewis (1967) has warned against the casual equating of 'anxietas' with our word anxiety. Whatever it is, the emotion was commonly referred to the heart in the Middle Ages, and certainly meant something more complex than palpitations.

Acedia tempted the monk in the heat of midday to doubt whether there was any point in it all, and stopped him from doing anything useful. *Acedia* made him sink through disgust and lassitude into the black depths of despair and hopeless unbelief (Huxley, 1948).

A century after Cassian, Gregory the Great rewrote his list. He changed it in a number of important ways, and in the process reduced the list to seven vices. The most significant change from our point of view was that he subsumed depression and *acedia* under the one heading, for which he kept the word *tristitia*. Why did he do this? I have been unable to find a convincing explanation, so I shall put forward one of my own. The evolution of a list of cardinal vices probably depends in part upon the keen observation of deviant behaviour by psychologically minded physicians of the soul. Perhaps Gregory was unable to detect any important difference in the psychological outcome of the vice of depression and that of the vice of *acedia*, and so he combined them. After all, both led to despair. It will be argued below that his inability in the sixth century to distinguish the symptoms of a depressive syndrome from the symptoms of boredom or inactivity or disgust with life in general was the same as the inability of the GHQ 1,300 years later.

For 600 years after Gregory, the idea of *acedia* retained its original meaning of spiritual torpor, and for 900 years it remained inextricably confused with depression. There were sporadic attempts to separate the two. The most important from our perspective was made by a Dominican friar in Milan, Fra Battista da Crema, who in 1531 wrote 'Della cognitione et vittoria di se stesso'. A scholarly analysis of this document has been carried out by Brann (1979). In it, Battista da Crema argued for a theological separation of *acedia* from depression partly on the basis of a medical distinction between the two. He pointed out that medical writers in the tradition of Hippocrates and Galen believed that all pathology including mental disorders was based on an imbalance of one of the four bodily humours, blood, black bile, yellow bile and phlegm. He reminded his readers of the similarity between the outcome of the vice of depression and the outcome of an excess of black bile, the disorder of melancholy. Then he reminded them of the similarity between the outcome of the vice of *acedia* and that of an excess of phlegm. This was a disorder known as lethargy, which had a long and established place in medical classifications as quite a separate disorder from melancholy. Lethargy, the result of too much phlegm, was classified separately from melancholy, the result of too much black bile, in the classifications of Cornelius Celsus writing in AD 100, Galen writing in 150, Posidonius in 375, Alexander of Tralles in 500, Caelius Aruelianus in the fifth century, Paul of Aegina in 700, Avicenna in 1000, Thomas Aquinas in 1250, Fernel, Schenck and Felix Platter in the 1500s, and Zacchias and Thoms Willis in the seventeenth century (Menninger, 1967).

Battista da Crema made one other astute observation, which for him reinforced the distinction between depression and *acedia* in the theological frame of reference, or melancholy and lethargy in the medical framework. He recalled the question originally put by Aristotle (1927): 'Why is it that all those who have become eminent in philosophy or politics or poetry or the arts are clearly of an atrabilious temperament, and some of them to such an extent as to be affected by diseases caused by black bile?'

This observation has been repeatedly made since the time of Aristotle: melancholics are generally capable of greater feats than the normal run of men; phlegmatics are not. As da Crema put it, 'the spirit of *acedia* exclaims through the mouth of its lethargic victim: "I am of a phlegmatic disposition, and am neither very agile nor mobile. I am unable to complete a thing which has been begun". . . .' We retain the word 'phlegmatic' today to describe the character who is torpid and sluggish, and difficult to arouse to emotion or activity.

Although melancholics succumb to depression, there is a good and a bad form of depression, as St Paul pointed out (Altschule, 1967). A person with the good form of depression is revolted by the unpleasantness of the world, but then turns his thoughts to God. A person with the bad form of depression is deluded and despairing, rejects God, and turns his thoughts to death.

Battista da Crema argued that melancholics were capable of the more spiritually valuable form of depression because they were filled with *ekstasis*, the spiritual equivalent of combustibility which in the medical frame of reference distinguished the melancholic from the phlegmatic temperament. It was true that phlegmatic *acedia* could induce symptoms indistinguishable from the bad form of melancholic depression. But even at its best, phlegmatic *acedia*, lacking *ekstasis*, could not begin to approach the sublime heights which were accessible to the melancholic with the exalted form of depression.

From the twelfth to the fifteenth century the original notion of *acedia* became corrupted, and the idea began to lose its relevance for us today. Its meaning was changed from that of a complex state of lassitude and disgust with life in general to a simpler idea of failing to observe certain religious practices such as church attendance, until by Elizabethan times it had come to mean nothing more than personal laziness.

There were two reasons for this, one to do with the church and one to do with the state. The fourth Lateran Council in 1215 made confession and penitance obligatory for everybody. The man in the street needed a list of sins which he could memorize to help him examine his conscience. The sophisticated idea of *acedia* was reduced to a notion of personal sloth to meet this need. The secular reason was to do with the rise of the bourgeoisie, who were keen to hear preached from the pulpit the dangers of sloth which they saw as typifying the idle nobility. On the other hand, the nobility encouraged preaching against avarice, which they saw as underlying the bourgeoisie's successful accumulation of capital.

MELANCHOLY AND LETHARGY

Let us return to the medical distinction between melancholy and lethargy which we briefly traced as far as the seventeenth century. The diagnosis of melancholy was very fashionable in Elizabethan England, as fashionable as the diagnosis of depression today. The myriad of conditions dissected by Burton in his *Anatomy of Melancholy* is testimony to this. Nevertheless, certain practitioners were concerned with the issues of differential diagnosis. Clear evidence of this can be found in Macdonald's fascinating study of the case notes of Richard Napier, an astrological physician who practised in Buckinghamshire (Macdonald, 1981).

The two most common non-psychotic disorders diagnosed by Napier were melancholy and 'mopishness', his word for lethargy. What differences did he discern between the two? Both conditions included symptoms of fear and sadness, but these symptoms were twice as common among those diagnosed as melancholic. One sees the parallel among the London women, where the true cases and the undiagnosed women complained of anxiety and depression, but the true cases complained more intensely.

The complaint of not doing anything useful was noted among both the mopish and the melancholic, but was more frequent among the mopish. Part of the explanation for this may have been that class influenced both the diagnosis of melancholy and whether idleness was recognized as a symptom of psychological disorder. With regard to the former point, Napier diagnosed peers and knights ten times more often as melancholic than as mopish. On the other hand, he diagnosed his lowest class of patients, those whom he did not even bless with the title Mr or Mrs, as melancholic or mopish in the ratio 1 : 1. With respect to the latter point, idleness was not seen as a symptom of a melancholic nobleman. It was the core of aristocratic life, not a symptom but a precipitating cause working on a melancholic temperament. In contrast, idleness was seen as a symptom of those patients who were born to work, a symptom of the disorder of mopishness. It is worth recalling in this context that the true cases among the London women were mainly the affluent women of Regent's Park, while the diagnosed women were distinguished by being unemployed or working-class.

The clearest distinction between Napier's diagnosis of melancholy and his diagnosis of mopishness lay in a third symptom, that of an impairment of the senses. Blunted sensibility is not a symptom about which we enquire today, but the phenomenon was perfectly familiar to Napier's contemporaries. Shakespeare, for example used the term to signify a kind of mental disorder that ruined people's capacity to perceive the world and to react properly to stimuli. Hamlet describes the effect of mopishness on the senses when castigating Gertrude for marrying Claudius:

> Eyes without feeling, feeling without sight,
> Ears without hands or eyes, smelling sans all,
>   Or but a sickly part of one true sense
>   Could not so mope.

Is this insensibility to the world around us what the Greeks understood by the phlegmatic temperament, the temperament which lacks the spirit of combustibility or *ekstasis*? Is it the same complaint which is expressed in twentieth century jargon as 'Nothing seems to turn me on'? I believe it is. It is mirrored in the following definition of *acedia* for which I am indebted to Father Michael Casey, of Tarrawarra Abbey, Victoria:

> I see acedia as a resistance to a personalisation of life which is expressed in Shoham's phrase [1974] as a 'depressive detachment' from people, things and courses of action which are potential sources of much happiness....

This is indeed the tenor of my title: disgust, or rather a-gust, no taste, for life in general.

CONCLUSIONS

An argument has been made for the rediscovery of a syndrome which can be differentially diagnosed from depression, and which has at various times been called *acedia*, lethargy, mopishness or insensibility. Other more recent epithets probably describe the same state: ennui, *welt-schmerz*, neurasthenia and the surburban neurosis.

The condition has three symptoms. First there is a mood disturbance of fear and sadness. Second, there is the complaint of doing nothing useful, and behaviour which supports that. Third, there is an insensibility to both the pain and the pleasure of the world.

Let us now speculate. Perhaps the cause of this condition is the lack of the satisfying activity called work. Lack of satisfying work will produce the complaint of doing nothing useful and of being bored. Boredom may be expressed as a relative insensitivity to both pain and pleasure. Boredom can also at times produce feelings of fear amounting to panic, and of misery which may be misdiagnosed as a depressive syndrome.

And what is the cause of the cause? Why do people find work unsatisfying? For three reasons. First, for many people their daily work is in fact boring, menial and unstimulating. Along this line of argument, one would expect to find *acedia* more prevalent among the suburban house-wife and the man on the factory production line. Second, many people have no work at all. One would expect to find *acedia* among the unemployed and the retired. It is noticeable that each of these four demographic groups is said to have rates of depression which are higher than usual: is the excess something else, something called *acedia*? Third, some people get no pleasure from work for apparently temperamental reasons. I do not know whether this is due to an excess of phlegm or a lack of endorphins, or simply because they live lives in which their labours have never been rewarded.

Does it matter if the diagnosis of *acedia* is not made? It does only in that there is probably a simple treatment for *acedia* which may be different to those prescribed for depression. It was described by Chaucer 600 years ago in his *Prologue to the Second Nun's Tale*. He called the remedy 'leveful bisynesse', or keeping oneself busy in a lawful way. It is probably rather good advice to offer a man on the eve of his retirement.

REFERENCES

Altschule, M. D. (1965)   Acedia: its evolution from deadly sin to psychiatric syndrome. *British Journal of Psychiatry*, 111, 117–19.
—— (1967)   The two kinds of depression according to St Paul. *British Journal of Psychiatry*, 113, 779–80.
Aristotle (1927)   Problemata. In *The Works of Aristotle* translated into English, vol. 7. Oxford: Clarendon Press, 953a.
Babb, L. (1951)   *The Elizabethan Malady*. Ann Arbor: Michigan University Press.
Bloomfield, M. W. (1951/67)   *The Seven Deadly Sins*. Michigan State University Press, 1951, 1967.
Brann, N. L. (1979)   Is acedia melancholy? *Journal of the History of Medicine and Allied Science*, 34, 180–99.
Bright, T. (1586   *A Treatise of Melancholie*. London: Vautrolier.
Burton, R. (1621)   *The Anatomy of Melancholy*. London.
Evans, B. (1946)   *The Psychiatry of Robert Burton*. New York: Columbia University Press.
Finlay-Jones, R. A. and Murphy, E. (1979)   Severity of psychiatric disorder and the 30-item General Health Questionnaire. *Psychiatry*, 134, 609–16.
Goldberg, D. P. (1972)   *The Detection of Psychiatric Illness by Questionnaire*, London: Oxford University Press.
Huxley, A. (1948)   Accidie. In A. Huxley, *On the Margin*. London: Chatto & Windus, 18–25.
Klibansky, R., Panovsky, E. and Saxl, F. (1964)   *Saturn and Melancholy*. London: Nelson.
Lewis, A. J. (1967)   Problems presented by the ambiguous word 'anxiety' as used in psychopathology. *Israel Annals of Psychiatry and Related Disciplines*, 5, 105–213.
Logan, B. C. (1973)   *The Voices of Melancholy*. London: Routledge & Kegan Paul.
Macdonald, M. (1981)   *Mystical Bedlam*. Cambridge: Cambridge University Press.
Menninger, K. (1967)   Appendix: attests and exhibits. In K. Menninger, *The Vital Balance*. New York: Viking, 419–89.
Schachter, S. (1971)   *Emotion, Obesity and Crime*. New York: Academic Press.
Shoham, S. G. (1974)   *Society and the Absurd*. Oxford: Basil Blackwell.
Wenzel, S. (1960)   *The Sin of Sloth*. Chapel Hill: University of North Carolina Press.
Wing, J. K., Cooper, J. E. and Sartorius, N. (1974)   *The Measurement and Classification of Psychiatric Symptoms*. London: Cambridge University Press.

13

Emotion Talk across Cultures

Paul Heelas

Emotional life has sparked the human imagination. Members of different societies talk about their emotions in a wide variety of ways, many of which strike us as distinctly imaginative. The Javanese of Ponorogo, for example, employ liver talk: 'it is the liver (*ati*) that appears in idiomatic expressions indicating emotion'; and 'the role of the liver is not altogether just a metaphor' (Weiss, 1983, p. 72).

In this chapter I shall take the reader on a 'Cooks tour' of societies whose members talk about emotions in an 'exotic' fashion. As we shall see, there are very considerable differences in the number of emotions clearly identified; what emotions mean; how they are classified and evaluated; how the nature of emotions is considered with regard to locus, aetiology and dynamics; the kind of environmental occurrences which are held to generate particular emotions; the powers ascribed to emotions; and management techniques. I hope I am justified in assuming that the relative inaccessibility of much of the ethnography means that many readers will not be aware of the extent to which emotion talk can diverge from our own. But what exactly has this to do with the social construction of emotions? Why do I plunge the reader into an assortment of ethnographic 'curiosities'?

By way of introduction, I shall indicate why I regard emotion talk to be of very considerable constructivist importance. I want to give some idea of the significance of the strange varieties of emotion talk to be encountered. For reasons which will become more apparent later, I shall indicate why emotion talk – clearly a product of the human imagination – does not have imaginary consequences. It in fact has great bearing on the nature of emotional life.

To argue this first means arguing against those who hold that emotions are endogenous. For, if emotions are part of our biological inheritance, emotion talk is adventitious. Just as the stars are impervious to cross-cultural differences in how they are conceptualized, so too are the emotions – at least, in their core properties. I must thus side with Geertz (1980), the constructivist, against Leach, who has written that Geertz's approach is 'complete rubbish' because it ignores 'genetic' factors (Leach, 1981, p. 32). This is not difficult to do. Perhaps the majority of those psychologists who have found evidence supporting the endogenous approach have also found it necessary to introduce exogenous determinants. Thus Leventhal, distinguishing between 'emotional elements' and 'emotional experiences', argues that biologically generated elements have to be 'enriched' by meanings ('conceptualizations of affect') before becoming emotional experiences (Leventhal, 1980, p. 192). Incorporating constructivist theorizing, Leventhal accords ample scope for the sociocultural to make impact. Meanings bound up with emotion talk can get to work.[1]

Granted this, what of the importance of emotion talk within the general context of sociocultural determinants? A number of theorists have argued for constructivism without mentioning emotion talk, let alone treating it as important. Mandler (1980) writes of 'languages of emotion' in this fashion: 'The label that something is good or the cognate facial expression of acceptance or approval influences the quality of the emotional experience' (p. 231). Mandler would certainly not want to discount emotion talk, but its *particular* importance is clearly diminished in that moral judgements as a whole can apparently function in generative fashion.

The particular importance I want to attach to emotion talk is seen by what happens when it is ignored. According to Kemper (1984), 'A very large class of human emotions results from real, anticipated, recollected, or imagined outcomes of power and status relations' (p. 371). More specifically, consider his explanation of how status loss generates anger:

> When we believe the other is the agent of our status loss, whether by insult, intentional infliction of pain, ignoring us when we have a right to be attended to, or depriving us of goods, services, money, or approval that we have earned or deserve according to our understanding ... the immediate emotional outcome ... is *anger*. (Kemper, 1978, p. 128)

Emotion talk, enabling participants to understand the emotional significance of status loss, does not enter the picture. This is unfortunate. It is true that we have acquired a strong tendency to respond to insults and the like in terms of anger, but by no means do we always do so: my status is affected by a public insult and I feel shame; my status is affected when I do not get what I deserve and I feel inadequate; I am deprived of the attention of my wife and feel jealous. Events of the kind mentioned by Kemper, in other words, need not mean that we respond with *anger*. How we respond depends on how we use our knowledge of our emotional life, interpreting an episode as shaming, for example, because it accords with our understanding the episode as being bound up with what we take shame to mean. In short, the fact that we attribute emotion-specific meanings to those more general sociocultural varieties discussed by Kemper explains why the 'immediate emotional outcome' is not always anger.

I do not want to conclude that the meanings provided by emotion talk are the only ones which constructivists should attend to. One consideration is that emotion talk does not exist in isolation from other domains of knowledge. The meaning of 'anger', for example, is obviously bound up with how we have learnt to use this word in connection with the moral domain (cf. Kemper's 'insults'). The term enables us to know (and so have) the emotion in connection with particular moral events precisely because its meaning is not purely psychological. That emotion talk is often bound up with the moral domain is also clearly seen in Peter's (1974) observation: 'emotions, such as pride, ambition, guilt and remorse, imply a certain view of ourselves. They are probably not felt in cultures in which little importance is attached to individual effort and responsibility' (p. 402).

Other reasons for not limiting emotionally significant meanings to emotion talk are provided by all those psychologists who do not limit themselves to this domain (cf. Mandler, 1980; and Lazarus et al., 1980, who include all 'transactions that the person judges as having implications for her or his *well-being* (p. 195)). One final consideration, to do with the fact that the constructivist cannot simply attend to emotion talk when exploring the management of emotions, concerns what social learning theorists such as Bandura (1965) call 'attentional shift'. Do we not often try to manage distressful emotions by thinking of something other than our emotional states?

Having said this, the fact remains that meanings are necessary for the construction of emotions and that particular meanings (of some kind) are necessary for the construction of particular emotions. In the absence of such particular meanings, we are left with those differentiations in experience which occur at the level of what Leventhal calls emotional 'elements'. And it is difficult not to conclude that these particular meanings have more to do with emotion talk than with anything else. Indeed, it might be possible to argue that meanings can constitute different emotions only if they involve emotion terms which provide knowledge of differences. This certainly is what is implied by Lazarus (1980) when he writes that 'each emotion quality and intensity – anxiety, guilt, jealousy, love, joy or whatever – is generated and guided by its own particular cognitive theme' (p. 192). And is not the importance of emotion terms suggested by experimental research (e.g. Schachter and Singer, 1962) apparently showing that emotions are states of physiological arousal defined by the actor as emotionally induced? If, indeed, such research shows that differences in knowledge (this situation means 'anger', this 'euphoria') are crucial in determining which emotions are experienced, then emotion talk, providing the linguistic distinctions, lies at the heart of the matter. To an extent, these distinctions *are* the differences in experience.

It is considerations such as these which explain why Lewis and Saarni, for example, place emotion talk at the very heart of the constructivist enterprise. For them, 'emotional experience ... requires that organisms possess a language of emotion' (Lewis and Saarni, 1985, p. 8). Other theorists who have emphasized the importance of emotion talk include Malatesta and Haviland ('the emotion words of a culture exert a powerful influence on the actual experience of emotion': 1985, p. 110); Levy (who introduces 'the idea of emotion as involving information about the relations of a person to his socially constituted world': 1984, p. 222); Gordon ('Arousal is socially interpreted in terms of sentiment vocabularies, which are sets of meaningful categories that connect sensations, gestures, and social relationships': 1981, p. 577) and Lutz ('Emotions are culturally constructed concepts which point to clusters of situations typically calling for some kind of action': 1981, p. 84).

I hope that the ethnographic material now to be presented is not merely of curiosity value. It concerns how people understand their emotional lives. Being those culturally provided forms of knowledge which are most explicitly focused on emotions, they are perhaps the first thing the constructivist should attend to. They involve the attribution of the kind of meaning which is of paramount significance to those interested in exploring how emotions are constructed in the everyday life of other cultures. We might even learn how other cultures so manage things as to diminish, even do away with, distressful emotions such as 'jealousy' or even 'anger'.

Finally, a word about the survey. A number of cultures, we shall see, do not make distinctions of the 'mental–physical', 'body–mind' and 'emotion–cognition' variety. Ethnographers studying societies which do not employ the category 'emotion' clearly have not found it easy to identify what counts as emotion talk. It is difficult to elicit satisfactory replies to the question, 'Does "x" term refer to an emotion?' if respondents' replies could be referring, for example, to what we consider to be bodily states of affairs (such as physiological arousal). There are in fact many interpretative and linguistic problems to do with establishing what counts as emotion talk – and, for that matter, to do with establishing the nature of forms of emotion talk. Although some of these are mentioned in passing, I side-step more thorny problems. I rely on the insights of the ethnographers concerned.

VARIETIES

Perhaps the most obvious and arresting way in which emotion talk varies from culture to culture concerns the number of emotions which are clearly identified. Hallpike (1979) reports 'a general absence of terms to describe inner states' in connection with the Ommura of Papua (p. 394). Marsella (1976) also writes of cultures which do not label inner mood states. Then there are those cultures which appear to have an extremely limited lexicon. According to Howell, ethnographer of a small aboriginal group in central Malaysia, Chewong emotional vocabulary is limited to: *chan* (glossed as 'angry') *hentugn* ('fearful', 'frightened'), *punmen* ('like something'), *meseq* ('jealous'), *lidva* ('ashamed', 'shy'), *hanrodn* ('proud'), *imeh* ('want') and *lon* (want very much') (Howell, 1981, p. 134). In contrast, neighbouring Malays use some 230 words referring to emotion states (Boucher, 1979, p. 170; cf. Boucher and Brandt, 1981). Going further afield, Chinese (Taiwanese) work with some 750 words (Boucher, 1979). The Taiwanese, it appears, have a richer lexicon than we in the West: Davitz (1969), using *Roget's Thesaurus* to note 'every word that seemed at all likely to be used as the label of an emotional state' (p. 10), arrives at some 400 English terms.

Although there are grave difficulties in establishing what counts as a member of the emotional lexicon of any culture, it certainly appears that numbers vary.[2] So do meanings of emotion terms. As will become apparent, classificatory differences, differences in how emotions are associated with circumstances, differences in the powers ascribed to emotions and so on all function to ensure that supposedly 'basic' emotions, such as 'anger', show little cross-cultural constancy in meaning. To introduce the subject, I simply draw attention to how emotion terms which are broadly similar to our own nevertheless differ in what they mean. Although such terms involve distinctions which allow translation in terms of our emotion concepts, they also derive their meaning by including states of affairs which do not suit our concepts; which do not suit our understanding of what counts as being afraid, being angry and the like. Consider, for example, La Barre's portrayal of 'guilt' in classical Greek culture:

> Greek guilt was not an agonizing consciousness of sin and not necessarily earned by conscious moral choice after a wrangle with conscience, but rather a quasi-material contamination as the result of sometimes innocently blind acts as in the case of Oedipus. (La Barre, 1972, p. 448)

Little to do with wilful action, Greek 'guilt' diverges from how we understand the roughly corresponding emotion in our culture. Other illustrations are provided by Davitz's comparison of how emotional experiences are described by Ugandans speaking Luganda, Ugandans speaking English, and Americans. It is true that Davitz found that the first two groups of subjects described 'happiness', 'sadness' and 'anger' in much the same fashion (1969, pp. 178–9). However, comparison of the two Ugandan groups with American subjects show clear differences. Concerning 'happiness', the 'Ugandan adolescent's stress on freedom from pain and worry . . . reflects an important contrast with . . . the American adolescent' (Davitz, 1969, p. 185). Concerning 'anger',

> in the Ugandan sample, both moving away from others and crying were reported more often than aggression. Moreover, impulses to extreme aggression (e.g., killing, severe mutilation), general discomfort, and various subcategories of inadequacy were far more frequent in the Ugandan sample. Among the United States Ss, impulses to moderate aggression (striking out, hurting, a sense of hyperactivation, and aggressive behaviour) were emphasized. (Davitz, 1969, p. 183)

Lutz (1985) argues that children learn the meaning of emotion words by attending to the sum of the contexts in which the words are used. Greek 'guilt' and Ugandan 'anger' indicate how variegated contexts can be. The way emotions are talked about shows that the context for 'guilt' includes 'blind acts', while the context for 'anger' includes 'crying'. It is particularly striking that Ugandan 'anger' does not mean what it does for us when it is recalled that half the sample speak 'English'.

Countless examples could be given of emotion terms which are used in connection with states of affairs and activities which diverge from what we take translated 'equivalents' to be about. Malatesta and Haviland (1985) write: 'To judge from semantic differential studies, the phenomenology of what we have come to regard as the basic, fundamental human emotions can vary in shades of experience, in accord with particular patterns of socialization, for example, by culture and gender' (p. 98). Studies surveyed show differences of meaning within American society and between two not radically dissimilar language users, American and Norwegian. Thinking now of cross-cultural differences in how the emotions are classified, the implications are considerable. If, indeed, members of those societies employing classifications broadly similar to our own (in that it is relatively easy to effect translation) are working with somewhat different meanings, even these classifications show cross-cultural divergence. If 'English'-speaking Ugandans do not distinguish between 'sadness' and 'anger', as we do (crying being an important feature of our distinction but not for Ugandans), what differences in classification can we expect to find embedded in more alien languages?

The answer is that classifications, and so meanings, vary very considerably. Obvious illustrations are provided by emotion terms which in effect conflate what we keep distinct. Leff (1973), for example, reports that 'in a number of African languages a single word stands for both being angry and being sad' (p. 301). And, he continues, 'these two emotions are not clearly distinguished linguistically.' Leff also points out that 'Chinese' employ one word 'to stand for worry, tension and anxiety' (Leff, 1977, p. 322). Another illustration of how the indigenous terms of alien languages can subsume distinctions made in English is provided by Boucher. In his study, 'anger, rage and furious were all translated into the single term *marah* by bilingual Malays' (Boucher, 1979, p. 171). A yet more striking example is provided by Rosaldo (1980). Examining the key emotion term of the Ilongot, a small group living in the remote reaches of northern Luzon, she points out that the expression is used in a wide range of contexts, including those which she considers to involve 'anger' and 'envy' (pp. 44–7).[3]

Not operating with our distinctions, subsuming what we think of as distinct emotions in alien categories, in general working with meanings which show little (if any) cross-cultural constancy, the evidence suggests that no one classificatory system is the same as another.[4] To emphasize how cultures differ in how emotions are classified, I now present evidence that which emotions are 'hyp*er*cognized' and which 'hyp*o*cognized' varies with setting. In accordance with Levy's (1984) usage, the first of these terms refers to processes whereby emotions come to be well known, the second to processes whereby understanding is 'force[d] ... into some private mode' (p. 227). For present purposes, what matters is that hypercognized emotions are those which are culturally identified, hypo-cognized being those which receive much less conceptual attention.

It appears that classifications always accord pride of place to particular emotions. 'Love' and 'guilt' for us; 'pressure' for the Rastafarian; 'fear' and 'shyness' for the Chewong (Howell, 1981, p. 141) and the neighbouring Semai (Robarchek, 1977; 1979); 'passion' or *liget* for the Ilongot (Rosaldo, 1980); 'fear' and 'shame' for the Tahitian (Levy, 1973); *lek* for the Balinese (Geertz, 1973); *sungkan* for the Javanese (Geertz, 1959); *whaka-momore* for the Maori (Gudgeon, 1906), 'gentleness' and 'mild-ness' for the Utku Eskimo (Briggs, 1970) – all are hypercognized or focal emotions.

It is hardly worth pointing out that herein lies evidence for cross-cultural differences in classification. What is worth dwelling on, however, is the extent to which these core emotion terms are culturally specific. Additional evidence can thus be provided for the claim made earlier to the effect that classificatory systems differ in that there is little (if any) constancy in what emotion terms mean.

Culturally valued focal emotions draw together and otherwise bear on many domains of experience. They are highly ramified. Since what they draw on, bind together, are particular details of particular cultures, it is easy to see why these terms should be so culturally specific.[5] I illustrate with two examples, the first being a term described by Geertz as 'something peculiarly Javanese' (1959, p. 233). She writes,

> Roughly speaking, *sungkan* refers to a feeling of respectful politeness before a superior or an unfamiliar equal, an attitude of constraint, a repression of one's own impulses and desires, so as not to disturb the emotional equanimity of one who may be spiritually higher. (Geertz, 1959, p. 233)

The second example is a yet more distinctive term. According to Rosaldo,

> *Liget* is associated most readily with a variety of words suggesting chaos, separation, and confusion, words that point to the disruptive qualities of 'anger' uncontrolled by 'knowledge' – 'anger' that derives from someone else's fury or success. Red ornaments, signifying the *liget* of a killer, can irritate the unaccomplished members of his audience; boasts testify, as they give rise, to *liget* among 'equals'; red in the sky at sunset is a form of *liget* that can make people ill. (Rosaldo, 1980, p. 47)

It is already apparent that *liget* includes more than is bound up with what we take 'anger' to mean. But this is not all: *liget* is also associated with what is good in life, and not as a distressful or dangerous emotion:

> Opposed to the chaotic energy of a distracted heart is *liget* that is given form or focus, an 'energy' shaped by 'knowledge', and directed to some end. 'I am full of *liget* when I hunt', a man says, 'because I do not fear the forest'; 'I am moved by *liget* at the thought of eating game'. Unlike wild 'anger', such 'energy' is creative, and whereas unfocused *liget* breeds distraction, *liget* that is concentrated toward a desirable object transcends the challenge and irritation at its roots. Concentrated *liget* is what makes babies, stirs one on to work, determines killers, gives people strength and courage, narrows vision on a victim or a task. (Rosaldo, 1980, p. 49)

Having introduced hypercognized emotion talk, it remains to say a few words about emotions that are hypocognized. Variations in this regard also reflect differences in classification. Thus, if what we think of as distinct emotions are subsumed by more general categories, they obviously cannot be conceptualized as such by members of the cultures under consideration. Thinking back to Leff's point (that a single word stands for both 'anger' and 'sadness' in a number of African languages), both terms must be missing from the lexicon. A related way in which hypocognition is bound up with more general categories occurs when categories allow for only partial recognition of those emotions which ethnographers report them as subsuming. Ilongot emotion talk serves to make the point: 'Ilongots describe this state [of 'envy'] as *ngelem*, and with a sort of pungent pleasure indicate that the *liget* that underlies it, although disturb-ing, may also be desirable' (Rosaldo, 1980, p. 47). Ilongot can talk of 'envy', but not in a fashion which clearly differentiates it from *liget*.

When emotion terms are hypocognized in this fashion, they clearly vary in accord with cross-cultural differences in core emotions. Hypocognition can also occur when classificatory systems do not emphasize emotions which conflict with what is culturally valued. The point can be made by referring to Tahitian emotion talk: not suiting Tahitian values, 'sadness' and 'guilt' receive little conceptual attention (Levy, 1984, p. 219).

Finally, mention should be made of a form of hypocognition which does not appear to be as cross-culturally variable as those bound up with different classificatory systems. I am thinking of 'depression'. Marsella's review of the literature leads him to the conclusion that the term 'is not well represented among the lexicon of non-Western people' (Marcella, 1980, p. 242; see also Leff, 1977, p. 323; Levy, 1984, p. 230). Why a term with which we are so familiar should be hypocognized in this fashion is something of a mystery.

I have indicated that hypercognized emotions tend to be culturally valued whereas hypocognized states do not tend to be thought of so highly. This leads on to another way in which classifications vary cross-culturally – variations to do with the moral significance of emotion talk. A useful approach is to contrast societies which adopt a 'Dionysian' assessment of the emotions with those which favour the 'Apollonian' strategy. Drawing on Nietzsche, this is how Benedict (1935) formulates the contrast:

> The desire of the Dionysian, in personal experience or in ritual, is to press through it towards a certain psychological state, to achieve excess. The closest analogy to the emotion he seeks is drunkenness, and he values the illuminations of frenzy. With Blake, he believes 'the path of excess leads to the palace of wisdom'. The Apollonian distrusts all this, and has often little idea of the nature of such experiences. He finds means to outlaw them from his conscious life. He 'knows but one law, measure in the Hellenic sense'. He keeps the middle of the road, stays within the known map, does not meddle with disruptive psychological states. In Nietzsche's fine phrase, even in the exaltation of the dance he 'remains what he is, and retains his civic name'. (Benedict, 1935, pp. 78–9)

Members of Apollonian societies regard the majority of emotions as dangerous threats to themselves and to their institutions. Typically, emotions to do with anything other than those which enhance the power of the established order are accorded negative moral value. The Chewong, for example, encourage 'fear' and 'shyness' but regard all other emotions as dangerous. 'Wanting', 'liking' and so forth are treated as morally reprehensible; they are considered to incur the wrath of supernatural beings (Howell, 1981, p. 141). The Ommura are another case to hand: 'Generally speaking, what we would describe as "inner states" etc. tend to be treated in most contexts as dangerous, unpredictable, and "asocial" and to be closely associated with sorcery activities' (Hallpike, 1979, p. 394, reporting a personal communication from Mayer). In contrast, members of Dionysian societies regard the majority of emotions as vital to both themselves and the social order. The Tauade of Papua thus treat 'pride', 'self-assertion', 'envy', 'rage' and so on as 'the normal basis of all behaviour' (Hallpike, 1979, pp. 80–1; 234). These are 'the very stuff out of which social processes are generated' (p. 77). 'Fear', 'shyness' and the like, it seems, are little valued.[6]

However, the Apollonian–Dionysian distinction, though useful, does not provide an adequate basis for capturing the intricate ways in which moral assessments of the emotions vary from culture to culture. This will become apparent when we come to discuss how emotion talk includes reference to the powers and management of emotional life. First, however, it is necessary to turn to the matter of how emotions can be described. Talk of powers and management has to wait until this has been done because it often makes use of ways of describing the emotions which ring strange to our ears.

Cursory examination of our own talk of emotions shows that they can be described in various ways. Moving from talk which concentrates on internal states to talk which takes an externalized form, 'vehicles' employed include direct reference to emotions as inner experiences ('I feel angry'; 'I hide my fear'); use of bodily parts including organs ('I vented my spleen'); use of physiological phenomena ('I tingled with fear'); use of behavioural manifestations ('her smile said it all'); appeal to contexts, including social activities ('You can imagine how I felt when I saw the Alps'; 'That cocktail party!'); and use of extremely diverse metaphors and other figures of speech ('Love is like a red, red rose').[7]

It is not surprising that we use various vehicles for talking about the emotions. Psychologically speaking, emotions as inner states are indeed located within the body, associated with physiological arousal and ways of behaving, associated with various contexts, and often experienced as coming from without. But what bearing does this have on cross-cultural differences in how the emotions are described? Rather than members of any other cultures doing what we do – namely, using various vehicles to talk about emotions essentially understood as inner experiences – the evidence suggests that differences in the vehicle employed are (more) literally bound up with different ideas of the nature of emotions: their loci (where they are seated), their generation, their powers and so on.

First, then, how have the possibilities raised by the different ways of describing the emotions been put to use in talk of loci? Regarding emotions as inner experiences, experiences which cannot be reduced to or seen as physiological arousal, intellectual activity or behavioural display, we favour a mentalistic locus. A great many other cultures 'somatize' the emotions. Emotions are talked of as 'bodily' occurrences, whether in terms of 'organs' such as the liver, which are rarely (if ever) experienced, or in terms of bodily parts such as the stomach and the back of the neck, which can be felt.

Before giving illustrations, I should explain why I have just placed several words in quotation marks. This is to remind the reader that 'somatization' should not be taken to mean that emotions are identified with what we take to be bodily, as opposed to mental, states. As indicated in the introduction to this chapter, many cultures do not make this distinction. Read's point for the Gahuku-Gama of New Guinea almost certainly stands for a great range of societies:

> The biological, physiological and psychic aspects of [man's] nature cannot be clearly separated. They exist in the closest inter-dependence, being, as it were, fused together to form the human personality. To an extent to which it is perhaps difficult for us to appreciate or understand, the various parts of the body ... are essential constituents of the human personality. (Read, 1967, p. 206)

'Organs' are, so to speak, 'psychologized'. Organ talk does not mean that emotions are understood to belong to 'organs' as we understand the term.

This said, however, ethnographers have often found it necessary to report a close association between emotions and organs. It is hard to dispute that members of the cultures concerned treat the nature of the emotions in a more organic fashion than we would dream of doing. After all, organ talk provides a way of differentiating between emotions. Thus, Howell writes of the Chewong, 'Whenever they do express verbally emotional and mental states and changes, this is done through the medium of the liver. Thus they may say, "my liver is good" (I am feeling fine) or "my liver was tiny" (I was very ashamed)' (Howell, 1981, p. 139). The Elema, discussed by Williams, also concentrate on the liver. Emotion talk is somewhat more sophisticated, however, in that members of this society do not simply refer the states of the liver as a whole:

> The Elema have a simple physical psychology by which they allocate all emotion [and] desire ... to the liver, *iki*. (n. Thus the terms *iki vere*, desire; *iki heaha*, bad temper; *iki bereke*, good temper; *iki haroe*, compassion; ....) Of the two sides of this organ the right (*mai-keva*) is the seat of kindliness, sociability; the left (*mai-keva*) of the angry passions, strong talk, un-sociability. (Williams, 1940, pp. 90–1)

Other illustrations of somatization are provided by Onians ('For Homer the heart and lungs were the emotional centre of the body': 1973, p. 84);

Read (in Gahuku-Gama thought, 'the seat of the emotions is located in the stomach': 1967, p. 214); Johnson (Israelites conceived man in such a way that 'the various members and secretions of the body, such as the bones, the heart, the bowels, and the kidneys, as well as the flesh and the blood, can all be thought of as revealing psychic properties': 1964, p. 87); Levy (Tahitians treat the intestines as 'the seat of the emotions': 1973, p. 515); Smith (for Maori, *ngakau* (associated with the intestines) 'could "feel well", "laugh", "be satisfied" or "sweet"; it could "feel pain", "be weak" or "dark" ': 1981, pp. 152–3); Rosaldo (the Ilongot saying, 'If "anger" and "intent" on action, our hearts may "tense" and "knot" themselves, displaying "hardened" strength and purpose': 1980, p. 39); and Leff (the Yoruba talk of 'depression' as 'the heart is weak', 'anxiety' as 'the heart is not at rest': 1977, p. 322).[8]

When organs (and the like) provide the loci, emotions must somehow be thought of as organic in nature. Another option, adopted by a number of societies, is to talk about the emotions as taking place in behaviour. Occurring here, attention is directed to emotions being a form of public action. So let us move from the inner world of organs to explore this more 'Austinian' world of public acts (see also chapter 8 above).

I first give an example of how emotions can be seen as bound up with public activities of bodily parts. Discussing how ancient Israelites thought of emotions in terms of a variety of such activities, Johnson includes material on the eye:

> the behaviour of the eye is found to be related to a wide range of psychical activity, i.e. pride or humility, favour or disfavour, desire and hope, or disappointment; and in view of the ease with which the eye may be affected by distress of any kind it is not surprising that it should be capable of pity. (Johnson, 1964, p. 48)

That the eye 'should be capable of pity' suggests that it was not simply regarded as a way of expressing and identifying inner emotions. Emotions were thought of as occurring on the surface.[9] Moving further into the external domain, emotions can be talked about in ways which suggest that they are considered to be as much bound up with social activities as they are with what we think of as inner states. A good illustration is provided by Onians (1973). Homeric Greeks identified 'joy' with going to battle to the extent that the same word ($\chi \acute{\alpha} \varrho \mu \eta$) is used for both the emotion and the activity. Joy is 'the spirit of battle' (Onians, 1973, p. 21). More generally on the Homeric Greeks, Simon and Weiner (1966) write that 'What we consider as *inner* mental states or functions are preferentially represented in terms of their concrete, observable, behavioral aspects' (p. 306). As they continue to make the point,

Homer is generally much more interested in portraying details about how a
character appears, while engaged in a particular mental process, than in the
details of the process itself. Thus, the poet does not elaborate the indecision
of Penelope but rather Penelope as indecisive – tossing and turning, and
unable to sleep. (Simon and Weiner, 1966, p. 306)

If talk is entirely about behaviour, then it is perhaps best not to regard it as
emotional in meaning. The examples I have given count as emotion talk
because, although behavioural loci are emphasized, inner experiences are
not entirely left out of the picture. Instances of 'emotion' talk which are so
bound up with activities, which are so institutionally and morally laden as
to lead one to suspect that the talk might not be about the emotions at all,
are provided by the Chewong and by the Japanese notion *amae*. I have
discussed the problem of deciding whether the Chewong talk about
emotions or simply about behaviour elsewhere (see Heelas, 1983a; 1984);
amae is discussed by Leff (1977, p. 336) in an interesting albeit brief
fashion;[10] see also chapter 15 below.

Having begun this discussion of the various kinds of loci accorded the
emotions with internalized representations, I close with some examples of
the most externalized varieties of talk, namely, those forms which, so to
speak, take the emotions away from the 'experiencing' individual and
locate them in external agencies. Least radically, this can be effected by
talking about inner experiences in terms of figures of speech. Discussing
the role of 'visibilia' during the European Middle Ages, Lewis gives a good
example of how externalized idioms were employed to communicate
emotions: 'If you are hesitating between an angry retort and a soft answer,
you can express your state of mind by inventing a person called Ira with a
torch and letting her contend with another person called Patientia' (Lewis,
1958; p. 45). More radically, emotions can be talked about as though they
are largely bound up with external states of affairs. Their loci are
dissociated from human subjects – or so it is claimed by Hallpike. He
reports 'a great deal of evidence ... that mental states and feelings are
often regarded by primitive peoples as external to the person, and as
entities whose existence is independent of their being thought or felt'
(Hallpike, 1979, p. 402).

Evidence for the externalization of loci is provided by a number of
cultures, including Homeric Greece (Simon and Weiner write of 'strong
emotions' as 'outside agencies': 1966, p. 307). Lienhardt's (1961) account
of the Dinka (south Sudan) provides one of the best illustrations. Having
'no conception which at all closely corresponds to our popular modern
conception of mind' (p. 149), Dinka talk about emotions as though they
were occurring in others. Consider, for example, the role played by the
fetish Mathiang Gok:

This fetish, according to Dinka accounts, works analogously to what, for Europeans, would be the prompting of a guilty conscience. The European emphasis here is upon an integrally interior subject of activity, the conscience. For the Dinka, Mathiang Gok is a presence acting upon the self from without, and employed by someone to do so. The image (as we have called it) of the experience of guilty indebtedness (to take the usual situation in which Mathiang Gok is thought to operate) is extrapolated from the experiencing self. It comes (as memories often do) unwilled by the debtor, and is interpreted as a Power directed by the creditor. (Lienhardt, 1961, p. 150)

Or consider how 'envy' is conceptualized in terms of beliefs about witchcraft:

it is possible to interpret them [witchcraft beliefs] as imaging, in another person, states of a person's own conscience. An envious man, for example, not recognizing the envy in himself, transfers to another his experience of it, and sees its image in him, 'the witch'. (Lienhardt, 1961, p. 151)

Dinka imagination has worked on a possibility provided by the natural phenomenology of emotions, namely, that emotions are felt as happening to us.[11] Coming from outside the 'self', emotional experiences lend themselves in being understood as taking place elsewhere. Lienhardt uses a derivative of the late Latin term *passio* ('The fact or condition of being acted upon or affected by external agency; subject to external force': *OED*) to make the point that 'If the word "passions", *passiones*, were still normally current as the opposite of "actions", it would be possible to say that the Dinka Powers were the images of human *passiones* seen as the active *source* of those *passiones*' (Lienhardt, 1961, p. 151; my emphasis).

It will be noted that externalization is not quite so comprehensive as is suggested by Hallpike. The Dinka, employed by Hallpike to make his point, do not entirely ignore the natural phenomenological fact that people experience emotions as happening to themselves. Thus, although 'the experience of guilty indebtedness' is accorded a predominantly external locus, it is also acknowledged that it 'comes' to the debtor. Other cultures retain the idea that emotions happen outside the 'self', while giving more explicit acknowledgement that it is people who experience them. This is effected by talking of emotions as external agencies which invade or possess people. The Pintupi Aborigines of the Western Australian Desert sometimes appear to think in this fashion: *kurrunpa* ('fear') is 'having a "wet spirit" ' (Myers, 1979, p. 349).

I close this introduction of loci by reminding the reader that our own emotion talk is derived from an externalized variety. Discussing names of 'feelings' and 'passions' employed by our ancestors, Barfield writes,

The nomenclature of the Middle Ages generally views them from without, hinting always at their results or their moral significance – 'envy', 'greedy', 'happy' (i.e. 'lucky'), 'malice', 'mercy', 'mildheartness', 'peace', 'pity', 'remorse', 'repentance', 'rue', 'sin' . . . Even the old word 'sad' had not long lost its original sense of 'sated', 'heavy' (which it still retains in 'sad bread'), and 'fear' continued for a long time to mean, not the emotion, but a 'sudden and unexpected event'. Hardly before the beginning of the seventeenth century do we find expressed that sympathetic or 'introspective' attitude to the feelings which is conveyed by such labels as 'aversion', 'dissatisfaction', 'discomposure', . . . while 'depression' and 'emotion' – further lenient names for human weaknesses – were used till then of material objects. (Barfield, 1954, p. 169)

I now turn to different ways of talking about the generation and dynamics of emotions. The most widely employed option for us in the West is to consider emotions (inner states) to be generated by external events. Combination of internal locus and external aetiology is probably the option most frequently adopted by other cultures. A number of these cultures also share our emphasis on 'natural' causation. Read (1967) reports that the Gahuku-Gama consider 'anger' and 'enmity' to be the consequence of adultery within the clan (p. 205); Hallpike (1977) writes that 'For the Tauade, behaviour is the product of particular situations, and of the emotions generated thereby' (p;. 233)' and in his discussion of Norse culture Wax (1969) states, 'Trouble and sorrow are seen not as the result of unseemly or offensive conduct toward Beings and Power, but as the logical outcome of an individuals foolish and naïve conduct' (p. 122).

Emphasis on 'natural' causation is likely to go together with a 'Bandurian' understanding of the dynamics of emotional life. Seen as generated by external events, emotions can be talked about in something akin to the fashion favoured by social learning theorists such as Bandura. Pintupi Aborigines, for example, regard their emotions as being very much bound up with social activities. The (social learning) nature of their indigenous understanding of dynamics is seen in Myers's account:

How their cultural understanding of 'happiness' works is clear in the following example. Informants frequently told me that Yayayi was 'not a happy place' (*pukulpa wiya ngarrin*); there were fights all the time because there were 'no *corroborees*' (a pidgin term for any ceremonies or organized singing). There should be, they said, '*corroborees* all the time'. On a day of numerous fights and arguments, several men suggested that a 'sing' be organized, in order to stop the fighting, to make everyone 'happy'. (Myers, 1979, p. 353)

While 'naturalistic' understanding of causation is widespread (see for example Hallpike, 1979, p. 407), it is by no means always emphasized. Members of most societies believe in gods. Most deities are taken to have emotions. 'Supernatural' causation is thus possible. A deity gets angry at a human transgression and threatens punishment: the outcome is 'fear'. Christians would find nothing strange about this extremely widespread way in which deities generate emotions. What is more alien, except perhaps for devout fundamentalists, are those societies whose gods are believed to generate emotions which we would ascribe to 'objective' causes. Smith (1981) provides a good illustration: 'The Maori did not consider the emotion of fear to be caused by what we would see as a fear-causing event such as a forthcoming battle, but rather believed it to be inflicted upon a man by a hostile *atua* angered by some violation of a *tapu* rule' (p. 149). So does Onians. Functioning to 'breathe' emotion into man, gods do more than send distressful states such as *ate*: 'A sudden access of courage or impulse or resolve with its accompanying sense of energy and power as was conceived as the work of a god' (Onians, 1973, pp. 56, 51). Or we can think of Dinka powers (being the 'active source' of '*passiones*') – indeed, of all those societies which place emotions in the hands of their gods.

In these societies the dynamics of emotions obviously include the workings of gods. This sometimes means that emotions are considered to be outside the control of man. We read in the *Odyssey*, for example: 'We soon made Tenedos, and there, all agog to be home, we sacrificed to the gods. But Zeus had no intention of letting us get home so soon, and for his own cruel purposes he set us all at loggerheads once more.' More frequently, dynamics are thought to include human agency. In Smith's example, the person who violates a *tapu* rule knows the consequences. Emotions are not simply under the control of *atua*. Maori have a role to play in the process. A long and detailed account of a similar form of emotion dynamics is provided by Harris (1978).

External agencies can also include other human beings, operating in 'magical' fashion. Discussing Dinka witchcraft, Lienhardt writes:

> If a man hates another, is spiteful towards him, is thought to resent the other's material (not moral) good and envy his possessions, then the Dinka believe that he intends harm towards him, and can cause him to suffer simply by being what he is in relation to his victim – an enemy, but without material weapons or demonstrated hostility. (Lienhardt, 1951, p. 317)

Neither should the reader forget that Simon and Weiner include 'strong emotions' among Homeric Greek agencies. That a great variety of things can be called upon to generate the emotions from without is shown by Anderson's analysis of the indigenous psychology of Shakespeare's time:

> The elements of all matter (celestial as well as earthly) possess qualities, and the qualities of one substance are capable of acting upon those of another.

Man thus lives in close relationship with the world about him. Diet, climate, and the stars may alter his temperament and his spirits. (Anderson, 1934, p. 46)

In diametric contrast to those cultures where talk is of external causation, there are those which understand causation in terms of something akin to Freud's theory of the id. Emotions well up from within, according to the dynamics of internal organs and the like. The Elema provide a case to hand: Williams writes of 'the man whose liver so to speak secretes the corresponding thoughts, emotions, or desires' (Williams, 1940, p. 91; cf. Onians, 1973, pp. 84–5). Generally speaking, however, societies which talk of internal causation do so by combining this with talk of external causation. Such applies to Elizabethan psychological thought: diet and so forth influence 'temperament'; so does, for example, the spleen, as Anderson points out:

The spleen may incline man to a variety of passions. Its function is to draw to itself and purge the melancholy excrement, normally cold and dry, an excrement which breeds fearful passions, checks passageways, and defiles the whole supply of humours. When it performs this task successfully, man is disposed to mirth. The spleen is thus sometimes said to be the seat of laughter. If the spleen flourishes, the body withers; if the spleen withers, the body flourishes. (Anderson, 1934, pp. 75–6)

Cultures which combine external and internal talk of determinants can often be thought of as possessing indigenous 'psychodynamic' explanations. This is certainly the case for those societies where it is believed that the emotions can be controlled by the ('mental') efforts of participants. Whether because of external or internal ('organic') processes, emotions well up; participants have the responsibility to hold them in check. Thus, Anderson (1934) writes of Elizabethan 'psychological treatises' which 'accord high praise to the man who is at all times master of himself. They enumerate devices to be used in control of the passions and continually urge to patience' (p. 174).

Another variant is when (negative) emotions are seen as generated by something other than the 'self' – stored inside, but then regulated by ritualistic activities. Such societies include the Kalabari and the Tallensi (Horton, 1961, pp. 110–16) and the Utku (Briggs, 1970). Utku Eskimos are especially interesting in that their emotion talk makes reference to those psychodynamic processes which we know of as repression and catharsis (see Heelas, 1983b, p. 394).

Emotions, we have seen, can be regarded as being generated by 'objective' states of affairs, by gods, 'magically' by other people or stars and the like, and by internal organs. They can also be seen as influenced by activities of the 'self'. Dynamics vary accordingly: workings of the gods, of organs, of social activities, of the 'self' – all can be brought to play, and, I should add, all can be combined in various ways. More generally, I have pointed out that some societies favour 'sociodynamics', others 'psycho-dynamics' and yet others 'id-dynamics'.

Discussion of dynamics has introduced us to differences in how participants of various cultures talk about the management of their emotions. First, though, there is one other important consideration to be raised in connection with aetiology: namely, that there are considerable cross-cultural differences in *what* is held to generate particular emotions.

Chagnon's study of the South American Yanomamö provides a by no means exceptional illustration. Husbands treat their wives, as we would see it, in an abominable fashion – they beat them, hold glowing sticks against them, even kill them. Yet women 'measure their husband's concern in terms of the frequency of minor beatings they sustain', and Chagnon overheard a woman commenting 'that the other's husband must really care for her since he has beaten her on the head so frequently' (Chagnon, 1968, p. 83). What for us would elicit anger here elicits something akin to 'endearment'. Another example is provided by the Semai and Chewong. In both these cultures people who are not given food and the like interpret their state in terms of 'fear', rather than in terms of anger or irritation, as might be expected if our Western understanding is brought to bear.

Ethnographic material provided by Robarchek (1977, 1979) for the Semai, and by Howell (1981, 1984) for the Chewong, shows that members of these two societies have learnt to interpret frustrating situations in terms of emotion words which do not accord with how we would evaluate such situations. The situations are interpreted in terms of 'rules' (*pehunan*, Semai; *punen*, Chewong) which call supernatural agencies into play. These agencies are intent on punishing those who have been frustrated – people who thus have cause to be 'frightened'. The rules in effect mean 'fear'. (See Heelas, 1983a, 1984, for further discussion.)

Moving on to a subject which has already raised its head – indigenous understanding of the *management* of emotions – I should first point out that this is an extremely large and complex subject. This is because indigenous understanding of management can be approached from at least three (interrelated) points of view. One avenue is to concentrate on moral aspects; another is to explore the powers which are ascribed to emotions; the third is to concentrate on indigenous 'theories' to do with loci, generation and dynamics.

Myers (1979) points out that 'The determination of when one ought to be angry, when sad, when sorry, when lonely, and how to act, is largely a cultural matter' (p. 349). A number of theorists have recently drawn attention to the role played by 'display' and 'feeling' rules in this regard (Ekman, 1982; Hochschild, 1983). Myers explicitly attends to the moral significance of emotion terms themselves. These are what he has in mind when he writes of 'the ideology of the emotions' (Myers, 1979, p. 365). (Emotion terms are also what Rosaldo (1983) has in mind when she writes, 'Psychological idioms that we use in offering accounts of the activities of our peers – or our companions in the field – are at the same time "ideological" or "moral notions" ': p. 136).

The point is that emotion terms provide information to do with how people should or should not feel (or display their feelings) in particular circumstances. When emotion terms are taken to be associated (in meaning) with particular activities, they provide information as to how participants should feel when they are engaged in the activities. I illustrate by reference to Myer's analysis of how the emotion terms of the Pintupi are bound up with their institutions and morality. Consider his account of 'happiness': 'the central themes of the Pintupi moral order revolve around the ideal of closely cooperating kin, and it is in terms of this understanding that Pintupi attempt to define when and how one should be "happy" (*pukulpa*)' (Myers, 1979, p. 353). Articulating the values of the kin ideal, the morally laden term *pukulpa* conveys the information that Pintupi should feel happy when acting with kin and should not feel happy when alone. The anthropological literature on kinship terms in a variety of societies suggests that something similar pertains: that kin terms are bound up with 'conventional' emotions, telling people how they ought to feel towards their mother's brother and so on (cf. Needham, 1971, pp. lii–lix).[12]

The implications for indigenous understanding of management are obvious. Often reflecting, perhaps better encapsulating, what society is about, attention to emotion talk enables us to see why participants should feel obliged to manage their emotions as they do. Reflecting cross-cultural differences in moral orders, attention to emotion talk enables us to see why members of different societies select different emotions to emphasize or attempt to do away with. Nor is this all. Emotion talk differs from culture to culture with regard to what people should do if their emotions are to remain in accord with the moral order.

Before exploring this further I want to say a few words about the second way of looking at cross-cultural variations in management. Attention is directed at what has to be handled – specifically, the powers which are ascribed to emotions. The matter is clearly not divorced from moral considerations. As I have already pointed out, Apollonian societies tend to treat emotions as dangerous threats to the moral order, whereas Dionysian societies tend to treat them as essential for that order. But I want to focus on the subject in order to indicate the extent to which cultures have arrived at different ideas of which emotions are associated with which powers, and in which contexts.

Harris (1978) reports that Taitian 'anger' can kill: 'Mystical agents, including those lying within human persons, were subject to anger and that anger could be manifested in the sickness and death of human adults, their children, and their livestock, or in plague and drought affecting humans in the mass' (p. 27). More specifically, she reports that

> the rights of persons as members of families and narrow circles of kin, and the rights of domesticated animals as quasi-members, could not be transgressed without mystically endangering the wronged. When such transgressions occurred, the offended one's heart, the locus of the sentiments, became 'hot', or he was 'injured in the heart' (*waβaβwa ngolonyi*), that is, the wronged person or beast became angry and resentful. There followed, as divination would later reveal, suffering of the transgressor. (Harris, 1978, pp. 31–2)

The theme of the mystical powers of the emotions of the wronged contrasts nicely with Lienhardt's discussion of Dinka witches: the reader will recall that powers are here those of the wrongdoer. Both of these societies can then be contrasted with the Ilongot. *Liget* (which has an 'anger' aspect) is culturally approved and is exemplified in head-hunting. 'Anger' is one of the factors in motivating Ilongot to go out and 'toss a head': 'Grieving for lost kin, envious of past headhunting, angry at an insult, and bent upon revenge, he and his fellows are concerned, primarily, to realize their *liget*' (Rosaldo, 1980, p. 55). The positive power of *liget* is seen in the fact that only when it has been 'realized' in this fashion are youths allowed to marry and become adults.

With different views as to the powers of 'anger', the three societies just mentioned employ different management techniques. These are referred to in the following discussion, indicating how different mangement techniques also go together with different ways of talking about loci, generation and, of course, dynamics.

The third paragraph of the Confucian *Book of Rites* reads:

> The ancient Kings were watchful in regard to the things by which the mind was affected. And so they instituted ceremonies to direct men's aims aright; music to give harmony to their voices; laws to unify their conduct; and punishments to guard against their tendencies to evil. The end to which ceremonies, music, punishments and laws conduct is one; they are the instruments by which the minds of the people are assimilated, and good order in government is made to appear.

Attributing the generation of emotions to ceremonies, these kings operated in a fashion which would win the approval of modern-day social learning theorists and constructivists. Other examples of management strategies involving this kind of understanding of the loci, generation and dynamics of emotion are provided by the Pintupi (their management of 'happiness' has already been introduced) and the Ilongot. Ilongot, it can be noted, are interesting because they combine sociodynamic and psychodynamic understanding of the emotions in a fashion reminiscent of the Western theorist, Berkowitz. Psychodynamic management (' "heavy" feelings were what made men want to kill; in taking heads they could aspire to "cast off" an "anger" that "weighed down on" and oppressed their saddened "hearts" ') combines with management couched in terms of sociodynamics. (Adults, exemplifying the social order, teach successful head-hunters *beya*, the 'knowledge' which 'organizes affective life': Rosaldo, 1980, pp. 19, 98.)

Confucians, Pintupi and in some regards Ilongot attach great importance to 'learning models'. A related strategy, found in many societies, involves working on the emotions in a fashion not dissimilar to that advocated by cognitive therapists, such as Beck. Buddhists in Thailand and northern Nepal, with whom I have talked, favour cognitive strategies. And we can recall what Anderson says of Elizabethan 'psychological treatises' (cf. Wax, 1969, p. 123, on Norse management). This strategy, however, is probably less common than that of taking practical steps to manage emotions. It is no doubt true that members of all societies are sufficiently aware of the 'natural' sociodynamics of emotions to do what is necessary to maintain the emotional order. The variety of management discussed by Geertz (1959) when she writes that, if a quarrel in a Javanese village 'threatens to erupt into an uncontrollable fight, the opponents forestall it by cutting off relationships with one another' (p. 227) is frequently encountered in the literature.

The reader should not need reminding that, remaining close to our own cultural understanding, members of many societies think in psychodynamic fashion. Whether sent by supernatural or natural agencies or coming from within, certain emotions are thought to well up and cause harm unless released. Utku, Taita and Ilongot provide illustrations, members of each society practising what they understand as 'catharsis'. If dangerous emotions remain 'stored', the consequences are grave (Utku, for example, say that 'a man who *never* lost his temper could kill if he ever did become angry': Briggs, 1970, p. 47). Another way in which psychodynamic understanding can be employed is provided by the Gisu (Kenya): Gisu male initiation rituals involve the idea that fierce 'anger' (*lirima*) is generated when youths are frustrated (see Heald, 1982).

Then there are those techniques found when externalization is important. Generated by the gods, the gods must be placated, for example by sacrifice. As well as pleasing gods, sacrifice can also function to get rid of distressful human 'emotions'. Dinka sacrificial beasts are 'made the vehicle for the *passiones* of men' (Lienhardt, 1961, p. 293). Sent by *atua*, Maori 'fear' is exorcised in another fashion:

Since a man in this position [feeling fear before a battle] was not held to be personally responsible for his fear, he could not be held responsible for overcoming it. Fear was instead removed by ritual means: one method used was to crawl between the legs of a high-born woman or chief, the sexual organs (particularly the vagina) having the power to to remove supernatural influences. (Smith, 1981, p. 149)

Yet another way of handling the emotions of gods is provided by the Chewong. For example, they make an effort to avoid subjecting each other to those frustrations which lead supernatural beings to implement the *punen* rule (Howell, 1981, p. 136).

One could go on and on. There is the literature on witchcraft (witches being external sources of distressful emotions among the Dinka, for example – see Lienhardt, 1951); there is the literature on those societies where distressful emotions are thought to derive from food (see e.g. Weiss, 1983, p. 88); there is the literature on curing rites (see the bibliography provided by Favazza and Faneem, 1982); there is the literature on classical Greece (see e.g. Simon and Weiner, 1966, on *ate*); and of course, there is the literature on Eastern and Western traditions (see e.g. Rawlinson, 1981; Matthews, 1980). Our own psychotherapeutic techniques can all be found elsewhere; but, given the variety of ways in which the emotions are understood, it is not surprising to find techniques which also strike us as strange.

It is time to draw our 'Cooks tour' to a close. Pulling together a number of themes, I now want to emphasize something that many of the societies we have visited have in common: they are less 'psychologically' minded than we in the West.

Hallpike (1979) writes that 'the realm of purely private experience and motives, as distinct from the evaluation of actual behaviour, is given little attention in many primitive societies' (p. 392). This is certainly born out by the Pintupi. Myers (1979) backs up his claim that 'Pintup use of concepts of the emotions frequently does not present an introspective view of a person's feelings' by drawing attention to the fact that he 'found it very difficult to elicit private or individual interpretations of experience, as in the matter of a parent's death' (p. 347). Members of the Western psychological subculture, intent on exploring their own innermost feelings, would not be happy in this culture, where, as we have already seen, 'emotions' are understood as highly social in nature. Neither would we be happy with the Maori: 'psychology did not interest the Maori very much', writes Johansen (1954); 'conflicts in the mind, unconscious motives, or the like are never mentioned' (p. 249). Even members of those societies which emphasize emotions as inner states would not make good companions in, e.g., encounter groups. The Ilongot might attach 'commendable' importance to emotions ('without *liget* to move our hearts, there would be no human life':

Rosaldo, 1980, p. 47), but the ethnographer presents little evidence that Ilongot are interested in pondering the subtle inner dynamics of emotional life. And it is not without significance that it is the Tahitians ('anxious and concerned when the[ir] inner sense of "enthusiasm" decreases') whom Levy (1984) has in mind when he presents an externally orientated characterization of emotion talk: it is used to 'convey and represent information about one's *mode of relationship* as a total individual to the social and nonsocial environment' (Levy, 1984; p. 230; 1973, p. 271).[13]

The emotion talk of these cultures is clearly not much concerned with emotions as inner experiences. Such experiences are not thought of as important, as we might put it, *in* themselves. The implications of this, and of what their emotion talk is concerned with, are addressed in the final section of this chapter, along with the implications of the fact that some cultures, such as the Chewong, appear to be even less concerned with psychological matters.

SIGNIFICANCE

First, though, a few words on what is involved in exploring the constitutive significance of emotion talk. Anthropologists, classicists and others provide material on the subject. Psychologists (and philosophers, with their discussion of the 'aboutness' of emotions) find evidence for constructivism, and so provide a way of exploring the significance of emotion talk for emotional life. This, broadly speaking, is the picture. However, the division of labour between ethnographic and theoretical work has meant that not all that much has been done to effect the exploration. In 1979 Boucher wrote that 'systematic studies of the socially learned aspects of emotion in the cross-cultural context are extremely small in number' (Boucher, 1979, p. 175). The last few years have witnessed a growth of interest in the subject. But I think it is incontestable that we are far from knowing much about how emotions are learnt in 'exotic' societies. And, despite the pioneering work of a number of anthropologists-cum-psychologists, we know even less about the role played by emotion talk.

Perhaps this is not surprising. The subject is fraught with difficulties, it indeed being one thing to claim, on the basis of evidence from experimental psychology, that emotions are socially constructed, and quite another to explore the significance of cross-cultural differences in emotion talk. Consider what is involved in establishing whether or not particular emotions are universal. Can we identify cultures where certain emotions are not conceptualized, and infer from this that the emotions are absent? First, we have to establish that the emotions do not enter into emotion talk. This raises formidable problems to do with identifying emotion talk, for until we know what counts as emotion talk we do not know whether or not certain emotions are being conceptualized. There are also, of course, translation problems to do with the 'logical geography' of terms which might apply to those emotions thought to be absent from emotion talk.

Second, we have to consider the possibility that meanings other than those involved in emotion talk are actually generating those emotions which are not identified in the emotional lexicon. This possibility is raised by those psychologists (such as Lazarus, 1980, 1982) who work with broad definitions of what counts as an 'appraisal'. Until we have a clearer idea of the constitutive significance of various domains of meaning (the reader will recall my earlier mention), we cannot rule out the possibility that emotions are generated when not identified as such.

Finally, we have to settle what role to accord to endogenous processes. In this chapter I have been concentrating on differences in representation. But this is not to say that there is not evidence of cross-cultural constancy. Together with evidence for endogenous differentiation and the like, this suggests that culture does not have an entirely free hand in laying down emotions. As I have already argued, the evidence suggests that endogenous processes alone do not generate 'true' emotions. But we still have to take into account the fact that members of cultures which do not provide meanings for particular emotions almost certainly experience, say, 'anger' as a quasi-emotion.[14]

These and other considerations explain why we are far from knowing much about the exact significance, the exact impact, of emotion talk. The following explorations are thus speculative in nature. They are not unrealistically speculative, though. We might not be able to specify the exact signifiance of emotion talk, but surely we know that it provides the most obvious domain for the constructivist to explore; for it is here that meanings are 'experience-near' (Geertz, 1984, p. 124), are most directly focused on emotional life.

Emotion talk functions as a kind of spotlight. Depending on culture, it dwells on whatever is taken to be associated with those raw experiences (cf. Leventhal's 'elements') necessary for emotions. Sometimes the beam picks out organs, sometimes witches, sometimes behaviour and social activities, sometimes the gods. How raw experiences are constituted as emotions depends on how they are illuminated. Emotions experienced in the light of organ talk are not the same as emotions experienced in the light of gods (emotions coming from a god will be associated, in *meaning*, with the attributes of that god; emotions coming from an organ will almost certainly be associated, in *meaning*, with different attributes). Emotional elements which have no light thrown on them remain in the dark. And emotions which are focused on become enriched and highlighted in experience.

Anthropological evidence, together with constructivist theorizing, allows us to say that the differences encountered on our tour are not simply metaphorical ways of talking about 'the same thing'. 'Emotional elements' might be universal; 'emotional experiences' are not. As meaningful experiences, emotions differ according to the various meanings which have been introduced in this chapter. Differences in 'representation' are actually differences in construction. Dinka understanding of envy in terms of witches means that envy cannot be the same emotion for them as it is for us. To a degree, then, differences in emotional life can simply be read off from differences in emotion talk. But we can do more than this. We can try and spell out the ways in which emotion talk makes impact.

Attending to ways in which emotional activity might be diminished, consider Leff's claim that 'there is a strong link between the availability of the appropriate words for the various emotions and the ease with which people distinguish between the experiences' (Leff, 1973, p. 304). More specifically, 'words for denoting emotion whose meaning largely relates to ... somatic accompaniments cannot be used to distinguish a variety of emotional states with any clarity' (p. 300). Indeed, Leff implies that somatized emotion talk does not function to construct fully fledged emotions, but refers to relatively inchoate bodily states (Leff, 1973; p. 301; 1977, p. 324). Levy's account of Tahitian terms to do with 'mild or moderate longing' serves to illustrate. There are, he writes,

> no unambiguous terms which represent the concepts of sadness, longing, or loneliness. . . . People would name their condition, where I supposed that the context called for 'sadness' or 'depression', as 'feeling troubled' (*pe'ape'a*, the generic term for disturbances, either internal or external); ... as 'feelng heavy' (*tōiaha*); as 'feeling fatigued' (*haumani*); and a variety of other terms all referring to a generally troubled or subdued state. These are all nonspecific terms, which had no implication of any external relational cause about them, in the sense that 'angry' implies an offense or a frustration. (Levy, 1973, p. 305)

As Levy elsewhere concludes, 'In dealing with what I took to be "sadness" as, say, "fatigue", the Tahitians were accepting the "feeling" but denying that it was an "emotion" ' (Levy, 1984, p. 220). But there is more to it than this. Hypocognition is not simply facilitated by a somatized mode of attention. There is also the point that 'sadness' can be interpreted in terms of 'the effect of spirits' (Levy, 1984, p. 223). Attention is thus taken away from what 'really' is 'sadness'-inducing: namely, some loss or another.

There is much more to be said about ways in which cultures so devise things that emotional elements do not get transformed into emotions, or so that particular emotions are not identified and developed. Since it is not my intention now to do anything other than indicate some of the moves which can be made in exploring the constructivist importance of emotion talk, I shall make only one or two more points.[15] One is that absence of linguistic differentiations (as between 'anger' and 'irritation', with regard to Ilongot *liget*) clearly means that particular 'emotions' remain hypocognated. Another is that it could be the case that some cultures do not provide learning models (even of a somatic variety) for certain of what we might want to consider as 'core' emotions. Some might think that it would be a foolhardy person who would try and argue that certain cultures do not provide learning models for, say, 'anger'. Taking my cue from Robarchek (1977, 1979), although perhaps paying more attention to emotion talk than he does, this is what I have tried to argue for the Chewong (Heelas, 1984). Organ (liver) talk is also discussed. (I argue that it directs attention-away from emotions as inner experiences by virtue of the fact that it has to do with social behaviour.) And I explore the significance of Chewong 'rules': rules, the reader will recall, which ensure that any 'natural' connection between, say, a frustrating event and 'anger' is overridden by supernaturally implemented 'fear'. Hypocognition gives way to 're-cognition', as perhaps it does with Tahitian 'sadness' when spirits come into play. Attention to supernatural beings, more exactly to the human behaviour which has 'angered' them, comes to the fore.

Chewong, I conclude, are not experts at suppressing their emotions. That they never seem to 'lose control' (Howell, 1981, p. 135) is because they do not have many strong emotions to get excited about. What, then, of the reverse situation? How can emotion talk function to increase emotional activity? As a rule of thumb, the greater the importance of emotion talk, the greater the importance of emotionality; the greater the number of emotions which are identified, the greater the number of experienced emotions; and the more an emotion is valued, the more likely it is to be hypercognized and to be at the forefront of experience. In our own society, some have come to have richer, more intense, emotional lives by virtue of their belonging to the psychological subculture. Certain drug rehabilitation units, for example, might claim to uncover repressed emotions but actually are employing emotion talk in such a way as to teach people how to be more angry. Every society, it should go without saying, provides contexts to teach emotions. Generally informed by the moral domain, rituals very often dramatize and thereby enrich whichever emotions have, so to speak, been selected for attention.

Just as emotion talk is of the utmost importance in our psychological culture, so is it important in many of these rituals (see, for example, Kapferer, 1979).[16] On more general ways in which emotions are taught by way of emotion talk, see Geertz (1959), Myers (1979), Lewis (1958), Levy (1973, 1984) and Gordon (1981). Rather than dwell on this relatively well discussed topic, I want to end by making the point that there is a considerable difference between the way in which emotion talk of the Western psychological subculture generates core emotions and the way in which a different kind of emotion talk, found in many other societies, generates emotions of a core or hypercognated variety.

Gordon (1981) points out that 'A vocabulary of sentiments is a linguistic expression of experiences shared by group members, and mirrors their interests and concerns' (p. 578). In many of the societies introduced in this chapter, the 'self' is defined as a social being. This means that the 'interests and concerns' mirrored in emotion talk belong to the social or moral order. People thus define how and what they should feel in terms of externalized forms of emotion talk. In other words, since emotion talk articulates the moral order and defines what people should feel if they are to be 'themselves' as social beings, it is externalized in terms of that order.

Social locus of identity is reflected in forms of emotion talk which function to bind participants to their true (socially defined) identities. Reflecting the public domain, emotion talk directs the attention of participants away from the 'private' and instead concentrates on what it means to be emotional as that is socially defined. Even when the Pintupi are talking about the 'private self', their emotion talk takes a sociocentric form. As Myers (1979) writes, 'they seem to present it [private experience] in terms that reflect more about the cultural system than about the individual' (p. 348). Whether it is by way of emotion talk as an extension of social institutions or by way of emotion talk incorporating gods as bound up with the moral order, or both, the outcome is that emotions of the private self are little attended to in many cultures. And if they do erupt, as antisocial or private states of affairs, it is not surprising that they are managed by the external representatives of true identity.

From a functional point of view, we gain an idea of how emotion talk in many societies works to bind, 'cathect' in some cases, the emotional lives of participants to the moral order. Detailed examination of how emotion talk facilitates this process in different societies will probably show us that cross-cultural differences in emotional experiences can be co-ordinated with differences in both morality and notions of self. This is indicated by comparing what has just been said about some other cultures with how core emotions are generated by the Western psychological subculture. Here, with a highly individualistic morality and self-concept, emotion talk is of course directed within. The locus is internalized. And the outcome of 'psychobabble' is a different kind of emotional life than that found (for example) among the Pintupi. Emotions are not judged as 'right' or 'wrong'; emotions are not experienced (or at least should not be experienced) as bound up with public presentations of the self; and in general, emotional life is differentiated, complex, if not more powerful as a whole. Mirroring individualistic 'interests and concerns', the emotion talk of the psychological subculture almost certainly opens experiences unavailable to those whose emotional lives are bound – by way of emotion talk – to particular social orders. But then, members have to put up with emotions (such as 'anger') which might well be more or less absent in those societies which organize things differently.

To sum up, emotion talk differs from culture to culture. We are still a long way from knowing how to handle all the differences. It seems clear, though, that they can generate quite radical differences in emotional experience; that they can generate differences at the very heart of what it is to have an emotion. It also seems clear that the study of emotion talk provides a fruitful path for exploring the relationship between emotional and social life. It can function to keep the former in alignment with the latter. All this is recognized by Lutz, who has provided what I think is one of the clearest statements on the matter:

> Ethnotheories of emotion describe a fundamental and ubiquitous aspect of psychological functioning. They are used to explain why, when, and how emotion occurs, and they are embedded in more general theories of the person, internal processes, and social life. As they play a central role in the organization of experience and behavior, an examination of the structure of emotion ethnotheories can contribute to both cultural and psychological models of emotion and social action. (Lutz, in press)

NOTES

1 See Heelas (1983b; 1984, pp. 33–9). The evidence strongly suggests that Izard's (1971, p. 267) claim that 'the subjective experience component of emotion determines Emotion Labeling' be reversed.
2 Concerning numbers, see e.g. Hiatt (1978, pp. 182–7) (Australian Aborigines), Briggs (1970, pp. 375–6) (Utkuhikhalingmiut Eskimo), Needham (1972, pp. 25–8) (Nuer), Weiss (1983) (Ponogoro), Izard (1980) and Averill (1975). See Heelas (1983a; 1983b; 1984) for a discussion of difficulties.
3 More evidence for cross-cultural variations in differentiation is provided by Levy (1973, e.g. p. 322; 1984, e.g. p. 230), Lewis (1967, pp. 70–85), Sorenson (1975, e.g. p. 367) and Marsella (1980, e.g. p. 242).
4 In passing, it can be pointed out that semantic variations, complex differences in contexts of use, mean that classifications take a polythetic form (see Averill, 1980a, p. 308; cf. Needham, 1983, pp. 36–65).
5 Culture-specific emotion terms, it can be noted, need not be culturally valued: see, for example, Newman (1964) on 'wild man' behaviour among the Gururumba of New Guinea.
6 Another illustration of how Apollonian and Dionysian societies differ in their attitudes towards particular emotions is provided by the Tallensi and Kalabari of West Africa: the former accord high value to timidity; the latter to aggressive emotionality (see Horton, 1961).
7 Cf. Davitz (1969), Harris (1985) and Frijda (1969). On the particular point of how we employ body talk, see Leff (1973, p. 301; 1977, pp. 321, 323); on our use of what I have called metaphors, see Hallpike (1979, p. 393).

8   For more on somatization see Johansen (1954) (Maori) and Weiss (1983).
9   Cf. Strathern's (1975) 'Why is Shame on the Skin?
10 Rosaldo (1980; 1983), Myers (1979), Hallpike (1979, pp. 388–409) and Heider (1984) all present interesting material and observations on this topic.
11 See Averill (1980b); cf. Heelas and Lock (1981, e.g. pp. 49–50).
12 The anthropological literature is relatively rich on the topic of 'conventional' emotions (see e.g. Mauss, 1921; Williams, 1932), although emotion talk is generally not dwelt on.
13 Other cultures which to varying degrees are not so concerned with emotions as inner experiences as Westerners include: Chewong (Howell, 1981, p. 141), Zapotec (Selby, 1974) Hindus (Miller, 1984; Schweder and Bourne, 1984). See also Leff (1977, p. 344) and Marsella (1976).
14 Ekman and Scherer (1984) present an excellent guide to evidence pertaining to such matters as endogenous elicitation and the kinds of meaning which have to be present. Evidence for cross-cultural constancy has been provided by many: see, for example, Osgood et al. (1975), Ekman (1982) and Levy (1984). Scher et al.'s (1983) work might prove of great use in this regard. On the issue of establishing what counts as emotion talk, see e.g. Needham (1972; 1981). For general discussion of problems, see Heelas (1983a, 1983b, 1984).
15 Other avenues which could be explored include the ways in which externalization bears on emotional experience: could it be that the significance of 'guilt' is diminished when gods (etc.) are held to be the locus of responsibility? What happens to the experience of 'envy' when it is externalized in Dinka fashion?
16 See also Heald (1982) and Munn (1969), the latter referring to Geertz's (1973) work on 'symbolic models of emotion'. Marsella and White (1982) present a number of articles bearing on the topic.

REFERENCES

Anderson, R. (1934)   *Elizabethan Psychology and Shakespeare's Plays.* University of Iowa Humanistic Studies, vol. III, no. 4.

Averill, J. (1975)   A semantic atlas of emotional concepts. JSAS Catalogue of Selected Documents in Psychology, 5, 330 (MS. no. 421).

—— (1980a)   A constructivist view of emotion. In R. Plutchik and H. Kellerman (eds), *Emotion Theory, Research and Experience.* Vol. I: *Theories of Emotion.* London: Academic Press (pp. 305–39).

—— (1980b)   On the paucity of positive emotion. In K. Blankstein et al. (eds), *Assessment and Modification of Emotion Behavior.* London: Plenum Press (pp. 7–45).

Bandura, A. (1965)   Vicarious processes: a case of no trial learning. In L. Berkowitz (ed.), *Advances in Experimental Social Psychology*, vol. 4. London: Academic Press (pp. 167–223).

Barfield, O. (1954)   *History in English Words.* London: Faber.

Benedict, R. (1935)   *Patterns of Culture.* London: Routledge & Kegan Paul.

Boucher, J. (1979)   Culture and emotion. In J. Marsella et al. (eds), *Perspectives on Cross-cultural Psychology.* London: Academic Press (pp. 159–78).

—— and Brandt, M. (1981)   Judgement of emotion from American and Malay antecedents. *Journal of Cross Cultural Psychology*, 12 (3), 272–83.

Briggs, J. (1970)   *Never in Anger*. London: Harvard University Press.

Chagnon, N. (1968)   *Yanomamö: The Fierce People*. New York: Holt, Rinehart and Winston.

Davitz, J. (1969)   *The Language of Emotion* London: Academic Press.

Ekman, P. (ed.) (1982)   *Emotion in the Human Face*. Cambridge: Cambridge University Press.

—— and Scherer, K. (1984)   Questions about emotion. In K. Scherer and P. Ekman (eds), *Approaches to Emotion*. Hillsdale, NJ: Lawrence Erlbaum (pp. 1–8).

Favazza, A. and Faheem A. (1982)   *Themes in Cultural Psychiatry*. Kansas City and London: University of Missouri Press.

Frijda, N. (1969)   Recognition of emotion. In L. Berkowitz (ed.), *Advances in Experimental Social Psychology*, vol. 4. London: Academic Press (pp. 167–223).

Geertz, C. (1973)   *The Interpretation of Cultures*. New York: Basic Books.

—— (1980)   *Negara: The Theatre State in Nineteenth-Century Bali*. Princeton: Princeton University Press.

—— (1984)   From the native's point of view. In R. Schweder and R. LeVine (eds), *Culture Theory*. Cambridge: Cambridge University Press (pp. 123–36).

Geertz, H. (1959)   The vocabulary of emotion. *Psychiatry*, 22, 225–37.

Gordon, S. (1981)   The sociology of sentiments and emotion. In M. Rosenberg and R. Turner (eds), *Social Psychology*. New York: Basic Books (pp. 562–92).

Gudgeon, C. (1906) *Journal of the Polynesian Society*, 15, 163–74.

Hallpike, C. (1977)   *Bloodshed and Vengeance in the Papuan Mountains*. Oxford: Clarendon Press.

—— (1979)   *The Foundations of Primitive Thought*. Oxford: Clarendon Press.

Harris, G. (1978)   *Casting out Anger*. Cambridge: Cambridge University Press.

Harris, P. (1985)   What children know about the situations that provoke emotion. In M. Lewis and C. Saarni (eds), *The Socialization of Emotions*. London: Plenum Press (pp. 161–86).

Heald, S. (1982)   The making of men. *Africa*, 52 (1),15–36.

Heelas, P. (1983a)   Indigenous representatives of the emotions: the Chewong. *Journal of the Anthropological Society of Oxford*, 14 (1), 87–103.

—— (1983b)   Anthropological perspectives on violence: universals and particulars. *Zygon*, 18 (4), 375–404.

—— (1984)   Emotions across cultures: objectively and cultural divergence. In S. Brown (ed.), *Objectivity and Cultural Divergence*. Cambridge: Cambridge University Press (pp. 21–42).

—— and Lock, A. (eds) (1981)   *Indigenous Psychologies*. London: Academic Press.

Heider, K. (1984)   Emotion: inner state vs. interaction. Paper delivered to the American Anthropological Association.

Hiatt, L. (1978)   Classification of the emotions. In L. Hiatt (ed.), *Australian Aboriginal Concepts*. Princeton, NJ: Humanities Press (pp. 182–7).

Hochschild, A. (1983) *The Managed Heart*. Berkeley and London: University of California Press.

Horton, R. (1961)   Destiny and the unconscious in West Africa. *Africa*, 31 (2), 110–16.

Howell, S. (1981) Rules not words. In P. Heelas and A. Lock (eds), *Indigenous Psychologies*. London: Academic Press (pp. 133–44)

—— (1984) *Society and Cosmos: Chewong of Peninsular Malaysia*. London: Oxford University Press.

Izard, C. (1971) *The Face of Emotion*. New York: Meredith.

—— (1980) Cross-cultural perspectives on emotion and emotion communication. In *Handbook of Cross-Cultural Psychology*. Boston: Allyn and Bacon.

Johansen, J. (1954) *The Maori and his Religion*. Copenhagen: Ejnar Munks-gaard.

Johnson, A. (1964) *The Vitality of the Individual in the Thought of Ancient Israel*. Cardiff: University of Wales Press.

Kapferer, B. (1979) Emotion and feeling in Sinhalese healing rites. *Social Analysis*, 1, 153–76.

Kemper, T. (1978) *A Social Interactional Theory of Emotions*. Chichester: John Wiley.

—— (1984) Power, status and emotions: a sociological contribution to a psycho-physiological domain. In K. Scherer and P. Ekman (eds), *Approaches to Emotion*. Hillsdale, NJ: Lawrence Erlbaum (pp. 369–83).

La Barre, W. (1972) *The Ghost Dance*. London: George Allen & Unwin.

Lazarus, R. (1980) Thoughts on the relations between cognition and emotion. *American Psychologist*, 37, 1019–24.

—— et al. (1980) Emotions: a cognitive–phenomenological analysis. In R. Plutchik and H. Kellerman (eds), *Emotion Theory, Research and Experience*. Vol. 1: *Theories of Emotion*. London: Academic press (pp. 189–218).

Leach, E. (1981) A poetics of power. *The New Republic*, 4 April.

Leff, J. (1973) Culture and the differentiation of emotion states. *British Journal of Psychiatry*, 123, 209–306.

—— (1977) The cross-cultural study of emotions. *Culture, Medicine and Psychiatry*, 1 (4), 317–50.

Leventhal, H. (1980) Toward a comprehensive theory of emotion. In L. Berkowitz (ed.), *Advances in Experimental Social Psychology*. London: Academic Press (pp. 149–207).

Levy, R. (1973) *Tahitians*. London: Chicago University Press.

—— (1984) Emotion, knowing, and culture. In R. Shweder and R. LeVine (eds), *Culture Theory. Essays on Mind, Self, and Emotion*. Cambridge: Cambridge University Press (pp. 214–37).

Lewis, C. (1958) *The Allegory of Love*. London: Oxford University Press.

—— (1967) *Studies in Words*. Cambridge: Cambridge University Press.

Lewis, M. and Saarni, C. (1985) Culture and emotions. In M. Lewis and C. Saarni (eds), *The Socialization of Emotions*. London: Plenum Press (pp. 1–17).

Lienhardt, G. (1951) Some notions of witchcraft among the Dinka. *Africa*, 21 (1), 303–18.

—— (1961) *Divinity and Experience*. Oxford: Clarendon Press.

Lutz, C. (1981) Situation-based emotion frames and the cultural construction of emotion. In *Proceedings of the Third Annual Conference of the Cognitive Science Society, Berkeley* (pp. 84–9).

—— (1985) Cultural patterns and individual differences in the child's emotional meaning system. In M. Lewis and C. Saarni (eds), *The Socialization of Emotion*.

New York: Plenum Press (pp. 37–116).

—— (in press) 'Goals, events, and understanding in Ifaluk emotion theory'. In N. Quinn and D. Holland (eds), *Cultural Models in Language and Thought*, Cambridge: Cambridge University Press.

Malatesta, C. and Haviland, J. (1985) Signals, symbols and socialization. In M. Lewis and C. Saarni (eds), *The Socialization of Emotions*. London: Plenum Press (pp. 89–116).

Mandler, G. (1980) The generation of emotion: a psychological theory. In R. Plutchik and H. Kellerman (eds), *Emotion Theory, Research and Experience*. Vol. 1: *Theories of Emotion*. London: Academic Press (pp. 219–42).

Marsella, A. (1976) Cross-cultural studies of depression: a review of the literature. Paper presented at the Symposium on Cross-Cultural Aspects of Depression, Tilburg.

—— (1980) Depressive experience and disorder across cultures. In H. Triandis and J. Draguns (eds), *Handbook of Cross-Cultural psychopathology*. London: Allyn and Bacon (pp. 237–89).

—— and White, G. (eds) (1982) *General Conception of Mental Health and Therapy*. London: Reidel.

Matthews, G. (1980) Ritual and the religious feelings. In A. Rorty (ed.), *Explaining Emotion*. London: University of California Press (pp. 339–54).

Mauss, M. (1921) Obligatory expression of emotion. *Journal de Psychologie*, 18.

Miller, J. (1984) Culture and the development of everyday social explanations. *Journal of Personality and Social Psychology*, 46 (5), 961–78.

Munn, N. (1969) The effectiveness of symbols in Murngin rite and myth. In R. Spencer (ed.), *Forms of Symbolic Action*. New York and London: American Ethnological Society (pp. 178–207).

Myers, F. (1979) Emotions and the self. *Ethos*, 7 (4), 343–70.

Needham, R. (1971) Introduction. In R. Needham (ed.), *Rethinking Kinship and Marriage*. London: Tavistock Press (pp. xliii–cxvii).

—— (1972) *Belief, Language, and Experience*. Oxford: Basil Blackwell.

—— (1981) Inner states as universals: sceptical reflections on human nature. In P. Heelas and A. Lock (eds), *Indigenous Psychologies*. London: Academic Press (pp. 65–78).

—— (1983) *Against the Tranquility of Axioms*. London: University of California Press.

Newman, P. (1964) 'Wild man' behavior in a New Guinea Highlands community. *American Anthropologist*, 1–19.

Onians, R. (1973) *The Origins of European Thought*. New York: Arno.

Osgood, C. et al. (1975) *Cross-Cultural Universals of Affective Meaning*. Chicago and London: University of Illinois Press.

Peters, R. (1974) *Psychology and Ethical Development*. London: George Allan and Unwin.

Rawlinson, A. (1981). Yoga psychology. In P. Heelas and A. Lock (eds), *Indigenous Psychologies*. London: Academic Press (pp. 247–64).

Read, K. (1967) Morality and the concept of the person among the Gahuku-Gama. In J. Middleton (ed.), *Myth and Cosmos*. New York: Natural History Press (pp. 185–230).

Robarchek, C. (1977) Frustration, aggression and the nonviolent Semai. *American Ethnologist*, 4, 762–79.
—— (1979) Learning to fear: a case study of emotional conditioning. *American Ethnologist*, 6, 555–67.
Rosaldo, M. (1980) *Knowledge and Passion*. Cambridge: Cambridge University Press.
—— (1983) The shame of headhunters and the autonomy of the self. *Ethos*, 11 (3), 135–51.
Schachter, S. and Singer, J. (1962) Cognitive, social, and physiological determinants of emotional state. *Psychological Review*, 69 (5), 379–99.
Scherer, K. et al. (1983) Cross-national research on antecedents and components of emotion: a progress report. *Social Science Information*, 22 (3), 355–85.
Selby, H. (1974) *Zapotec Deviance*. Houston and London: University of Texas Press.
Shweder, R. and Bourne, E. (1984) Does the concept of the person vary cross-culturally? In R. Shweder and R. LeVine (eds), *Culture Theory: Essays on Mind, Self, and Emotion*. Cambridge: Cambridge University Press (pp. 158–99).
Simon, B. and Weiner, H. (1966) Models of mind and mental illness in ancient Greece. I: The Homeric model of mind. *Journal of the History of the Behavioural Sciences*, 11 (4), 303–14.
Smith, J. (1981) Self and experience in Maori culture. In P. Heelas and A. Lock (eds), *Indigenous Psychologies*. London: Academic Press (pp. 145–59).
Sorenson, E. (1975) Culture and the expression of emotion. In T. R. Williams (ed.), *Psychological Anthropology*. The Hague: Mouton (pp. 361–72).
Strathern, A. (1975) Why is shame on the skin? *Ethnology*, 14, 347–56.
Wax, R. (1969) *Magic, Fate and History*. Kansas City: Coronado Press.
Weiss, J. (1983) *Folk Psychology of the Javanese of Ponorogo*. Ann Arbour, Mich.: University Microfilms International.
Williams, F. (1932) *Sentiments and Leading Ideas in Native Society* (Anthropological Report no. 12). Port Moresby, Papua New Guinea.
—— (1940) *Drama of Orokolo*. Oxford: Clarendon Press.

14

The Domain of Emotion Words on Ifaluk

Catherine Lutz

Internal feeling states have commonly been assumed to be the primary referents of emotion words in Western thought, both social–scientific (Gardiner et al., 1937; Solomon, 1976, 1978) and lay (Davitz, 1969). In these views, the function of the emotion word is to label an internal state and perhaps to communicate that state to others. To an important extent, however, scientific conceptions of emotion and person are rooted in American ethnopsychological themes (LeVine, 1980; Lutz, 1981a) and everyday uses of emotion language (Kagan, 1978). Examination of the use of emotion words among several Oceanic peoples, including Samoans (Gerber, 1975), Pintupi Aborigines (Myers, 1979), and A'ara speakers of the Solomon Islands (White, 1981), reveals an alternative view of emotion. In these societies, emotion words are seen as statements about the relationship between a person and an event (particularly those involving another person), rather than as statements about introspection on one's internal states. In addition, physiological descriptions of emotion do not frequently occur naturally and in some cases are extremely difficult to elicit (Gerber, 1975, p. 183).

A study of emotion words on the Micronesian atoll of Ifaluk indicates that these words are defined and sorted by informants based on the situations in which the emotion usually occurs. The way in which people talk about emotion words is related to broader ethnotheories about the nature of the self. The world view and values within which emotion words have meaning are therefore emphasized. The clusters and dimensions that

The data on which this chapter is based were collected in 1977 and 1978 during 12 months of fieldwork on the atoll of Ifaluk in the Western Caroline Islands. The research was supported by a grant from the National Institute for Mental Health. I am grateful to John Whiting, Beatrice Whiting, Robert LeVine, Martin Etter, Geoffrey White, the late Michelle Rosaldo, and anonymous referees for their constructive comments on drafts of this chapter. An earlier version received the 1980 Stirling Award in Culture and Personality Studies.

emerge from card-sorting by Ifalukian informants display both some universal features of semantic meaning and some culturally specific foci that are related to the central values and ethnotheories of many Ifaluk. Although the differences between emotion words and emotions are clear, both cultural differences and universals in the meaning of emotion words can provide important evidence about the nature of the emotion itself (Lutz, 1981b).

ETHNOGRAPHIC BACKGROUND AND METHOD

The Ifaluk are a Malayo-Polynesian group inhabiting a one-half square mile coral atoll in the Western Pacific.[1] The 430 members of this densely populated society subsist on taro, breadfruit, coconut and fish. Hereditary chiefs head the several matrilineal clans and meet periodically to decide on island-wide issues, but they are accorded few special privileges. Extended matrilocal households average 13 members each and, as adoption is quite common, consist of members of several clans and of varying degrees of biological relatedness.

The most striking feataures of Ifaluk values are their emphasis on non-aggression, on co-operation and sharing within and between households, and on obedience within a system of ranking. Murder is unknown; the most serious incident of aggression in a year involved the touching of one man's shoulder by another, a violation that resulted in the immediate payment of a severe fine. People are expected to share their labour, food and goods, and those who shirk such responsibilities are sharply criticized. Communal labour and food sharing are daily occurrences, and the value of sharing one's children is expressed in an adoption rate of over 40 per cent. Finally, the system of rank hierarchically orders clans, lineages and individuals. The main prerogative of rank is that of exacting obedience from others. The status of rank carries with it, however, the obligation to speak and act 'kindly' to those of lower rank.

These values and their behavioural expressions are intimately linked to the environmental pressures and constraints of an island that is small, bounded and subject to periodic devastation by typhoons. In such a context, co-operation, obedience to authority, sharing of resources and non-aggression may contribute to survival. The cultural order that is built against this backdrop will be seen below to be reflected in the meaning and cognitive ordering of emotion words.

The methods by which the domain of emotion words was investigated will now be reviewed. Although no word in the Ifalukian languages translates as 'emotion', 31 words that were identified as 'about our insides' were selected for use in the formal testing according to the following procedure. From the beginning of the fieldwork period, all terms were collected that could conceivably have relation to emotion, thought, personality or expressive behaviour. These words came from (1) a search of Sohn and Tawerilmang's (1976) dictionary of the virtually identical dialect of the neighbouring island of Woleai; (2) daily conversations in which states or traits of individuals were discussed; and (3) a collection of words 'relating to emotion' from a bilingual informant.[2]

Interviews based on the resulting list of 208 words revealed several classes of words, including *wegitegil* (behaviour) and *ununul varemat* (personal style). These words were said 'not [to be] about our insides' (*tai kofal niferash*). An informant was asked to sort the 208 words into three groups: 'behaviour', 'personal style' and 'all others'. The latter group consisted of 58 words, the definitions of which were obtained from between three and ten informants of both sexes. These words, written on small cards, were free-sorted into piles by six literate informants. The sorters were told that the piles could be of any size and that words should be sorted according to whether they were similar (*hafiteg*) or a little similar. Any two words that were sorted into one pile by all six people were considered synonymous. Several people were asked to identify the more commonly used word of the pair, and the other was then omitted from further testing. Based on the definitions, archaic or non-native words were also eliminated.

This process resulted in a list of 31 words that were then sorted by 13 informants into piles according to the procedure described above. The order of, and changes in, sorting of each word were noted, and when the task was complete each individual was asked why all of the words in each group went together.[3]

The process just outlined constituted an attempt to elicit the domain and classification of emotion words in the absence of an overarching category of emotion, as distinct from thought or will. Although there is not one word like 'emotion' that exclusively defines the list that resulted, all of the words are 'about our insides'. While some related terms may never have been discovered, informants agreed on the cohesiveness of the group that constituted the list.

EMOTION WORD CLUSTERS AND THE MEANINGS OF SITUATIONS

The groupings made by informants were analysed both for structure (which will be examined first) and for underlying dimensions of meaning. A 'hierarchical clustering' program was used which bases its calculations on a similarity matrix consisting of the number of times each word was paired with each of the others by informants.[4] The criteria used to combine the similarity measure between each pair of emotion words and each subsequent cluster were the average measures of similarity between

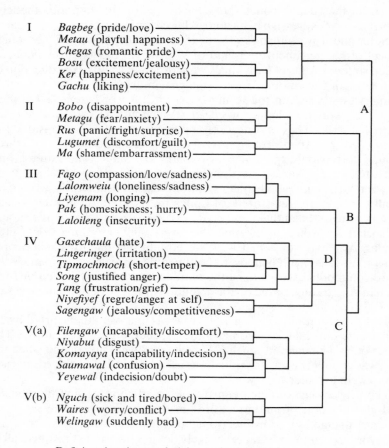

Figure 1 Hierarchical clustering diagram of 31 Ifalukian emotion words (not to scale): index of structure = 0.94

the clusters. The diagram that this program produced may be conceptualized as the 'average sorting' performed by the Ifaluk and is presented in figure 1. There are five major clusters in this domain, and they will be interpreted below in view of the explanations that those who did the sorting gave for their inclusion of words in a single pile.

The most frequent criterion on which informants sorted and defined each emotion word was *situation*. Typical explanations for the sorting of several words into the same pile included, 'If my child dies, I will feel all of them', or 'If there is gossip about me in the village, I'll feel _____, and then I'll feel _____.' Two words were grouped together if (1) the emotions are felt in the same or similar situations, or (2) the emotions may follow one after the other in a hypothetical sequence of situations. An example that includes both types of sorting rationale is the following explanation given for one four-word pile:

> If someone goes away on a trip, you feel *livemam* [longing] and *lalomweiu* [loneliness/sadness], and if you had nothing to give them [as a going away gift] you feel *tang* [frustration/grief] and *filengaw* [incapable/uncomfortable].

Other bases besides situation were sometimes used for sorting explanations, and these will be noted in the analysis of each cluster which follows.*

Cluster I: the emotions of good fortune

This group of words is separate from all others at the highest level of branching in figure 1. These words were rarely sorted with others outside of this group. When situations were mentioned as the basis for sorting, they were often situations in which 'good' things happen. Definitions also reveal that all of these emotions are pleasant ones that occur in the context of good fortune. The reasons that sorters gave for including them in one pile included the following: 'They all involve something happening that we *tipeli* [want/desire it]'; 'They all mean *ker* [happiness/excitement]'; and, a frequent response, that they all are associated with having a boyfriend or a girlfriend. Many of the emotions also occur when a person has a valuable object. This cluster includes several words that are taboo in mixed company, as they refer specifically or especially to emotions associated with sexual situations. No other cluster contains a taboo word.

In several cases, common behaviours that follow the emotions in this cluster were mentioned as one of the bases of sorting. A person in these states walks about the village, is talkative, and tends to act in a disruptive, 'show-off' or improper manner. Hence, the emotions in this cluster are not morally good or the outcome of ethically correct behaviour in a certain situation; rather, they simply occur in rewarding situations. These rewards are not conceived of as internal or physiological, and in only one case was

---

* Notice how these 'explanations' are narratives through which *both* the constitutive and regulative rules are expressed (see chapters 5 and 6). (*Ed.*)

the internal state itself elaborated as a basis of sorting – 'You feel like you are great, the number one person.'

Cluster II: the emotions of danger

This cluster contains words that all refer to dangerous situations. Several people said that they linked *metagu* (fear/anxiety), *lugumet* (discomfort/guilt) and *ma* (shame/embarrassment) because each is felt when one must go someplace where respectful behaviour is required. These situations include walking past a seated group of elders or past one's brother (if female), walking on the chief's property, or when one goes to visit someone but has nothing to give them, especially food. They are also sorted together because they are felt when one walks up to a group of people. The danger in the latter situation is due to the expectation that such people 'will laugh at you'.

Bobo (disappointment) was most often sorted with *rus* (panic/fright/surprise) because they both involve 'something bad happening that you don't expect'. *Metagu* (fear/anxiety) was the word that formed a bridge between *rus* and *bobo*, *ma* and *lugumet* in many people's sortings. It is important to note that this second cluster was also quite distinct from any other (see figure 1). The perception of danger in a situation may be of a higher order of importance than any other factor besides that of the pleasantness or unpleasantness of the consequence of a situation.

Cluster III: the emotions of connection and loss

This cluster is a generally unified one; that is, almost all individuals sorted the words in it together. There is also uniformity in the reasons given for the sortings. Each of the four emotions – *fago* (compassion/love/sadness), *pak* (homesickness), *liyemam* (longing), and *lalomweiu* (loneliness/sadness) – is felt in the context of separation or the threat of it. Adolescent boys who must go to the distant island of Ulithi to attend high school were said to experience all four emotions; in these states, 'their thoughts are random' and 'they think only of home.' Death also causes all four emotions to be evoked and was mentioned as the basis for sorting.

In cases where *laloileng* (insecurity) was sorted with the other words in cluster III, it was due to their common evocation during sickness. According to one older man, 'If I'm sick, I feel both *laloileng* and *lalomweiu* that I will die and no one will get food and sweet coconut toddy for my children. I feel *liyemam* if a relative dies who used to always be in my house, and it made me feel good to see him. But I feel *liyemam* because there's no one to talk to me.'

Although this cluster may be decribed as the 'emotions of loss', it also contains most of the emotion words that refer to positive connections between individuals, even while those connections may be in jeopardy owing to death, travel or sickness. The most commonly used word in the cluster, *fago*, refers to one's relationship with a more unfortunate other, rather than to a more atomistic internal feeling such as 'sadness'. Similarly, *lalomweiu* and *liyemam* are felt by those who remain in the more fortunate position of being on the island and healthy. Thus, the core words of this cluster focus both on attachment to a more unfortunate other, and on the loss suffered by self.

Cluster IV: the emotions of human error

This cluster contains most of the emotions that are considered the most unpleasant to experience. The focus on this aspect of emotion is shown by the fact that here internal feeling tones were the basis for sorting more often than in any other cluster. It was frequently said that these emotions belong together because 'they all feel bad inside'. *Song* (justified anger), the most commonly used term in the cluster, is considered 'good'; however, this 'goodness' is of a higher, moral level, as it indicates that one has taken proper notice of the violation of a cultural norm by another.

The situations that each of these emotion words refer to include the element of human error, and each word further distinguishes between whether that error is one's own or another's. *Lingeringer* (irritation/small anger) and *tipmochmoch* (short-temper) are milder and less justifiable responses to frustration than *song*, as they refer to the thwarting of individual, rather than culturally defined goals. *Tang* (frustration/grief) refers to the response to situations where one is thwarted either justly or unjustly, but in either case one is powerless to do anything about it. Thus, one person said that all of the words in cluster IV belong together because they can all occur when one is interrupted in one's work. *Song* will be felt if this interruption is uncalled for; *lingeringer, tipmochmoch* and *tang* are all felt if one is called away from work to perform an errand for someone of higher rank. As the value of obedience to elders is paramount, such a request is acceptable and supercedes other culturally constituted goals. *Gasechaula* (hate) is also felt in the same situations, but is said to follow upon the other feelings.

Less centrally related to this core group of words in cluster IV are *sagengaw* (jealousy/competitiveness) and *niyefiyef* (regret/anger at one's self). Unlike the others, these words focus on the self and what one could have done to prevent, or should now do to alleviate, the situation. Men often stated that they sorted these two emotions together because they are both felt 'if someone goes fishing and catches a lot and you do not'. *Niyefiyef* will be felt if the reason for that discrepancy is that one did not go fishing at all, while *sagengaw* is felt if one did go fishing but caught little.

The two were also sorted together as sequential emotions; one woman stated that if her mother died and had not yet taught her how to weave, she would feel *niyefiyef* that she had not asked her mother to teach her previously. She would then feel *sagengaw* and would try to learn to weave as well as other women.

This latter pair of words and the more central words in the cluster were often linked through such situations of differential fortune for the self and for 'other'. 'If I feel *sagengaw* to someone because they are smarter than me, I'll be both *lingeringer* and *tipmochmoch* with him and then *gasechaula* him.' Similarly, 'If someone catches a lot of fish you feel *niyefiyef*, and then you feel *sagengaw* to that person. You also become *lingeringer*, which causes *song*. And then you *gasechaula* that person.'

Cluster V: the emotions of inability

All of the words in this cluster are unified by their common elicitation in situations where one is unsure about what to do or is incapable of doing what seems to be required by the situation. As a whole, this is the least unified of all the five clusters. Several of the words in this group have strong connections with other clusters; that is, many people sorted individual words in this cluster with words from other clusters. Many of those same words were among the last to be sorted by people during the task itself, as they were obviously less clearly members of any one particular group.

A close relationship is found between *komayaya* (incapable/indecisive), *saumawal* (confused) and *yeyewal* (indecisive/doubtful). Most people said that they belong together because all involve 'not knowing something'. Some mentioned specific situations – most particularly, work situations – where one does not know what to do. The other words in the cluster were variously sorted with this core group, or members of it, on the basis of situation. Some examples include the following:

> If you are making thread, you can feel *waires* [worried/conflicted] if you don't know if you can finish it [in time]. You feel *welingaw* [suddenly bad] if you are not able to.
>
> If you don't like a certain kind of food, you feel both *welingaw* [suddenly bad] and *niyabut* [disgusted] if you have to eat it.
>
> If you are always doing things wrong, you feel *saumawal* [confused] and *filengaw* [incapable/uncomfortable].
>
> When the teacher puts an assignment on the board at school, you look at it and feel all three *nguch* [sick and tired/bored], *saumawal* and *waires*.

Although the words in this cluster share the eliciting situation of a work or social obligation of which one is unsure, or unable to fulfil properly, there are two subclusters within it, labelled (a) and (b) in figure 1. These will be discussed below in reference to variation in classification.

The five clusters to emerge from the sorting task reflect an 'average' cognitive map of this domain for the Ifaluk in the sample. Although there was significant agreement between individuals about the interrelations and similarities among these words, it is important to examine in particular those emotion words that were sorted into widely different groups by different individuals. Those links between words which are not reflected in figure 1 will be termed *secondary classifications*. They are important because they may reflect the use of different dimensions of meaning of the words (for example, situation versus feeling tone, or different aspects of a situation) by different individuals in their sorting. Secondary classifications may also reflect ambivalence or ambiguity (White, 1978) about the situations in which a particular emotion is evoked. These classifications will be examined by cluster and in terms of the meaning of the nonmodal pairings for the individuals who made them.

Cluster I, being the most distinct and different group, had only five links with other words outside itself. These included *ma* (shame/embarrassment), *lugumet* (discomfort/guilt), *sagengaw* (jealousy/competitiveness) and *fago* (compassion/love/sadness). These links illustrate that the good fortune that is the basis of cluster I may provoke ill feeling in others (e.g., *sagengaw*). Responsibility for this ill feeling lies with the individuals who may have 'shown off' their good fortune. The person who was originally happy and excited then feels ashamed (*ma*) or guilty (*lugumet*) for having flaunted his or her more favourable position. *Fago*, which may be glossed as 'sad love', is exclusively the love that is felt for the less fortunate. This is confirmed by the minimal linkage made between the happy emotions of cluster I and *fago*, and contrasts with the strong similarities between the connotations of love and happiness in English.[5]

The most important secondary classification not reflected in cluster II includes a number of links made between itself and *laloileng* (insecurity). Although the latter word is included in cluster III with other emotion words having to do with loss and connection, feelings of insecurity are elicited both in situations which are dangerous to the self and in situations where the danger is to a significant other. The most important context in which danger and potential loss occur is during the illness of a relative.[6] *Laloileng* is also connected to the other words in cluster V through their mutual elicitation in situations where one does not know what will happen.

Cluster III is linked to the emotion words in cluster IV through *tang* (frustration/grief). The people who sorted *tang* and *fago* (compassion/

love/sadness) together did so on the basis that they are both felt in a situation where one feels for an unfortunate other but is somehow blocked through circumstance from acting on those compassionate feelings. As one woman stated, 'If someone is sick or leaving the island, and I have nothing to give them, I feel *fago* and *tang*.' On the other hand, the loss that causes *fago* may also lead to a form of anger: 'We *fago* someone who is far away. We then feel *nguch* [sick and tired/bored] at work and get *song* [justifiably angry] at people who talk to us while we are thinking [of our *fago* for that person].'

Although *nguch* is in cluster V with other words indicating uncertainty, it is also linked to cluster III by mutual elicitation during separation from significant others. *Nguch* has even stronger links to cluster IV, and in particular to *song*. *Nguch* is a much-used emotion word that labels feelings in situations where one must accept that one's individual goals are thwarted. Although *nguch* and *song* are related to the blocking of goals, *nguch* is an 'unjustified' or ambivalent anger. For this reason, it is not surprising that *nguch* was also sorted with *waires* in cluster V. This is in line with the use of *nguch* in daily life to describe the frustration engendered by the obedience required to those of higher rank. While this frustration cannot legitimately cause anger in one's self, it is with some ambivalence and difficulty that the label of *nguch*, rather than *song*, is used in structurally similar (i.e., frustrating) situations.

The secondary classifications in cluster V include links between *nguch*, *filengaw*, *welingaw*, *niyabut* and words outside the cluster. *Filengaw* (incapable/uncomfortable) has links to the emotions of *ma* (shame/embarrassment) and *lugumet* (discomfort/guilt) in cluster II through their common elicitation in situations where one 'stands out in the crowd' because of ineptitude. *Welingaw* (suddenly bad) is a more general term than most of the others. It is a 'turning-of-the-stomach' (feeling that may result from either disgust (*niyabut*) or the sudden and simultaneous pull of conflicting definitions of the situation (*waires*). *Welingaw* may also result from the same situations that cause *song* and therefore has links to cluster IV. *Niyabut* (disgust) has the weakest links of any word in the domain with any particular other word. *Niyabut* is in fact only a 'quasi-emotion', as it refers exclusively to the physical revulsion experienced on seeing a spoiled or fetid object.[7] The strongest link between *niyabut* and others outside cluster V is that with *gasechaula* (hate). The latter emotion can, like *niyabut*, also be felt towards a repulsive object.

Members of cluster V are loosely related to *ma*. In two closely related explanations, it was said that 'If there's gossip going around about me, I'll be *ma*, and then *waires* (worried/conflicted) about whether to go out or to hide at my house.' Another informant also sorted these two words together on the basis of their co-occurrence when one tries to make something for the first time: 'I'll be *waires* because I'll be *ma* that it will come out poorly, and people will laugh.' Although *niyabut* and *waires* were never sorted together, a similar situation to those above was used to explain the sorting together of *ma* and *niyabut*: 'If our clothes are old and people feel *niyabut* when they look at us, then we feel *ma*.'

What, then, do these clusters of emotion words reveal about the nature of emotions on Ifaluk? Most significantly, they show the importance of 'situation' in the definition and sorting of emotion words. Emotion is elicited in social interaction and in interaction with environmental events. A person on Ifaluk does not look inward to 'discover' the emotional state being experienced so much as he or she evaluates the existing situation. I do not mean to imply that only situations are coded in these emotion words. In the foregoing analysis I have noted instances where individuals explained their sorting on the basis of similarity of internal feeling tone. While the evaluation of the environment must occur before a situation can truly 'elicit' a linguistically labelled emotion, in individual retrospect the strength of a feeling may take precedence (in sorting) over situational similarity.

When a situation is evaluated on Ifaluk, it is in terms of its rewards for the self (cluster I); dangers (cluster II); negative consequences for others and (through them) for the self (cluster III); frustration, through human error, of ego needs, including culturally constituted needs (cluster IV); and, finally, comprehensibility or the potential for individual mastery of the situation (cluster V). These broad evaluations of situations and the finer distinctions made within each cluster have important reference to (1) cultural values that are being either conformed to or violated, and (2) the reactions of other individuals to the behaviour of the self within the situation. Individuals must appraise a situation as rewarding, punitive, dangerous, frustrating or overly complex within the constraints and with the aid of cultural values, as well as in relation to significant others, in order to label themselves with a specific Ifalukian emotion word.

THE DIMENSIONS OF EMOTION WORDS

Multidimensional scaling is less responsive than hierarchical clustering to cultural and linguistic nuances of meaning, but it can give a more holistic picture of the dimensions of meaning and of the relations between words on those dimensions. The same similarity matrix of the sorted emotion words used in the clustering analysis was submitted to a multidimensional scaling procedure. Figure 2 presents the two-dimensional results.[8] A three-dimensional model resulted in only slight reduction of stress and will not be considered here (stress = 0.0882 for the two-dimensional model and 0.0507 for the three-dimensional model).

The clearest and most striking dimension along which the emotion

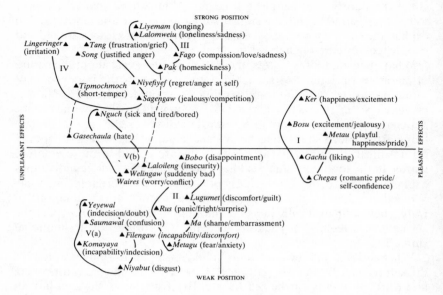

*Figure 2 Two-dimensional picture of 31 Ifalukian emotion words
(stress = 0.0882). Circles indicate groups found in cluster analysis. Dashes connect
outlying members of cluster*

words fall is what I have called *pleasant* versus *unpleasant* effects of the
emotion-eliciting situation. This dimension sharply divides cluster I from
all the others and is similar to the 'evaluation' dimension that Osgood
(Osgood et al., 1975) found in his cross-cultural studies of meaning. Of
interest here is what the Ifaluk evaluate when they sort their emotion
words. It is necessary to return to the cultural data that are the source of a
multidimensional scaling in order to name and explain the dimensions.
While it appears to be universally the case that people sort the environment into the categories of 'good' and 'bad', these latter words are
themselves multidimensional and must be placed and interpreted in cultural context.

Words on the right side of figure 2 are not distinguished (in either use,
ethnotheory or expressed rationale for sorting in the task situation) as
being morally good emotions; neither are the situations in which they are
elicited. *Ker* (happiness/excitement) and other emotions in this cluster
may, in fact, be 'bad' in the sense that the emotion may result from an
inequitable distribution of resources in ego's favour, which then causes
envy or excitement in others. An individual who 'shows off' his or her good
fortune is reprehensible, and such behaviour is said to cause others to feel

bosu (excited/jealous). It is also said that a child who is *ker* is antithetical to feelings of *metagu* (fear/anxiety). It is *metagu* that is the emotion considered most responsible for obedient and good behaviour. Moreover, the unpleasant end of this dimension contains emotions that are considered necessary and morally good to feel in the correct situations. Prominent among those is *song* (justified anger). *Song* is said to be 'good' for people (and especially parents) to feel and express when a wrongdoing has occurred. It is only through the observation of their parents' *song* in particular situations that children are said to learn the difference between right and wrong.

The sorting and uses of these emotion words indicate that what distinguishes the two ends of this first dimension are the nature of the consequences of the situation associated with each emotion word. Many informants stated that all of the emotions on the right of figure 2 are evoked when something happens 'that we want' to happen, while the opposite is true of all the emotions on the left side. In addition, but secondarily, feeling tone itself maps on to this dimension. 'Our insides feel good' is used to describe all terms to the right, and 'our insides feel bad' to describe those on the left.

The second dimension in the scaling model refers to ego's position *vis-à-vis* other actors in the emotion-eliciting situation. This position may be one of relative strength or weakness. It may be the result of moral rectitude (strength) or wrongdoing (weakness), or it may reflect an individual's possession of higher social rank, more resources or greater cognitive control or understanding of the situation (strength) – or the lack of the same (weakness). Thus, this second dimension refers to ego's encounter with the environment, and the appropriate emotional response is one that takes account of one's position in relation to it.

The emotions of danger (cluster II) and the emotions of inability (cluster V) are both found at the 'weak position' end of the dimension and share an uncertainty about performance or about the consequences of the situation that elicits them. The emotions that arise out of a 'strong position' include those emotions that entail certainty about oneself in relation to the environment. The emotions of connection and loss (cluster III) and the emotions of human error (cluster IV), found at the 'strong position' end of the dimension, are generally emotions that are felt towards an individual who is 'weaker' than oneself, either through illness or other misfortune (for example, *fago* (compassion/love/sadness)), or through participation in a morally reprehensible act (for example, *song* (justified anger)).

This dimension does not refer to the strength or weakness of the feeling tone which accompanies each emotion. Two of the emotions that the Ifaluk say produce the most disruptive physiological symptoms – *rus* (panic/fright/surprise) and *niyabut* (disgust) – are found at the 'weak' end of this dimension. Similarly, cluster I words (the emotions of good fortune) include reference to excited hyperactivity and have 'strong' behavioural expressions such as shouting or running, but they are located near the midpoint of the dimension. In addition, cluster I emotions may cause one to misbehave and lead to 'jealousy' in others. This indicates that the second dimension refers to interpersonal relationships of strength and weakness more than to an atomistically defined strength, such as might emerge from the possession of material goods.[9]

Although this dimension parallels that of 'potency' (Osgood et al., 1975), it takes its particular meaning on Ifaluk in reference to the institutions and values of rank. In a political and economic system that is based on individual achievement and that encourages the differential distribution of resources, 'potency' may carry stronger connotations of superiority and unidirectional control. On Ifaluk, by contrast, rank carries the responsibility of benevolence and nurturance towards those 'lower' or more 'needy' than oneself. The orthogonality of the dimensions based on evaluation and potency (figure 2) indicates that the Ifaluk do, as their values insist, differentiate rather sharply between strength and self-aggrandizement. This is not meant to imply that there are no ego rewards to the altruism that ideally accompanies strength on Ifaluk: rather, it is exactly the cultural moulding and social desirability of an emotion like *fago* (compassion/love/sadness) that gives this dimension the meaning attributed to it here.

In definitions of emotion words, in conversational use and in explaining their sorting decisions, the Ifaluk primarily define the emotions by the situations during which they are felt, and this is reflected in the foregoing analysis. The two most important dimensions of emotion-eliciting situations are the rewards that they hold for ego (horizontal dimension) and the strength of ego relative to the people and objects in the situation (vertical dimension). Figure 3 illustrates this with the situational elicitors (as revealed in folk definitions and in the uses of the terms in everyday conversations) for some of the emotions located at outlying points in the dimensional space defined by the scaling procedure.

The emotions at the top of figure 3 are generally felt by individuals of higher rank towards those of lower rank. An elder is more often *song* (justifiably angry) at a younger person than at a peer or at a higher-ranked individual. The chiefs are often said to be *song* at those who have broken rules or taboos. *Fago* is more frequently directed from parents to their children than in the other direction, and the ideal chief is one who feels *fago* for his subjects. Note that *gasechaula* (hate) may occur in the same situations that elicit *song*, but the former is more often used between peers, and even here only rarely. This is reflected in the place of *gasechaula* at a midpoint between the strong and the weak position ends of the vertical dimension.

In a dyadic interaction, the *song* of one person (usually of higher rank)

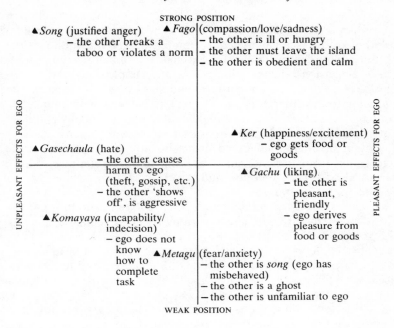

STRONG POSITION

▲ *Song* (justified anger)
 – the other breaks a
 taboo or violates a norm

▲ *Fago* (compassion/love/sadness)
 – the other is ill or hungry
 – the other must leave the island
 – the other is obedient and calm

UNPLEASANT EFFECTS FOR EGO

PLEASANT EFFECTS FOR EGO

▲ *Ker* (happiness/excitement)
 – ego gets food or
 goods

▲ *Gasechaula* (hate)
 – the other causes
 harm to ego
 (theft, gossip, etc.)
 – the other 'shows
 off', is aggressive

▲ *Gachu* (liking)
 – the other is
 pleasant,
 friendly
 – ego derives
 pleasure from
 food or goods

▲ *Komayaya* (incapability/
 indecision)
 – ego does not
 know
 how to
 complete
 task

▲ *Metagu* (fear/anxiety)
 – the other is *song* (ego has
 misbehaved)
 – the other is a ghost
 – the other is unfamiliar to ego

WEAK POSITION

Figure 3 Situational elicitors of emotion at outlying points in two dimensions

produces the emotion of *metagu* (fear/anxiety) in the other (usually of lower rank). *Metagu* and *komayaya* (incapability/indecisiveness) are felt primarily in situations in which ego has done something morally wrong or performed incapably. To the right in figure 3 are two emotions that are both spatially and situationally orthogonal to the system of rank that informs the vertical dimension. *Ker* (happiness/excitement) occurs in situations where the other is neither *song* nor *metagu*, but this fact makes *ker* a somewhat dangerous, 'uncontrolled' emotion. Like *gasechaula*, *gachu* (like) is most often used to describe one's feelings towards peers. *Ker* and *gasechaula* hold extreme positions at the ends of the horizontal dimension, in contrast to their shared orthogonality to the vertical dimension. As can be seen in figure 3, ego is punished by the situations that elicit *gasechaula* and is rewarded by those that elicit *ker*.

DISCUSSION

The Ifalukian cognitive organization of the domain of 31 emotion words is based on the eliciting situation. The five major groupings of emotion words in the hierarchical clustering analysis were named according to five basic situation types: good fortune, danger, loss and connection with others, human error, and overly complex and misunderstood events. The multidimensional scaling procedure pointed out two major dimensions of emotion words that were also interpreted in terms of eliciting situation. Those dimensions include the pleasant or unpleasant nature of the consequences of the situation for ego and the strength or weakness of ego in relation to the other. Stressed throughout is the meaningfulness of the groupings and dimensions for Ifalukian individuals. Equally emphasized is the articulation of the dimensions of meaning with dimensions that are present in Ifalukian values and social institutions. It is these cultural factors that structure and give meaning to the situations which are associated with each emotion and which in fact create the emotional meaning of the situation.

The similarity between the dimensions found here and those found by several other researchers across various types of semantic domains is clear. Osgood (Osgood et al., 1975) has described the dimensions of 'evaluation, potency and activity' as universal aspects of meaning. White (1980), in a comparison of the scaling of Melanesian and Indian personality descriptives, finds 'solidarity/conflict' and 'dominance/submission' to be the most important dimensions. He relates them to Osgood's evaluation and potency dimensions, respectively. There have been numerous analyses of English emotion words which find some of these same dimensions.[10]

The evidence from other domains and other cultures suggests a universal tendency to perceive 'the meaning of things' with broadly similar criteria. It is crucial, however, to examine what in particular is the *focus* of perception. This focus will vary in similar domains across cultures and across semantic domains within particular cultures. Most importantly, this variation may be very informative about both culturally framed perceptions (for example, Ifalukian views of emotion versus Samoan views of emotion) and the domain in question (for example, emotion words or personality trait terms). These two types of variation in the focus of perception are briefly examined in conclusion.

In terms of variation across cultures within the same domain, the dimensional analyses of English emotion words mentioned above are very instructive. A comparison of these analyses reveals that the two most common dimensions found are the pleasantness/unpleasantness of the feeling state and the level of activation. The first dimension is called 'hedonic tone' (comfort/discomfort) by Davitz (1969) and 'pleasant/ unpleasant' by others (e.g., Schlosberg, 1954; Block, 1957; Frijda and Philipszoon, 1963). The second most common dimension is 'level of activation', which refers to physiological and/or behavioural activity (Schlosberg, 1954; Block, 1957; Abelson and Sermat, 1962; Davitz, 1969; Bush, 1973). Although these and other investigators have posited some secondary dimensions of emotion that relate to the position of ego in relation to the environment,[11] the focus of perception in emotional situations is presumed to be primarily *internal.*

The focus of these latter studies on the psychological, physiological and more generally, internal dimensions of emotion contrasts with the Ifalukian focus on the external dimensions of emotion, that is, on the eliciting situation. Cultural differences in the meaning of the dimensions of evaluation and potency are related, in this case, to ethnopsychological beliefs about the nature of emotion and self. While Americans define emotions primarily as internal feeling states (see also Gardiner et al., 1937; Solomon, 1976, 1978), the Ifaluk see the emotions as evoked in, and inseparable from, social activity (Lutz,1980).

Another aspect of focus is illustrated by the organization of the domain of emotion words in Samoan (Gerber, 1975). The dimension of evaluation is central to Samoan emotion words as well as to American English and Ifalukian terms. This dimension is focused on pleasant and unpleasant feeling states in the English case, and on the pleasant or unpleasant consequences of the situation on Ifaluk. An analysis of sorted Samoan emotion words reveals that the focus of evaluation there, however, is on the social good rather than on pleasant feeling or consequences. The positively evaluated emotions are the ethically correct emotions. These 'socially virtuous' emotions are, moreover, strongly associated with submission, and they are considered more unpleasant than pleasant to experience.

The extent of overlap between socially valued emotions and pleasant or egocentrically rewarding emotions is thus culturally variable, as is the extent to which one or the other is seen as central to the meaning of emotion words. The 'pursuit of happiness' may be a cultural value and is portrayed as such, for example, in American public ideology. In Ifalukian belief, the group of ethically correct or good emotions is not the same as the group of emotions that occur in situations bringing personal reward. Involvement in a rewarding situation is not always, or perhaps even usually, culturally sanctioned. Variation in the focus of evaluation in Samoan, Ifalukian and American emotion word meanings can shed important light on the effects of the cultural values and theories that inform the perception of emotion.

Variation across semantic domains in the focus of meaning is a second important source of information. One would then ask how the meaning of emotion words differs from, for example, that of personality trait terms. Several investigators have noted a close relationship both between states and traits themselves (Izard, 1977) and between emotion terms and personality trait terms (Plutchik, 1980). Both sets of words can be used to describe the characteristics of individuals, with emotion words focusing on more temporary than permanent characteristics. Both types of words are also interpersonal judgements which, as White (1980, p. 776) points out, rely on common 'conceptual themes in folk interpretations of social behavior generally'.

The difference between the dimensions found by White to inform personality descriptives ('solidarity/conflict' and 'dominance/submission') and those found here for emotion words is instructive about the nature of these two domains. White (1980, p. 767) sees these dimensions as based on 'inferential knowledge', which is much more complex than the 'simple connotations of "goodness" and "strength" '. The dimension of solidarity/conflict emerges from the possibility for matching or mismatching between the goals of two actors, while the dimension of dominance/submission arises from the fact that individuals influence each other. Personality terms are most frequently used to predict or explain the behaviour and presumed motivations of the other (White,1980, p. 767).

Although a predictable other is one who can be counted on to either support of block ego's goals, the focus is on the other. Psychological studies among American populations have shown, in fact, that people observing the behaviour of others tend to see the actor as 'figural against the ground of the situation' (Jones and Nisbett, 1971, p. 15). In describing the causes of their own behaviour, however, actors speak in terms of more immediate situational demands. Trait descriptors would therefore be used most frequently to depict others rather than self.

Emotion words, by contrast, simultaneously code changing situations and ego's stance in relation to those situations. Although it has been seen that the primary referent of emotion words may be either psychological or external events, these words are more readily used to describe the state of the self (either alone or in relation to the environment) than are personality trait terms.

Finally, we may ask about the relation between emotion words and emotion itself. Emotion words are used for giving accounts of experience. The extent to which culture provides conceptual and ethnotheoretical tools for constructing emotion experience itself, as well as accounts, has not as yet been fully realized. In part this is due to the influence of Western views of emotion as an essentially private, unlearned and physiological process. There is evidence accumulating in other domains that the personal and cultural theories that people use in constructing accounts of experience have powerful, direct and generative effects on such things as problem solving (Gentner, 1981), the perception of and action within a marital relationship (Quinn, 1981) and the production of metaphor (Lakoff and Johnson, 1980).

Divergence between what people say and what they presumably know (and feel) has been presented as the central flaw in research that uses verbal reports (Nisbett and Wilson, 1977) and in many studies in cognitive anthropology (Laboratory of Human Cognition 1978, pp. 63–6). Rather than dismissing verbal reports as inaccurate, however, it would seem more useful to investigate 'the transformations that lead to introspective accounts' (Mandler, 1980, p. 242) and, in particular, cultural conventions for communicating personal experience to others or for concealing it (LeVine, 1981, p. 5). Explicitly examining the various contexts in which emotion words are used, including structured and unstructured interviews with an ethnographer and use in conversations with a wide variety of others, can move us in the direction of understanding the relation between emotion words and emotion experience.

The distinctive nature of emotion as a phenomenon lies in the fact that it appears to the individual to originate both in the self and in the world. Cultural variation exists in the extent to which either the former or the latter is emphasized. In either case, emotion words do not simply serve to bring the private into the social realm. The cultural values and theories that inform the meanings of emotion words give those words an important role in aiding individuals in the interpretation and understanding of their situated selves.

NOTES

1 Further ethnographic description of Ifaluk is available in Burrows and Spiro (1953). Burrows (1963), and Lutz (1980).

2 These words were cross-checked with several other informants by asking them to free-associate to a cue word from the list. This process added few words to the list and consisted mainly of terms already acquired by the other methods mentioned here. It is certain, however, that there are rarely used emotion words that were not discovered here.

3 The sorting task was performed by six females and seven males, of whom all but one were literate. The sorting of that one individual did not differ significantly from the others and is included in the analysis. Literacy of at least a minimal sort is nearly universal among islanders under the age of 40. The task seemed to be easy as well as enjoyable, and most peopled completed it within a half hour.

4 The program used was Cluster Analysis PIM, designed by John Hartigan and described in Dixon and Brown (1977). An 'index of structure' for the domain was computed following the method presented by Von Glascoe (1979, p. 308).

5 The two pairings of *fago* (compassion/love/sadness) and *ker* (happiness/excitement) were made by men with some knowledge of English. On questioning, these men translated *fago* as 'love'. The possibility that some sortings were made on the basis of a translation into English is problematic, but it may point to important structuring effects of language.

6 *Metagu* (fear/anxiety), *rus* (panic/fright/surprise) and *laloileng* (insecurity) were sorted together in several cases. One young man said that he feels all three emotions in relation to the possibility that his father may fall out of a coconut tree. One person sorted them together because they can be elicited sequentially in a situation: *laloileng* is felt when one does not know what will

happen in the future, which then causes *rus*; one is then *metagu* of the thing which has caused one's *rus*.

7   *Niyabut* (disgust) was kept in the sample despite the statements by several informants that it is 'a bit different' from the other words. This was done in order to allow comparison with 'disgust', which is considered by many to be a universal emotion (Tomkins, 1973; Ekman, 1974).

8   The scaling program used was KYST, designed by Kruskal et al. (1973).

9   Note that *gachu* (like) and *chegas* (romantic pride), both of the 'weak position' side of the second dimension, refer more than the others in that cluster to interpersonal satisfactions. To 'like' or be 'proud' of another may involve an element of weakness *vis-à-vis* the other.

10   The data on which these dimensional analyses have been based vary from coded interview material and judgements of facial expression through introspection and *post hoc* theorizing. In any case, they reflect an important aspect of American (both scientific and lay) cognitive organization of emotion words.

11   One such posited social dimension that relates to the dimension of strength/weakness found in the present study has been variously but similarly labelled by several individuals 'social submission/condescension' (Frijda and Philipszoon, 1973), 'feel superior/feel inferior' (Krech and Crutchfield, 1965), 'competence (Davitz, 1969) and 'dominance/submission' (Russell and Mehrabian, 1977).

REFERENCES

Abelson, Robert P. and Sermat, Vello   (1962) Multidimensional scaling of facial expressions. *Journal of Experimental Psychology*, 6 (3), 546–54.

Block, Jack (1957)   Studies in the phenomenology of emotions. *Journal of Abnormal and Social Psychology*, 54, 358–63.

Burrows, Edwin G. (1963)   *Flower in My Ear*. Seattle: University of Washington press.

—— and Spiro, Melford (1953)   *An Atoll Culture: Ethnography of Ifaluk in the Central Carolines*. New Haven: HRAF.

Bush, Lynn E. (1973)   Individual differences MDS of adjectives denoting feelings. *Journal of Personality and Social Psychology*, 25, 50–7.

Davitz, Joel R. (1969)   *The Language of Emotion*. New York: Academic Press.

Dixon, W. J. and Brown, M. B. (eds) (1977)   *Biomedical Computer Programs P-Series*. Berkeley: University of California Press.

Ekman, Paul (1974)   Universal facial expressions of emotion. Robert le Vine (ed.), In *Culture and Personality: Contemporary Readings*. (pp. 8–15). Chicago: Aldine.

Frijda, Nico H. and Philipszoon, Els (1963)   Dimensions of recognition of expression. *Journal of Abnormal and Social Psychology*, 66: 45–51.

Gardiner, Harry, Metcalf, Ruth and Beebe-Center, John (1937)   *Feeling and Emotion: A History of Theories*. New York: American Book Company.

Gentner, Dedre (1981)   Generative analogies as mental models. In *Proceedings of the Third Annual Conference of the Cognitive Science Society* (pp. 97–100). Berkeley, California: CSS.

Gerber, Eleanor (1975) The cultural patterning of emotions in Samoa. PhD dissertation, University of California, San Diego.

Izard, Carroll E. (1977) *Human Emotions.* New York: Plenum Press.

Jones, Edward E. and Nisbett, Richard E. (1971) *The Actor and the Observer: Divergent Perceptions of the Causes of Behavior.* Morristown, NJ: General Learning Press.

Kagan, Jerome (1978) On emotion and its development: a working paper. In Michael Lewis and Leonard Rosenblum (eds) *The Development Affect.* (pp. 11–41) New York: Plenum Press.

Krech, David and Crutchfield, Richard S. (1965) *Elements of Psychology*, New York: Knopf.

Kruskal, Joseph, Young, Forrest and Seery, Judith (1973) *How to use KYST: A Very Flexible Program to Do Multidimensional Scaling and Unfolding.* Murray Hill, NJ: Bell Laboratory.

Laboratory of Comparative Human Cognition (1978) Cognition as a residual category in anthropology, *Annual Review of Anthropology*, 7, 51–69.

Lakoff, George and Johnson, Mark (1980) *Metaphors We Live By*, Chicago: University of Chicago Press.

LeVine, Robert (1980) Anthropology and child development. In Charles M. Super and Sara Harkness (eds), *Anthropological Perspectives on Child Development.* (pp. 71–86). San Francisco: Jossey Bass.

—— (1981) The self in culture: person-centered ethnography and psychoanalytic anthropology. Unpublished paper.

Lutz, Catherine (1980) Emotion words and emotional development on Ifaluk Atoll. PhD dissertation, Harvard University.

—— (1981a) Talking about 'our insides': Ifalukian conceptions of the self. Paper presented at the Annual Meeting of the Association for Social Anthropology in Oceania,February 1981, San Diego.

—— (1981b) Situation-based emotion frames and the cultural construction of emotions. In *Proceedings of the Third Annual Conference of the Cognitive Science Society* (pp. 84–9) Berkeley, California: CSS.

Mandler, George (1980) *The generation of emotion: a psychological theory.* In Robert Plutchik and Henry Kellerman (eds), *Emotion: Theory, Research, and Experience*, (pp. 219–43). New York: Academic Press.

Myers, Fred (1979) Emotions and the self: a theory of personhood and political order among Pintupi Aborigines. *Ethos*, 7, 343–70.

Nisbett, Richard E. and Wilson, Timothy D. (1977) Telling more than we can know: verbal reports on mental processes. *Psychological Review*, 84, 231–59.

Osgood, Charles, May, William H. and Miron, Murray S. (1975) *Cross-Cultural Universals of Affective Meaning.* Urbana: University of Illinois Press.

Plutchik, Robert (1980) A general psychoevolutionary theory of emotion. In Robert Plutchik and Henry Kellerman (eds), *Emotion: Theory, Research, and Experience*, (pp. 3–33). New York: Academic Press.

Quinn, Naomi (1981) 'Commitment' in American marriage: analysis of a key word. Unpublished paper.

Russell, James A. and Mehrabian, Albert (1977) Evidence for a three-factor theory of emotions. *Journal of Research in Personality, 11, 273–94.*

Schlosberg, Harold (1954) Three-dimensions of emotion. *Psychological Review*, 61, 81–8.

Sohn, Ho-min, and Tawerilmang, Anthony (1976) *Woleaian-English Dictionary*. Honolulu: University Press of Hawaii.

Solomon, Robert C. (1976) *The Passions*. New York: Doubleday-Anchor.

—— (1978) Emotions and anthropology: the logic of emotional world views. *Inquiry*, 21, 181–99.

Tomkins, Silvan S. (1963) *Affect, Imagery and Consciousness*. Vol. 2: *The Negative Affects*. New York: Springer.

Von Glascoe, Christine (1979) Evidence for multiple cognitive realities in Yucatec game cognition. In Madeleine Mathiot (ed.), *Ethnolinguistics: Boas, Sapir and Whorf Revisited* (pp. 297–312). New York: Mouton Publishers.

White, Geoffrey (1978) Ambiguity and ambivalence in A'ara personality descriptors. *American Ethnologist*, 5, 334–60.

—— (1980) Conceptual universals in interpersonal language. *American Anthropologist*, 82, 759–81.

—— (1981) 'Person' and 'emotion' in A'ara ethnopsychology. Paper presented at the Annual Meeting of the Association for Social Anthropology in Oceania, February 1981, San Diego.

15

A Japanese Emotion: *Amae*

H. Morsbach and W. J. Tyler

... and never, never try to prolong his or her dependence. ...
Advice to British parents in B. and S. Jackson, 'Teenage tripwires',
Sunday Times Magazine, 1974

Few Western visitors will deny that Japan is a thoroughly industrialized society. Since it is the first Asian society to achieve parity with (or even exceed) Western societies concerning gross national product, it is often easy to conclude that this has been achieved by wholesale borrowing and 'Westernization' in most aspects of Japanese life.

At a superficial level this is, of course, the case. The Western visitor is usually greeted by English-speaking Japanese who wear modern Western dress and who escort him or her to the Tokyo Hilton where bedding and plumbing are indistinguishable from the conveniences back home.

Yet, why all this smiling? Why all the funny squiggles instead of having changed long ago to the 'obviously superior' alphabet? Why this eternal bowing to each other, or, at best, the limp handshakes? Why the maddening absence of street names, the curious disincentive to take tips? Why all this slurping and hissing? Don't 'they' know how to behave 'properly'?

Thus confusion sets in. Most trappings are obviously Western, but what lies 'underneath'? How can this puzzle be solved? A promising approach, which might help to clarify these conditions, is to see how words or phrases regarded as especially 'Japanese' are used in literature and daily life. These would be words unique to the language that are difficult or impossible to translate exactly.

One of the most interesting studies in this respect is the theory by the Japanese psychiatrist Doi (1973) that the concept of *amae* is a key to the understanding of Japanese personality structure. Doi points out that there is no single equivalent for *amae* (the noun form) or *amaeru* (the verb form) in the Indo-European languages, and even a phrase fails to get the feeling of *amae* across to the non-Japanese. Of course there are other

Japanese words and phrases which, as a result of historical circumstances unique to Japan, are equally untranslateable. Likewise, certain Anglicisms like 'stiff upper lip' may not find their counterparts in Japanese or even in the nearby romance languages. What makes *amae* so exceptional is that it seems so universal and fundamental to all human beings. Japanese find it hard to believe that there is no exact translation in English. As one astonished colleague of Doi's put it, 'Why, even puppies do it!' (Doi, 1973, p. 15).

Kenkyusha's New Japanese–English Dictionary (1974) translates *amaeru* as '(to) presume upon another's love; behave like a spoilt child; play the baby to; be coquettish; coquet; coax; fawn on a person; . . . take advantage of (another's kindness)'.

Unfortunately, not one of these phrases has a favourable connotation although *amaeru* can, in Japanese, be used both favourably and unfavourably. Aware of this discrepancy, Doi has tried to provide a more exact translation with 'to depend or presume upon another's love', 'to bask in another's indulgence' or 'to indulge in another's kindness'. He calls it 'a sense of helplessness and the desire to be loved', and he feels that the psychoanalyst Balint (1965) comes closest to identifying *amae* with the term 'passive object love'. Put into Freudian parlance, *amae* expresses the desire 'to seek restoration of the once-lost quasi-union of mother and infant', or 'the oceanic feelings'.

At any rate, *amaeru* has the aura of sweetness and permissiveness which Doi finds common to the psychology of normal and neurotic Japanese alike. His first-hand experience with US–American culture confirms him in the opinion that non-Japanese also *amaeru*, but in a far more restricted way.

As is apparent even from Doi's definitions, *amae* has several levels of meaning and will not readily yield to a comprehensive definition. To make matters more difficult, although Japanese may often *amaeru* they seldom speak about it. This is chiefly because *amae* has its setting in those familial, matrimonial and social relations where communication is primarily nonverbal (Morsbach, 1973). To articulate the desire, or to go so far as to identify it in another, would be unnecessary and, in some instances, downright gauche. Finally, as will be shown, *amae* intrinsically avoids verbalization, as Doi indicates:

> Japanese feel that the use of words can chill the atmosphere, whereas Americans, in contrast, feel encouraged and reassured by such communication. I think this is clearly related to the psychology of *amae*, because the Japanese idea is that those who are close to each other – that is to say, who are privileged to merge with each other – do not need words to express their feelings. One surely would not feel merged with another (that is *amae*), if one had to verbalize a need to do so! (Doi, 1972, p. 387)

On the basis of the following examples from Japanese life and literature, and with the help of Doi's observations, this paper will attempt to convey some of the 'flavour' which *amae* has in Japanese social interaction.

I

> You're pitying me, aren't you? There's no reason to . . .'
> I'm sorry for you, Moriya.'
> 'Don't be absurd. I have no intention of *taking advantage of others' sympathy* [*ninjō ni amattareyo*]. . . . I have some affection for other people at times, but *I don't expect anything in return* [*tanin ni nanika o kitai shivo to omowanu*]. When you've lived abroad you learn to get that way. You've got to. . . . That old Japanese feeling of just because they are kin they can go overboard in *amaeru* to you and hate you for not letting them. But that's not for me. I figure I've graduated from at least that much. How different it is from the way they act with their neighbours!'   Osaragi, 1952, pp. 130–1)

Quoted from the best-selling postwar novel *Kikyo* (Homecoming) by Osaragi Jiro (1898–1966), this example illustrates the following aspects of *amae*.

1   The central character dismisses his companion's solicitude by saying that he has no intention of taking advantage of other people. He suggests that *amae* is 'to expect something from others', or at least to secretly nurse such expectations.

2   *Amae* is a typically Japanese feeling. The central character has been living abroad for a number of years. No doubt foreigners' independence from their families and the ease with which they make friends impressed him as somehow different from the Japanese.

3   *Amae* is chiefly expressed within the family (and not within society at large). Because it cannot usually be freely expressed towards outsiders, it may even be particularly intense in the family.

4   The statement, 'I figure I've graduated from at least that much' suggests that *amae* is a childish feeling to be outgrown. The vehemence with which the character deprecates 'that old Japanese feeling' makes one wonder if he has really outgrown it after all (cf. Doi, 1967, pp. 169–72).

II

The woman left off her conversation with the maid who sat next to her and suddenly – or rather, spastically – began going 'bum-bum' at the lips and plastering or, if you will, 'cauterizing' kisses in the Japanese style on the infant's neck and cheeks. The baby smiled and squirmed all over, as though tickled. Then, projecting her lovely neck out of her kimono and tilting her bunned head to one side, the woman did the same thing under the baby's chin, only more vigorously. Kensaku, a witness to all this, suddenly felt the business to be sickeningly sweet and could no longer stand it. He turned and looked out of the window as though nothing had happened. He thought how far more adroit the woman was at the art of *playing baby* [*amattarete iru*] than the infant who hadn't even yet learned how [*amattare-kata o shiranu*]. (Shiga, 1967, p. 65)

This example is taken from the semi-autobiographical novel *Anyakōro* (Dark Night's Journey) by Shiga Naoya (1883–1971), which highlights the following aspects of *amae*:

1 *Amae* is something to be learned: the infant is still too small to know about it.
2 The mother's spasm of mushiness is considered to be *amattare*.

III

Now Hata is married. Next Yodono. Then Shimizu. Everyone's becoming king of his own castle. The longer my wedding is postponed, however, the more I can get away with *amaeru*ing to mummy and daddy.... '... and the newlyweds will just love to have him over for dinner' – what'll you bet that this is the shameless sort of thought that just flashed through your mind, and you are smiling to yourself (I know, don't say it: *amaekko* psychology). (Kajii, 1967, p. 184)

Taken from a collection of letters by a minor novelist, Kajii Motojirō (1901–1932), who died of tuberculosis, this excerpt was written at the age of 26. He is denied the happiness of his friends, all recently married, because, one gathers, his parents are experiencing difficulty in finding a bride willing to marry their ailing son. Here *amae* has the following features:

1 The person involved refers to himself as an *amaekko* (an *amae* child), which is commonly used in Japanese to describe a child, and in some cases an adult, who likes to be spoiled. Kajii owns up to the idea to be indulged. In fact, he likes it.

2   As long as a Japanese child lives under his parents' roof, he can get away with *amaeru*ing. Marriage, or being 'king of one's own castle', seems to be the official termination of the childlike dependence on one's parents. In this case it appears that because the son is denied the right to a wife he will be entitled to *amaeru* a bit longer.

3   He anticipates that his newlywed friends will also be only too glad to spoil him.

IV

'Come on, let's run back!'
It would be an exaggeration to say that I did not want to see Mother in the slightest. Not that I had no feeling for her. The fact was probably that I disliked being confronted with the straightforward expression of love that one receives from one's blood relatives, and that I was simply trying to rationalize this dislike in various ways....
Only in my hatred was there something authentic. For I myself was a person who should be moved with hate.
'There's no point running,' I replied. 'It only makes one tired. Let's take our time going back!'
'I see,' said Tsurukawa. 'So you *want to make up [amattareru]* to your mother and get her sympathy by pretending to be too exhausted to walk fast.'
(Mishima, 1959, p. 74; trans. Ivan Morris)

Mishima Yukio (1925–1970) wrote *Kinkakuji* (The Temple of the Golden Pavilion) in 1956 as an attempt to reconstruct the psychology of a young misfit who burned down the famous building in Kyoto in 1950.
   The character is depicted as having extremely ambivalent feelings towards his mother because at a tender age he had witnessed her having sexual intercourse with a family friend. His hatred is no doubt authentic. Dragging his feet is an expression of his dislike for his mother rather than a desire to *amaeru* or get her sympathy, as his friend believes. A subsequent passage adds:

Thus Tsurukawa was invariably interpreting my behaviour and was invariably mistaken about it. But he did not bother me in the slightest and had in fact become quite indispensable – an irreplaceable friend who could translate my words for me into the language of the real world.

The association between 'making up' and 'getting sympathy' indicates that there has to be a degree of empathy or receptivity in the other if a person is to *amareu* successfully.

V

'Mother.' Shigemoto called her again. He knelt on the ground and pressed his body against his knees, gazing all the while into her face. Dimmed in the translucent light of the moon, his mother's face appeared sweet, small and haloed in its white habit.

The memory of that spring day forty years ago when she had held him in the shade of a sail suddenly came vividly back to life, *and for the moment he felt as though he was still only a six or seven-year-old boy.* In his reverie he brushed aside a branch of small yellow flowers she held in her hand, and drew his face closer to hers. And, while the trace of incense in her sleeve brought back the scent of the past long, long ago, he – almost as though *amaeru*ing – he once more pressed his tears into her black robes. (Tanizaki, 1956, p. 261)

This is an example from another popular postwar novel, *Shūshō Shige-moto no Haha* (The Mother of General Shigemoto) by Tanizaki Junichirō (1886–1966). It is the story, in a historical setting, of Shigemoto's separa-tion from and forty-year search for his mother. In this, the final scene, she has become a Buddhist nun and they are at last reunited. One literary critic, Kamei Katsuichirō, has referred to the mother in this story as the 'madonna' type, which, he points out, appears frequently in Japanese novels. Obviously the mother's attributes are very madonna-like. The significant point is that Shigemoto suddenly feels himself to be no more than a little boy. He experiences a momentary psychological regression. Furthermore, the desire to *amaeru* is shown here by gestures, not words, and the scene is cast in a romantic tone.

VI

Almost two years have elapsed without a house-mother in the student's hall. ... For the students who were living far away from home she was a person who could take the place of their mother in times of sickness and emergency. At times she was even *an object to which they could amaeru [amaerareru taisho)* without reserve or anxiety.

This example is quoted from a letter in a 1968 edition of the *Student Office News* from International Christian University, Tokyo, devoted to hostel life and problems. The female student writer discusses how the hostel has, through self-government, successfully managed without a substitute mother figure to whom one could, at times, *amaeru*. The remark 'without reserve or anxiety' suggests that people may have inhibitions about *amaeru*ing out of fear that others may take advantage of or laugh at the naked exposure of their feelings of helplessness.

VII

It is hardly necessary to go into the nobility of the love between teacher and pupil here, but in this case love is beyond the shadow of a doubt the severity the pursuit of truth requires. It is not to be confused with the teacher's pampering his students [*gakusei o amayakasu*], nor the students' *playing up* [*amaeru*ing] to their teacher. (Kamei, 1962, p. 45)

In this quotation a clear distinction is drawn between love and *amae*. True love does not admit pampering or being pampered. Kamei (1907–1966) suggests that such severity is necessary for the pursuit of academic truth; *amae*, then, is a kind of softness or looseness that does not aim at a truthful statement of reality. The statement indirectly suggests that *amaeru* could be an element in teacher–pupil relations, though it ought not.

VIII

People who imagine that romance is a vaguely beautiful, pleasant thing are, quite frankly, spoilt (*amattare*) and counting on the sympathy and support of society. (Mishima, 1966, pp. 20–1)

Here, too, as in examples II, IV and XIII, the word *amattareru* (another conjugation of *amaeru*) is used, and the connotation is derogatory. There is the association that a person being *amattare* is being romantic or sentimental, and the passage implies that the realization of such dreams depends 'on the sympathy and support of society'.

IX

The nearer the novel *Shinsei* (New Life) approaches the end, the more a vague 'sugariness' – if one might call it that – appears. This 'sugariness' stems partly from the nature of romantic love – even if it can't help looking more like the romance of a school pupil than that of a middle-aged man – but chiefly from Tōson's rather vulgar interpretation of religiosity.

One cannot escape the impression that the more Tōson employs a calm feeling of pity for example, telling Setsuko that although they are apart they will always be together, or in the way he fans her religiousness or *takes advantage of the lyricism of the situation* [*jōjosei ni amaeru gotoku*] – the more the novel becomes 'beautiful hypocrisy' or the 'skilful beautification of lust'. (Kamei, 1966, p. 177)

Once again, *amaeru* is associated with romantic love, especially of the 'saccharine' and infantile sort.

Shinsei (1920) was an autobiographic novel written by Shimazaki Tōson (1871–1943) in which he confesses an incestuous relationship with his neice. After getting the girl pregnant, Tōson has neither the courage nor the courtesy to mention the matter to his brother, head of the household, until he is in Shanghai on his way to France. In France he spends four lonely years repenting his misconduct. On his return to Japan he meets his neice again and finds her strengthened by her suffering. He suggests she become a nun and then proceeds to write a novel revealing the whole scandal which his brother had been careful to conceal. The novel resulted in Tōson being disinherited. He was, however, able to put the matter right with his readership by taking advantage of the 'lyricism of the situation', as Kamei, his critic, suggests. Kamei also suggests that it was only Tōson's position as a famous poet and novelist that made it possible for him to act and write with such licence.

X

Rainbow in My Heart
1   I trusted you
      and came this far, but . . .
      the rainbow we found
      oh, where did it go?
2   To the grey skies
      send sadness
      for the frail butterfly
      oh, where did it go?
3   On the day
      we are finally one
      hug me,
      hug me,
      and *you'll let me play baby, won't you?* [*amaete ii no ne*]
4   My heart
      trembles in tears, but . . .
      that sad butterfly
      goes back to the big, big sky
      goes back to the big, big sky.
(Lyrics by Hashimoto Jun, sung by the 'Blue Comets' in 1968)

In this popular song the singer is asking permission of her lover if it will be all right to *amaeru*. The expression is very affectionate, cute and innocent. Note the general romanticism and sentimentalism of the lyrics. The fact that this is a song helps to explain the straightforwardness with which the singer speaks of her desire to *amaeru*. It is worth noting that at the time this song was popular there were no less than three pop tunes in which the word *amaeru* was used.

Figure 1 Picture-card illustrating Japanese mother–son relationship.
(Reproduced from Caudill, 1962. Copyright 1962 by the Wenner-Gren Foundation for
Anthropological Research, New York)

XI

In an investigation of Japanese patterns of emotion, Caudill (1962) administered pictures depicting various scenes in Japanese households to patients as well as nurses in mental hospitals and asked his subjects to tell stories about them. One of the cards (figure 1) shows an adult male in a Japanese-style bed on the tatami floor while an older female, kneeling by his bedside, holds her hand to his forehead:

> there is a nice story that illustrates the relation of mother and son, along with the conflict with the potential daughter-in-law. The nurse, in telling of this experience, used the Japanese word *amaeru* which is translated as 'to coax' here.
>
> (Miss H.) '. . . The doctor has just gone and the mother is very much worried, and the son has a temperature and is "coaxing". Why I say this is that recently my fiancé became sick and I went to see him. His mother was there, so there wasn't any such 'coaxing' thing. To tell you the truth, I wanted to have him 'coax', and to talk with him. The day he got sick his mother called and said that he was sick. She didn't tell me that I should come or that he wanted anything. . . . When I talked with him at the house he said he had a person who would take care of him, so he didn't need anybody, and didn't want to make me worry. . . . (Caudill, 1962, p. 120)

XII

The Secret of Getting the Girls to Dote on You
—Extol, *coax* [*amae*], and *importune* [*nedaru*]
    First, you must become the kind of guy that Mme Beauvoir calls the type
girls *dote on* [*kawaigarareru-ko*].
    Feed your woman a line like, 'oh-you-are-the-most-beautiful-girl-in-the-world-especially-when-you're-being-cold-to-me', and if you can use the
stunt of staring sheepishly into her eyes with a look of, 'you'll-never-date-the-likes-of-me', nothing could be better.
    That's because nothing appeals to her vanity more than enthusiastic praise
and sheepishness.
    Secondly, create the impression that you are a timid, talentless man unable
to do anything without the help of a stronghearted woman.
    At that point, if you have a fairly nice face and look frail enough, and can
by *words and gestures skilfully amaeru to a woman*, your success is assured.
    Thirdly, and most importantly, if she has really taken a liking to you, slowly
turn on the sweetness [*amae*] and importune [*nedaru*] her first for things to
wear: a sweater, a sports shirt, a wrist watch, and then even for pocket money.
She will only too gladly *respond to your amae* [*amae ni ōjite kurere*] out of
the pleasure of having her own superiority recognized and of having given
when importuned. (Kitahara, 1968, pp. 46–7)

This example is from *Heibon Panchi*, a precursor of the Playboy-type
magazine in Japan, which became a pace-setter for the teen generation in
the 1960s. The article is intended to be read in jest. The younger
generation probably found it amusing; the older generation, absurd. What
makes it amusing is that tradition demands that males dote on (*kawaigaru*)
females, and not *vice versa*. Here the roles are reversed, and the male is
instructed in the art of coquetry. *Amaeru* is described as one of the
techniques of such an art.

    Note the distinction between *amaeru* (coaxing) and *nedaru* (importun-
ing). Both are a form of ingratiating oneself, but *nedaru* (importuning)
contains an ulterior motive such as the receipt of clothes or money. The
article also suggests that a person responds to another's *amae* because it
appeals to his/her vanity and sense of self-importance to do so. Note the
vertical structure of the relationship: the male *amareus* 'upwards' (by
creating the impression that he is mentally and physically small and weak –
the timidity, the sheepishness, etc); on the other hand, the female dotes
'downwards' (from her position of superiority).

    Finally, note that the writer says *amaeru* is done by both words and
gestures.

XIII

His wife had promised to go to the theatre next Sunday when relatives had asked them out.

'They haven't gotten seats yet, so they won't mind if we decline', Tsuda said.

'But Yoshio, you know that's not right', she said. 'To refuse after they were so kind to ask us out.'

'What could be wrong? It's not like we don't have a good reason.' She hesitated. 'But I wanted to go. . . .'

Tsuda noticed a kind of sneaky calculation in her look. It was a strange gleam that did not match in the least the sweet things she had been saying until then. '. . . I'm only fooling', she added. 'I don't care about the old play anyway. I was just *acting spoilt [amattareta no yo]*, that's all.' (Natsume, 1965, pp. 14–16)

This is an example of *amae* in a husband–wife relationship from the novel *Meian* (Light and Darkness) by Natsume Sōseki (1867–1916), who is widely regarded as one of Japan's greatest modern novelists. Note the importance given to the eyes as a means of communicating desire (even more is given in the original, not quoted here), and the wife's sweet, pouting way of speaking.

XIV

Being strict with oneself.

When I look back on the years of my life, I am pained at the thought of my weakness and folly. If I were to give one example – I used to *amaeru* to the fact that I was sickly and weak. Actually, I was very sickly . . . but the truth is I should have fought harder against my infirmity. (Tamiya, 1966, p. 108)

This is an example of *jibun ni amaeru* (to *amaeru* to oneself). The person uses his frail constitution as an excuse to avoid responsibility.

XV

I must go on living. And, though it may be childish of me, *I can't go on in simple compliance [amaete bakari mo orarenai]*. From now on I must struggle with the world. I thought that Mother might well be the last of those who can end their lives beautifully and sadly, struggling with no one, neither hating nor betraying anyone. In the world to come there will be no room for such people. . . . Now that it was clear that Mother would soon die, my romanticism and sentimentality were gradually vanishing, and I felt as though I were turning into a calculating, unprincipled creature. (Dazai, 1965, pp. 227–9)

Shayo (The Setting Sun) is Dazai Osamu's (1909–1948) chronicle of the decline of the Japanese aristocracy just after the defeat in World War II. The dying mother is symbolic of the passing away of the old order. As she lies dying, word arrives that the Japanese emperor has renounced all claims to divinity.

The daughter suggests that people like her mother had been able to get along in the world by *amaeru*ing, i.e., by having all their needs fulfilled and desires gratified without struggle or pettiness. (The translation of *amaeru* as 'compliance' is interesting but ultimately incorrect. 'I can't go on having my own way' might be a better approximation of the real meaning.)

She also suggests that in the new order it will no longer be possible to do as her mother did, or at least only partially. Consequently, she will have to struggle. No longer able to *amaeru* her way through life, she will have to hate and even betray people. For her, the end of *amae* is the end of living beautifully.

Note the association of a life based on *amae* and a romantic or sentimental view of life.

In passing, it is also worth mentioning that on one occasion Doi defines the prewar position of the Japanese emperor as 'psychologically speaking ... the absolute gratification of dependency wishes' (Doi, 1966, p. 10). It is interesting that the emperor's renunciation of divinity in this novel is timed to coincide with the demise of the aristocracy and of *amae* as a way of life.

As these fifteen examples illustrate, *amae* has a variety of meanings centring around passive dependency needs in hierarchical relationships. '*Ama-*', the root of *amae*, means 'sweet', as opposed to sour or bitter. The Chinese ideography is regarded as originally depicting the breast at which the baby suckles.

In the majority of the examples, *amae* has its setting in the family. The central character in example I even goes so far as to say that the fact of being kin is, in itself, sufficient excuse for relatives to impose upon one another. The mother is, in particular, the principal target for *amae* feelings (examples IV, V, VI, XI, XV).

Examples VIII, IX and XV also suggest that *amae* can be directed at society at large or, as in example III, to a teacher who is not a blood relative. The creation of surrogate mother and father figures is a psychological phenomenon by no means confined to the Japanese, but there is a marked tendency in Japan for non-familial, primary social groups to be patterned on the family unit (Nakane, 1970).

The Japanese have habitually used terms of family address such as *niisan* (big brother) and *neesan* (big sister) to address friends and helpful strangers, much like revivalist religious groups refer to fellow-believers as 'brother' or 'sister', or Catholics refer to a priest as 'father'. Nowadays the custom is considered boorish among the young Japanese, but it still remains very much alive in the reference to, for example a bar proprietress as *mama-san*, and, noticeably, in minority groups such as gangster organizations or gay subculture. Doi (1966), p. 7) notes that *amae* is only rarely applied to descriptions of the behaviour of a social superior. Mothers are not normally said to *amaeru* to their babies. Superiors do, in fact, *amaeru* to subordinates; role reversals do occur, as the charcter Kensaku perceives in example II or in the exaggerated and humorous romancing of 'Getting the Girls to Dote on You' (example XII).

If the existence of two distinct vocabulary words is any indication, the Japanese language distinguishes between the desire to *amaeru* (*amaetai*) and the desire to be loved (*aisaretai*), although most Japanese feel ill-at-ease with such declamations as 'I love you', which have come into their language through contact with the romantic literature of the West. The distinction is drawn in example VII, where the writer differentiates between the rigorousness of true love among teacher and pupil on the one hand and the kind of moral laxity that results from academic cliquishness, or confusing love with licence, on the other. His view of love is of course idealistic, but it may be that he felt he was expressing a somewhat revolutionary idea.

It is easy enough to imagine situations in which a person wishes to be loved passively in the sense of desiring kindness, forgiveness or solicitude – in the parlance of Eric Berne (1966), 'stroking'. It is a manifestation of narcissistic selfishness (if that can be said in a non-pejorative way without at the same time getting too clinical) in which the person wishes to merge with others in a loving, heartwarming relationship (Doi, 1972, p. 385). It is the expectation that one's dependency is at the same time the other's delight.

In the child–parent relationship the child *amaerus* and the parent bestows affection (*kawaigaru*). To use a Japanese metaphor, the child wags its tail and the parent pets it. The verb *kawaigaru* is a compound of the adjective *kawaii* – the meaning lies somewhere between the English 'cute' and the French '*petit*' – and the suffix *-garu*, which means 'wanting to do'. Hence, 'wishing to be sweet upon', 'wishing to dote upon'. The word *kawaii* probably rivals *kanashii* (sad) as the most commonly used adjective in the language, and the proverbial description of a lovable child is, 'You are so *kawaii* (cute) that it wouldn't hurt to pop you in my eye'.

> In Japan . . . the mother views her baby much more as an extension of herself, and psychologically the boundaries between them are blurred. . . . Thus, in Japan, there is a greater emphasis on interdependence, rather than independence, of mother and child, and this emphasis extends into adulthood. . . . The Japanese child will ordinarily sleep with his parents until he is approximately ten years of age. (Caudill, 1972, p. 43)

This could explain the importance of *amae* in Japanese life which can be seen as, 'ultimately, an attempt psychologically to deny the fact of separation from the mother' (Doi, 1973, p. 75).

The language seems to recognize that there is an active, conscious aspect about this desire to be loved passively. The term is not applied to infants' behaviour until they reach the age of about one year (see example II); and the average mother can probably cite a point in time at which she feels that her baby has ceased to stop acting instinctively in its demands for feeding or caressing. It is probably at this point that the child reaches an awareness of its separation and isolation from the mother. This is referred to in Japan as *monogokoro ga tsuku*, 'when a child begins to take notice (of its surroundings)' and of its need to find ways to keep her physically nearby. In cases where *amae* finds its reciprocal gratification there is minimal desire to manipulate the other. Thus, although there is an element of manipulation even in *amae*, the Japanese language clearly provides one with alternative terminology to indicate a high degree of manipulative behaviour. Example XII uses the word *nedaru* (importuning); other words are *kobiru* (coquetting) and *toriiru* (taking someone in or flattering him/her in order to get one's way). Not only is flattery often used in Japanese social settings, it is also institutionalized in the many honorific forms that permeate the language. A ready example of 'taking in' can be seen in comparing the two questions in English, 'Do you remember me?' and 'Don't you remember me?'. Their meanings seem almost identical, but, on second thought, one realizes that the latter expression is a bit *amaeta* because it attempts to 'take in' or to *toriiru*. The implication of 'Don't you remember me?' is that one ought to (because I am lovable, perhaps?) and that, if not, you should feel slightly embarrassed. The phrasing is thus less straightforward and more latently aggressive. The person addressed is put on the defensive and, unless his memory serves him well, he/she is obliged to apologize, however insipidly.

Even though Japanese society sanctions dependency wishes, *amae* frequently ends in frustration. This may result in pouting spells or feeling that one is not receiving one's fair share in life. Space does not permit more elaboration of the words *higamu* and *suneru* used in this context. But these frustrations do not seem to be so strong or frequent as to inhibit the desire to *amaeru* in most Japanese. 'The normal adult knows when and where he can satisfy his *amae*. If that involves a little hard work he does not begrudge it' (Doi, 1967, p. 178).

There is always an ambivalent element about *amaeru*ing. One never knows for certain whether the desire will be gratified (see example VI). Doi claimed, moreover, that there was a clear connection between some neuroses in his Japanese patients and their troubled feelings concerning *amae*. He found that neurotic patients could rarely allow themselves to *amaeru* freely because the desire had been blocked in childhood. He hypothesized that, although they might have been successful in suppressing their hostility at not having been allowed to *amaeru*, this very frustration often heightened their desire to *amaeru*. However, Doi found that, because *amae* was acceptable in their environment, they could at least verbalize this desire without constraint or embarrassment in the therapeutic setting. This contrasts strongly with the following observation:

> A Caucasian patient says with anxiety and every evidence of constriction, and perhaps only after many weeks or months of therapy, 'I had the thought that I want to be held in your arms and cuddled.' As with the Japanese patient, when the patient finds that the wish is acceptable to the therapist, even though the activity may not be indulged in, improvement occurs. (Babcock, 1962, p. 181)

Compared with Anglo-Americans, for instance, the Japanese seem to have a relatively greater need and ability to openly show their desire for dependence on others, especially in hierarchically structured face-to-face relationships. The ideal of reaching self-sufficient maturity, so frequently accepted as an unquestioned belief in the West, seems to be far less important in Japan.

De Vos and Wagatsuma (1973, p. 50) stress that for Japanese adults passive, dependent, yet manipulative roles are acceptable. In the West such roles run counter to ideals of personal autonomy. In particular, the Japanese son's dependence on his mother tends to be lifelong. This is possible because, according to Beardsley (1965, p. 378), 'institutionalized male roles in Japanese society tolerate self-centred, juvenile dependency as one way of performing the role.'

This makes sense if seen in the total context of Japanese society where, according to Dore (1958, p. 70), 'By traditional Japanese moral standards the submissive client's role is neither humiliating nor irksome. An old proverb – "wrap yourself up in something long" – gives it explicit sanction.'

There is a strong tendency in the Japanese culture towards creating *oyabun–kobun* (leader–follower) relationships. Among men there is often the desire to yield oneself to a superior completely. In the language of the *samurai*, or his modern-day equivalent the *yakuza* (Japanese gangster), men fall for other men and wish to become their faithful retainers. This is often misinterpreted by Westerners, as Doi (1965, pp. 140–1) notes, 'Let me put down what is approved of as *amae* among Japanese often appears among Occidentals as homosexual feelings in the broadest sense of the word.'

Furthermore, dependency should not be confused with passivity. Wagatsuma (1973, p. 368) stresses that many Japanese (especially males) may be dependent, but they are not always passive. For instance, diverse roles can be played by the same person, depending on the time of day. Thus, many Japanese male employees, dependent but active during daytime working hours, enjoy their need for passivity after hours, for example at a bar, a Turkish bath or at home.

It is unfortunate that Japanese behaviour is mostly contrasted with that prevalent in Anglo-American-type societies. It is quite possible that *amae*-type dependency behaviour occurs and is tolerated in countries such as Italy – but to date comparative studies with Japan are sadly lacking. Bronfenbrenner (1971, pp. 7–8), however, remarks on the large differences found between babies raised in the US and the USSR: 'the Russian child receives considerably more hugging, kissing and cuddling. On the other hand, the infant is held more tightly and given little opportunity for freedom of movement or initiative. . . .'

It is this particular insistence on individual choice (perhaps largely due to the basically Protestant heritage) that de-emphasizes emotional dependence in the Anglo-American culture which most readers basically accept as the norm. Whereas it is regarded as polite in Western society to present a visitor with as large a choice as possible when offering, say, food or drink, it is thought far more polite for the Japanese host to pre-select what his/her guest is likely to want. A dialogue such as the one described in Kingsley Amis's *The Anti-Death League* (set in England) would tend to embarrass the guest if he were a Japanese, whereas in its Western setting it is a ritual absolved with ease by most hosts and guests:

> 'Now,' said Dr Best, 'what's it to be? Sherry or Martini?'
> 'Sherry, please', said Leonard.
> 'Manzilla, fino or amontillado?'
> 'Amontillado, please?'
> 'Pedro Domeq or Harvey's?'
> 'Harvey's, please'
> 'A lot or a little?'
> 'A little please'
>
> (Amis, 1966, p. 156)

In its broadest sense, *amae* can be thought of as one important factor in the harmonizing of everyday human relationships in Japan, as such stock phrases as *Go-shinsetsu ni amaete* ('availing myself of your kind offer') and *O-kotoba ni amaete* ('taking you at your kind word') suggest. In a society where relative status is so very important, one has to be especially polite to those persons who are closest in standing, especially one's superiors. Group harmony can easily be disrupted by inattention to details in etiquette which most Westerners would find trifling. In Japan, however, this easily leads to resentment. Caudill remarks:

The combined traits of social hierarchy and the wish to *amaeru* in human relationships contribute to understanding both the 'genius' and the 'curse' of Japanese life. When the individual feels taken care of and secure in a tight vertical structure he can work successfully and creatively. The vulnerabilities of the system are evident in the trauma experienced by persons who have been rejected by their group and have nowhere to turn. (Caudill, 1970,p. 46)

AMAE IN THE WEST

Although there is no special word for them, *amae*-type feelings do exist in Western culture, since the ideal of individualism and independence is far from realized in practice. In recent years the emergence of, for example, encounter groups, the communal sharing of drugs, etc., has shown that psychological interdependence is a powerful need. Furthermore, North European Protestantism has been the religion which stressed individualism most strongly, whereas Catholicism retained socially acceptable channels for *amae*-type feelings, such as the cult of the Virgin Mary or the practice of Confession. Outside childhood and religion there are, however, relatively few opportunities to *amaeru* in ways approved by society. Terms of endearment during courtship and lovemaking, such as 'darling', 'baby', etc., come to mind, and during pregnancy a woman is often urged to behave in an especially passive and dependent way. In the recent BBC-TV film, *Family of Man: Birth*, a pregnant upper-middle class Englishwoman was asked about her husband's behaviour during her pregnancy. She replied:

> My husband is very much more attentive. He is much more outwardly loving, since he is a very reserved character normally. It has given him, not necessarily the excuse, but the freedom. He feels, 'Ah well, she is pregnant and *I can really cuddle up a bit more*.' It's gorgeous! And if it didn't last nine months I'd do it every year for this reason alone.

But the ideal has been in the past for adults to outgrow *amae*-type feelings and to show the desire for independence, as voiced by Ibsen's Nora.

Finally, the question remains whether some Westerners, knowing about Japanese customs, could bring themselves to *amaeru* more if they wanted to. But here the many years of different childhood socialization stand in the way, plus a social environment which is quick to censure this kind of behaviour. Broadly speaking, the relative absence of *amae* in the West may contribute towards loneliness and feelings of anomie in a cold, harsh world where all have to fight basically on their own and where there are precious few, if any, shoulders to cry on. But once the childlike innocence is lost, who can retrieve it?

REFERENCES

Amis, K. (1966)   *The Anti-Death League.* Harmondsworth: Penguin.
Babcock, C. G. (1962)   Reflections on dependency phenomena as seen in *Niesei*

in the United States. In R. J. Smith and R. K. Beardsley (eds), *Japanese Culture: Its Development and Characteristics*. London: Methuen (pp. 172–85).

Balint, M. (1965)   *Primary Love and Psychoanalytic Technique*. London: Tavistock.

Beardsley, R. K. (1965)   'Personality psychology'. Chapter 8 in J. W. Hall and R. K. Beardsley (eds), *Twelve Doors to Japan*. New York: André Deutsch.

Bronfenbrenner, U. (1971)   *Two Worlds of Childhood – US and USSR*. London: Allen and Unwin.

Caudill, W. (1962)   Patterns of emotion in modern Japan. In R. J. Smith and R. K. Beardsley (eds), *Japanese Culture: Its Development and Characteristics*. London: Methuen (pp. 115–31).

—— (1970)   The study of Japanese personality and behaviour. In E. Norbeck and S. Parman (eds), 'The study of Japan in the behavioural sciences', *Rice University Studies*, 56, 37.

—— (1972)   Tiny dramas: vocal communication between mother and infant in Japanese and American families. In W. Lebra (ed.), *Transcultural Research in Mental Health*. Honolulu: University Press of Hawaii.

Dazai, Osamu (1965)   *The Setting Sun* (trans. Donald Keene), Tokyo: Hara Shobō.

De Vos, G. A. and Wagatsuma, Hiroshi (1973)   Status and role behaviour in changing Japan: psychocultural continuities. In G. A. De Vos (ed.), *Socialization for Achievement – Essays on the Cultural Psychology of the Japanese*. Berkeley: University of California Press (pp. 1–60).

Doi, Takeo (1965)   *Seishinbunseki to Seishinbyōri* (Psychoanalysis and Psychopathology). Tokyo: Igaku Shoin.

—— (1966)   Giri-Ninjō: an interpretation. *Psychologia*, 9, 7.

—— (1967)   *Seishinbunseki* (Psychoanalysis). Osaka: Sogen Igaku Shinsho.

—— (1972)   A Japanese interpretation of Erich Segal's *Love Story*. *Psychiatry*, 35, 385.

—— (1973)   *The Anatomy of Dependence*. Tokyo: Kodansha International.

Dore, R. P. (1958)   *City Life in Japan*. Berkeley: University of California Press.

Jackson, B. and Jackson, S. (1974)   Teenage tripwires. *Sunday Times Magazine*, 6 October, p. 44.

Kajii, Motojirō (1967)   *Wakaki Shijin no Tegami* (Letters from a Young Poet). Tokyo: Kadokawa Bunko.

Kamei, Katsuichirō (1962)   *Seishunron* (On Adolescence). Tokyo: Kadokawa Bunko.

—— (1966)   *Shimazaki Tōson Rōn* (On Shimazaki Tōson). Tokyo: Shinchō Bunko.

Kenyusha's New Japanese–English Dictionary (1974)   Ed. K. Masuda. Tokyo: Kenkyusha.

Kitahara, Takeo (1968)   Onna ni kawaigarareru hiketsu (The secret of getting the girls to dote on you). *Heibon Panchi*, 1 April, pp. 46–7.

Mishima, Yukio (1959)   *The Temple of the Golden Pavillion*. New York: Avon.

—— (1966)   *Hantei Onna Daigaku* (School for Women Against Charity). Tokyo: Shinchōsha.

Morsbach, H. (1973)   Aspects of nonverbal communication in Japan. *Journal of Nervous Mental Diseases*, 157, 262.

Nakane, Chie (1970) *Japanese Society*. London: Weidenfeld and Nicolson.

Natsume, Sōseki (1965) *Sōseki Zenshū: Meian* (Collected Works of Natsume Sōseki: Light and Darkness). Tokyo: Iwanami Shoten.

Osaragi, Jirō (1952) *Kikyō* (Homecoming). Tokyo: Shincho Bunko.

Shiga, Naoya (1967) *Anyakōro* (Dark Night's Journey). Tokyo: Kadokawa Bunko.

Tamiya, Torahiko (1966) *Watashi o Sasaeta Hitokoto* (Words to Live By), ed. Ogiya Shōzō. Tokyo: Seishun Shuppansha.

Tanizaki, Junichirō (1956) *Shōshō Shigemoto no Haha* (The Mother of General Shigemoto). In *Sengō Mondaisakū Zenshū* (Principal Postwar Works). Tokyo: Kawade Shōbo.

Wagatsuma, Hiroshi (1973) Ishiwara Shintarō's early novels and Japanese male psychology. *Journal of Nervous Mental Diseases*, 157, 358.

Affiliations

Claire Armon-Jones, Linacre College, Oxford.

James R. Averill, Department of Psychology, University of Massachusetts, Amhurst, Mass., USA.

Errol Bedford, Department of Philosophy, University of Edinburgh, Scotland.

J. Coulter, Department of Sociology, Boston University, Boston, Mass., USA.

Eduardo Crespo, Department of Psychology, Universidad Complutense, Madrid.

Robert Finlay-Jones, Research and Evaluation Unit, Mental Health Services of Western Australia, West Perth, Western Australia.

Rom Harré, Linacre College, Oxford.

Paul Heelas, Department of Religious Studies, University of Lancaster, England.

Catherine Lutz, Department of Anthropology, Suny, Binghamton, USA.

H. Morsbach, Department of Psychology, University of Glasgow, Scotland.

J. Sabini, Department of Psychology, University of Pennsylvania, Philadelphia, USA.

M. Silver, Department of Psychology, University of Pennsylvania, Philadelphia, USA.

Theodore R. Sarbin, Department of Psychology, University of California at Santa Cruz, USA.

W. J. Tyler, Department of Psychology, University of Glasgow, Scotland.

C. Terry Warner, Department of Philosophy, Brigham Young University, Utah, USA.

Linda A. Wood, University of Guelph, Ontario, Canada.

Index